The Future of the Capitalist State

Bob Jessop

polity

First published in 2002 by Polity Press in association with Blackwell Publishing Ltd.

Reprinted 2003, 2005, 2007

Polity Press
65 Bridge Street
Cambridge CB2 1UR, UK

Polity Press
350 Main Street
Malden, MA 02148, USA

ISBN 978-0-7456-2273-6

A catalogue record for this book is available from the British Library and has been applied for from the Library of Congress.

Typeset in 10 on 12 pt Times
by SNP Best-set Typesetter Ltd., Hong Kong
Printed and bound in Great Britain by MPG Digital Solutions, Bodmin

For further information on Polity, visit our website: www.polity.co.uk

The Future of the Capitalist State

For Ngai-Ling

Contents

List of Boxes

List of Tables and Figure

Preface

In addition to the three giants, Gramsci, Poulantzas and Luhmann, whose intellectual shoulders I have attempted to straddle in developing the argument below and whose contribution is detailed in the Introduction, there are many immediate personal debts incurred in writing this book that I would like to acknowledge. These are owed to the scholars and friends with whom I have shared or, at least, debated my ideas over many years. Singling out the most influential is invidious and, in any case, they know who they are. So I will simply note that special mention is due for various reasons, large and small, to Elmar Altvater, Ash Amin, Bjørn Terje Asheim, Henrik Bang, Jens Bartelson, Mats Benner, Werner Bonefeld, Robert Boyer, Neil Brenner, Terrell Carver, Hee-yeon Cho, Myung-Rae Cho, Simon Clarke, Chris Collinge, Ryan Conlon, Robert Delorme, Alex Demirovic, Frank Deppe, Bülent Diken, Gérard Duménil, Josef Esser, Norman Fairclough, Steve Fleetwood, Ann Haila, Colin Hay, Jerzy Hausner, Joachim Hirsch, John Holloway, Carsten Jensen, Jane Jenson, Joo Hyoung Ji, Martin Jones, Tetsuro Kato, Eleonore Kofman, Ernesto Laclau, Patrick Le Galès, Alain Lipietz, Gordon MacLeod, Rianne Mahon, Birgit Mahnkopf, James Martin, Margit Mayer, Marguerite Mendell, Timothy Mitchell, Lars Mjøset, Chantal Mouffe, Yoshikazu Nakatani, Klaus Nielsen, Claus Offe, Joe Painter, Leo Panitch, Ove Kai Pedersen, Markus Perkmann, Sue Penna, Jamie Peck, Sol Picciotto, Moishe Postone, Martin Rhodes, John Roberts, Ralf Rogowski, Andrew Sayer, Takeshi Shinoda, George Steinmetz, Gerry Stoker, Gunther Teubner, Adam Tickell, Bruno Théret, Adam Tickell, Chao-Ming Tseng, Constantine Tsoukalas, John Urry, Jenn-hwan Wang, Helmut Willke and David Wolfe. None of them can be held responsible for the errors in this book – indeed only two of them have read even one of its successive drafts in its entirety and few have followed its tortuous development from beginning to end – but they have nonetheless helped to make it better than it would otherwise have been through their influence at various stages in its gestation. I have also benefited immensely from the encouragement, criticism and, sometimes, blank incomprehension of countless other scholars and students over many years.

For institutional support at different times I would also like to thank the Zentrum für Interdisziplinäre Forschung at Bielefeld University for a year's fellowship as part of its joint research project on *Staatsaufgaben* (1988–9), Manchester University for a Hallsworth Senior Research Fellowship (1996–7), the Japan Society for the Promotion of Science for a productive two-month visit to Hitotsubashi University, Tokyo (1997), the Danish Social Research Council for a visiting Research Professorship at Roskilde University (1997–8), and the Centre for Organization and Management, Copenhagen Business School, for support during a whole series of academic visits. Many of the arguments developed here came together during a three-year research project on economic development and local governance financed by the Economic and Social Research Council (United Kingdom) under grant L311253032.

For his interest and commitment as I began this book, I wish to thank David Held. For their continuing encouragement and their polite responses to increasingly incredible excuses for the delays involved in its completion, I would like to express my gratitude to Lynn Dunlop and Rachel Kerr. And for judicious copy-editing, thanks go to Sarah Dancy.

Finally, the most important influence on my life in the last twelve years has been Ngai-Ling Sum. As well as being my constant intellectual companion during these years, she has also proved my closest friend and devoted partner. It is to her that this book is dedicated with the warmest love and the deepest appreciation for everything.

Bob Jessop
Lancaster

Abbreviations

B2B	Business-to-business
B2C	Business-to-consumer
CIS	Commonwealth of Independent States
Comecon	Council for Mutual Economic Assistance
EC	European Commission
EMU	European Monetary Union
EU	European Union
FDI	Foreign Direct Investment
G2B	Government-to-business
GATT	General Agreement on Trade and Tariffs
ICT	Information and Communication Technologies
ILO	International Labour Organization
IPR	Intellectual Property Rights
IMF	International Monetary Fund
KBE	Knowledge-based economy
KWNS	Keynesian Welfare National State
MNC	Multinational Company
NAFTA	North American Free Trade Agreement
NET	'Natural Economic Territory'
NGO	Non-governmental Organization
NIC	Newly Industrializing Country
OECD	Organization for Economic Cooperation and Development
OPEC	Organization of Petroleum Exporting Countries
R&D	Research and development
SEM	Single European Market
SWPR	Schumpeterian Workfare Postnational Regime

TNB   Transnational Bank
TRIPS   Trade-Related Aspects of Intellectual Property Rights
UN   United Nations
UNESCO   United Nations Education and Science Commission
WTO   World Trade Organization

Introduction

This book is a product of many years of intermittent reflection on the capitalist state and its role in postwar capitalism and involves a systematic attempt to move beyond sympathetic critiques of other theoretical currents in order to present my own analysis of the actually existing capitalist state. Its primary aim is to elaborate the theoretical foundations for a research agenda on the capitalist type of state in contemporary capitalism rather than to present detailed accounts of particular political regimes. It does so by setting out a research agenda and some preliminary conclusions regarding the changing forms, functions and effectiveness of economic and social policy in the advanced western capitalist states over the last fifty years. Moreover, whilst recognizing that this is still an open question, it also comments on their likely future development.

The analysis presented here is inspired by Marx's predisciplinary critique of political economy but draws, in a postdisciplinary manner, on a wide range of scholarship and research by social scientists. Starting out from the basic features of capitalism as a mode of production and object of regulation, it highlights the inherent improbability of stable capital accumulation based solely on market forces. It then considers the main contributions of the capitalist type of state in conjunction with other non-market mechanisms in securing crucial preconditions for accumulation. The basic features of capitalism as a mode of production and object of regulation assume different patterns in different varieties and stages of capitalism. The state apparatus and state power are critical factors here in shaping the dynamic of accumulation as well as being shaped by that dynamic. In order to illustrate these arguments, therefore, I will focus on the form of state that developed after the Second World War in those advanced capitalist economies integrated into Atlantic Fordism; and then reflect on its recent development and speculate on its future prospects following the crises in/of Fordism from the 1970s onwards.

I examine the general form of the postwar state, its specific variants and its contributions to economic and social reproduction. I interpret this form of state as a historically specific political regime that corresponds (in complex ways to be discussed in successive chapters) with a historically specific stage of capital accumulation in a particular economic and political space within the world economy. To highlight its historical specificity, I characterize this form of state in ideal-typical (or stylized) terms as a Keynesian welfare national state (hereafter, KWNS). Each of the four terms used in defining this ideal type is linked to a basic dimension of economic and social reproduction. I then consider the crisis-tendencies of the KWNS along these four dimensions and comment on the trial-and-error attempts to resolve or transcend them. The concluding chapter draws the arguments together to identify a plausible but still emergent form of the capitalist type of state that is replacing the KWNS, albeit unevenly and at different speeds.

The KWNSs that developed in many advanced capitalist societies during the postwar boom have long been regarded for good or ill as being in some sort of crisis, if not in terminal decline. There is far less agreement about the exact nature and causes of this crisis, however; or, again, about what could or should replace this particular form of state and its associated mode of regulation. If the crisis of the KWNS essentially involves a crisis *in* that regime and its role in reproducing the accumulation regime with which it is linked, then piecemeal reforms in one or both might restore its role without changing its basic organizational form. But, if there is a crisis *of* the KWNS, a new regime of economic and social reproduction would be necessary. One of the most provocative claims in this regard comes from Claus Offe, who, writing as questions of crisis, crisis-management and crisis resolution moved up the political agenda, argued that 'while capitalism cannot coexist *with*, neither can it exist *without*, the welfare state' (1984: 153; italics in original). I return to this argument in my last chapter to suggest how 'Offe's paradox' can be resolved.

In relating my analysis of the Keynesian welfare national state to capitalism, I do not want to suggest that state forms and functions are somehow fully determined in the last – let alone in the first – instance by some fully autonomous logic inscribed within capitalism. Indeed, my analysis attempts to move away from a simple, economic interpretation of the state. It does so in three main ways. First, it adopts a far broader interpretation of the economic than is usual in conventional economic analysis; second, it argues that the economy, whether considered in narrow or broad terms, is co-constituted by what are conventionally considered extra-economic factors; and, third, it identifies important structural and strategic limits to economic determination rooted in the relative intractability of other institutional orders and in resistance from a wide range of social forces within and beyond the economic system. In particular, in addition to showing how the dynamic of state forms and functions are shaped by changes in capital accumulation, I also indicate how the accumulation process is co-constituted in turn by many other processes, including the dynamic of state forms and functions. Thus I focus on the structural coupling and co-evolution of accumulation regimes and political regimes and how this is influenced by the attempts of different social forces to steer their individual and/or conjoint development.

Given my previous work, three cautions are in order to advise readers what (not) to expect from this particular study. First, this is not a primer in Marxist political economy or Marxist state theory. Although I draw heavily on Marx's critique of the economic categories of political economy and his sadly incomplete analysis of the capitalist mode of production, this is not the latest of many attempts to reconstruct historical materialism. Hence it advances no general ontological, epistemological or methodological claims. Nor have I tried to develop a systematic analysis of capitalism that starts with its most abstract and simple determinations and proceeds dialectically and stepwise to an account of the actually existing capitalist world market in all its concrete-complex details. Instead, I introduce only those economic categories that are necessary for my limited purposes and ignore much that would be necessary even for a largely economic analysis of contemporary capitalism. Likewise, while I have been inspired by the rich tradition of Marxist theorizing on the state, this work is not intended to provide a detailed commentary on Marxist state theories. Instead, it takes the critiques I have presented elsewhere for granted and develops only those analytical concepts and theoretical lessons that are essential for the limited tasks in hand. It also introduces categories from other theoretical traditions, especially institutionalist work on the state, where relevant and compatible with my overall approach. Moreover, since it focuses on economic and social policy, there are important aspects of the capitalist state that it ignores. Most notable of these are the military and police apparatuses, their changing forms and functions, the nature of modern warfare, and their overall connections to the broader state system.

Second, this book is not a primer on the welfare state. What is conventionally included under this rubric refers to only one of the four dimensions of the state's form and functions that are of interest in this study. Moreover, even in regard to this one dimension, social policy is approached primarily in terms of the state's role in the social reproduction of labour-power and many other important aspects of welfare are ignored. Thus, although I touch upon gender, ethnicity and 'race' as key aspects of the strategic selectivities of modes of regulation, the social division of welfare and the institutional matrix of the state, these are not themselves central topics of enquiry in this work. For this study is intended primarily to develop a *form analysis* of the state and state intervention rather than to offer concrete institutional analyses of particular welfare regimes or detailed accounts of specific welfare outcomes. It is in this more limited context that I discuss social policy. Thus my starting point is specific social forms, the extent to which they are – or could ever be – relatively unified in a given social formation (my preferred form-analytic term for the conventional, but ideologically imbued, and theoretically contested, category of 'society'), and the ways in which form problematizes function rather than guarantees it (on this last aspect, see Jessop 1982). Of most interest are the effects of the (always tendential, always socially reproduced) dominance of particular social forms (especially those linked to capital as a social relation) on the improbable reproduction of capital accumulation (including the reproduction of labour-power as a fictitious commodity) and the tendential emergence of the bourgeois nature of contemporary social formations. This particular ambition does not mean that there is nothing else worth saying about social relations theoretically, empirically or normatively. But I leave this to others (and, perhaps, myself on other occasions) to narrate.

Third, this book does not contribute directly to the growing body of theoretically informed empirical research on comparative capitalisms, comparative welfare regimes or other currents in the new institutionalist research agenda. Nonetheless I have learnt much from this literature and hope my own critical reflections on the political economy of accumulation regimes and the role of capitalist states in their reproduction will influence this research agenda in turn. But my project in this primarily form-analytical work remains relatively abstract and must therefore leave open many concrete comparative issues. In this sense I aim to elaborate the basic concepts for a new research agenda on capitalism and the capitalist state. I hope to refine this analysis in a future collaborative research report that compares Britain, Denmark, Germany and Sweden and, if so, this may provide a means to show how the current approach can be applied in specific case studies.

In analysing the capitalist state and its future in this and other texts, I have drawn freely on three complementary theoretical perspectives concerned with the discursive and extradiscursive aspects of economic, political and other social phenomena: (1) institutional and evolutionary economics, especially the regulation approach to the political economy of the capitalist economy; (2) an approach to the political economy of the state and politics that has been inspired above all by Gramsci and Poulantzas; and (3) critical discourse analysis and allied approaches to the discursive constitution of economic and political (as well as other social) relations. One major reason why these three perspectives can be rendered complementary is that they are all premised on a critical realist ontology, epistemology and methodology (Jessop 1982, 2001b; Sayer 2000). Moreover, in exploring the co-evolution of the economic and political aspects of the KWNS and its potential replacement, I also draw on: (4) recent analyses of self-organizing (or autopoietic) systems and the problems of governance posed by the interdependence of a plurality of self-organizing systems. While the autopoieticist theories are often seen as having constructivist theoretical underpinnings, I believe they can be appropriated and integrated into a critical realist analysis. Let me briefly sketch the relevance of all four modes of enquiry.

First, as regards capitalism, the regulation approach suggests that market forces are merely one contributing factor to capitalist expansion. Adherents of the regulation approach reject the key assumption of classical economics that there is a clearly delimited, socially disembedded sphere of economic relations with a tendency towards general equilibrium. Instead, they emphasize that economic rationality and dynamics cannot be adequately analysed in terms of pure exchange relations in perfect markets – even as a first approximation. They also deny that exchange is entirely driven by the optimizing, economizing conduct of inherently rational individuals who have pregiven and stable preference functions and who are solely oriented to the price mechanism and its implications for individual profit-and-loss. Instead, regulationists are concerned with the socially embedded, socially regularized nature of capitalist economies rather than with pure, self-regulating market phenomena; and they are concerned with changing economic norms and modes of calculation rather than with the transhistorical egoism of a *homo economicus* who is allegedly the active subject in all economies, precapitalist as well as capitalist. The regulation approach analyses capitalism very broadly, then, critically examining its anatomy as an 'integral economy' or 'economy in its inclusive sense'. Seen in integral or inclusive terms, specific forms of capitalism can be interpreted as an 'accumulation regime + mode of social regulation'. This comprises an ensemble of socially embedded, socially regularized and strategically selective institutions, organizations, social forces and actions organized around (or at least involved in) the expanded reproduction of capital as a social relation. This ensemble typically acquires its structural coherence, to the extent that it displays one, within the limits of a specific social fix that is historically variable in both its spatial and temporal dimensions. Such a spatio-temporal fix helps to secure the always partial, provisional and unstable equilibria of compromise that seem necessary to consolidate an accumulation regime and its mode of regulation. It is in these terms that I locate the role of the KWNS in the expanded economic and social reproduction of capitalism (on the regulation approach, see especially Boyer 1990; Boyer and Saillard 2002; Jessop 1997)

Second, following the prewar Italian Communist, Antonio Gramsci, and the postwar Greek Marxist theorist, Nicos Poulantzas, I consider the state as a social relation. The former proposed an inclusive definition of the state in its integral sense as 'political society + civil society' (Gramsci 1971); the latter analysed state power as a form-determined condensation of the balance of political forces operating within and beyond the state (Poulantzas 1978). Combining their ideas, one can define the state as an ensemble of socially embedded, socially regularized and strategically selective institutions, organizations, social forces and activities organized around (or at least actively involved in) making collectively binding decisions for an imagined political community. State power can be understood in turn as a power relation that is mediated in and through this institutional ensemble. It is not exercised by the state as such: the state is not a subject. Nor does it originate entirely within the state itself or from among the state's personnel. Instead, it depends on the balance of forces within the wider society as well as within state apparatuses. There are three further major themes to be drawn from Gramsci's work: hegemony, historic bloc and the role of intellectuals. He defines hegemony as the exercise of political, intellectual and moral leadership within and over a given political space in such a way as to bring social forces and institutions into conformity with the requirements of capitalist reproduction in a particular period. Where hegemony is successfully exercised it is reflected in what Gramsci terms an historic bloc. This can be defined for present purposes as a historically specific, contingent correspondence between the economic, the juridico-political, and the ethical dimensions of a given social formation. Following Gramsci's pioneering work, I argue that a key role in the exercise of hegemony and construction of an historic bloc is played by intellectuals who develop alternative economic strategies, state projects and hegemonic visions and may thereby help to consolidate an unstable equilibrium of compromise among different social forces around a given economic, political and social order. I draw on these ideas in addressing the social bases of different welfare regimes and their role in consolidating specific accumulation regimes and their corresponding modes of regulation (on state theory, see Jessop 1982, 1985, 1990b, and 2001a).

Third, inspired by critical discourse analysis and recent work on the narrative features of the social world, I emphasize the contribution of discourse to the construction of the capitalist economy as an object of regulation and of the national state as an imagined institutional ensemble. I also insist on the cultural as well as social embeddedness of economic and political institutions and power relations. Thus, the economy as an object of regulation is viewed as an imaginatively narrated system that is accorded specific boundaries, conditions of existence, typical economic agents, tendencies and countertendencies, and a distinctive overall dynamic. The state system is treated as an imagined political entity with its own specific boundaries, conditions of existence, political subjects, developmental tendencies, sources of legitimacy and state projects. Discourse analysis is also very relevant, of course, to the analysis of hegemony. In emphasizing the discursive moments of the economy and the state I do not intend to argue that they are somehow 'purely' discursive and lack any institutional materiality. Instead, I wish to highlight two issues. First, economic and political relations are so complex that any action oriented towards them requires some discursive simplification (hence an economic or political imaginary) that constitutes specific subsets of social relations as its social, material and spatio-temporal horizon of action. In this regard there are many economic and political imaginaries competing for hegemony or, at least, a dominant position in contemporary society. And, second, such discursive simplifications have a key role in their turn in the always tendential constitution and consolidation of the economic, political and other systems, shaping the forms of their institutional separation and subsequent articulation. Thus, while the dynamic of the capitalist economy has long unfolded within the framework of a more or less extensive and changing world market, it is often conceived as a series of more or less clearly demarcated national or regional economies. The recent discourses around globalization involve a shift in economic and/or political understandings and are reflected both in the restructuring of economic and political relations and in the reorientation of economic and political strategies. They thereby help to modify the institutional materiality and strategic bias of accumulation regimes and their associated political frameworks. I will deploy similar claims at other levels of economic and political analysis in order to show the key contribution of discourses to the overall shaping of economic and political structures and strategies in different contexts and conjunctures (on critical discourse analysis, see especially Fairclough 1992 and 2000).

Fourth, in exploring the institutional and social interconnections between the economic and the political, I draw on theories of self-organization. My initial source of inspiration here was Marx's analysis of the self-valorization of capital, that is, capital's capacity to reproduce itself through the profitable reinvestment of past profits as it moves repeatedly through the successive stages of what Marx termed the circuit of capital. However, while Marx confined his analysis of self-organization mainly to the capitalist mode of production, it is worth considering several other potentially self-organizing (or autopoietic) systems with major significance for social order in modern societies. These include the legal system, the political system, science, the educational system, religion and art. Each has its own operational code, organizational principles, institutional dynamics, instrumental rationalities and logics of appropriateness. Together they form a self-organizing ecology of instituted systems that develops through the interaction between their respective operational autonomies and material interdependencies. This approach has major implications for studies of the structural coupling and co-evolution of the economic and political in regard to both capital accumulation and the exercise of state power. Alongside the system domain there also exists a rich and complex lifeworld (sometimes inadequately described as 'civil society'), which is irreducible to such systems and their logics. It provides multiple sites of resistance to these logics as well as constituting a major sphere in its own right for conflicts and struggles as well as mutual recognition and solidarities (on Luhmann's approach to autopoiesis, see Jessop 1990b; Lange and Schimank 2000; Rasch 2000; Thornhill 2000; Willke 1992, 1997).

It is clear from this brief account of my principal theoretical sources and substantive concerns that the arguments in this book are indebted to many scholars. Among these, three, all now dead, merit special attention. The strongest influence is undoubtedly that of Nicos Poulantzas: I met him only once but have long been inspired by his state theory and more general analyses. Antonio Gramsci's work has also been influential – especially regarding the organic connections between the economic and the political, the contingent development of historic blocs, and the relational nature of power. And, perhaps surprisingly to many readers, I learnt much from the late Niklas Luhmann about the role of systems theory in social analysis. Luhmann would have profoundly disapproved of the use to which I have put his ideas – especially my attempt to synthesize his autopoietic systems theory with Marxism, which he claimed was a premodern theory that was quite inappropriate for the analysis of contemporary societies. One aim of this work is to refute that claim.

The rest of the book is organized into seven chapters. Chapter 1 presents the main theoretical concepts that will be used in my analysis of the postwar form of state in the circuits of Atlantic Fordism and my speculations on its future. Chapter 2 sketches the nature of Atlantic Fordism, the Keynesian welfare national state, which had a key role in the regulation of Atlantic Fordism, the more general spatio-temporal fix that helped to stabilize the Atlantic Fordist accumulation regime, and the crises that emerged in Fordism from the mid-1960s onwards. Chapter 3 explores the nature of post-Fordism and suggests that, following initial uncertainty about the substantive features of a feasible post-Fordist accumulation regime, it is gradually assuming the form of a globalizing knowledge-based economy. The extent to which this will occur is not secured purely by an economic logic but depends on its co-constitution by extra-economic forces that contribute to its stabilization and governance. The chapter sketches the main features of post-Fordism in these terms, the inherent structural contradictions and dilemmas of capital accumulation, and explores the complexities of globalization and the new forms of competition in the emerging knowledge-based economy. It concludes with a discussion of the distinctive functions of the Schumpeterian competition state that is steadily replacing the Keynesian full employment state and assesses whether this emerging state form is adequate to post-Fordism. Chapter 4 continues this line of analysis by examining the redesign of the welfare state, its changing role in social reproduction and the changing articulation between economic and social policy. It first considers in more detail the specificity of the welfare state and critiques some of the main alternative approaches to its restructuring, recalibration and reorientation in response to economic crisis and globalization. Three main changes in the welfare state are then examined: the increasing subordination of social policy to economic policy, downward pressure on the social wage considered as a cost of production, and the restructuring of collective consumption. I also emphasize the limits to welfare retrenchment rooted in the state's role in reproducing labour-power and the extra-economic conditions for accumulation as well as in the nature of politics in capitalist democracies.

Chapter 5 focuses on the rescaling of the capitalist type of state in response to the crises of Atlantic Fordism, new forms of competition, and the emergence of a globalizing, knowledge-driven economy. It also identifies three main trends in the restructuring of the national state and their countertrends. I then consider whether there is still a major role for the national state in the overall reproduction of capital accumulation and maintenance of social cohesion. I conclude that, despite the challenges to the primacy of the national state, it still has key roles in organizing the global economy, the global polity and an emerging global civil society. In other words, the national state is being reimagined, redesigned and reoriented in response to these challenges rather than withering away. The next chapter explores the material bases for the survival and co-existence of market forces, corporatist concertation and imperative coordination throughout the history of capitalism, and then considers some basic tendencies towards market, network and state failure. It then examines the crisis of the mixed economy paradigm of governance that characterized the Keynesian welfare national state and the tendency towards greater reliance on network forms of governance in the globalizing, knowledge-based economy. The chapter ends with observations on governance failure, metagovernance and metagovernance failure as potential sources of future crisis-tendencies in capitalist social formations.

The concluding chapter pulls together the main threads of the arguments that were presented in previous chapters. It claims that what is tendentially replacing the Keynesian welfare national state is the Schumpeterian workfare postnational regime. I suggest how this new form of state could contribute to the structural coherence of a new spatio-temporal fix for capital accumulation. I then consider possible variant forms of this new state form and show how these forms are linked to different path-dependent varieties of capitalism. Finally, in setting out the changing articulation of capital accumulation and the state, I propose a solution to Offe's paradox.

1

Capitalism and the Capitalist Type of State

This chapter develops three main themes to be elaborated in the rest of the book. First, neither capitalism as a whole nor the capital–labour relation on which its contradictory and conflictual dynamic depends can be reproduced purely through market relations. Both require supplementary modes of reproduction, regulation and governance – including those provided in part through the operations of the state. Second, and in particular, since labour-power is essentially a fictitious commodity, it cannot be reproduced solely through the wage form and labour market. Thus, non-market mechanisms of various kinds play a key role here too. And, third, as capital accumulation expands on an increasingly global scale, its dynamic becomes more ecologically dominant in shaping the overall evolution of social systems and the lifeworld.[1]

In developing these three themes I do not intend to argue that the dynamic of capital accumulation explains everything significant about the architecture and operation of states and the modern state system, let alone every last detail of their development. On the contrary, it is precisely because capitalism cannot secure through market forces alone all the conditions needed for its own reproduction that it cannot exercise any sort of economic determination in the last instance over the rest of the social formation. This requires us to pay close attention to the co-constitution of capital accumulation through the interaction of market-mediated and non-market social relations and, in turn, to the complex and overdetermined nature of its impact on the overall development of social relations. It follows that this chapter cannot limit itself to a presentation of economic concepts for analysing capitalism as a mode of production and object of regulation but must also introduce other concepts appropriate to the analysis of politics and the state, the lifeworld and civil society, and their connections to the economic categories and each other. In developing this more complex conceptual instrumentarium it will also prepare the ground for a four-dimensional analysis of recent changes in the state's role in capitalist reproduction and its institutional, social, and discursive mediation.

1. Capital as a Social Relation

In terms of surface appearances, capitalism can be defined initially as an economic system in which goods and services are produced for sale (with the intention of making a profit) in a large number of separate firms using privately owned capital goods and wage-labour (Bowles and Edwards 1985: 394). Most observers would probably broadly support this definition but this might well be explained by its vagueness over such key issues as the nature of labour-power, the labour process, the powers of capital and the dynamic of accumulation. Digging into these four issues is bound to arouse theoretical and political controversy, but this cannot be avoided if we are to establish capitalism's historical specificity as a mode of production and its implications for economic and social policy. Accordingly, I first explore some of the more abstract and simple preconditions of organizing commodity production on capitalist lines, and then expand and deepen the initial definition through several spiral steps that specify some more concrete and complex features of capitalism. This essentially theoretical exercise should generate a richer set of categories with which to begin an analysis of the forms of economic and social policy and their changing roles in the overall reproduction and expansion of capitalism. Paradoxically, it will also help to reveal the limits of a purely capital- and class-theoretical approach to the myriad complexities of actually existing states and thereby establish the importance of combining it with other theoretical approaches that start out from different sets of social relations.

The capitalist mode of production

What most distinguishes capitalism from other forms of producing goods and services for sale is the generalization of the commodity form to labour-power. This entails the historical development and subsequent reproduction and expansion of a labour market in which workers offer their labour-power for sale to capitalists in a formally free and equal commercial transaction. In abstract terms, the capital–labour relation operates as follows. Workers exchange their capacity to work for a wage and accept capital's right to (attempt to) control their labour-power in the production process and to appropriate any profits (or absorb any losses) that result from its effort to produce goods or services for sale. Workers spend their wages on means of consumption according to the prevailing social norms of consumption and thereby reproduce their labour-power so that it can be sold once more.[2] In this way the wage serves as a cost of production (for all capitals), a means of self-reproduction (for labour) and a source of demand (in the first instance, for those capitals that produce consumer goods and, indirectly, for those capitals that produce capital goods). Although capital appropriates and transforms natural resources and also draws on the productive powers of nature (so that these resources and powers contribute to the production of use-values and any resulting increase in wealth), the socially necessary labour-power that is consumed in producing commodities is the sole source of real added value (and hence profit) for capital taken as a whole. This point holds in the aggregate regardless of how the resulting surplus may later be divided among particular capitals. Moreover, far from excluding the possibility that superprofits may derive from innovation, other temporary advantages, or monopoly positions at the expense of below-average profits for other capitals, it highlights how competition to generate such superprofits is an important souce of capital's overall dynamic.

The generalization of the commodity form to labour-power does not mean that labour-power actually becomes a commodity. Instead it becomes a *fictitious commodity*. The latter is something that has the form of a commodity (in other words, that can be bought and sold) but is not itself created in a profit-oriented labour process subject to the typical competitive pressures of market forces to rationalize its production and reduce the turnover time of invested capital. There are four key categories of fictitious commodity: land (or nature), money, knowledge and labour-power. Each is often treated as a simple factor of production, obscuring the conditions under which it enters the market economy, gets transformed therein, and so contributes to the production of goods and services for sale. But this tendency to naturalize fictitious commodities as objectively given factors of production leads to the fallacious belief, strongly criticized by Marx, that economic value arises from the immanent, eternal qualities of things rather than from contingent, historically specific social relations.

'Land' comprises all natural endowments (whether located on, beneath or above the earth's surface) and their productive capacities in specific contexts. The current form of such natural endowments typically reflects the past and present social transformation of nature as well as natural developments that occur without human intervention. Virgin land and analogous resources are not produced as commodities by capitalist enterprises but are appropriated as gifts of nature and then transformed for profit – often without due regard to their specific reproduction cycles, overall renewability, or, in the case of land, water and air, their capacities to absorb waste and pollution. Money is a unit of account, store of value, means of payment (for example, taxes, tithes and fines), and a medium of economic exchange. Regardless of whether it has a natural form (for example, cowrie shells), a commodity form (for example, precious metals) or a fiduciary form (for example, paper notes, electronic money), the monetary system in which such monies circulate is not (and could not be) a purely economic phenomenon that is produced and operated solely for profit. For money's ability to perform its economic functions depends critically on extra-economic institutions, sanctions and personal and impersonal trust. Insofar as money circulates as national money, the state has a key role in securing a formally rational monetary system; conversely, its increasing circulation as stateless money poses serious problems regarding the reregulation of monetary relations. Knowledge is a collectively produced common resource based on individual, organizational and collective learning over different time horizons and in varied contexts – non-commercial as well as commercial. Since knowledge is not inherently scarce (in orthodox economic terms, it is a non-rival good), it only gains a commodity form insofar as it is made artificially scarce and access thereto is made to depend on payment (in the form of royalties, license fees, etc.). Thus a profound social reorganization is required to transform knowledge into something that can be sold (Schiller 1988: 32). Finally, the ability to work is a generic human capacity. It gains a commodity form only insofar as workers can be induced or coerced to enter labour markets as waged labour. Moreover, even when it has acquired a commodity form, labour-power is reproduced through non-market as well as market institutions and social relations.

Some of the structural contradictions[3] and strategic dilemmas[4] that arise from extending the commodity form to land, money and knowledge are discussed in later chapters. Here, I focus briefly and commonsensically on labour-power as a generic human capacity. Human reproduction is not organized capitalistically – not yet, at least. Babies are rarely brought into this world as commodities (despite the commercial possibilities of surrogacy and new reproductive technologies); and they are typically cared for in families (or family surrogates) without serious resort to the cash nexus for such care. Mass education is still largely provided by not-for-profit public or private bodies (despite the neoliberal vogue for league tables and market proxies). Employees do not systematically orient their entire lives to opportunities for increased income (despite growing pressures on us all to become enterprising subjects and to welcome the commodification of our entire lives) at the cost of other social relations. In short, although most people must sell their labour-power to be able to live and to participate fully in social life, they are not actually commodities – merely treated as if they were.

It is only when labour-power acquires a commodity form that the market-mediated self-valorization of capital becomes possible. Self-valorization is the process by which capital expands through the profitable reinvestment of past profits. This occurs through the repeated self-transformation of capital as it passes through the circuit of capital. This begins with the stage of money capital, when money as capital is used to purchase materials, means of production and labour-power, which are then combined in a production process through which value is added (the stage of productive capital). Capitalist production involves not only the material transformation of nature to add use-value but also the valorization of capital through the successful appropriation of any exchange-value added by the socially necessary labour time expended during the production process. Any exchange-value so created is only realized, however, by selling these commodities at a profit for money as revenue (the stage of commercial capital). Such sales are not guaranteed. The circuit is completed and renewed with the reinvestment – in the same and/or other areas of production – of the initial capital as augmented by part or all of this profit. As the circuit of capital becomes more developed and differentiated, distinct fractions of capital may emerge around specific functions within the circuit. Thus one can distinguish in elementary terms between money capital, productive capital and commercial capital – whilst recognizing that any individual capital, even if it is specialized in one phase of the circuit, must also engage in its other phases (Bryan 1995: 94–5). At more concrete-complex levels of analysis, richer sets of distinctions may be necessary or appropriate.

With the fictitious commodification of labour-power, the appropriation of surplus labour gains its distinctive capitalist mediation in and through market forces. In short, exploitation[5] takes the form of exchange. The formal subordination of 'commodified' labour-power to capital through the emergence of the market for wage-labour was reinforced historically when the exercise of labour-power in production was brought directly under capitalist control through machine-pacing in the factory system.[6] Commodification turns both the labour market and labour process into sites of class struggle between capital and workers.[7] The basic economic forms of this struggle are shaped by the wage form, the technical and social division of labour and the organization of capitalist production as an economy of time. But the dynamic of economic class struggle also has many other economic and extra-economic determinants and, in addition, class struggles typically spread beyond the economy in its narrow sense to other areas of social organization. The nature of labour-power as a fictitious commodity also shapes the competition among capitals to secure the most effective valorization of labour-power and the appropriation of the resulting surplus value. Competition and class struggle are major sources of capitalism's open-ended dynamic as a mode of production. Lastly, when capital accumulation becomes the dominant principle of organization within the economy in its narrow sense, it also gains a significant influence on the overall nature of societies and, in certain circumstances, it may become the dominant principle of societal organization (see pp. 22–30).

The most important general law in capitalism is the law of value. This describes the tendency of capitalists to allocate resources to different fields of production according to expectations of profit (see box 1.1). Although this law is mediated through market forces and the price mechanism, the operation of which may or may not socially validate these private decisions, it is ultimately grounded in the sphere of production. For it is only here that new value is created through the application of socially necessary labour time and thereby becomes available for any subsequent validation, redistribution or even destruction.[8] Marx also described other laws and tendencies of capitalist economies. These need not concern us for the moment.[9] But we should note that he did not treat the law of value or other tendencies as iron necessities. Instead he emphasized their mediation through capitalist competition and class struggles.

Marx identified an essential contradiction in the commodity form between its exchange- and use-value aspects (Marx 1967). Exchange-value refers to a commodity's market-mediated monetary value for the seller; use-value refers to its material and/or symbolic usefulness to the purchaser. Without exchange-value, commodities would not be produced for sale; without use-value, they would not be purchased.[10] This was the basis on which Marx dialectically unfolded the complex dynamic of the capitalist mode of production – including the necessity of periodic crises and their role in reintegrating the circuit of capital as a basis for renewed expansion. Building on this argument, I suggest that all forms of the capital relation embody different but interconnected versions of this basic contradiction and that these impact differentially on (different fractions of) capital and on (different strata of) labour at different times and places. I discuss different forms of this contradiction in the next section.

These contradictions also affect the wider social formation and are necessarily reproduced as capitalism itself is reproduced. But they need not retain the same relative weight or significance for accumulation or regulation. Indeed, as we shall see, differences in this regard provide one way to distinguish different stages and/or varieties of capitalism. We

Box 1.1   *The 'law of value' in capitalism*

In general terms, the law of value suggests that more time will be spent on producing commodities whose market price is above their price of production as measured by the socially necessary labour time involved in their creation. Conversely, less time will be spent on producing commodities whose market price is lower than their price of production. In capitalist economies this mechanism is complicated, as competition tends to equalize rates of profit even though individual capitals may employ different ratios of physical capital and wage-labour – although the latter is the only source of 'added-value'. Accordingly it is fluctuations in *profits* (market price less cost price) which mediate the law of value in capitalism. In response to these fluctuations and in anticipation of how they might develop in future, individual capitals decide how to allocate not only labour-power but also physical capital to production, distribution and circulation. Whether or not these calculations prove correct and they can sell the resulting commodities at a profit depends on the subsequent operation of market forces and is therefore inherently uncertain. Total production in capitalist economies depends on the uncoordinated decisions of competing capitals about opportunities for profit from different patterns of investment and production. Profit depends not only on the demand for different commodities (reflecting their prevailing use-value) but also on the rate of economic exploitation in different branches of production. It is therefore crucially related to the course and outcome of struggles between capital and labour at many different points in the circuit of capital and in the wider social formation.

should also add here that 'the reproduction of these contradictions with their contradictory effects and their impact on the historical tendency of capitalist development depends on the *class struggle*' (Poulantzas 1975: 40–1; italics in original). I discuss later how appropriate it is to describe different forms of social struggle bearing on capital accumulation in terms of class struggle (see pp. 31–2). It is enough to argue for now that various class-relevant social struggles shape the forms in which the various contradictions and dilemmas of the capital relation come to be expressed in specific conjunctures; they also affect the manner and extent to which possible bases for renewed expansion, if any, get established, blocked or overturned. This explains why accumulation involves an ever-changing balance among repeated cycles of self-valorization, continuous self-transformation, bouts of crisis-induced restructuring and other modalities of change. These are often linked to new patterns of time–space distantiation and compression (see p. 112) as well as to shifts in the dominant spatio-temporal horizons and the leading places and spaces for accumulation. The complexity of these aspects vitiates any unilinear account of the stages of capitalism because they permit different trajectories in different sets of circumstances. For the same reason it precludes any attempt to interpret accumulation in terms of some kind of equilibrium theory.

Capital as an object of regulation

Together, these contradictions and dilemmas mean that the capital relation cannot be reproduced entirely through market exchange and is therefore prone to what is often expressed ideologically as 'market failure'. This means that the improbable self-valorization of capital cannot be explained in terms of some alleged self-correcting, self-expanding logic. This leads us to consider the mechanisms through which, despite capital's contradictions, accumulation may get regularized and reproduced. These extend well beyond the capitalist economy in its narrow sense (profit-oriented production, market-mediated exchange) to include various direct and indirect extra-economic mechanisms. Moreover, insofar as these extra-economic mechanisms also reproduce the contradictions and dilemmas inherent in the economic mechanisms of the capital relation, they further expand the scope for agency, strategies and tactics to shape the course of accumulation and the manner in which these contradictions and dilemmas are expressed. This in turn requires any analysis of the improbable nature of capital accumulation to take agency seriously.

We can best understand what is involved here if we ask why capitalism needs regulating. The answer lies in the indeterminate but antagonistic nature of the capital relation and its dynamic. This has three key aspects:

- the incompleteness of capital as a purely economic (or market-mediated) relation such that its continued reproduction depends, in an unstable and contradictory way, on changing extra-economic conditions;
- the various structural contradictions and strategic dilemmas inherent in the capital relation and their changing structural articulation and forms of appearance in different accumulation regimes, modes of regulation, and conjunctures; and
- conflicts over the regularization and/or governance of these contradictions and dilemmas as they are expressed both in the circuit of capital and the wider social formation.

The first aspect refers to the inherent incapacity of capitalism to achieve self-closure in economic terms or, in other words, to its inability to reproduce itself wholly through the value form in a self-expanding logic of commodification. This is linked to the fictitious nature of land, money, knowledge and, above all, labour-power as commodities and to the dependence of accumulation not only on these fictitious commodities but also on various non-commodity forms of social relations. This incompleteness is a constitutive, or defining, feature of capitalism and has major implications for its overall dynamic. Even at the most abstract level of analysis, let alone in its actually existing forms, the reproduction of capitalism depends on its achieving an inherently unstable balance among market-mediated economic supports and other, extra-economic supports whose efficacy depends on their location beyond market mechanisms. This excludes the eventual commodification of everything and, a fortiori, rules out a pure capitalist economy. The resulting instability explains uneven waves of commodification, decommodification and recommodification as the struggle to extend the exchange-value moments of the capital relation encounters real structural limits and/or increasing resistance and, likewise, as new ways to overcome these limits and resistance are sought (Offe 1984). It is also associated with uneven waves of territorialization, deterritorialization and reterritorialization (Brenner 1999a,b) and the search for new forms of spatio-temporal fix as prevailing fixes begin to decompose (Jessop 1999a; 2000; 2001b; and section 4 below). Such structural limits and contradictions (and their associated 'market failures') provide chances to shift direction insofar as capitalism is constantly oriented, under the pressure of competition, to new opportunities for profit. This open-ended dynamic excludes any final destination towards which the logics of capital accumulation and/or class struggle ineluctably draw it (for elaboration, see Postone 1993). In short, viewed substantively, capitalism has no pregiven trajectory.

Second, accumulation within the capitalist economy as a whole depends essentially on profit-oriented, market-mediated exploitation of wage-labour in the labour process. For, while markets mediate the search for added value and modify its distribution within and across classes, they cannot themselves produce it. Moreover, the very process of commodification rooted in the spread of the market mechanism generates structural contradictions that cannot be resolved by that mechanism. Many of these contradictions and their associated strategic dilemmas are different expressions of the basic contradiction between exchange- and use-value in the commodity form (see table 1.1).

Thus productive capital is both abstract value in motion (notably in the form of realized profits available for reinvestment) and a concrete stock of already invested time- and place-specific assets in the course of

Table 1.1 Sources of tension in basic forms of the capital relation

Form	Exchange-value moment	Use-value moment
Commodity	Exchange-value	Use-value
Labour-power	(a) abstract labour as a substitutable factor of production (b) sole source of surplus value	(a) generic and concrete skills, different forms of knowledge (b) source of craft pride for worker
Wage	(a) monetary cost of production (b) means of securing supply of useful labour for given time	(a) source of effective demand (b) means to satisfy wants in a cash-based society
Money	(a) interest bearing capital, private credit (b) international currency (c) ultimate expression of capital in general	(a) measure of value, store of value, means of exchange (b) national money, legal tender (c) general form of power in the wider society
Productive capital	(a) abstract value in motion (or money capital) available for some form of investment in future time and place (b) source of profits of enterprise	(a) stock of specific assets to be valorized in specific time and place under specific conditions (b) concrete entrepreneurial and managerial skills
Land	(a) 'free gift of nature' that is [currently] unalienable (b) alienated and alienable property, source of rents	(a) freely available and uncultivated resources (b) transformed natural resources
Knowledge	(a) intellectual property (b) monetized risk	(a) intellectual commons (b) uncertainty
State	Ideal collective capitalist	Factor of social cohesion

being valorized; the worker is both an abstract unit of labour-power substitutable by other such units (or, indeed, other factors of production) and a concrete individual (or, indeed, a member of a concrete collective workforce) with specific skills, knowledge and creativity;[11] the wage is both a cost of production and a source of demand; money functions both as an international currency exchangeable against other currencies (ideally in stateless space) and as national money circulating within national societies[12] and subject to some measure of state control; land functions both as a form of property (based on the private appropriation of nature) deployed in terms of expected revenues in the form of rent and as a natural resource (modified by past actions) that is more or less renewable and recyclable; knowledge is both the basis of intellectual property rights and a collective resource (the intellectual commons). Likewise, the state is not only responsible for securing certain key conditions for the valorization of capital and the reproduction of labour-power as a fictitious commodity but also has overall political responsibility for maintaining social cohesion in a socially divided, pluralistic social formation. In turn, taxation is both an unproductive deduction from private revenues (profits of enterprise, wages, interest, rents) and a means to finance collective investment and consumption to compensate for 'market failures'. And so forth.

These structural contradictions are inherent in the capital relation, and the tensions and dilemmas that they generate provide an important entrypoint into the general analysis of capital accumulation. Nonetheless it is also important to recognize that they can assume different forms and different weights in different contexts. They can also prove more or less manageable depending on the specific spatio-temporal fixes and institutionalized class compromises with which they are from time to time associated. These differences provide in turn an important entrypoint for analysing different stages and/or varieties of capitalism. It is in this context that I will argue that the KWNS is just one set of mechanisms among several through which the always problematic delivery of capitalist economic and social reproduction comes to be organized. It coexists with other such mechanisms to produce a specific reproduction regime involved in the overall regulation of capitalism and its embedding into the wider society (see chapters 2 and 4).

Third, modes of regulation and patterns of governance vary considerably. There are various ways in which to seek the closure of the circuit of capital and/or to compensate for lack of closure in securing continued accumulation. Which of these patterns comes to dominate depends on the specific social and spatio-temporal matrices in which these attempts occur. Indeed, despite the inherent tendency for capital accumulation to continue expanding until a single world market is created, there are major countertendencies and other limits to the complete realization of globalization, especially but not only in its neoliberal form (see chapters 3 and 5; also Altvater and Mahnkopf 1999; Polanyi 1944). Thus specific accumulation regimes and their modes of regulation are typically constructed within specific social spaces and spatio-temporal fixes. Taken together, these three sets of factors imply that there is no single best solution to the regularization of capital accumulation – instead, various accumulation regimes and modes of regulation will be associated with their own distinctive forms of appearance of the basic contradictions, dilemmas and conflicts noted above. The overall course of accumulation will depend in turn on how these different solutions complement each other and/or win out in competition in the world market.

2. Accumulation as a Principle of Societalization

The self-valorization of capital can occur where most of the key inputs into capitalist production take the form of (real or fictitious) commodities; there is effective control over labour-power within the labour-process; the environment is sufficiently stable to enable capitals to systematically orient their activities to opportunities for profit; and profits can be realized and reinvested. None of this requires that all social relations have been subsumed under the commodity form and entirely subordinated to market forces. Indeed, capitalism would be impossible if this were so. On the contrary, there is wide variation in how far capitalist market forces (and the associated logic of profit-seeking) come to dominate the overall organization and dynamics of social formations. This raises questions about the conditions under which accumulation can become the dominant principle of societal organization (or societalization). For there are always interstitial, residual, marginal, irrelevant, recalcitrant and plain contradictory elements that escape subordination to any given principle of societalization and, indeed, serve as reservoirs of flexibility and innovation as well as actual or potential sources of disorder. This implies in turn that there is ample scope for conflict over societal projects that privilege radically different organizational principles as well as for conflict over rival projects based on the same principle. Thus social formations may be relatively unified under the dominance of religion (theocracies), military-police considerations (national security states), nation-building (new nations), socially constructed 'racial' demarcations (apartheid), capital accumulation (bourgeois societies), etc. (on societalization, see Jessop 1990b: 4–6).

In this sense bourgeois societalization involves far more than continuing accumulation. This can also occur in theocracies, national security states, new nations, revolutionary situations or state socialist societies.

What bourgeois societalization really involves is the relative subordination of an entire social order to the logic and reproduction requirements of capital accumulation. This could be described as 'the embedding of the market economy in a market society' (Polanyi 1944); as the development of an 'historic bloc' between the economic base, juridico-political superstructure and forms of consciousness (Gramsci 1971); or as the rise of a 'bourgeois civilization'. Four different mechanisms can contribute to such a situation: economic determination, ecological dominance, economic domination and bourgeois hegemony. The first principle is a systemic feature of the operation of the economy, the second concerns the systemic relations between the economy and other systems, the third concerns the institutional and organizational dimensions of structural power in the economy and/or the relation between economic agents and extra-economic forces, and the fourth mechanism operates in the first instance on an ideational or discursive plane – although successful hegemony also tends to become structurally embedded and dispositionally embodied.

Economic determination

Many orthodox Marxists have argued for determination in the last instance of the extra-economic by the economic. This amounts to the claim that the social relations of production ultimately determine the form and functions of juridico-political institutions and the so-called ideological superstructure. There is little merit in this argument and, indeed, even on casual inspection, it is incoherent. For the social relations of production could play this determining role only on two conditions: (1) if they were wholly self-contained and self-reproducing and thus operated as a cause without cause; and (2) if there were a necessary correspondence between the economy, other institutions and the lifeworld. Once we allow for the interdependence of the economic and extra-economic, however, the economic alone could never be determinant in the first, last or any intermediate instance. For the economic lacks the self-closure necessary to determine the extra-economic without being reciprocally determined by the latter in turn. The same argument applies even more forcefully to claims about technological determinism, which assert the ultimately determining role of the forces of production. An alternative way of dealing with this general issue, in terms of ecological dominance, is suggested just below.

Dismissing the ultimately determining role of the forces of production and/or the technical and social relations of production for an entire society does not, however, exclude their importance within the economy. Here the principle of economic determination can be stated in terms of the primacy of production in the overall circuit of capital. By extension, it means the primacy of productive capital (not to be equated solely with industrial capital) over money or commercial capital. This involves no more (but certainly no less) than the fact that wealth must first be produced before it can be distributed or, in Marxist terms, that value must first be produced before it can be realized. The recent rise and fall of the so-called new economy based on the dot.com bubble illustrates this well because the cash-burn rate of dot.com firms was unsustainable and their collapse destroyed value created elsewhere. Likewise, an expansion of state credit to stimulate demand without a matching increase in production can trigger inflation (on inflation in Atlantic Fordism, see chapter 2).

This means in turn that the course of capital accumulation is primarily shaped by the organization of the capitalist economy under the dominance of the value form and its dynamic mediation through the capitalist law of value. Because production lies at the heart of the circuit of capital, productive capital's performance is vital to the overall accumulation process. This implies that the real rates of return on money capital (including credit), commercial capital and landed capital depend in the long term on continued valorization of productive capital. In turn this depends on capital's continued ability to control the terms, conditions and performance of wage-labour and, since added value can be realized only through sale of commodities at appropriate volumes and prices, to ensure that its products are marketable. Owing to the multiplicity of distinct, autonomous centres of production and their output of goods and services in the form of commodities, however, the coordination of the capitalist economy is essentially anarchic, mediated through market forces and competition. Market forces operate *ex post* rather than *ex ante* and this always poses problems regarding the eventual validation of capital's decisions and production (for an extended discussion of market failure, see chapter 6). This holds true even though firms themselves rely more on top-down organization and internal networking than on internal markets and may also cooperate with other economic agents in joint projects. For the underlying competitiveness and current competitive strategies of such firms and alliances will still be exposed to the audit of the market's invisible hand. This account of economic determination, with its emphasis on production, has major implications for analysing the contradictions and dilemmas of so-called post-industrial or knowledge-based capitalism (see chapter 3).

Ecological dominance

This concept was initially developed in the biological sciences. Ecological dominance refers there to the fact that one species exerts an overriding influence upon the other species in a given ecological community.

This idea can usefully be extended to social systems. This requires that due allowance be made both for the latters' specificities as communicatively or discursively mediated systems and for the capacity of social forces to reflect on, and learn about, their own evolution, to engage in deliberate attempts (successful or not) to guide it, and even to modify the forms in which evolution itself evolves (Willke 1997: 48–51). Thus understood, ecological dominance refers to the structural and/or strategic capacity of a given system in a self-organizing ecology of systems to imprint its developmental logic on other systems' operations far more than these systems are able to impose their respective logics on that system.[13] This capacity is always mediated in and through the operational logics of other systems and the communicative rationalities of the lifeworld. For example, the ecological dominance of capitalism over modern states is mediated in part through state managers' calculations about the likely impact of their decisions on alterations in the money markets and fisco-financial system on which state revenues depend. Conversely, state activities and performance tend to impact on the economy through market actors' calculations about their impact on opportunities for profit (or other forms of income). For example, whereas the imperialist roles of Britain and the USA have been associated with strong military-industrial complexes, we find a well-developed 'social-industrial' complex in social democratic welfare regimes (O'Connor 1973). Another example of the relatively path-dependent structural coupling and co-evolution of economic and political regimes can be found in the forms of labour flexibility encouraged by different welfare regimes. Thus liberal welfare regimes with hire-and-fire labour markets encourage employers to exercise their rights to manage, discourage workers from investing in firm-specific skills, and promote the expansion of low-wage private sector services. In contrast, social democratic and Christian democratic (or corporatist-conservative) welfare regimes are associated with economic and social rights that produce relatively inflexible, high-wage labour markets; this encourages workers to acquire firm- or branch-specific skills, prompts firms to take advantage of a skilled labour force and develop high-tech, high-productivity processes and products to recover their higher wage costs, and discourages the expansion of low-wage, low-productivity services sectors (Estevez-Abe et al. 2001; Scharpf 1997). As for the lifeworld, the ecological dominance of capitalism depends on the extent to which monetized, profit-and-loss calculation penetrates the lifeworld at the expense of other modes of calculation and subjectivity. In turn, other identities, values and modes of calculation will affect the capitalist economy mainly insofar as they shape opportunities for profit (or other forms of income) – for example, as sources of labour market segmentation, threats to wage differentials, or an opportunity to develop new markets. I explore what this implies for resistance to capitalism in the next section.

Ecological dominance is always differential, relational and contingent. Thus a given system can be more or less ecologically dominant; its dominance will vary across systems and in different spheres or aspects of the lifeworld; and its dominance will depend on the development of the entire social ecosystem. This does not mean that the ecologically dominant system will not be affected by the operation of other systems or that specific social forces will not attempt to reverse, brake or guide that dominance. Rather, as its name implies, ecological dominance involves an *ecological relation* where one system becomes dominant in a complex, co-evolving situation; it does not involve a one-sided *relation of domination* where one system unilaterally imposes its will on others (cf. Morin 1980: 44). There is no 'last instance' in relations of ecological dominance – they are always contingent. Thus we must study the historically specific conditions under which accumulation tends to become the ecologically dominant process in the wider social formation.

The relevance of ecological dominance to our concerns becomes clear once we recall that capitalism cannot be reproduced solely through the value form. It depends on other systems and the lifeworld to help close the circuit of capital and to compensate for market failures. Outside a fully imaginary pure capitalist economy, then, capitalism is structurally coupled to other systems and the lifeworld. Thus the development of the capitalist (market) economy is closely tied to non-economic factors. It never follows a purely economic logic.

Since other systems and the lifeworld are structurally coupled to the economy as well as each other, we should ask which, if any, of them could become ecologically dominant. There are at least five analytically distinct, but empirically interrelated, aspects that affect a system's potential in this regard in the social (as opposed to biological) world:

- the extent of its internal structural and operational complexity and the resulting degrees of freedom this gives it in securing a given outcome;
- its ability to continue operating, if necessary through spontaneous, adaptive self-reorganization, in a wide range of circumstances and in the face of more or less serious perturbations;
- its capacities to distantiate and compress its operations in time and space to exploit the widest possible range of opportunities for self-reproduction;
- its capacity to resolve or manage its internal contradictions, paradoxes and dilemmas, to displace them into its environment, or defer them into the future; and

- its capacity to get actors in other systems and the lifeworld to identify its own operations as central to the reproduction of the wider
  system of which it is always and necessarily merely a part – and thus
  to get them to orient their operations more or less willingly to their
  understanding of its particular reproduction requirements.

In general terms, the capitalist economy, with its distinctive, self-
valorizing logic, tends to have just those properties that favour ecological
dominance. It is internally complex and flexible because of the decentralized, anarchic nature of market forces and the price mechanism's dual
role as a stimulus to learning and as a flexible mechanism for allocating
capital to different economic activities. Moreover, as capitalism develops,
different organizations, institutions and apparatuses tend to emerge to
express different moments of its contradictions, dilemmas and paradoxes
and these may then interact to compensate for market failures within the
framework of specific spatio-temporal fixes. Capital also develops its
capacity to extend its operations in time and space (time–space distantiation) and to compress them (time–space compression), making it easier
to follow its own self-expansionary logic in response to perturbations.
Through these and other mechanisms it develops the capacity to escape
the particular structural constraints of other systems and their attempts
at control even if it cannot escape from its overall dependence on these
systems' general contribution to its own operation or, of course, from the
crisis-tendencies associated with its own internal contradictions and
dilemmas. Attempts to escape particular constraints and particular
attempts at control can occur through its own internal operations in time
(discounting, insurance, risk management, futures, derivatives, etc.) or
space (capital flight, relocation, extra-territoriality, etc.), through the sub-
version of the logic of other systems through their colonization by the
commodity form, or through simple personal corruption. In certain conditions it can also win support for the primacy of accumulation over other
principles of societalization in the continuing struggle for political, intellectual and moral leadership.

   Nonetheless, ecological dominance, insofar as it exists, is always contingent and historically variable. It depends on the specific properties of
accumulation regimes and modes of regulation, the nature of other
systems in its environment, and specific conjunctural features. Other
systems and their actors will be more or less able to limit or resist commodification and to steer economic activities by imposing their own systemic priorities and modes of calculation on the economy. By way of
illustration, consider the impact of a territorial state committed to an
alternative principle of societalization and willing to accept the political
costs of de-coupling from the world market.[14] Conversely, the rise or

re-emergence of globalization, especially in its neoliberal form, is important in enhancing the ecological dominance of capital by expanding the scope for accumulation to escape such constraints (Jessop 2000: 328–33; chs 3 and 5). Yet this will also enhance the scope for the contradictions and dilemmas of a relatively unfettered (or disembedded) capitalism to shape the operation of other systems and may thereby undermine crucial extra-economic conditions for accumulation.

Moreover, even when conditions do favour the long-term ecological dominance of the capitalist economy, other systems may gain short-term primacy in response to crises elsewhere. For no individual system represents, or can substitute for, the whole. Each autopoietic system is both operationally autonomous and substantively interdependent with other systems. Even an ecologically dominant system depends on the socially adequate performance of other systems and a normally subordinate system may become dominant in exceptional circumstances. This would occur to the extent that solving a non-economic crisis becomes the most pressing problem for the successful reproduction of all systems – including the capitalist economy. For example, during major wars or preparations for them, states may try to plan or guide the economy in the light of perceived military-political needs. This can also be seen in Cold War national security states (for example, Taiwan, South Korea). After such states of emergency have ended, however, the primacy of accumulation is likely to be re-asserted. This does not exclude path-dependent traces of such exceptional conditions in the normally dominant system (for example, the distinctive features of peacetime war economies or legacies of total war on postwar economic trajectories). But, even given such path-dependency, the 'quasi-transcendental meta-code'[15] of the ecologically dominant system will still impact more on other systems' development in the multilateral process of structural coupling and co-evolution than they can on it.

Economic domination

Economic domination has two dimensions. The first is internal to the economy and concerns the power of one or another fraction of capital (or simply a cartel or even a single firm) to impose its immediate interests on other fractions, regardless of their wishes and/or at their expense. Such domination can derive directly from the position of the relevant fraction (cartel, firm) in the overall circuit of capital in a specific economic conjuncture and/or indirectly from the use of some form of extra-economic coercion (including the exercise of state power). Interestingly, many business strategy handbooks provide advice on how best to build and defend such dominant market positions to avoid exposure to the raw winds of perfect competition. There is wide scope for variation in the incidence and exercise of economic domination – subject to the requirement that this must ultimately be compatible with continued valorization of productive capital. If the latter does not occur on an appropriate scale (up to the global), there will be a declining mass of surplus value for distribution among all capitals. In turn, this will provoke a crisis in the accumulation regime or long-run decline, which can only be resolved capitalistically by developing an effective new accumulation strategy and institutionalizing it. How this tension between economic domination and the valorization of productive capital plays itself out is one of the key differentiating factors across varieties of capitalism and specific accumulation regimes, with their distinctive modes of regulation and governance (for an early discussion of economic domination in this sense, albeit in different terms, see Veblen 1958, 1967; and, for a recent interpretation of Veblen in similar terms, see Nitzan 1998).

The second dimension of economic domination involves the articulation of the economic and extra-economic. Here, it refers to the capacity of capital in general, a given fraction of capital, or particular capitals to steer the evolution of other institutional orders in line with the demands of capital accumulation, either through sheer structural power or through specific strategic capacities. Such domination is grounded in the nature of capitalism, can express itself in several ways and can, in certain circumstances, become a major element in the more general ecological dominance of capitalism. First, and most crudely, capital can use its 'strike', 'sabotage' and 'flight' powers to secure the compliance of other systems (such as the state) with its specific reproduction requirements. In the long term this capacity is grounded in the tendential ecological dominance of the capitalist economy; in the short term, it depends on specific forms of material interdependence between the economic and non-economic. Second, as capital searches for new sources of valorization, commodity relations can be extended into spheres not currently subject to the logic of accumulation. This process is seen in commodification of political, educational, health, scientific and many other activities, so that they come to be primarily and directly oriented to opportunities for profit. Third, capital can seek to impose an economizing, profit-seeking logic on other systems, even though their activities remain largely non-commercial. This becomes evident when the choice among these non-commercial activities is shaped by calculations about the economic profitability of applying the relevant primary code in one way or another. For example, neoliberal educational, health, scientific and other 'reforms' are intended to induce decision-makers in these systems to become more business-like. They are induced to make judgements on educational, medical or scientific matters not only in terms of their respective primary codes, but also in terms of their financial implications. This is reflected in careerism, the influence of market proxies in non-commercial organizations and the subordination of diverse institutions to the (perceived, alleged) imperatives of a strong and healthy (internationally competitive) economy.

Economic hegemony

Accumulation strategies involve efforts to resolve conflicts between the needs of capital in general and particular capitals by constructing an imagined 'general economic interest' that will always and necessarily marginalize some capitalist interests. Economic hegemony exists where a given accumulation strategy[16] is the basis for an institutionalized compromise between opposed social forces for coordinating, governing or guiding activities within and across different institutional orders around the pursuit of a particular economic trajectory. Interests are not only relational but also relative, such that a given actor only has interests in relation to others and relative to different spatial and temporal horizons. The imagined general interest limits the identities and relations relative to which interests are calculated; and it defines the spatial and temporal horizons within which this occurs. It involves specific notions about which identities and interests can be synthesized within a general interest, about the articulation of different temporal horizons (short-, medium- and long-term, business cycle, electoral cycle, long wave, etc.), and about spatial horizons (local, regional, national, supranational, etc.). Thus a conception of the general economic interest privileges some identities, interests and spatio-temporal horizons and marginalizes or sanctions others. It also refers to what is needed to secure an institutionalized class compromise appropriate to that accumulation strategy and to address wider problems of social cohesion. In all these respects it is closely related to spatio-temporal fixes (see below).

The conditions for accumulation and regulation often get identified only through a trial-and-error search that reveals them more through repeated failure than sustained success. Moreover, there is nothing in the economic logic of accumulation that entails that it will inevitably subordinate other institutional orders or colonize the lifeworld. To the extent that this occurs, it depends on the outcome of political and ideological struggles around political projects and hegemonic visions as well as on the ecological dominance of the circuit of capital (for further discussion, see Jessop 1990b: 196–219, 307–37).

Capitalist societalization and resistance

Approaching capitalist societalization in these terms enables us to identify sources of resistance to capitalist dominance, domination and hegemony. First, where valorization dominates, class struggles emerge. This happens not only in the capitalist economy narrowly seen – the main field of the economic class struggle between capital and labour – but also in various extra-economic contexts linked to capitalist exploitation. Moreover, if commodification is pushed beyond certain limits, 'market failure' will threaten capital accumulation as a whole. Second, where another system code or non-class identities remain primary, the imposition of profitability as a secondary code may be resisted. For institutional orders and social relations outside the immediate logic of valorization typically have their own values and norms, bases of social inclusion or exclusion, their own forms of structured conflict, and so forth. This tendency is also structurally limited by market failures of different kinds. Third, attempts to establish capitalist hegemony often provoke counterstruggles to resist the claim that accumulation is the key precondition for realizing other social goals. This takes us well beyond actions to modify or challenge system logics to include the lifeworld, which, with its wide range of identities, values and interests, can be a major source of resistance to (as well as site for struggles to establish) bourgeois hegemony.

On class struggle

It is only through a very elastic and imprecise use of the concept that all these forms of resistance can be entirely reduced to class struggle. I prefer to restrict the latter term to struggles to establish, maintain or restore the conditions for self-valorization within the capitalist economy understood in its inclusive sense. This certainly extends well beyond struggles over wages and working conditions to include such aspects of modes of economic regulation as the money form, modes of competition, economic and social policy regimes, or international economic regimes. Moreover, even in this broad (but far from all-embracing) context, it is useful to distinguish explicit 'class consciousness' from the actual impact of different struggles. This distinction matters for two main reasons: first, the proclaimed class identity of a given social force and/or form of struggle could be deliberately misrepresented, simply mistaken or wholly imaginary; second, the polyvalence of all social struggles means that their provisional outcomes can often be recuperated or subverted at later dates. The class relevance of particular struggles is never given once and for always but is both fought for and played out over time and space. There is certainly no univocal correspondence between the declared class belonging (i.e. location, affiliation or membership) and the actual class impact of particular social movements or forms of struggle. Nor, equally obviously, can class interests or their impact be derived from abstract positions in the capital relation. Any calculation of such interests requires participants or observers to undertake a strategic-relational analysis of specific conjunctures – including the extent to which accumulation is the dominant principle of societalization (see Jessop 1982: 241–7).

The remaining sites and stakes of resistance to capitalism are less suited to a simple class analysis (see table 1.2). They often involve conflicts over the very principle of accumulation itself rather than over class interests within capitalism. They involve both the extension of the logic of capital to other spheres and attempts to establish bourgeois hegemony over society as a whole. Such conflicts often mobilize popular movements organized around issues of social exclusion and marginalization and/or 'elite' social movements concerned to realign diverse institutional orders, identities and interests. 'Civil society' can become a major stake in many of these conflicts. It is the site both of colonizing struggles to integrate civil society more effectively into the service of one or another specific institutional order (for example, through commodification, juridification, scientization, the rise of the 'learning society', politicization, militarization, etc.) and also of struggles to resist and roll back such colonization attempts in defence of identities and interests that lie outside and/or cross-cut them (for example, class, gender, sexual orientation, 'race', nation, stage in the life-course, disability, citizenship, human rights, or the environment). In this sense, popular or elite movements organized around extra-economic institutional orders, with their own modes of domination and exclusion and their own politics of identity and difference, have no necessary class belonging (Laclau 1977). But they still have a conjuncturally determined – thus hard to calculate and provisional – class relevance. The opposite problem occurs as ostensibly non-class movements (such as feminism or anti-racist movements) seek to calculate the strategic or tactical value of alliances with class-based or largely class-relevant movements. All such struggles involve serious strategic dilemmas. These include the relative weight to be attached to different bases of mobilization in broad coalitions; and the risks of political fragmentation when there are no attempts to build lasting coalitions when there are many such bases (Poulantzas 1978). The struggle to establish accumulation as a dominant/hegemonic principle of societalization typically extends well beyond class struggles, even broadly understood.

Some preliminary conclusions and caveats on capitalism

I have now presented the initial set of concepts to be used in the following analysis of capital accumulation and its implications for the future of the capitalist state. Different sets of concepts would be appropriate if my main interest were in other aspects of capitalism and/or social

Table 1.2 Bases of capitalist societalization and resistance thereto

Base of bourgeois societalization	Mode of resistance	Typical actors mobilized for or against this basis
Development of the market 'Fictitious' commodification and imposition of the value form in economic relations	Class struggles in their proper sense – including struggles against the extra-economic conditions for the dominance of value forms	(a) Individuals and/ or collectivities with class identities (b) Other social forces whose struggles are relevant to consolidation of this basis
Imposition of 'economizing' logic in non-economic areas	Struggles for the primacy of other modes of calculation	Various social categories identified with and/or supportive of other values and modes of calculation
Ecological dominance of capitalist economy	Struggles to privilege the operational logic of some other system or systems	Advocates of other logics (e.g., legality, military security, health, religion)
Economic hegemony of a given accumulation strategy	Struggles to consolidate a counter-hegemonic project that prioritizes values other than the logic of permanent capitalist expansion	Forces based in 'lifeworld' allied with social categories from non-economic systems and with subordinate social classes Such struggles may become the basis for a new hegemonic bloc, i.e., a durable alliance based on alternative hegemonic project

formations. As my approach to these issues is rooted in Marxist theory but departs from many orthodox interpretations, it is worth listing some of the conceptual innovations that distinguish the proposed form-analytic and strategic-relational reading of Marxism from some of the more orthodox interpretations that have been developed during its long and troubled history. Many of these innovations have either been adumbrated or more fully developed elsewhere: for example, in the regulation approach, recent Marxist state theory and critical discourse analysis. My other source of inspiration is the theory of self-organizing systems, their structural coupling and co-evolution. Table 1.3 presents some of the main innovations (including some to be introduced later in this chapter) for the research programme enabled by this approach but the initial test of their heuristic and explanatory power must await more detailed analyses in other chapters.

Five caveats are also needed before we consider the form and functions of the capitalist type of state. First, while many institutions are related to fundamental categories of the capital relation (such as the commodity, labour-power, money, capital or price), the different forms they adopt are irreducible to these basic categories. Institutions matter.[17] The extensive body of work on successive stages of capitalist development and/or varieties of capitalism illustrates this well. Such work examines how different configurations of structural forms can be stabilized and will lead to different weights being attached to different contradictions and dilemmas and to their different aspects, to different patterns of conflict and compromise, and to different prospects of displacing and/or deferring problems and crisis-tendencies. Such work can be taken yet further by considering the complementarities and conflicts over different time horizons and on different scales not only within but also across different varieties of capitalism. Second, particular structural and institutional forms are always constituted in and through action, always tendential and always in need of stabilization. In particular, any tendencies linked with particular accumulation regimes or modes of regulation, let alone with capitalism itself, are themselves always tendential. This doubly tendential nature of tendencies means that the very presence of the tendencies linked with a given accumulation regime or mode of regulation (whether or not such tendencies are also actualized in specific circumstances) depends on the extent to which the social forms that generate them are themselves reproduced. This implies that the incomplete realization and/or subsequent decomposition of a given social form will attenuate what would otherwise be regarded as its otherwise naturally necessary tendencies. Third, structural forms and institutions never wholly constrain actions. For our purposes this means that struggles will tend to overflow structural forms that were instituted to contain them or

Table 1.3 Some new concepts in the strategic-relational approach

Some orthodox Marxist arguments	The strategic-relational alternatives
Economic determination in the last instance of overall social formation and its development. This occurs through the development of productive forces and/or the development of the social relations of production	(a) Necessary tendential primacy of productive capital within circuit of capital (b) Contingent ecological dominance of capital accumulation in wider society
Relative autonomy of the capitalist state as an 'ideal collective capitalist' with no more nor less autonomy than is required to secure the complex economic, political and ideological conditions for accumulation	(a) Operationally autonomous, institutionally separate political system such that (b) this separation problematizes state's performance for and on behalf of capital
Either Unilateral determining role of the economic base in relation to the juridico-political superstructure and major forms of social consciousness *Or* Mutual functional linkages between economic base, juridico-political superstructure and ideologies serve to reproduce the capitalist economy	(a) Mutual structural coupling of operationally autonomous systems under 'ecological dominance' of accumulation (strongest when the world market is fully developed) (b) 'Spatio-temporal fix' *may* help to displace or defer contradictions, dilemmas, etc.; but this is always limited, provisional, and may not coincide with state boundaries (c) An 'historic bloc' *may* emerge from structural coupling and co-evolution of different institutional orders in a social formation
Civil society is a distinct sphere beyond the state and the market where individuals pursue their own egoistic self-interests	'Lifeworld' is a realm of identities, values, modes of calculation and social relations not anchored in specific systems or their logics
Class struggle develops to the extent that objectively pre-given classes (defined by their place in the relations of production) become more active, class-conscious 'classes-for-themselves' and also develop the appropriate forms of economic and political organization to serve their interests The latter are also objectively pre-given by classes' respective places in production, the wider social formation and the general logic of capitalist development	(a) Distinguish 'class identities' from the 'class relevance' of social forces and struggles (b) Discourse has a key role in defining all identities ('class' and non-class alike) (c) Objective interests linked to any given subjective identity are relative and can only be calculated for specific fields of struggle and conjunctures rather than on a permanent and comprehensive basis

have resulted from institutionalized compromises. This is one of the key themes of the strategic-relational approach and highlights the contingency and relativity of structural constraints (Jessop 1982, 1985, 1990b, 2001a,c; and pp. 40–1 below). Fourth, strategies cannot be explained purely as products of contradictions even though contradictions and their associated dilemmas do open a space for strategic choice. For strategies are always elaborated in and through discourses; and their implementation depends on organizational and learning capacities. Fifth, and finally, strategies are implemented on a strategically selective terrain which makes some strategies more viable than others. This terrain is not purely economic, however broadly the economy may be defined. It is always the product of the interaction of economic and extra-economic systems and social relations.

3. Capital, the State, and Policy Regimes

This section presents some basic categories for analysing the capitalist type of state and relates these to economic and social policy regimes. Its historical premise and conceptual starting point is the institutional separation of the economic and extra-economic in capitalism. This separation is rooted in the generalization of the commodity form to labour-power so that coercion can be excluded from the operation of labour markets, and is also required to manage the unstable balance between the inherent capitalist drive to ever greater commodification and its dependence on non-commodity forms of social relations. This separation does not involve a single, fixed and immutable boundary; instead, it involves plural, contested and mutable boundaries. Nor are these boundaries identical to the (always complex) institutional separation between economy and state; instead, they involve a wide range of often heterogeneous, if not irreconcilable, distinctions between the economic and the extra-economic. These typically undergo major shifts when accumulation regimes and modes of regulation change. For example, as later chapters argue, the changing forms of competitiveness associated with globalizing, knowledge-based economies lead to a major rearticulation of the economic and extra-economic. More generally, this is linked to changing forms of state intervention that affect the definition, regulation and operation of market forces narrowly conceived as well as to the broader restructuring, rescaling and retemporalizing of market–state–civil society relations. This conceptual triplet has the merit of indicating that the 'extra-economic' includes not only the state or juridico-political system but also the family, household and forms of civic association. This is helpful when showing how neoliberal 'rollback' of the state tends to displace the burdens of adjustment to market failure onto the family (for which, read, in most cases, women) or the institutions, networks and solidarities of civil society. But these three terms are really only convenient shorthand for a much more complex and variable set of social relations.

The capitalist type of state

The modern state is often characterized in terms of its claim to a legitimate (or constitutionalized) monopoly of organized coercion in a given territorial area, its other distinctive state capacities (for example, the ability to raise taxes or the right to make decisions that are collectively binding on individuals and collectivities present in its sovereign territory), or its distinctive political logic, rationality or governmentality (for example, its maintenance of territorial integrity, its formal responsibility for promoting a socially constructed 'public interest' in the face of private egoism, its key role in maintaining social cohesion). However, while these arguments may help to establish the distinctiveness of the state and politics, they must be complemented by an understanding of the historical preconditions of the modern state and the complexities of its subsequent articulation and interpenetration with other institutional orders and civil society. Otherwise they risk fetishizing and naturalizing the institutional separation between economic and political, the juridical distinction between public and private, the functional division between domestic and foreign policy, etc. This risk is most marked in the state-centred approach that sought to 'bring the state back in' as a key independent variable in social scientific analysis (classically, Evans et al., 1985). In contrast, along with many other critical state theorists, I view such boundaries as discursively constituted, institutionally materialized, structurally coupled to other institutional boundaries, essentially contested and liable to change (on the critical role of the imaginary state–society boundary, see especially Mitchell 1991).

It is important nonetheless to recognize that the capitalist type of state has features that distinguish it both from states in precapitalist or non-capitalist formations and from atypical forms of political regime (for example, predatory military dictatorships) in societies where capitalism in some form[18] is nonetheless a significant feature of economic organization. For the capitalist type of state has a distinctive, form-determined strategic selectivity with major implications for the organization and effectiveness of state intervention (see especially Gramsci 1971; Krätke 1984; O'Connor 1973; Offe 1972; Pashukanis 1978; Poulantzas 1973, 1978; Théret 1992). I present some of these basic form-analytic features in table 1.4, but take them for granted hereafter in order to highlight more

Table 1.4 Some key features of the capitalist type of state

Articulation of economy and state in capitalism	Implications for the economy and class relations	Implications for the state and politics
Institutional separation between market economy, sovereign state and a public sphere (civil society) located beyond market and state	Economy is organized under dominance of capitalist law of value as mediated through competition between capitals and economic class struggle	*Raison d'état* (autonomous political rationality) distinct from profit-and-loss logic of market and from religious, moral, or ethical principles
Constitutionalized claim to a monopoly of organized coercion within the territory mapped by the state. Role of legality in legitimation of the state and its activities	Coercion is excluded from immediate organization of labour process. Thus value form and market forces, not direct coercion, shape capital accumulation. Nonetheless coercion has a key role in securing external conditions of existence of the operation of the capitalist economy	Specialized military-police organs are subject to constitutional control. Force has ideological as well as repressive functions Subject to law, state may intervene to compensate for market failure in 'national' or 'public' interest
State is a tax state. Income derives largely from taxes on economic property, actors and activities and from loans raised from market actors Tax capacity depends on legal authority + coercion Ideal bourgeois tax form is a continuing and general contribution to government revenue that can be applied freely by state to legitimate tasks – not ad hoc, specifically levied for specific tasks	Taxes deducted from private revenues may be used to produce 'public goods'. Thus a possible tension between exchange- and use-value aspects of tax state activities If state-owned and operated production is profitable, this reduces state's dependence on private economic forces and/or weakens institutional separation. Unprofitable activities may socialize losses, redistribute losses or destroy wealth and value	Subjects of the state in its territory have a general duty to pay taxes, regardless of whether or not they approve of specific state activities National money issued by the state is also the means of payment for taxes Taxation capacity acts as security for sovereign debt Taxes and their application are one of the earliest foci of class and political struggles

Table 1.4 Continued

Specialized administrative staff with own channels of recruitment, training, and *ésprit de corps*. This staff is subject to the authority of the political executive. It forms a social category (not a class) that is internally divided by market and status position	State occupies specific place in general division between manual and mental labour. Officials and political class tend to specialize in mental labour with close relationship between their specialized knowledge and their power. Knowledge becomes major basis of state's capacities	Official discourse has a key role in the exercise of state power. Public and private intellectuals formulate state and hegemonic projects that define the national and/or 'national-popular' interest. State derives its legitimacy by reflecting national and/or 'national-popular' interest
Rechtstaat: state is based on the rule of law, not of men. A division between private, administrative and public law. International law governs relations between states. No formal monopoly of political power in hands of dominant economic class(es) but formal 'equality before the law' of all citizens	Economic subjects are formally free and equal owners of commodities, including labour-power Private law develops on the basis of property rights and contract law State has a key role in securing external conditions for economic exchange	Formal subjects of state are individuals with citizenship rights, not feudal estates or collective economic classes. Struggles to extend these rights play a key role in the expansion of state activities Public law organized around the individual–state, public–private, and the national–international distinctions
Formally sovereign state with distinct and exclusive territorial domain in which it is free to act without direct, authoritative interference from other states or actors Substantively, states are constrained in exercise of sovereignty by balance of international forces as well as by domestic balance	Conflict between economy as abstract and apolitical 'space of flows' in the world market and as the sum of localized activities, with an inevitably politically overdetermined character Particular capitals may try to escape state control or seek support in world competition from their respective states	Ideally, states are recognized by other states as sovereign in their own territories but they may need to defend this territorial integrity by force Political and military rivalry depends in part on strength of national economy. Need to balance pursuit of geo-economic and geo-political goals and social cohesion

specific institutional features of this type of state as it was instantiated in the circuits of Atlantic Fordism. It is perhaps worth noting nonetheless that the generic features listed in the table do not include democratic institutions, even though the current 'normal' form of the capitalist type of state involves representative democracy based on universal adult suffrage for the citizens of a given territorial state and an executive authority and/or legislative power formally accountable to its citizens. This feature is not coeval with the capitalist type of state. It has developed more recently and rather unevenly in the twentieth century in the advanced capitalist societies and was still absent in the three peripheral Fordist capitalist economies of Southern Europe until the mid-1970s. Representative democracy nonetheless has important implications for the forms of political struggle, especially for the increased influence of mass politics within and at a distance from the state and for significance of the orientation to the 'national-popular' interest in attempts to define state and hegemonic projects (see Gramsci 1971; Jessop 1982, 1990b; Poulantzas 1973, 1978).

The general form-analytic, strategic-relational approach adopted below treats the state as a social relation (Poulantzas 1978). This implies that the exercise of state power (or, better, state powers in the plural) involves a form-determined condensation of the changing balance of forces. In other words, state power reflects the prevailing balance of forces as this is institutionally mediated through the state apparatus with its structurally inscribed strategic selectivity. Adopting this approach, the state can be defined as a relatively unified ensemble of socially embedded, socially regularized, and strategically selective institutions, organizations, social forces and activities organized around (or at least involved in) making collectively binding decisions for an imagined political community. By strategic selectivity, I understand the ways in which the state considered as a social ensemble has a specific, differential impact on the ability of various political forces to pursue particular interests and strategies in specific spatio-temporal contexts through their access to and/or control over given state capacities – capacities that always depend for their effectiveness on links to forces and powers that exist and operate beyond the state's formal boundaries.[19] It follows that to talk of state managers, let alone of the state itself, exercising power is at best to perpetuate a convenient fiction that masks a far more complex set of social relations that extend far beyond the state apparatus and its distinctive capacities. Interestingly, this is reflected in the practices and discourses of state managers themselves. For, whilst they sometimes proudly claim the credit for having initiated and carried through a general strategic line or a specific policy, at other times they happily seek to offload responsibility for state actions and/or outcomes to other social forces (or to *force majeure*) at one or more points else-where in the ongoing struggle over power. While the constitutionaliza-tion and centralization of state power enable responsibility to be formally attributed to named officials and bodies, this should not lead us to fetishize the fixing of formal political responsibility at specific points and/or in specific personages. We should always seek to trace the circu-lation of power through wider and more complex sets of social relations both within and beyond the state. This is especially important where the growing complexity and mass mediatization of the exercise of state power lead to a search for charismatic figures who can simplify political realities and promise to resolve them. For, as Grande (2000) shows, charisma actually serves to hide complex, if not chaotic, behind-the-scenes practices which would be hard to explain or defend in public.

This approach is inconsistent with any attempt to treat the state as a simple instrument or functional mechanism for reproducing capitalist relations of production. Indeed, it suggests that the typical form of the capitalist state actually problematizes its overall functionality for capital accumulation and political class domination. For the institutional sepa-ration of the state from the market economy, a separation which is a nec-essary and defining feature of capitalist societies, results in the dominance of different (and potentially contradictory) institutional logics and modes of calculation in the state and the economy (for example, Hirsch 1976; Offe 1984; Poulantzas 1978; Reuten and Williams 1989; Wood 1981). Thus there is no guarantee that political outcomes will serve the needs of capital – even assuming that these could be objectively identified in advance in sufficient detail to provide the basis for a capitalistically ratio-nal plan of state action and inaction. The operational autonomy of the state is a further massive complicating factor in this regard. Indeed, to the extent that it enables the state to pursue the interests of capital in general at the expense of particular capitals, it also enables it to damage the interests of capital in general. Accordingly, one must pay careful attention to the structurally inscribed strategic selectivity of the specific state forms and political regimes; and move away from abstract, often essentialist theorization towards more detailed accounts of the complex interplay of social struggles and institutions. A key element in such inves-tigations is a concern with the changing state and/or hegemonic projects that define the nature and purposes of state actions (and inaction) in particular periods, stages and phases of social development and/or in different varieties of capitalism with their distinctive institutional configurations. It also requires attention to statecraft (the art of govern-ment) as a repertoire of skilled, discursive practices that reflexively monitor events and activities beyond as well as within the state and thereby inform state projects and attempts to exercise state power.

In this regard, the state can be studied in terms of six interrelated dimensions. Three primarily concern formal institutional aspects of the state regarded as a social relation: (1) modes of political representation and their articulation; (2) the internal articulation of the state apparatus; and (3) modes of intervention and their articulation. Each of these has its own structurally inscribed strategic selectivities and, while analytically distinct, they typically overlap empirically. Corporatism, to give a clear example of such overlap, involves representation, decision-making and intervention on the basis of function in the division of labour. These aspects can be studied at different levels of abstraction and complexity, ranging from the most basic state forms through to quite concrete-complex descriptions of specific regimes. The other three dimensions mainly concern substantive and strategic aspects of the state regarded as a social relation: (4) the political projects articulated by different social forces that are represented within the state system, seek such representation, or contest its current forms, functions and activities; (5) the prevailing state project with its *raison d'état* – or governmental rationality – and statecraft that seeks to impose an always relative unity on the various activities of different branches, departments and scales of the state system and that also defines the boundaries between the state and its environment as a precondition of the ongoing attempts to build such an improbable internal unity; and (6) the hegemonic projects that seek to reconcile the particular and the universal by linking the nature and purposes of the state into a broader – but always selective – political, intellectual and moral vision of the public interest, the good society, the commonweal, or some analogous principle of societalization. These projects give content to the more formal features of the state and it is the contest among social forces over competing projects that mediate structural and strategic changes in the state in given conjunctures.

Capital and the state

Even a pure capitalist economy, notwithstanding the claims of some classical economists and neoliberal ideologues, would be prone to market failure. Individual capitals compete for profit, act self-interestedly and try to avoid limits on their freedom of action. Competition discourages individual capitals from undertaking activities necessary for economic and social reproduction that are unprofitable from their individual viewpoint and it may also lead them into activities that undermine the general conditions for economic and social reproduction. Regarding economic reproduction, for example, there is no guarantee that the general external conditions for production (such as law, property and money) will be secured through market forces; nor that certain general economic conditions of production ('public goods') will be offered at the right price in the right quantities. This suggests the need for extra-economic institutions to compensate for partial or total market failure in the provision of the important conditions for capital accumulation. These include a formally rational monetary system, a formally rational legal system and the reproduction of labour-power as a fictitious commodity. But, as I have indicated above and will elaborate below, there are many other conditions too. In this sense, state intervention is not just a secondary activity aimed at modifying the effects of a self-sufficient market but is absolutely essential to capitalist production and market relations. For commodities must be produced before they can be distributed via the market and/or political action. Thus, given the institutional separation between the economic and the political, the state must ensure that capital accumulation occurs before it can begin its redistributive activities (Müller and Neusüss 1975: 43–6; Offe 1972).

There are many ways in which the state can and does intervene in these respects. In abstract terms, state support for the valorization of capital and social reproduction can be provided through force, law and regulation, money, goods and services, knowledge, or 'moral suasion' and in the form of meta-, macro-, meso- or micropolicies. The relative weight and adequacy of such means of intervention, as we shall see, vary significantly over time and in relation to specific accumulation regimes. Economic and social policies can be oriented in turn to supply-side conditions and/or the demand for (fictitious) commodities or non-traded goods and services. Metapolicies address the wide variety of extra-economic factors that affect the systemic competitiveness based on society's overall organizational patterns (Messner 1998) and their character will change along with notions of competitiveness (see chapter 3). Macropolicies focus on the general external conditions of production (for example, formally rational legal and monetary systems) and on the provision of general conditions of production (for example, infrastructure and the supply of labour-power) within the spatio-temporal horizons of a discursively and institutionally constituted economy. In the era of imperialism, for example, this was a plurinational economy organized in terms of centre–periphery relations. In the case of Atlantic Fordism, the macrolevel was naturalized as the national economy managed by the Keynesian welfare national state. More recently, European Economic Space is being imagined and instituted as the appropriate macroeconomic framework for European Union (EU) intervention. In all three cases, of course, states also pursued policies concerned to insert the relevant macrolevel economy into wider sets of economic relations up to the world market. Mesopolicies concern specific branches/sectors and/or specific spaces/places within this broader economic system. And, finally, micropolicies affect 'individual' economic units (such as house-holds, individual workers or individual firms).

These distinctions are always relative to particular scales of analysis. This can be seen in the partial rescaling of the macrolevel up to Europe for EU member states and in the changing scope of the meta- and mesolevels in the present era of globalization. The distinction between supply- and demand-side policies is likewise relative to specific markets, commodity chains, and so forth. Moreover, as the taken-for-granted meanings of these distinctions began to decompose as a result of the crisis of the postwar national mixed economy, space has opened for debates over what should replace the conventional set of policy goals for the Keynesian welfare national state.

A brief and incomplete list of general functions that states might perform regarding the capitalist economy is presented in box 1.2. These general functions acquire institutionally specific forms in specific stages and varieties of capitalism and are articulated to more distinctive functions related to these particular stages and varieties and their accumulation regimes and modes of regulation. There can be no guarantees (let alone guarantees inscribed in the general nature of the capitalist type of state) that these complex and interrelated functions will be performed adequately from the viewpoint of accumulation. For, as I have argued above, the capital relation is inevitably incomplete and contradictory so that, even at a purely techno-economic level, performance of these functions inevitably has contradictory effects. Further, as a glance at this incomplete list indicates, state intervention in these matters involves far more than narrow techno-economic issues. It always affects more than the forces of production, the profitability of capital, or more general economic performance. And it always occurs in a wider political context concerned with state and governmental legitimacy as well as social cohesion and exclusion. Thus choices among economic and social policies are typically linked to prevailing accumulation strategies, state projects, hegemonic projects and more general philosophical and normative views of the good society. One area where the inevitably political character of economic and social intervention is especially clear is the reproduction of labour-power as a fictitious commodity. For this is also associated in the capitalist type of state with a citizen's right to existence (cf. Reuten and Williams 1989).

Labour-power and social reproduction

I have already referred briefly to the centrality of the capital–labour relation in the valorization of capital and to the state's role in securing the wage relation and capital's rights to manage the labour process. I will

Box 1.2 *Some functions of the capitalist type of state*

1. Securing the general external conditions for capital accumulation, such as a formally rational legal order and protection of property rights.
2. Securing the fictitious commodification of land, money, labour-power and knowledge and modulating their subsequent de- and recommodification in the light of the changing forms of appearance of capital's structural contradictions and strategic dilemmas and of the changing balance of forces contesting the extent and consequences of such fictitious commodification. In relation to labour-power, this involves managing the supply of labour-power, labour markets and the terms of employment within the labour process.
3. Securing the rights and capacities of capital to control labour-power in the production process and regulating the terms and conditions of the capital–labour relation in the labour market and labour process.
4. Defining the boundaries between the economic and extra-economic and modifying the links between the economic and extra-economic preconditions of capital accumulation in the light of changing materially and discursively constituted forms of competition and in the light of resistance to the colonization of the extra-economic by the logic of capital.
5. Promoting the provision of the general conditions of production, especially capital-intensive infrastructure with a long turnover time, appropriate to a given stage and/or variety of capitalism.
6. Managing the fundamental contradiction between the increasingly social nature of productive forces and the continuing private and competitive nature of the social relations of production and the appropriation of surplus labour.
7. Articulating the interlinked processes of de- and reterritorialization and de- and retemporalization associated with the remaking of the spatio-temporal fixes necessary for relatively stable periods of accumulation.
8. Addressing the wider political and social repercussions of the changing forms of appearance of capitalist contradictions and dilemmas as these are mediated in and through specific forms of political organization and social mobilization.

now consider the state's role in social reproduction. This involves the day-to-day, lifetime and intergenerational reproduction of social subjects in accordance with specific principles of societalization. In capitalist social formations, social reproduction is organized mainly through and/or around the (changing) wage relation and its insertion into an economy dominated by accumulation for the sake of accumulation. The capitalist wage relation has three features that militate against a harmonious, market-mediated solution to social reproduction – especially when the latter goes beyond daily survival as an active member of the labour force to include maintenance over the life-course and intergenerational reproduction. First, employees and their dependants (if any) are free to spend their wages without regard to the needs of capital and may be objectively unable to do so, even if they were so inclined. Thus workers may not reproduce their labour-power (including specific skills, knowledge and commitment as well as generic working capacity) to satisfy the material needs of capital; and they may not enter the labour market (or remain within it) on terms favourable to its continuing valorization. Moreover, insofar as consumption norms are co-constituted by particular capitals offering particular commodities, workers may adopt patterns of consumption that are harmful to capital in general (even if profitable for some particular capitals) as well as to themselves. Even where labour-power is adequately reproduced, employment may not be available at an appropriate wage, or at all. Second, once wage-labour is subject to capitalist control in the labour process, it may be destroyed or weakened through over-exploitation (excessive hours or work intensity) or through 'collateral' damage (such as accidents or occupational diseases). For capital tends to prioritize its self-valorization rather than the reproduction and welfare of labour-power. Particular capitals are certainly not obliged to invest in improving their 'human capital' or to compensate for its depreciation unless it is profitable to do so and, indeed, it is widely recognized that there is a general tendency for capital to under-invest in education and training. This problem is linked to the contradiction between labour-power as one substitutable factor of production among others and labour-power as a specific set of skills and competencies; and to the contradiction between the wage as cost of production and source of demand. Nonetheless some types of production regime and modes of regulation do manage to institutionalize partial solutions. Third, regarding both its private consumption and its exploitation in the labour process, workers find it hard to defend their collective interests in reproducing their labour-power – especially where there is a large pool of unemployed but employable workers.

These problems concerning a purely market-mediated reproduction of labour-power create a space for one or more extra-economic (here, non-market) institutions that can help to reproduce the labour force to the extent that the market cannot achieve this. The role of domestic labour performed outside the cash nexus is obviously important here and this is why the family and/or household forms (hence gender and inter-generational relations too) are always major objects of governance as well as sites of struggle. The present work is mainly concerned, however, with the key roles of the state in these matters. The latter operates on one or more scales from the local to the supranational to contribute directly or indirectly to the reproduction of labour-power over the life cycle, affecting daily, lifetime and intergenerational reproduction. Its twin tasks are, if possible, to ensure a continuing and adequate supply of appropriately qualified labour-power in relation to the changing (and often unpredictable) demands of the labour market and to compensate for the effects of commodification on social reproduction and social cohesion (Aumeeruddy et al. 1978; de Brunhoff 1978; Offe 1985b; Reuten and Williams 1989).

The wage relation is therefore the starting point for a wide range of policies directed at the 'social question', which involves more than social policy. For, as Kaufmann notes:

> What we generally term the welfare state refers not only to the state, but also, as German social scientists precisely formulated in the mid-19th century, to civil society. The 'mediation' between the private sphere of the market economy and the public sphere of government under law was referred to around 1850 as 'Sozialpolitik' (Pankoke 1970). 'Sozialpolitik' may be translated into English as 'social policy' or 'social politics'. In the German context the main concern addressed by social politics was the political and social integration of the emerging working classes into the newly constituted German Reich. In the British and Scandinavian tradition there was, for a long time, no comprehensive concept for the emerging policies of labour protection, social security and social services. The term 'welfare state' was accepted in Scandinavia in the 1930s, but was only widely used in Great Britain after World War II. 'Welfare state' here is less concerned with social politics than with social policies. (2001: 17)

Kaufmann's reference to national traditions illustrates once more the role of discourse in constituting state policy. He also indicates significant variations in individual national states over time as issues of economic and social policy are reproblematized in different ways and as appropriate new governmental solutions are proposed, instituted and pursued.

The fact that neither employees nor individual capitals can solve these dilemmas unaided does not mean that the state *can* (or must) solve them. Indeed, as with the other state functions discussed above, it is unlikely that the state could ever know in advance how to solve them even were such total solutions possible. Such economic and social functions require active management of changing conjunctures within an inherently contradictory system rather than pursuit of predetermined and autonomous economic and social policies. They are always mediated in and through political struggles broadly defined rather than determined in narrow technical and economic terms. And they are affected by the state's own distinctive failures and crisis-tendencies, rooted in the distinctive nature of politics in capitalist societies. Although these dilemmas are handled on various economic levels from the firm upwards and on various non-economic sites, the state has not only been a major addressee of demands in these areas but has also gained a major role in managing these dilemmas directly or indirectly through its labour market and social policies.

4. On Spatio-temporal Fixes

I have already suggested that reproducing and regularizing capital as a social relation involves a social fix (mode of regulation) that compensates for the incompleteness of the pure capital relation in specific contexts and gives it a specific dynamic through the articulation of its economic and extra-economic elements. This social fix helps secure a relatively durable structural coherence in managing the contradictions and dilemmas inherent in the capital relation, so that different forms, institutions and practices tend to be mutually reinforcing. This includes the imposition on these economic and extra-economic elements of a spatio-temporal fix. This concept will be elaborated in later chapters, but some brief comments are appropriate here.

Structurally, these fixes emerge when an accumulation regime and its mode of regulation co-evolve to produce a certain structural coherence within a given spatio-temporal framework but not beyond it. This is typically associated with a distinctive hierarchy of structural forms that affects interactions within the institutional architecture as a whole and thereby shapes the overall logic of the spatio-temporal fix. This hierarchy involves giving greater priority to the regularizing of some structural forms (and giving greater priority, perhaps, to one or other aspect of their associated contradictions and dilemmas) than to other structural forms. These priorities will vary with accumulation regimes, modes of growth and governance capacities (cf. Petit 1999). In Atlantic Fordism, for example, the wage and money forms were the principal structural forms at the heart of the mode of regulation; in post-Fordism, other forms have become more important (see chapters 2 and 3). Or, again, while liberal market economies may give more weight to labour-power as a substitutable factor of production and to the wage as a cost of production, more coordinated capitalist economies may prioritize labour-power in its guise as so-called human capital and the wage as a source of demand. Strategically, because capitalism's contradictions and dilemmas are insoluble in the abstract, they are resolved – partially and provisionally, if at all – through the formulation-realization of specific accumulation strategies at various economic and political scales in specific spatio-temporal contexts. Once again, then, because of the significance of accumulation strategies (and their associated state projects and, where relevant, hegemonic visions), we observe the importance of agency and discourse in capital accumulation. Such spatio-temporal fixes delimit the main spatial and temporal boundaries within which structural coherence is secured, and externalize certain costs of securing this coherence beyond these boundaries. Even within these boundaries some classes, class fractions, social categories or other social forces located inside these spatio-temporal boundaries are marginalized, excluded or oppressed. Thus, spatio-temporal fixes also facilitate the institutionalized compromises on which accumulation regimes and modes of regulation depend, and subsequently come to embody them. This can involve super-exploitation of internal or external spaces outside the compromise, super-exploitation of nature or inherited social resources, deferral of problems into an indefinite future and, of course, the exploitation and/or oppression of specific classes, strata or other social categories. I discuss the spatio-temporal fix of Atlantic Fordism and its breakdown in the next chapter.

Nonetheless, insofar as such compromises marginalize forces that act as bearers of functions or operations essential to long-run accumulation, the growth of significant imbalances, disproportionalities or disunity in the circuit of capital will tend to strengthen the hand of these forces, enabling them to disrupt the institutionalized compromises involved in a particular accumulation regime, mode of regulation, state form and spatio-temporal fix (cf. Clarke 1977). Such crises typically act as a steering mechanism for the always provisional, partial and unstable re-equilibration of capital accumulation insofar as they prompt attempts to guide the forcible reimposition of the unity of the circuit of capital through new accumulation strategies and modes of regulation (cf. Hirsch 1976, 1977; Lindner 1973; Wirth 1977).

The primary scales and temporal horizons around which such fixes are built and the extent of their coherence vary considerably over time. This is reflected in the variable coincidence of different boundaries, borders or frontiers of action and the changing primacy of different scales. Political boundaries, for example, have been characterized by medieval polymorphy, Westphalian exclusivity and post-Westphalian complexity. Likewise, the consolidation of capitalism witnessed the national eclipse of the urban scale as cities were integrated into national economic systems and subordinated to the political power of national territorial states. And the national scale has since been challenged by the rise of global city networks more oriented to other global cities than to national hinterlands (cf. Braudel 1984; Brenner 1999a, 1999b; Taylor 1994). I consider some implications of rescaling in chapter 5.

These ideas have important implications for accumulation strategies, state projects and hegemonic projects on various scales of action and over different time horizons. For each of these involves an attempt to strategically coordinate activities across different systems and the life-world in order to achieve a limited, localized structural coherence in accumulation, state activities and social formations respectively. There is ample scope for competition among social forces over accumulation strategies, state projects and hegemonic visions, as well as for potential disjunctions between the strategies that emerge from such competition to dominate their respective imagined spheres. In this context a key role is played by the rivalries and struggles of intellectual forces, individually and collectively, in a free-floating or an organized manner, to articulate strategies, projects and visions that seek to reconcile contradictions and conflicts and to resolve dilemmas for various sites and scales of action (cf. Gramsci 1971; Jessop 1990b; Portelli 1973). The principal forces involved in these rivalries and struggles are organized interests, political parties and social movements, with the mass media rather than the public sphere now having a central position in the mediation of the struggle for hegemony in these matters. We will see many examples of this in later chapters.

As part of a given spatio-temporal fix, different institutions, apparatuses or agencies may specialize primarily in one or other horn of a dilemma, deal with it over different temporal horizons, or address different aspects at different times. The state may also alter the balance between institutions, apparatuses and agencies by reallocating responsibilities and resources, allowing them to compete for political support and legitimacy as circumstances change, etc. Such strategies may be pursued entirely within the state or extend to the division between state and non-state modes of governance. Another way to manage potential problems arising from the limits of different modes of policy-making or crisis-management is through variable policy emphases across different scales of action and temporal horizons. For example, in Atlantic Fordism, the national state set the macroeconomic framework, the local state acted as its relay for many nationally determined policies and intergovernmental cooperation in various international regimes maintained the conditions for national economic growth. Likewise, in contemporary neoliberal accumulation regimes, a relative neglect of substantive (as opposed to formal) supply-side conditions at the international and national levels in favour of capital flows in and through space is partly compensated by more interventionist policies at the regional, urban and local levels, where many material interdependencies among specific productive capitals are located (Gough and Eisenschitz 1996). This helps explain why local states are being reorganized as new forms of local or regional partnership emerge to guide and promote the development of local or regional resources (see chapter 5).

Another example of spatial-scalar divisions of labour is the distinction between foreign and domestic relations inherent in the modern state system such that some parts of the state apparatus specialize in external relations, some in internal relations. However, with the growing impact of globalization and new forms of competitiveness, inherited divisions of state labour change. Thus, not only is the distinction between domestic and foreign policy becoming blurred; but subnational governments are now getting engaged in foreign (economic) policy through cross-border cooperation, international localization, and so on, at the same time as supranational bodies get involved in the redesign and reorientation of subnational politics.

There can also be a temporal division of labour with different institutions, apparatuses or agencies responding to contradictions, dilemmas and paradoxes over different time horizons. This is reflected in the conventional distinction between planning and execution within organizations and in the primacy of different temporal horizons across organizations (for example, banks and central banks, computer-programmed arbitrage funds and long-term venture capital funds). Similarly, corporatist arrangements have often been introduced to address long-term economic and social issues where complex, reciprocal interdependence requires long-term cooperation – thereby taking the relevant policy areas outside the short-term time horizons of electoral cycles and parliamentary in-fighting. In both cases there is scope for activities to rebalance relations among these institutions, apparatuses or agencies through differential allocation of resources, allowing them to compete for legitimacy in changing circumstances.

5. Governance and Metagovernance

The constitutive incompleteness of the capital relation, the contradictions and dilemmas of accumulation, and the limitations of the spatio-temporal fixes that develop to contain, displace and defer these problems create a space for attempts at ongoing management, muddling through and crisis-management. Governance and metagovernance are useful concepts for addressing such issues and their implications for economic and social intervention. Governance refers here to any form of coordination of interdependent social relations – ranging from simple dyadic interactions to complex social divisions of labour. Three main forms are usually distinguished: the anarchy of exchange (for example, market forces), the hierarchy of command (for example, imperative coordination by the state) and the heterarchy of self-organization (for example, horizontal networks). Sometimes I will also refer to this third form as governance, but it will be clear from the context whether a narrow or broad meaning is intended. Because the other two forms are probably familiar, I will focus here on heterarchy. This involves the reflexive self-organization of independent actors involved in complex relations of reciprocal interdependence, with such self-organization being based on continuing dialogue and resource-sharing to develop mutually beneficial joint projects and to manage the contradictions and dilemmas inevitably involved in such situations (for more extended discussion of all three types, see chapter 6). Governance organized on this basis need not entail a complete symmetry in power relations or complete equality in the distribution of benefits: indeed, it is highly unlikely to do so almost regardless of the object of governance or the 'stakeholders' who actually participate in the governance process. All that is involved in this preliminary definition is the commitment on the part of those involved to reflexive self-organization in the face of complex reciprocal interdependence. In addition to any general relevance that these three forms of coordination may have, they also correspond to different aspects of the capital relation and capitalist societalization more generally (chapter 6). In this sense, all three tend to be reproduced, albeit with different weights at different times, as capital accumulation itself is reproduced.

Governance mechanisms and practices have key roles in modulating the scalar and spatial divisions of labour and allocating specific tasks to different time scales and periods. But, like modes of regulation more generally, they may be destabilized in the course of capital accumulation. For this always tends to escape the forms instituted to regulate and/or govern it and may thereby modify or even disrupt the unstable equilibrium of compromises around which that same accumulation process was previously organized. The neglect of some key condition for accumulation generates increasing tensions to address it (either through emergence of crises or through the mobilization of social forces that are critical to continued accumulation and adversely affected by such neglect). Within the economy, this is reflected in price movements as well as economic conflicts, in the political system in terms of shifts in public and elite opinion as well as political protests, etc. Metasteering (sometimes called metagovernance) enters here as social forces attempt to collibrate (modify the relative balance among) various governance mechanisms and modify their relative importance. Collibration, according to Dunsire (1996), is concerned with the overall organization and balancing of the different forms of coordination of complex reciprocal interdependence. In addition to metasteering practices within the more or less separate fields of anarchic market exchange, hierarchical organizations and heterarchic self-organization, there is also extensive scope for more general practices that steer the evolving relationship among these different modes of coordination. The need for such practices is especially acute owing to the wide dispersion of governance mechanisms in an emerging world society and the corresponding need to build appropriate macro-organizational and intersystemic capacities to address far-reaching increases in the complexity of interdependencies.

6. Concluding Remarks

This chapter has introduced some basic features of capitalism as a mode of production and object of regulation, noting in particular the role of spatio-temporal fixes in securing its relative stabilization, in order to contextualize the study of economic and social reproduction. It has introduced some basic ideas about the capitalist type of state, modes of state intervention, and the economic and social policy functions of the state and their relevance to welfare regimes. And it has also introduced some general themes and concepts regarding their connection to issues of governance and metagovernance, and their specific dynamics. These ideas are elaborated, supplemented and qualified in subsequent chapters.

These arguments have prepared the ground for a four-dimensional analysis of the changing form and functions of the state in regard to capital accumulation, social reproduction, scale and governance. The first dimension refers to the state's distinctive roles in securing the conditions for the improbable continuation of profitable private business from the viewpoint of particular capitals and capital in general. This is the field of economic policy. It is important because market forces alone cannot secure these conditions and must be supplemented by non-market mechanisms. The second dimension refers to how the conditions for the problematic reproduction of labour-power on a day-to-day, lifetime and intergenerational basis are secured from the viewpoints of particular capitals, capital in general and workers (considered both as workers and as citizens). This is the field of social policy as defined in this book. It matters, because labour-power is a fictitious commodity. For, although it is bought and sold in labour markets and may add value in production, it is not itself directly (re)produced within and by capitalist firms with a view to private profit. Labour-power enters the market economy from outside. This poses economic problems as regards its individual and collective suitability to capital's needs and its own survival in the absence of a secure income or other assets; social problems regarding social inclusion and cohesion – important in turn for attracting investment; and political problems regarding the legitimacy of state intervention in this area.

The third dimension concerns how a certain structured coherence is introduced into the scalar organization of these two sets of activities through spatio-temporal fixes in which, typically, one scale is primary. Thus the central issue here is the primary scale, if any, on which economic and social policies are decided – even if they are underpinned or implemented on other scales (see especially Collinge 1999). This is important because economic and social policies are politically mediated and the primary scales of political organization may not coincide with those of economic and social life. The fourth dimension concerns the chief mechanism, if any, for supplementing market forces in facilitating capitalist profitability and reproducing labour-power and, more generally, how the relative weight of these modes of regulation or governance is maintained in a coherent manner. This matters because the state is just one among several mechanisms through which attempts are made to overcome market failures and inadequacies. Capitalism's overall dynamic and the nature of the wider society depend on the particular mix of mechanisms. Deploying these four dimensions, I now present the key features of the Keynesian welfare national state, explain its crisis-tendencies and suggest that it is being tendentially replaced by a new form of welfare regime.

2

The Keynesian Welfare National State

This chapter constructs a stylized model of the postwar state in the economies of Atlantic Fordism, namely, the USA and Canada, Northwestern Europe, Australia and New Zealand. I characterize these economies as Atlantic Fordist for two reasons. First, despite its largely autocentric (or domestically based) growth dynamic, the spread of the Fordist accumulation regime occurred through diffusion of the American industrial paradigm to Northwestern Europe; and, second, because it was supported by various transatlantic international regimes (van der Pijl 1984; Rupert 1994). Australia and New Zealand are included because they were integrated during this period in an economic and political bloc that was organized under British hegemony and were included in American military alliances. Atlantic Fordism can be briefly defined as an accumulation regime based on a virtuous autocentric circle of mass production and mass consumption secured through a distinctive mode of regulation that was discursively, institutionally and practically materialized in the Keynesian welfare national state (or KWNS). I define Atlantic Fordism in more detail below and elaborate the four key features of its ideal typical state. But I also note how different national economies, societies and states deviate from the ideal type to give different modes of economic growth, different welfare regimes and different forms of governance within this broad ideal-typical matrix. I then suggest why the KWNS had a key role in securing the spatio-temporal fix of Atlantic Fordism. The chapter ends with the crisis-tendencies in the typical KWNS.

1. On Atlantic Fordism

This is not the place to engage in a critique of the literature on Fordism and post-Fordism (see Amin 1994; Boyer and Durand 1997; Jessop 1992a), but a brief account of Fordism is appropriate (on post-Fordism, see chapter 3). It can be analysed from five angles: (1) the labour process viewed as a particular configuration of the technical and social division of labour; (2) an accumulation regime, which comprises a macroeconomic regime sustaining a structurally coherent pattern of growth in capitalist production and consumption; (3) a mode of regulation, defined as an ensemble of norms, institutions, organizational forms, social networks and patterns of conduct that sustain and 'guide' a given accumulation regime; (4) a mode of societalization, that is, a pattern of institutional integration and social cohesion that complements the dominant accumulation regime and its mode of economic regulation, thereby securing the conditions for its dominance in the wider society; and (5) a social formation characterized by a contingent correspondence among all four of the preceding referents. This section considers Fordism from these viewpoints; in addition, section 4 explores its spatio-temporal fix, a sixth perspective that crosscuts these five dimensions and exposes some of the limitations of Atlantic Fordism as an accumulation regime and mode of regulation.

As a distinctive type of labour process, Fordism can be considered initially as a specific production process independent of any wider linkages. In this sense it involves mass production based on moving assembly-line techniques operated with the semi-skilled labour of the mass worker. This does not mean that an enterprise where mass production is dominant may not also employ other labour processes or types of worker and/or be linked to them within a given branch, region or wider economic space. The key point in such cases is that mass production would be the main source of economic dynamism.

As a stable mode of macroeconomic growth, Fordism in its strict, ideal-typical sense involves a virtuous circle of growth based on mass production, rising productivity based on economies of scale, rising incomes linked to productivity, increased mass demand due to rising wages, increased profits based on full utilization of capacity and increased investment in improved mass production equipment and techniques. Not every branch of the economy must be dominated by Fordist production techniques for this mode of growth to be realized: it is sufficient that the leading sectors are Fordist. Indeed, if the expansion of Fordist mass production is to find a mass market, there must be matching growth in the production of complementary goods (such as oil, steel, electricity, roads and housing) and services (such as retailing, advertising, consumer credit and the servicing of consumer durables) that will involve a wide range of labour processes, going well beyond Fordism as defined above.

As a mode of economic regulation, Fordism can be considered in terms of five structural forms of regulation: the enterprise form and modes of competition, the wage relation, the nature of monetary emission and credit relations, the form and functions of the state, and the manner of its insertion into international regimes (Boyer 1990). The typical Fordist enterprise form involves the separation of ownership and control in large corporations with a distinctive multidivisional, decentralized organization subject to central controls; a search for growth based on economies of scale and market share – including through mergers and acquisitions as well as internal expansion; and cost-plus pricing strategies. The Fordist wage relation rests on the recognition by big business as well as the state of the legitimacy of responsible trade unionism and collective bargaining; and by responsible trade unions (or, at least, trade union leaders) of management's right to manage. In this context wages are indexed to productivity growth and retail price inflation. Monetary emission and credit policies are oriented to securing effective aggregate demand in national economies and socializing losses and debts in an expansionary but mildly inflationary environment. In this context the key wage bargains will be struck in the mass production industries: the going rate will then spread through comparability claims among the employed and through the indexation of welfare benefits, financed from progressive taxes, for the economically inactive. Any tendencies towards underconsumption owing to insufficient demand and/or to a wage-induced profits squeeze[1] can be offset provided that wages and productivity in the consumer goods sector move in a similar range. In the form of the KWNS, the state contributes to this delicate balance by helping to integrate the circuits of the capital and consumer goods industries and by managing the conflicts between capital and labour over both the individual and social wage so that the virtuous circle of Fordist growth can be maintained. The expansion of public sector employment and collective consumption also played a role here (see below and chapter 4). This pattern does not require an end to dual labour markets or non-unionized firms or sectors as long as the general level of mass demand rises in line with productivity. Insofar as they are directed at conditions in the economic and political space of Atlantic Fordism, international monetary, trade, investment, energy and security regimes serve primarily to sustain Fordist growth in national economies under American hegemony and to promote an orderly expansion of international trade and investment in the capitalist world market.

As a general pattern of social organization (societalization), Fordism involves workers' dependence on an individual and/or social wage to satisfy their needs from cradle to grave; growth in the consumption of standardized, mass commodities in nuclear family households and in the provision of standardized, collective goods and services by the bureaucratic state; the latter's key role in managing the conflicts between capital and labour and the social tensions that result from the dominance of Fordism, bureaucratism, collective consumption, and so forth; and the important role of the city and suburbs as sites for Fordist consumption patterns or lifestyle. Thus we have, in short, an urban-industrial, 'middle-mass', wage-earning society.

In broad terms, the dynamic of global expansion after 1945 was based on the continuing spread of Fordism as a labour process from the United States (where it was already en route to dominance in the interwar period) to the other Atlantic Fordist economies and, in parallel, on the consolidation of its mass production and mass consumption dynamic in this expanded space. This held most notably for the big economies of Britain, France and Germany.[2] Their national economies acquired a mainly Fordist dynamic with growth based largely on expanding home markets. Small, open economies (such as Austria, Denmark, New Zealand, Sweden, Canada and Australia[3]) could also move towards a mass consumption society with a KWNS, because they occupied key niches in an international division of labour whose transatlantic dynamic was decisively shaped by the leading Fordist sectors in the leading economies. This enabled them to finance rising standards of mass consumption and expanding collective consumption based on growing export demand and profits in non-Fordist sectors (small batch capital goods, luxury consumer goods, agricultural goods, raw materials) as well as the expansion of any dynamic Fordist sectors they possessed. These small open economies also established a political as well as an economic logic appropriate to their distinctive variants of KWNS (see below). In short, where an economy that was included in Atlantic Fordism did not itself have a predominantly Fordist structure and logic, it needed a mode of growth that complemented the dominant Fordist logic if it was to share in, rather than be excluded from, the latter's overall growth dynamic. The structural coupling and co-evolution of production regimes and modes of regulation (including the KWNS) in these ways established a path-dependent (but not deterministic) structural coherence that shaped the forms of crisis and the prospects for crisis-management.

2. The KWNS

The form and functions of the capitalist type of state in Atlantic Fordism are usefully described in terms of the Keynesian welfare national state.

Table 2.1 The Keynesian welfare national state (KWNS)

Distinctive set of economic policies	*Distinctive set of social policies*	*Primary scale (if any)*	*Primary means to compensate market failure*
Full employment, demand management, provision of infrastructure to support mass production and consumption	Collective bargaining and state help generalize norms of mass consumption. Expansion of welfare rights	Relative primacy of national scale in economic and social policy-making with local as well as central delivery	Market and state form a 'mixed economy'. State is expected to compensate for market failures
Keynesian	*Welfare*	*National*	*State*

Each term in this fourfold construct highlights *distinctive* features of the KWNS and ignores any *generic* properties and functions it may share with other types of capitalist state. Several of these generic properties, as well as the basis of the fourfold schema for assessing relevant distinctive features, were presented in chapter 1. I can therefore move directly to present the KWNS in stylized terms on all four dimensions before considering how to distinguish its possible variant forms (see table 2.1).

First, in promoting the conditions for the profitability of private capital by helping to provide the external and internal conditions for capital accumulation, the KWNS was *Keynesian* insofar as it aimed to secure full employment in what was treated as a relatively closed national economy and to do so primarily through demand-side management. The KWNS attempted to adjust effective demand to the supply-driven needs of Fordist mass production with its dependence on economies of scale and full utilization of relatively inflexible means of production. Likewise, in reproducing labour-power as a fictitious commodity and helping to secure the conditions for social reproduction, the KWNS was oriented to *welfare* insofar as it tried to regulate collective bargaining within limits consistent with full employment levels of growth; to generalize norms of mass consumption beyond male workers earning a family wage in Fordist sectors, so that all full national citizens and their family dependants, if any, might share the fruits of economic growth (and thereby contribute to effective domestic demand); and to promote forms of collective consumption favourable to the Fordist mode of growth. This is reflected in indicators such as increasing replacement

rates for unemployment benefit, sickness benefit and pensions during the
heyday of the KWNS (Huber and Stephens 2001: 207–8; Marglin and
Schor 1990). Berthil Ohlin, a Swedish economist, anticipated this general
characteristic of Fordism in his argument that the Swedish model nation-
alized consumption, not the means of production (1938: 5). More generally, the economic and social policies of the KWNS were closely linked
to an expanding definition and progressive institutionalization of economic and social rights attached directly or indirectly to citizenship of a
national territorial state – whether this citizenship was based on descent,
acculturation, naturalization, political tests or some other criterion (on
different types of national state, as opposed to nation-state, see below
and chapter 5).

The KWNS was *national* insofar as the national territorial state
assumed the primary responsibility for developing and guiding
Keynesian welfare policies on different scales. This reflects the more
general importance of national economies and national states in the
'thirty glorious years' of postwar growth. For the national not only dominated the circuits of Atlantic Fordism, but also the so-called mercantilist
regimes or trading nations of East Asia and the import-substitution accumulation strategies of many Latin American economies. The various
postwar international regimes linked to Atlantic Fordism were mainly
intended to rescue European national states, to restore stability to
national economies, to create the conditions for domestic economic
growth, to promote international cooperation to underwrite the smooth
operation of national economies and, where possible, to secure and reinforce their complementarity rather than to abolish these economies or
integrate them into some superimperialist system. Likewise, local and
regional states tended to act mainly as relays for policies framed nationally, modifying them in the light of local conditions and the balance of
forces but not initiating radically different policies. In particular, economic and social policies at the urban and regional level were orchestrated in top-down fashion by the national state and primarily concerned
with equalizing economic and social conditions within each of these
national economies. This institutional and discursive 'naturalization' of
the national economy and national state was linked (within Atlantic
Fordism) to the relative closure of postwar economies undergoing reconstruction on the basis of mass production and mass consumption. This
period marks the highest stage of the national state form in Europe as
an economic, political and social power container, with its apogee occurring at the end of the 1960s after the success of the Marshall Plan and
the development of the European Community in 1945–68 (Milward et
al. 1993). In several East Asian economies, although they cannot be
described as Fordist, the same effect was achieved through 'national

security' discourses that connected the nation's internal and/or external security to close control over the domestic economy.

And, fourth, the KWNS was *statist* insofar as state institutions (on different levels) were the chief complement to market forces in the Fordist accumulation regime and also had a dominant role in the institutions of civil society. Thus it was the 'mixed economy' that provided the centre of gravity for economic, social and political regulation. To the extent that markets failed to deliver the expected values of economic growth, balanced regional development inside national borders, full employment, low inflation, a sustainable trade balance, and a socially just distribution of wealth and income, the state was called on to compensate for these failures and to generalize prosperity to all its citizens.

Variant forms of KWNS

Since each of its four distinctive features can be realized in different ways, one would not expect to find a pure form of KWNS. But this does not exclude more or less distinct variations on the basic stylized model. Indeed, institutional economists, social policy specialists and comparative political scientists have shown real taxonomic zeal in their efforts to identify historically significant, empirically verifiable types and subtypes of capitalism, welfare state and political regime in the postwar period. Some of the most extensive research in these regards has been undertaken on welfare regimes. Although this latter concept is less inclusive than the KWNS, the effort devoted to typologizing illustrates some of the general problems involved in such endeavours. While some authors simply use the generic term 'European social model' to describe the distinctive features of European welfare regimes (for example, Grahl and Teague 1997; Palier and Sykes 2000), others have invested much theoretical and empirical effort in identifying different welfare regimes within Europe and elsewhere. The most influential of the resulting typologies was developed by Esping-Andersen (1985, 1990). He derived his initial typology from simple quantitative criteria concerning the decommodification of labour-power in eighteen OECD countries in the postwar period and then, on the basis of their aggregate scores, simply divided these eighteen countries into three groups of six. He then studied the economic, social and political histories of the three groups and found their genealogies sufficiently different to justify the claim that there were three distinct clusters of welfare regime and that they coincided with those he had already identified. He has since added a Southern European model and suggested that the Japanese case is a hybrid of liberal and conservative welfare regimes (on Japan, see Esping-Andersen 1997; for the four main types, see box 2.1).

Box 2.1   *Esping-Andersen's fourfold typology of welfare regimes*

The *liberal* type has the lowest level of decommodification of labour-power. It rests on three main pillars: a minimal role for the state (including a residual role in providing social welfare); an emphasis on the individualization rather than socialization of the risks related to labour market participation; and a preference for market solutions to economic and social problems. These three pillars are reflected in more specific features: means-tested assistance, modest universal transfers, or market-based social-insurance plans; benefits for low-income, usually working-class, state dependants; strict, stigmatizing welfare eligibility rules; and state encouragement to the development of markets in providing for economic and social reproduction.

The *conservative* type has an intermediate level of decommodification (by definition) and is said to have three main traits: the key role attributed to familialism and corporativism in compensating market failure, a commitment to maintaining status differentiation, and the pooling of risks within particular occupational groups and/or social strata rather than on a universal basis across all national citizens. Welfare rights privilege the traditional family form, are attached to class and status rather than national citizenship, and have a limited redistributive impact because they reflect rather than reduce existing class and status inequalities. Conservative welfare regimes also allocate a key role to the voluntary sector.

The *social democratic* welfare regime has the highest level of decommodification on Esping-Andersen's chosen measures. It is most strongly developed in the Nordic economies, is linked to a strong labour movement, and is strongly committed to social redistribution. It accepts an extended role for state action in compensating for market failures, socializes a broad range of risks and offers generous levels of universal benefits and redistribution. Thus it displays universal benefits based on the notion of the 'work society' (*Arbeitsgesellschaft, société salariale* or wage-earning society). It is also committed to providing high and rising benefits premised on full employment and tied to overall economic growth; it extends decommodifying measures to the middle class, thereby locking them into support for the state; and it enables all citizens to integrate themselves into the labour market.

The *familial* or Southern European welfare regime is a residual welfare state. It relies on the extended family with a male breadwinner for economic and social reproduction in the face of market contingencies. It thereby provides a different form of intermediate decommodification.

Esping-Andersen's typology was mainly based on just one of the four dimensions central to the definition of the KWNS – and, indeed, on just one aspect of that dimension. This was the state's role in decommodifying men's waged labour. Thus, even for the state's role in reproducing labour-power as a fictitious commodity, Esping-Andersen did not consider the state's equally important roles in relation to women's waged and unwaged labour. Nor did he examine other dimensions of the state's involvement in social reproduction, such as education, health or housing – although his later work has extended into these areas. But he did give a secondary role to a related aspect of the fourth dimension, namely, the governance mechanisms used in the social reproduction of labour-power. In particular, in addition to liberal market forces, he referred to corporativist insurance schemes, formally rational state redistribution and, in later work, clientelism and the family. His typology was also initially developed to explore how distinctive national balances of social forces at the founding moments of welfare regimes led to different types of welfare regime and then exercised continuing path-dependent effects on their subsequent development.

Most subsequent taxonomies based on Esping-Andersen's influential pioneering work comprise four to six types of welfare regimes. These are the market liberal (sometimes subdivided into North Atlantic and Antipodean variants); the social democratic; the conservative-corporativist (or Christian democratic); the Mediterranean (or Southern European or Latin Rim); and, for some but not all, the Confucian (or East Asian) regime.[4] This expanded typology has been used for many purposes besides those for which it was first developed, but it is still shaped by Esping-Andersen's initial research question. This makes it less relevant for showing how different welfare regimes have come to be integrated into broader modes of economic regulation and/or distinctive 'historical blocs' (i.e., mutually implicated, structurally coupled and historically co-evolving ensembles of economic, political and sociocultural relations, the construction of which depends on the activities of organic intellectuals and collective projects as well as on the gradual and emergent co-adaptation of institutions and conduct). It may also be less useful for analysing the recent politics of *retrenchment* (as opposed to *expansion*) that has emerged in response to crises in and/or of welfare regimes (Pierson 1995; but see also Huber and Stephens 2001).

This suggests that any fresh typology should not only include cases missed out from Esping-Andersen's original study but also reflect the most incisive criticisms of its theoretical and empirical foundations[5] and integrate the other dimensions of the KWNS. Particular attention should be paid to modes of economic intervention – previously ignored – and modes of governance – previously treated rather perfunctorily. This would permit more sophisticated analysis of the path-dependent structural coupling of modes of economic growth, modes of regulation and the nature of welfare regimes (see next subsection). In terms of forms of economic and social intervention, for example, one might distinguish between liberal social market regimes; tripartite social democratic regimes; conservative-corporativist regimes in which social welfare is partly organized on occupational or status lines and therefore tends to conserve rather than weaken economic and social inequalities; dirigiste regimes with strong states and a relatively fragmented labour force; regulatory states that protect the workforce through their support for mandatory collective bargaining and labour legislation rather than through an extended universal welfare state; and more clientelist modes of economic and social intervention. These would correspond to the North Atlantic Fordist, Nordic, corporatist-conservative, French, Antipodean and Southern European welfare regimes respectively. Several other models would be needed for cases beyond the circuits of Atlantic Fordism, such as East Asian or Latin American societies.

Likewise, in terms of governance, one might distinguish between a liberal mixed economy model that privileges market forces with a residual compensatory role for the state; a negotiated economy model that rests on concertation between social partners with backup from the state as required; a statist model where the state defines and regulates the obligations of workers and employers as well as the activities of market, not-for-profit and civic welfare organizations; and the familial model in which the extended family and paternalist and/or 'familialist' organizations have key roles in redistribution. These types correspond to four ways of governing the division of labour in capitalist formations (see chapter 6). Liberalism corresponds to the principle of free exchange among owners of commodities – with no distinction being made in principle between owners of labour-power and owners of other so-called factors of production. The negotiated economy model is linked to a Ricardian account of capitalist class relations, focusing on returns to 'factors of production' from potentially positive-sum cooperation and on issues of distribution, rather than a Marxist account that focuses on the inherently antagonistic class relations in production considered as a valorization process. Conservative-corporativist models rest in turn on a functionalist approach to the division of labour – with different functions or roles being considered in estate-like, corporativist, or organicist terms and the state being charged with overall responsibility for organizing the conditions for self-organization and securing overall social cohesion. And the familial model is linked to a subsidiaritarian approach to collective social responsibilities within a trinitarian 'market–state–civil society' view of modern societies.

The political economy of scale is less germane to Esping-Andersen's typology because, during the time period covered by his research, his cases were all marked by the primacy of the national scale. Even here, policy dynamics and the scope for radical reform differ according to the unitary, federal or subsidiaritarian form and operation of the national state. The issue of scale is also worth incorporating to facilitate comparisons with earlier and later periods. On the one hand, the earlier period merits attention because it is particularly relevant to the origins and development of welfare regimes. Local state capacities and the forms of domestic politics significantly affected the balance of economic and political forces during the formative period of welfare regimes. For example, the conservative-corporativist and Southern European regimes tend to be associated with strong localist and/or regionalist tendencies; whereas the more universalist, social democratic regimes tend to be linked with more centralized national governments. On the other hand, the later period is significant because the continuing diversity of contemporary welfare regimes at the national scale is reflected in the pursuit of different projects and strategies to promote economic integration and build a Social Europe. NAFTA has likewise created problems for Canada and Mexico – albeit through the economic domination of key US capitals and the sheer ecological dominance of the US economy more generally rather than through the actions of an emerging supranational political regime. Some issues raised by EU economic and social policies are examined in chapter 5.

More concrete-complex analyses could consider secondary variations on what, from the regulationist- and state-theoretical perspective adopted here, are the four key features of the KWNS. These may include their internal articulation, social bases, gendered inflection, 'sexualized' and 'racialized' character, degree of family-friendliness, generational bias (for example, to children, working adults, or pensioners[6]), distinctive political projects and associated hegemonic projects.[7] To take one example, there is now a rich literature on the gendered dimensions, if not inherently patriarchal nature, of welfare regimes. This has revealed an important contrast between male-breadwinner and individual wage-earner types. The former assumes a gendered division of labour, prioritizes the employment opportunities and status of men as male breadwinner, treats the family as the unit of income transfers and welfare benefits, adopts joint taxation of spouses and gives husbands and wives different rights. The latter tends to be neutral regarding the gendered division of labour, or even promotes equality of opportunity, treats employment as the basis for welfare benefits in a 'work society', grants uniform entitlements on the basis of employment record, citizenship or residence rather than discriminating on the grounds of gender or marital status, and assesses taxes on individuals rather than households (see, for example, Bussemaker and van Kersbergen 1994; Jenson 1997; Lewis 1992; Sainsbury 1996; Siim 2000).

It is quite appropriate to develop different typologies for different purposes. Much empirical research has tended to confirm the relevance of the three basic regimes originally distinguished by Esping-Andersen and/or the improved descriptive and heuristic power of more complex typologies (see especially Pitruzello 1999). However, while his initial typology was defended in terms of the historical roots as well as contemporary properties of the three clusters, Esping-Andersen himself has also noted that

> the decisive period in which the basic components of postwar welfare regimes were put in place, when welfare capitalism was institutionalized so to speak, was not the postwar decades but during the 1960s and 1970s. This was when strong worker protection and labour market regulation emerged, when social citizenship was fully affirmed. And this was when the core features of welfare states crystallized. The essential differences between the Nordic, social democratic, the Continental European, and the Anglo-Saxon liberal welfare states were affirmed in these years. (1999: 4)

This was also the period, of course, when the accumulation regimes and more general modes of regulation with which these welfare regimes are associated were consolidated. This occurred in turn in the context of an evolving division of labour in Atlantic Fordism and the wider international economy. This division of labour is also closely related to different patterns of dynamic competitive advantages (Porter 1990). And the latter are closely related to the ways in which different modes of growth are embedded in wider sets of social relations (see Ashton and Green 1996; Crouch 1993; Hall and Soskice 2001b; Hollingsworth and Boyer 1997a; Huber and Stephens 2001; Streeck 1992; Streeck and Crouch 1997). Esping-Andersen seems to conclude from his observation that four distinctive and path-dependent types of welfare regime were consolidated in this period. An alternative conclusion is that various path-dependent welfare regimes continued to co-evolve with their respective modes of growth during this period, but that they also changed in response to changes elsewhere in the social formations in which they came to be embedded.

It is worth noting here a comment of Scharpf and Schmidt on their own slight revision to Esping-Andersen's original threefold typology of welfare regimes:

> In spite of these fundamental structural differences, all three models could be considered functionally equivalent solutions for the problems of income security at the end of the golden-age period. Under conditions of assured full employment, private top-ups on flat-rate benefits could be as satisfactory as earnings-related public benefits; as segmented contingent insurance systems expanded their coverage, they could approximate the universalism of Anglo-Saxon and Scandinavian systems; and within the boundaries of national economies, general taxation and wage-based social-security contributions did not differ in their economic viability. With the onset of the new international challenges, however, the functional equivalence was lost. As unemployment increased, Anglo-Saxon welfare states lost their capacity to assure income maintenance whereas Continental and Scandinavian welfare states had to bear the fiscal burdens of their institutionalized promises. With the integration of product and capital markets, finally, the differences between tax-financed and contribution-financed welfare states also increased in importance. (2000b: 9)

This important observation lends support to my own argument that there was a broad structural congruence across different forms of welfare regime during the 'thirty golden years' of postwar economic growth. Thus, for all the intrinsic interest and methodological significance of attempts to refine, reclassify, extend, distinguish and critique the available taxonomies for the purposes of concrete-complex research, an exaggerated concern with variant forms of welfare regime could prevent recognition of their basic congruence at more abstract-simple levels of analysis. This is definitely not a call to reject such taxonomic attempts or their empirical results. All I wish to emphasize is that, given the relative ecological dominance of the growth dynamic of Atlantic Fordism and its impact on the structural coupling and co-evolution of the market economy and capitalist states in this period, there were several possible path-dependent trajectories to the same broad functional outcome. Bonoli, George and Taylor-Gooby make a similar point for the period of welfare state retrenchment in Europe when they suggest that 'European welfare states, faced with similar challenges, develop different solutions, depending on the welfare institutions and political configurations of each country, to attain similar outcomes' (2000: 46). Conversely, when attention turns to more concrete-complex issues, such as those typically studied by aficionados of comparative welfare research, the path-dependent specificities of national welfare regimes acquire a key role as independent and/or dependent variables according to the specific problem(s) to be studied. I will most certainly refer to such specificities in subsequent chapters.

Worlds of welfare and welfare capitalism

In addition to their role in organizing social transfers, welfare regimes organize the productive sector of the capitalist economy in different ways (Goodin et al. 1999: 5; see also Ebbinghaus and Manow 2001b; Hall and Soskice 2001b). Adopting the Esping-Andersen typology, Goodin and his co-authors suggest that the liberal welfare regime is based on liberal politics, capitalist economics and residual social policies; the social democratic on class politics, socialist economics and redistributive social policies; and the conservative regime on group politics, communitarian economics and mutualist social policies (1999: 40–54). My own approach emphasizes how welfare regimes are structurally coupled with modes of economic growth (including their insertion into the international division of labour) and more encompassing modes of regulation. Four patterns can be distinguished in this regard in Europe and North America:

- liberal welfare regimes are linked to finance-based, market-regulated capitalist regimes where the money concept of capital tends to dominate;
- social democratic welfare regimes are linked to small open economies with strong Fordist export-oriented branches and/or niche market-oriented, high-skill, high-productivity, high-wage, flexibly specialized export-sectors;
- more conservative, corporativist welfare regimes are linked to larger economies, open or closed, with close coordination between industry and finance as well as between large industrial concerns and small and medium enterprises, an emphasis on craft production and guild organization, and a large traditional and new petite bourgeoisie, where the productive concept of capital tends to predominate; and
- the Southern European welfare model is linked to late developing, peripheral Fordist economies with large agrarian sectors, traditional social structures and family capitalism.

Such correlations need to be explained, of course, rather than merely posited. Fortunately, there is a growing body of institutionalist analysis that is concerned with this question (for example, Ebbinghaus and Manow 2001b; Hall and Soskice 2001b; Huber and Stephens 2001). A regulationist approach would examine at least three variables in this regard. First, how are different patterns of finance–industry relations connected to the relative dominance of a 'money-capital' or a 'productive-capital' concept of the economic process on the part of the leading fraction(s) of capital? The money-capital concept is more liberal (and, often, internationalist) in its concern with formally free circulation and exchange; the productive-capital concept is more attuned to the substantive interdependence (or socialization) of the productive forces and is more interventionist (and, perhaps, protectionist) in its concern with securing the substantive conditions for the production of surplus value (Overbeek 1990: 25–9; van der Pijl 1984: 8–34). This has implications not only for economic policy, including modes of intervention, capacities for state planning or economic guidance, the levels and incidence of taxation, and education and training policy, but also for the relative weight of market and state in social policy (cf. Boyer 1997; Hall and Soskice 2001b; Huber et al. 1999; Huber and Stephens 2001; Polanyi 1944; Soskice 1999).

A second important factor is the timing of the emergence of formally free labour markets in relation to the onset and development of industrialization, the timing of the breakdown of guild supervision of urban labour, and the timing of the abolition of feudal labour dues (Biernacki 1995; Crouch 1993). For, as Biernacki has shown, these affect the prevailing cultural conceptions of labour-power, especially whether it is regarded primarily as one substitutable factor of production among others or as a distinctive set of creative capacities bearing attached rights and duties. These cultural perceptions affect not only the organization of production, labour market institutions, industrial relations and the propensity for corporatist cooperation, but also the more general economic and political demands made by labour movements (Biernacki 1995).[8] The coupling between welfare regimes and labour market organization has also been studied by Visser (2000) for unemployment policies; and the coupling between welfare regimes and production regimes has been explored by Estevez-Abe et al. (2001), Huber et al. (1999), Huber and Stephens (2001) and Thelen (2001).

Third, we should examine how different modes of inter-firm competition and/or cooperation lead to the relative dominance of formal market exchange or different forms of networking in securing the conditions of valorization, innovation, etc.[9] These sets of factors operate initially at the level of branches and sectors (for example, the organization of the labour process, the structure of labour markets, training regimes, or the differential development of paternalism and occupational welfare), but, depending on the relative structural dominance and hegemonic capacities of specific economic sectors and fractions of capital, their specific effects can become more general (or even universal) within particular regional or national formations. This dominance is typically mediated through the strategic selectivity of state forms, which make it harder or easier to promote universal welfare, and the changing balance of political forces. The relative weight of different factors also varies with stages of capitalism. Thus, to take one highly topical example, the money concept of capital had a reduced significance during the period of Atlantic Fordism compared with the current period of neoliberal globalization (Duménil and Lévy 2001a,b; van Apeldoorn 1998; van der Pijl 1984).

An explanation in terms of the strategic selectivity of the state and its form-determined role in mediating political struggles would focus on the basic institutional and strategic factors of the state noted in chapter 1 (pp. 37–42). These include modes of representation, the articulation of the state apparatus across different branches, functional domains, territorial scales and modes of intervention; and, for the wider political system, the way in which party systems and patterns of industrial relations have been shaped by extra-economic as well as economic factors (see, for example, Crouch 1993; Martin 1995; Rokkan 1999). The strategic selectivity of the state system on different scales, especially at the national level, generates a more or less systematic pattern of constraints and opportunities on corporate strategies (as it does on other types of strategy pursued by other types of actor). This affects not only their immediate market situation and their expectations regarding the opportunities for profit (and threats of loss) but also their capacity to respond to these opportunities and threats both economically and politically. Moreover, through the mechanisms of structural coupling and co-evolution, it also shapes the extent of correspondence or disjunction between much wider aspects of the production regimes and welfare regimes in different economies (for recent analyses of these configurations and their implications for institutional complementarities, see the contributions to Hall and Soskice 2001b; on the link between state traditions, trade unionism, and industrial relations, see Crouch 1993).

The variant forms are most important in addressing the various national crises *in* and *of* the KWNS and their implications for any transition to newer forms of economic and social intervention. For, just as there is no pure KWNS, there is no pure crisis of the KWNS – only specific, path-dependent, nationally variable crises, often with regionally specific manifestations. Some cases reveal greater continuity, linked to the dominance of the view that there was a crisis *in* the welfare state for which incremental adjustments might be appropriate (for example, Denmark, Sweden, Germany). Other cases involve greater discontinuity – admittedly more marked in declared policy changes than actual policy outcomes – linked to a discursively constructed crisis *of* the welfare state (for example, New Zealand, Britain). It is in the latter cases that the biggest shifts have occurred institutionally (typically associated with a neoliberal regime shift) and where the most severe income polarization consequent upon adjustment has occurred.

3. Distinctive Features of the KWNS as a National State

Having considered the general features of Atlantic Fordism and the KWNS and possible taxonomies of welfare regimes, I now consider the distinctive features of the KWNS as a national state. These can be summarized as follows:

1   Among the various spatial scales of formal political organization, the sovereign state level was regarded as primary. Local and regional states served primarily as transmission belts for national economic and social politics. The key supranational institutions comprised various international and intergovernmental agencies – typically organized under US hegemony – and were designed to promote cooperation among national states to help secure postwar economic and political regeneration in Europe and economic growth in North America. Among the key concerns of the national state are population, reproduction, citizenship, migration and territorial defence. Each of these has gender, ethnic and 'racial' aspects. Thus, in reproducing the primacy of the national state and international state system, the KWNS also indirectly reproduces specific forms of patriarchal, ethnic and 'racial' domination.

2   State economic strategies and economic regulation were premised on the existence of relatively closed national economies. A complex multiscalar field of economic relations was handled as if it were divided into a series of relatively closed national economies. Economic regulation through the KWNS itself contributed to the material as well as discursive constitution of national economies as objects of regulation. The international economy was mainly understood in terms of financial and trade flows among distinct national economies. The object of national and international economic management was typically seen as the formal market economy operating on the basis of the capitalist logic of 'economic man'; or, at most, in a national context, as the 'mixed economy' formed by the articulation of market and state (see above). There was little awareness of, let alone conscious policy-making concerned to overcome, the capitalist and/or patriarchal features of this object of economic management.

3   Among the various spatial scales of economic organization, the national economy was accorded primacy for state action, defined and measured in terms of national aggregates, and managed primarily in

terms of targeted variation in these aggregates (Barnes and Ledubur 1991, 1998; Bryan 1995; Radice 1984). Local or regional economies were treated as sub-units of the national economy and interregional differences were regarded as relatively unimportant.

4   The primary object of welfare and social reproduction policies was seen as the resident national population and its constituent house-holds and individual citizens. Many of these policies assumed the predominance of stable two-parent families in which men received a 'family wage' and could expect lifetime employment, if not neces-sarily a job for life. The principal exception here is found in 'individ-ual earner' welfare regimes. Moreover, not only did the Keynesian welfare state assume the stability of the patriarchal family form, it also marginalized other forms of family or household and alternative sexualities (Carabine 1996).

5   The primary units of the state's social basis were individual political subjects, endowed, as citizens of the national state, with various legal, political and social rights and organized as members of economic-corporate organizations (trade unions and business associations) and/or as supporters of responsible political parties. Different types of citizenship regime were compatible with this basic model (Boris 1995; Fraser 1987, 1997; Jenson 1986, 1997; Williams 1995). But most had a patriarchal form and often there were informal as well as formal limitations on access to citizenship rights (see section 4 below on the spatio-temporal fix of Atlantic Fordism).

6   The axis of struggles over domestic political hegemony was the 'national-popular' and its realization in the expansion and protection of citizen rights in a political process that was mainly concerned with issues of economic and social redistribution in an economy whose essentially capitalist features were taken for granted.

In short, there was a close and mutually reinforcing linkage between the national state form and Keynesian welfarism. Indeed, the KWNS probably gave fullest expression to the organizational and societalizing possibilities of the national state in the large economies. It emerged at a time when formal plurinational empires were being dismantled under pressure from the USA and liberation movements and before serious attempts were made to consolidate supranational blocs among the advanced capitalist economies. The primacy of the national scale did not occur because of some teleological unfolding of this potential, but because of specific economic and political conditions associated with the organization of Atlantic Fordism under US hegemony. Thus, to argue counterfactually, had Nazi Germany secured through economic and military imperialism the conditions for its projected 'New Order', a much more strongly plurinational and far more polarized mode of economic regulation would have been established in Europe. But the Allied defeat of the Axis powers created some essential conditions for generalizing the American New Deal to Europe. This occurred – seemingly paradoxically – through the reassertion of the organizational principle of the national state. It was through the latter that the national economy would be regulated as a distinctive 'imagined' economic space and that efforts would be made to secure a complementary expansion of national production and consumption as the basis for a 'politics of prosperity' to overcome rightwing and leftwing extremism (Hall 1989; Maier 1978; Milward et al. 1993; Siegel 1988; van der Pijl 1984).

4. The KWNS and the Spatio-temporal Fix of Atlantic Fordism

No accumulation strategy on whatever scale can be completely coherent or fully institutionalized. I have already noted three basic reasons for this that are inherent in the very nature of capitalism itself (pp. 18–21). Here, I want to highlight four consequences for attempts to regularize accumulation through accumulation strategies organized around a specific spatio-temporal fix. First, given the incomplete, contradictory and dilemmatic nature of the capital relation, the specific conditions necessary for accumulation tend to be opaque, indeterminate and liable to variation. This explains in part the trial-and-error nature of attempts to regularize and govern accumulation within any given set of spatio-temporal horizons. Second, given the absence hitherto (and the inherent improbability) of a comprehensive spatio-temporal fix instituted at the level of the world market, there will always be factors and processes necessary to the success of the prevailing accumulation regimes that lie beyond the reach of their respective modes of regulation. This is the other face of the capacity of a spatio-temporal fix to displace and defer contradictions and crisis-tendencies. Third, consolidating a spatio-temporal fix requires building support in and across many conflictual and contested fields for the corresponding accumulation strategies, their associated state projects and, where relevant, hegemonic visions. Nonetheless, insofar as one such strategy does become dominant or hegemonic and is institutionalized within a specific spatio-temporal fix, it helps consolidate an accumulation regime in its corresponding economic space. And, fourth, because the underlying contradictions and dilemmas still exist, all such regimes are partial, provisional and unstable. The circuit of capital may still break at many points within and beyond the spatio-temporal fix. Economic crises will then provoke restructuring through the normal working of market forces as well as through more deliberate attempts to restore the conditions for accumulation. If such attempts are compatible with the prevailing accumulation regime, growth will be renewed within its parameters. If not, a crisis *of* – and not just *in* – the accumulation regime will develop, provoking a search for new strategies, new institutionalized compromises and new spatio-temporal fixes (on this distinction, see Boyer 1990; Lipietz 1988).

Whether or not the search for solutions to economic crisis restores the prevailing accumulation regime and its mode of regulation does not depend solely on the objective features of the crisis and whether it is objectively feasible in principle to resolve it within this framework. It also depends on the institutional, organizational and learning capacities of the social forces seeking to resolve the crisis and on the outcome of the contest to define the nature of the crisis, to explain its various objective causes, to attribute blame for its development and to identify the most appropriate solutions. Accordingly, while similar objective economic crises affected the economies of Atlantic Fordism during the 1970s and 1980s, they were not all resolved in the same way. In some cases they were largely managed as crises *in* Atlantic Fordism, in others they were handled as crises *of* Atlantic Fordism. It is in this context that more concrete-complex analyses of the articulation between accumulation regimes and modes of regulation (or production and welfare regimes) and more general state capacities need to be introduced. Yet more detailed studies would examine the changing balance of forces mobilized around different accounts of the crisis and possible solutions. The basis for these claims can be illustrated in the first instance from the structural coherence of accumulation and regulation in Atlantic Fordism and the factors leading to its breakdown.

Before addressing this issue directly, however, it is worth asking how one might evaluate the claim that the KWNS is the ideal-typical 'Fordist state' (and hence has specifically Fordist features that correspond to and co-evolve with Fordism) rather than comprising just one possible form among several that could be adopted by the modern state in a Fordist mass society. This question can be approached in four ways, corresponding to the alternative referents of Fordism. It has been assessed in terms of: (1) the nature of the labour process within the state sector itself (for example, Hoggett 1987); (2) the state sector's direct economic role in a Fordist accumulation regime (for example, Overbeek 1990: 114–19); (3) the state's wider role in the social mode of economic regulation linked to such a regime (for example, Moulaert et al. 1988; Painter 1991); or (4) its role in securing the institutional integration and social cohesion of a social formation within which Fordism in one or more of its possible guises is dominant (Hirsch and Roth 1986). The last three criteria also have implications, as we shall see, for the Atlantic Fordist spatio-temporal fix.

Although it may be interesting to investigate how far the labour process in the state is Fordist (or quasi-Fordist) in character, this would tend, in the absence of other criteria, to reduce the state to one among several sites of economic activity. It would thereby lose its distinctiveness as a state. Focusing on the direct economic role of the state or public sector could also lead to neglect of the distinctive features of the state as a whole. Conversely, looking at the state's role in securing Fordist societalization might make it hard to distinguish a Fordist state proper from a state that maintains social cohesion in a society that happens to be Fordist. This suggests that the most promising approach to the 'Fordist' nature of the KWNS is the distinctive contribution of its form and functions *as a* state to securing a distinctively Fordist accumulation regime and mode of regulation. This should not be taken to mean that the KWNS emerged in order to perform these functions nor that the accumulation regime pre-existed the development of its mode of regulation. Instead, it is an invitation to explore the structural coupling and co-evolution of the accumulation regime and its mode of regulation and the extent to which they were able to develop a degree of structured coherence (or institutional integration) that helped to secure the improbable reproduction of capital accumulation for a significant period of time (on the rejection of functionalism in the regulation approach, see Lipietz 1988; Jessop 1990a,b).

Approached in these terms, the distinctive contribution of the KWNS to the regulation of Atlantic Fordism was its capacity to manage, displace or defer, at least for a while, the contradictions in the different forms of the capital relation and their strategic dilemmas as these were expressed in Fordist accumulation regimes. These benefited from a spatio-territorial matrix based on the congruence between national economy, national state, national citizenship embracing social as well as civic and political rights, and national society; and from institutions relatively well adapted to combining the tasks of securing full employment and economic growth and managing national electoral cycles. This spatio-temporal fix, sometimes known as embedded liberalism (Ruggie 1982), enabled a specific but still partial and provisional resolution of the contradictions of capital accumulation as they were expressed under Atlantic Fordism. The principal structural forms (with their associated contradictions and dilemmas) around which this specific resolution was organized in and through the KWNS were the wage and money forms. I will now seek to justify this claim by elaborating the stylized model introduced in section 2 above.

First, the primary aspect of the wage form in Atlantic Fordism as far as the KWNS was concerned was its role as a source of domestic demand rather than as a cost of international production.[10] Thus the state focused its efforts on securing full employment levels of demand within the national economy and organized its interventions and policies in other areas to support this goal as far as possible. Indeed, although the attainment of full employment during this period is often attributed to successful Keynesian fine-tuning,[11] its achievement was actually more strongly rooted in the basic dynamic of Fordist expansion that the KWNS helped to secure through its promotion of mass production and mass consumption. The role of wages as a cost of international production had secondary importance for the KWNS. Indeed, the state was willing to live economically and politically with modest inflation and engage in modest devaluations if this was judged necessary to protect the full employment levels of demand that served the interests of industrial capital as well as the Fordist labour force (see also the discussion of money and inflation below). This does not mean that wage costs were of no interest to the state. For, in addition to its overall interest in continued economic growth, the state was also a major purchaser of goods and services from the private sector and an increasingly significant employer in its own right. But wages were generally viewed with benign neglect by the state provided that they rose in line with productivity and prices and thereby contributed to the virtuous circle of Fordist accumulation. This was relatively easy to achieve through the operation of market forces during the expansion phase of Atlantic Fordism in the 1950s and early 1960s, owing to the continuing growth of Fordist firms and branches with their economies of scale and collective bargaining indexed to productivity and prices. Labour market pressures were also alleviated in this period by processes such as the transfer of workers from low productivity agriculture, the mobilization of women into the labour force and, later, the recruitment of immigrant workers.

These arguments can be related to the more general role of the KWNS in securing the conditions for Fordist accumulation. First, given the key role of economies of scale in the Fordist labour process and the supply-driven ('just-in-case') nature of production, the state played an important role in compensating for the limited scope of microeconomic flexibility in Fordist production by minimizing the need for industry to make larger adjustments in output. In particular, in managing the wage relation and labour market policies, and guiding aggregate demand, it helped to balance supply and demand without the violent cyclical swings characteristic of competitive markets. Moreover, by holding out the promise of smoothing economic fluctuations and securing stable, calculable growth, it also permitted Fordist firms to secure increasing returns to scale and encouraged them to invest. Given the dominance of Fordist firms in the Fordist growth dynamic, this also provided opportunities for profit to other firms whose activities complemented those in the leading sectors. In this and other regards, then, a relatively consistent accumulation strategy helped to select, consolidate and impart a Fordist dynamic to the national economy as a whole through the interwoven logics of market competition and economic complementarity. Second, given the potential virtuous circle of expansion rooted in rising productivity, rising wages, rising demand, rising profits and rising investment, the state acquired a key role in integrating the capital and consumer goods industries and managing the wage relation to this end. Its activities here included promoting the general infrastructural conditions for nationwide diffusion of mass consumption (for example, electricity grids, integrated transport, modern housing), promoting economies of scale through nationalization and/or supportive merger policies, engaging in contra-cyclical demand management, legitimating responsible collective bargaining, and generalizing norms of mass consumption through public sector employment and welfare expenditure. Urban and regional policies oriented to reducing uneven development helped to secure the conditions for mass production, mass distribution and mass consumption and to reduce inflationary pressures due to localized overheating in a largely autocentric economy. Finally, as well as its general role in creating the conditions for mass production and consumption and in meeting expanded notions of the social rights of citizenship, the state's provision of collective consumption helped to socialize and to lower the social reproduction costs of labour-power.

Many of these activities relating to the wage relation were closely tied to the Fordist mode of regulation as well as to the labour process and Fordist accumulation regime. Particularly important here was state support for responsible trade unionism, collective bargaining, industrial modernization, the consolidation of big business and bi- or tripartite forms of corporatism. While rather different patterns of trade union organization could serve this purpose during the period of Fordist expansion, the onset of crisis made more demands on the industrial relations system. Thus, during the period of stagflation, bi- or tripartite concertation played a major moderating role and contributed to comparatively good economic performance on the three key macroeconomic criteria in Fordist economies – employment, inflation and growth – relative to non-corporatist systems (Garrett 1998; Katzenstein 1985; Keman et al. 1987; Notermans 2000; Scharpf 1991; Western 1997; Windolf 1990). At the same time the dominance of the Fordist mode of growth in these relatively closed economies enabled the KWNS to link the interests of organized domestic capital and organized labour (especially male skilled workers) in programmes of full employment and social welfare insofar as the individual and social wage could function as a source of demand for industry oriented to the domestic market. Such corporatist bargaining sometimes involved the use of improved pension entitlements as part of the social wage in exchange for wage restraint. Insofar as these entitlements were not fully funded, if at all, however, this form of deferred wage served to postpone rather than solve economic problems (see chapter 5).

The primary aspect of the money form in Atlantic Fordism as far as the KWNS is concerned was its character as national credit money. The development of adequate national, macroeconomic statistics and the steady expansion of the peacetime state budget gave the KWNS far more leverage in fiscal and monetary terms to steer the economy than the liberal state had in the period of competitive capitalism. While the success of fine-tuning can certainly be exaggerated (especially as it was often overdetermined by electoral calculation in cases where central banks lacked real autonomy), the general increase in public spending did make a major contribution to creating the conditions for continued expansion. In addition to the role of public spending and borrowing, private debt also played a major role in the postwar boom. Debt was an increasingly important element in financing fixed investment and working capital for business; and consumer credit had a major role in enabling the growth of mass consumption. In turn, lubricated by public and private credit, growth helped to legitimate Keynesian welfare policies, and to generate the tax revenues for collective consumption, welfare rights and social redistribution, as well as for infrastructure provision. It also helped to consolidate a social basis for the Fordist accumulation regime based on a class compromise between industrial capital and organized labour.

All of this meant that, at least during the expansion phase of Atlantic Fordism, the role of money as an international currency was secondary. This aspect was managed through the combination of the Bretton Woods monetary regime and the GATT trade regime. Indeed, most national economies were actually more closed on their capital than their trade accounts, with national states enjoying effective capital controls, fixed but adjustable exchange rates and significant and legitimate trade controls in place or to hand. This enabled them to manage the national economy with reference to what one Keynesian economist, Hicks (1959), termed a national labour standard (the commitment to full employment) rather than to some monetary standard (the commitment to a fixed exchange rate) so that economic policy adjustment and intervention were primarily oriented to economic growth and full employment rather than defence of a given exchange rate. The commitment to a national labour standard and the ability to maintain it was gradually undermined, however, as, in the face of increasing flows of stateless money and near-money instruments, national governments chose, sometimes reluctantly, sometimes willingly, to abandon capital controls and adopt a floating exchange rate system. The USA was a partial exception to this general picture, of course, because its national money was also the hegemonic international currency. During the expansion phase of Atlantic Fordism, it recycled its trade surpluses back to Europe through Marshall Aid, military spending and foreign direct and portfolio investment. In later phases, however, the initially beneficial role of the US dollar became another source of instability and crisis for Atlantic Fordism.

The apparent success of the KWNS was also grounded in the nature of the postwar boom and the tax revenues it generated. Moreover, insofar as full employment was achieved in a labour market that was relatively unified rather than segmented, it reduced the volume of primary poverty among working families. This in turn created room for more generous income maintenance programmes for other groups (thereby sustaining and generalizing mass consumption) and/or welfare expansion into other areas (often tied to the changing social reproduction requirements of Fordism). In short, if the KWNS helped secure the conditions for Fordist economic expansion, Fordist economic expansion helped secure the conditions for expansion of the KWNS.

Welfare rights based on national citizenship helped to generalize norms of mass consumption and thereby contributed to full employment levels of demand; and they were sustained in turn by an institutionalized compromise involving Fordist unions and Fordist firms. In some cases (notably in the USA), collective bargaining at enterprise and sectoral level was important in securing occupational welfare and thereby in setting possible benchmarks for later generalization in and through state-provided – but often still dualistic – welfare. Securing economic growth with full employment and extending welfare rights were important axes of party political competition in all Atlantic Fordist societies. Finally, we should note that some costs of the Fordist compromise and the KWNS were borne within Fordist societies themselves by the relative decline of agriculture, the traditional petite bourgeoisie, small and medium firms; by the decline of cities, regions and sectors that could find no competitive role in the circuits of Atlantic Fordism; by workers employed in disadvantaged parts of segmented labour markets; and, especially in liberal welfare regimes, by women subject to the dual burden of paid and domestic labour. Migrant labour also had an important role in this spatio-temporal fix. For, as Klein-Beekman notes, 'Fordist state–society relations were partly enabled by this shifting articulation of spatiality. International migration was inextricably linked to the attempt to establish an exclusionary political-economic order centred around the welfare state and based upon universal criteria of inclusion for its citizens' (1996: 440; see also Soysal 1994).

One of the mechanisms for deferring the contradictions of Atlantic Fordism and the KWNS and displacing (or redistributing) their costs was inflation. Based on the capacity of banks and the state to expand credit, inflation served to (pseudo-) validate otherwise unprofitable production and to maintain high levels of capacity utilization and employment (Lipietz 1985). Provided that all the relevant economies had similar mild rates of inflation or that higher inflation economies could engage in occasional modest devaluations, this was not a problem in terms of integrating the circuit of Atlantic Fordism (Aglietta 1982). But it came at the cost of increased economic problems later, reflected in the typical Atlantic Fordist problem of stagflation (a combination of stagnation and inflation that is improbable in liberal competitive capitalism but quite possible under the Fordist mode of regulation). It also had significant redistributive effects in class, sectoral and regional terms. Thus, among other effects, inflation tended to redistribute market share and profits in favour of big capital at the expense of small and medium enterprises (Galbraith 1967; Nitzan 1998, 2001). Other costs were borne beyond Fordist societies by economic and political spaces that were integrated into international regimes (such as those for cheap oil or migrant labour) necessary to Atlantic Fordism's continued growth, but were not themselves included within the Fordist compromise. Atlantic Fordism was also enabled through a Janus-faced temporal fix. On the one hand, it depended on accelerated (and unsustainable) superexploitation of nature (especially raw materials and non-renewable resources laid down over millennia, such as fossil fuels). And, on the other hand, it produced environmental pollution and social problems that it did not address within its own temporal horizons – as if working on the principle of *après moi, la déluge*. This involved the deferral of current environmental costs of Fordism (regarding both the renewability of resources and the 'sink' function of the environment) into an indefinite future (see, for example, Altvater 1993: 247–78; Brennan 1995; Stahel 1999). At the same time, the temporal rhythms of the KWNS were oriented to managing the business and electoral cycles rather than to problems associated with far shorter or longer horizons (such as those of round-the-clock financial trading or those of long waves of accumulation). It was increasing difficulties in maintaining this spatio-temporal fix of Atlantic Fordism that helped trigger attempts to transform the KWNS.

5. Crisis

The KWNS underwent a crisis in the 1970s and 1980s. This had various general economic, political and sociocultural causes. There were also more specific, conjunctural factors that affected the timing, forms and incidence of the crisis in particular cases. For crises in/of Fordism are inevitably overdetermined. The typical manifestation of the economic crisis *in* Fordism was a growing stagflationary tendency – that reflected the distinctive grounding of its mode of regulation in the wage and money forms – and a tendential decline in the rate and mass of profit as the Fordist growth dynamic was progressively exhausted. Stagflation problematizes the state's capacity to engage in contracyclical demand management and, in the face of increasing internationalization, leads to additional problems. These include the risk that increased demand is met from abroad rather than domestic production; the state's growing inability to control interest rates and/or exchange rates; and, with each successive round of stagflation, growing public debt at a time when internationalization was linked to rising interest rates. But this crisis-tendency was usually overcome through a combination of crisis-induced economic restructuring and incremental institutional changes. As such problems mounted, however, the crisis *of* Fordism began to manifest itself structurally in the breakdown of its typical crisis-management mechanisms or, as Offe expressed it, in a crisis of crisis-management (Offe 1984); and, strategically, in the attempt to realign social forces around alternative accumulation strategies, state projects and hegemonic visions. This was reinforced by crises in other aspects of the mode of regulation, mode of societalization and overall spatio-temporal fix with which Atlantic Fordism was associated.

Economic crisis

Economically, the continued growth of the KWNS undermined some of the conditions that had sustained Fordist accumulation. This illustrates how form serves to problematize function (Jessop 1982). Following the initial one-off boost to productivity that came from the transition to mass production in a given branch of production, further increments became harder to achieve both technically and socially. The search to achieve further economies of scale and to compensate for relative market saturation in their home markets prompted Fordist firms to expand into foreign markets. They also began to resort to foreign credit to reduce borrowing costs and to transfer pricing and/or foreign tax havens to reduce tax bills. Yet this also began to undermine the relative closure of the national economy as an object of economic management. There were also limits to the extent to which Fordism could be extended into all branches of production, including services. The growing capital intensity of production and the dependence of economies of scale on full capacity utilization increased the strike power of organized labour; and the continuing search for productivity increases through work intensification led to growing alienation on the shop floor.

Economic expansion more generally and the gradual consolidation of unemployment benefits and other forms of social security also altered the underlying (structural) balance of class forces in favour of organized labour in the economic sphere – a shift that was translated into greater militancy in the mid- to late 1960s. This became critical as the crisis in/of Fordism emerged (expressed, inter alia, in declining profits) and capital tried to restructure the labour process and restrain labour costs. Economic expansion also altered the underlying (structural) balance of forces in favour of oil suppliers, because the dynamism of the Atlantic Fordist accumulation regime depended not only on continued productivity growth, but also, and critically, on an increasing supply of oil at declining prices in real terms. The two oil shocks in the 1970s associated with the formation of the Organization of Petroleum Exporting Countries (OPEC) were a reflection of this. In addition, welfare expansion also institutionalized a social wage whose downward rigidity (if not its upward momentum) could act as a brake on profits and capital accumulation. These changes threatened the Fordist growth regime through their adverse impact on both sides of the capital–labour relation, affecting the monetary incentives to invest and to work.

In addition to these domestically generated crisis-tendencies and mechanisms, the economic and political effectiveness of the KWNS in regulation was further weakened by a variable mixture of extraversion (outward flows of goods, services and capital), penetration (inward flows) and interiorization (defined as integration into a regional, international or global division of labour that blurs the previous distinction between domestic and foreign capital). Some multinational companies (MNCs) and transnational banks (TNBs) could also locate some of their activities abroad in order to escape national controls, or plausibly threaten to do so in order to seek concessions from local, regional or national governments (on the significant extent to which place-dependence still matters, see chapter 5). Many macroeconomic policy instruments associated with the KWNS became less effective, leading state managers to attempt to replace or buttress them with other measures in the hope of still being able to maintain the typical economic policy objectives of the KWNS – full employment, economic growth, stable prices and a 'sound' balance of payments. At the same time, as the internationalization of both monetary and real flows proceeded apace and involved ever more firms, markets and countries, states could no longer act as if national economies were more or less closed and their growth dynamic were autocentric. Moreover, alongside the impact of internationalization on national economic policy, regional and local economies were also increasingly found to have their own specific problems. These could be solved neither by the usual national macroeconomic policies nor by standardized industrial and/or regional policies formulated at the centre. Overall, it no longer appeared so self-evident that national economic space was the best starting point for economic policies aimed at promoting growth, innovation or competitiveness.

This prompted more interest in, and a shift towards, supply-side intervention and policies that would insert local, regional or national economic spaces more effectively into the global economy in the hope of securing some net benefit from internationalization. Small open economies had already faced this problem during the postwar boom, of course; now, even the larger and previously relatively closed economies were being absorbed into the broader circuits of capital. More generally, an emerging crisis in the forms and long-term viability of US hegemony was reflected in struggles over the shaping of new international regimes and the extent to which they and earlier postwar international regimes should serve particular American interests rather than capitalism more generally.[12]

The impact of these changes prompted a shift in the primary aspects of the two principal contradictions of accumulation in the KWNS and gave renewed force to other familiar expressions of the underlying contradictions of capitalism that had nonetheless played a secondary role in the Atlantic Fordist type of spatio-temporal fix. The wage (both individual and social) came increasingly to be seen, rightly or wrongly, as an international cost of production rather than as a source of domestic demand; and money now increasingly circulates as international currencies and offshore money capital, thereby undermining Keynesian demand management on a national level and eventually forcing states to abandon their attempts to maintain fixed exchange rates. This switch in the primary aspect of the contradiction in the money form is related to the tendency for the dynamic of industrial capital to be subordinated to the hypermobile logic of financial capital and the tendency for returns on money capital to exceed those on productive capital. But this shift in economic domination within the circuits of capital is still subject, of course, to the principle of economic determination by the long-run performance of productive capital (see chapter 1).

A further disruptive factor was the paradigm shift from a Fordist growth model and associated accumulation strategy based on mass production, scale economies and mass consumption to one oriented to flexible production, innovation, scope economies, innovation rents and more rapidly changing and differentiated patterns of consumption. While this paradigm shift was rooted in ongoing changes in production and the search for alternatives to Fordism, it was often taken up and magnified as part of the more general attempt to restructure and reorient accumulation, regulation and even societalization. This shift has had major implications for enterprise, sectoral and spatial strategies, even where Fordism itself did not previously dominate given sectors or national economies. It provides a major framework for making sense of the current crisis and imposing some coherence on the search for routes out of the crisis. In addition, the attempt to move beyond the limitations of the Fordist labour process and the Atlantic Fordist accumulation regime was deemed by key economic and political forces to require not only a significant rebalancing of capital–labour relations but also a series of organizational and institutional changes to facilitate the adoption of new core technologies and products as the motive and carrier forces of economic expansion. This posed problems for firms and states concerning how best to manage the transition to the next long wave of economic expansion, and this, in turn, typically required changes in their spatio-temporal horizons, capacities and activities (see chapter 5).

Other economic factors that weakened the KWNS included the challenges posed by lower-wage but increasingly high-tech East Asian economies; the shift from more supply-driven to more demand-driven forms of production (often paradigmatically summarized, but never adequately described, as we shall see in chapter 3, as the shift from Fordism to post-Fordism); the feminization of the labour force (with its impact on the family form and the family wage that had both played key roles in the KWNS); and the growing recognition of the environmental limits of the Fordist mode of growth as it intensified in the pioneer cases and spread to other economies – a recognition that affected not only environmental movements but also the driving forces of Fordism.

Fisco-financial crisis

As one form of the capitalist type of state, the KWNS must be considered as a tax state (see table 1.4 in chapter 1). As the KWNS expanded, so did its tax take. Moreover, as public sector employment and spending expanded relative to the private sector, the income level at which taxes began fell to include more of the working class. The crisis of Fordism exerted a 'scissors' effect on KWNS finances. On the revenue side, it reduced the tax base for social security payments insofar as these were tied to wage-earner and/or payroll taxes at a time when unemployment began to increase. Capital's contribution to state revenues also fell because of the decline in gross profits and the redistribution of tax burdens to protect post-tax profit levels. This was reinforced to the extent that capital was mobile and thereby able to escape national taxes – or, with or without the connivance of state managers, could plausibly threaten to do so. At the same time, the crisis increased demands for expenditure on income maintenance (for example, unemployment, early retirement and family benefit payments) and, via the social repercussions of unemployment and recession, on other welfare services (such as housing, health and family policies). This was reflected in a more rapid increase in state expenditures than tax receipts during the 1970s and 1980s in most OECD countries. Moreover, insofar as the state increased its real and/or tax expenditures for technological innovation and economic restructuring and/or reduced its taxes on capital in general, this further limited the resources available for social spending.[13] The resulting general fiscal crisis of the state was associated with conflicts not only over the level and incidence of state expenditures, but also over the restructuring of the taxation and credit systems (on fiscal crisis, see especially O'Connor 1973). This was reflected in growing hostility to the tax costs of the welfare state and/or to the inflationary consequences of financing welfare expenditures through government borrowing, and was a major factor behind the neoliberal regime shift in the anglophone Fordist economies and neoliberal policy adjustments in other Fordist economies. Yet the chances of long-term retrenchment in social welfare spending (especially on the capital account) without deteriorating provision were (and still are) limited: at most, there could be a redistribution of their provision between the public, private and 'third' sectors, together with more or less marginal attempts at cost-cutting. This became one of the key elements, of course, in the neoliberal project of welfare state restructuring. At the same time, there was growing hostility to the social and economic repercussions of welfare retrenchment (especially in health, education and pensions) once cuts extended beyond more marginal state activities and/or threatened to affect core economic and political interests rather than marginal social groups.

In this sense, the objective economic and social functions of the KWNS – which are particular expressions of the more general functions of the capitalist type of state in relation to the contradictions, dilemmas, asymmetries and antagonisms of the capital relation – have set limits to state disengagement. However, as we shall see in chapters 5 and 6, there is more scope for change in the economic than the social dimensions of state intervention. The path-dependent institutional and political legacies of the institutionalized compromise associated with the KWNS also serve to reinforce these limits in the short- to medium-term. Nonetheless, these basic limits do not exclude (and may, indeed, even encourage, for want of anything better) marginal adjustments in programmes, the rescaling of activities or a significant *strategic reorientation* of more or less constant state budgets. This is one area where the differences in welfare regimes and state forms discussed above have had a major impact on the scope for pursuing a neoliberal regime shift in social policy. The strategic selectivity of states and the partisan nature of governments also matter here (see, for example, the contrast between the radical neoliberal regime shift in unicameral New Zealand and the less drastic neoliberal policy turn in a federal Australia).

If one were to consider only the fiscal and budgetary aspects of the welfare state, two key features of its economic crisis would fall from view. First, it is important to note that the crisis was not purely financial. The fact that the financial crisis of the state was interpreted at the time largely in terms of the excessive burden of social expenditures reflected a shift in the balance of economic and political forces rooted in the more general dynamic of Fordism. The emergence of new alliances with interests in other policies implied that renewed capitalist expansion would not produce a simple return to the situation that had existed before the crisis. And, second, the underlying structural causes of the crisis would not disappear with renewed expansion. The economic crisis of the welfare state was rooted in the growing discrepancy between its activities and the discursively constituted (but often materially rooted) needs of capital accumulation. Tasks that had benefited capital during the Fordist upswing acquired their own institutional inertia and vested interests even though the needs of capital had changed (or were held to have done so as the dominant Fordist accumulation strategies were challenged) and many of the policies inherited from the period of Fordist expansion were failing or even proving counterproductive. Thus, resolving the economic crisis would require the reorganization of the accumulation regime, its modes of regulation and its mode of societalization, as well as private and public economic retrenchment.

The fiscal, financial and budgetary dilemmas of the welfare state must be considered in relation to the overall structure and finances of state expenditure and the state's role in securing the extra-economic conditions for renewed capital accumulation. Thus, the tendential emergence of post-Fordism as a labour process, accumulation strategy and societal paradigm also began to pose new problems for welfare state finance. For example, even assuming that something approaching 'full employment' could be restored, the weight of part-time, temporary and discontinuous employment patterns would prove much greater than under Fordism. This indicated a need for new patterns of taxation and welfare entitlements almost regardless of the particular variants of the KWNS that existed in different countries. Likewise, with increasing international capital mobility (especially in the service sector) and increasing competition among states to attract investment in sunrise sectors, the contribution of taxes on capital converged downwards. This situation is likely to continue in the absence of a concerted transnational policy to raise corporate taxation. Similar problems are now being posed by new phenomena such as international electronic commerce, which further undermines national tax regimes. These shifts were also reflected in the balance of political forces and the type of demands placed upon the welfare state. More generally, as we shall see below, the alleged need for new forms of flexibility in the organization of the labour process and labour market has had major implications for the functions and organization of the welfare state. The crisis of Fordism and the transition to post-Fordism have affected not only the levels and methods of financing welfare expenditure but also the ways in which the post-Fordist welfare state attempts to perform its functions in the valorization of capital, social reproduction and social cohesion.

Political crises

Politically, the KWNS was vulnerable to growing political resistance to taxation and stagflation, the crisis in postwar compromises between industrial capital and organized labour, and new economic and social conditions and attendant problems that could not be managed or resolved readily, if at all, through continuing reliance on top-down state planning and/or simple market forces. In addition, new conflicts and/or forms of struggle emerged that could not be easily integrated into the postwar compromise: two major examples were the crisis of corporatism and the rise of new social movements. The latter have been especially important, as they developed in crisis-prone cities and were often oriented to global or local rather than national issues. Finally, new problems also emerged, such as pollution and new categories of risk, which proved less easy to manage, regularize or govern within the old forms.

It is also clear that the welfare state caused some of its own problems. The rational-legal form of welfare provision is associated with bureaucratism, the juridification of social relations, political empire-building, centralization, clientelism and the intensification of personal dependence. Moreover, the professionalized and bureaucratized forms of help and support aggravated social problems and increased dependence. In addition, in liberal welfare regimes, the combination of taxation, national insurance and means-tested benefits systems created (and continues to create) two problems: a poverty trap confronting the low-wage employed (for whom increased earnings from employment are countered by loss of benefit) and the unemployment trap (which concerns the net real increase in income when an unemployed person takes a job). This double trap is avoided in social democratic welfare regimes and some conservative-corporatist welfare regimes. At the same time, the forms in which welfare policies were administered aggravated distributional and status conflicts in both the middle and working classes. It is often the middle classes who make greater use of welfare benefits and especially of the more expensive benefits (for example education, housing and health), whether these are provided through the public welfare system or through the so-called 'fiscal welfare state' rooted in tax reductions on certain classes of consumer spending. Indeed, the relationships among public, fiscal and occupational provision serve both to disguise the extent to which the state supports the social reproduction of the middle classes and to provide new foci for distributional and status conflicts.

There is also some truth in criticisms that the welfare state has an inherent expansionary dynamic insofar as welfare needs are often defined by those with a vested interest in their expansion.[14] This holds not only for politicians (spurred on by electoral competition) and welfare administrators and professionals (for whom welfare expansion implies jobs, career development and empire-building), but also for client groups and the political lobbies that articulate their interests. This has major structural as well as resource implications for Fordism, including the increasing social welfare budget during the postwar boom and beyond and the resulting need to restructure the tax and credit systems to generate the necessary revenues to finance that spending. This problem became more acute as the social and environmental costs of Fordist expansion and the dynamic of welfare policy-making created new issues and new interests around which social movements could organize. Among these issues we can note the growing decomposition of the nuclear family form that played a key role in Fordist societalization both as a locus of privatized consumption and as the site for social and emotional integration in an atomized society (Hirsch and Roth 1986). The proportion of households that conform to the nuclear family pattern also began to fall. This continues to be reflected in greater needs for state support (for education, sickness, single parent families, old age, etc.) and attempts to encourage families to bear the burdens of youth unemployment, sickness and care for the elderly. Likewise, inner-city decline concentrated social as well as economic problems in areas with a declining tax base and increasing needs for welfare expenditure and programmes. It is here, above all, that one finds the social problems of education, housing, health, single households and single parents, social isolation and mental illness, and demographic imbalance.

New forces became active in lobbying for state support. These ranged from capital–labour cartels in declining industries and regions, through ethnic minorities and single parents, to alternative cultural and social movements. The expansion of 'tax expenditures' to support the private provision of social reproduction goods and services (from pensions through housing and medical insurance to education) also created a new set of policy-taking interests among tax-payers as well as creating vested interests among capitalist concerns (such as pension funds) that service them. In the boom years there were few financial or electoral checks on these incremental processes – especially as the years of welfare expansion coincided with reduced military expenditures, rising productivity and full employment. These checks became more pressing during the 1970s and 1980s. Thus the crisis of Fordism was linked to the fiscal crisis of the state and with growing electoral resistance to the taxation for welfare needs. In some cases the electoral reaction was temporary, in others it provided the basis for a neoliberal regime shift.

A further aspect was that the monetary and legal forms of social policy are less adequate to the problems that the social state was having to handle. At first, it dealt with simple economic contingencies (such as ill-health, cyclical unemployment, pregnancy, etc.) that disrupted the earnings stream of individuals and/or families; then it expanded from a social security state into a welfare state through increasing interventions into the field of collective consumption – providing a widening range of basic welfare services such as education, housing and health that were linked to notions of equality, social democracy and social redistribution; later still, it got deeply involved in personal social services and the handling of sociopsychological problems ('people-processing' and the 'governance of the soul') – leading some to talk of the rise of the 'therapeutic state'. Increasing attention was also paid to the deeper, structural roots of individual economic contingencies (such as the operation of the labour market or health and safety at work) and, apart from the case of liberal welfare regimes, there was closer coordination between economic and social policy in these areas. Finally, the state moved into new fields of social policy (such as the crisis of the inner city, race relations and gender inequalities), which have complex roots in the overall mode of societalization rather than the operation of the capitalist economy narrowly conceived.

Social crisis

The KWNS was also undermined by two sets of emerging trends in the lifeworld. The first of these was a continuing tendential 'denationalization' of civil society. This is reflected in the development of cosmopolitanism and 'tribalism' (or the rediscovery or invention of primordial, affectual identities at the expense both of liberal individualism and of civic loyalty to an 'imagined' national community), and an expansion of diverse social movements that now operate across national boundaries. This was (and still is) associated with a crisis in the national state, which takes different forms according to the nature of the imagined national community on which it is based (see chapter 5). Together, these phenomena weakened the sense of national identity[15] that shaped the KWNS in its formative period and thereby weakened the coalition of forces that sustained it. The second set of social trends concern more specific values, social identities and interests associated with the welfare state and the growth of social movements opposed to one or more aspects of the KWNS. This is reflected in rejection of the social democratic and/or Atlantic Fordist normative commitment to class-based egalitarianism and its accompanying class-based redistributive politics; in a pluralistic identity politics and 'politics of difference' in which there is greater emphasis on mutual respect, authenticity and autonomy; in a shift from national citizenship to 'a more universal model of membership [in a state], anchored in deterritorialized notions of persons' rights' (Soysal 1994: 3); in increased concern for personal empowerment rather than for the bureaucratic administration of legal rights, monetized entitlements and uniform public services; and in the expansion of the so-called 'third' sector, which supposedly operates flexibly outside of the framework of pure markets and the bureaucratic state (but often in close conjunction with them as a 'shadow market' and 'shadow state').

The interrelated crisis-generating dynamics of accumulation, changes in social relations intelligible in terms of the dynamic of Fordist societies, and the welfare state were reinforced by important exogenous factors.[16] Chief among these is demographic change. This has affected both the scope and the finances of the welfare state. In particular, the ratio of contributors to beneficiaries has changed dramatically in the last 35 years, as the number of those in retirement has increased (especially among the oldest cohorts with their greater need for long-term medical attention) and the number of those who are economically active has fallen (in part because of the resort in the 1980s and 1990s to forced or voluntary early retirement as a means of reducing the active labour force). Immigration as a partial solution to this latter problem has generated its own social and political problems in turn. Costs in the welfare state also tend to rise disproportionately – education lasts longer, medical progress has increased costs, one-parent families require more support and Fordist productivity-raising techniques are less applicable to welfare activities (but see chapter 3 on the contingent nature of this differential price and productivity trap and on alternative exits therefrom). This intensified the fiscal squeeze on welfare policies and made the search for solutions more urgent.

Initial responses to the crises in/of Fordism and the KWNS

The development of the KWNS was still marked by temperate and optimistic reformism in the 1960s. The initial response to the crisis of Fordism did not produce demands for a radical transformation of the economy or the state. Instead, it intensified the features of the KWNS, supplementing and reinforcing them with other measures. What occurred was a conjunctural transformation of the KWNS rooted in its attempts to manage the crisis of Fordism and to limit the repercussions of that crisis on its own internal organization and unity. Thus:

> Governments first responded to the economic difficulties by following traditional formulas that entailed maintaining or increasing entitlements and expenditure in an effort to fight recession and unemployment and mitigate their social consequences. After a decade of 'fumbling', government after government regardless of political color embarked on new policies that often involved reining in the increase in expenditure and increasing revenue. (Huber and Stephens 2001: 207)

In the initial 'fumbling' period, political actors initially faced the false dilemma of mounting a one-sided attack on wages as a cost of production or providing one-sided support for wages as a source of national economic demand. An analogous dilemma concerned abandoning demand management in favour of monetarism (national or international) versus an equally one-sided resort to 'Keynesianism in one country' and subsidies for crisis-hit industries. This, in turn, was linked to the choice between a one-sided liberalization of economies (especially financial markets) that would initially reinforce the dissociation of financial and industrial capital and subordinate the latter to the former, and a one-sided pursuit of neo-mercantilist or protectionist strategies that might encourage or impose greater cooperation between these two rival fractions of capital. A related dilemma for the political managers of the KWNS concerned retrenching the welfare state and attacking the social wage as a cost of international production versus defending welfare employment, public services and transfers without regard to their impact on international competitiveness. What unified these opposed but equally false solutions to the crisis of Atlantic Fordism and the KWNS was their one-sided emphasis on tackling one or other moment of the principal contradictions of the prevailing accumulation regime and its mode of regulation. They differ in opting for unilateral commitment to reinvigorating the national scale of economic and political organization in these regards or else in unconditionally supporting (or surrendering to) the illogic of an abstract capital in potentially unrestricted global motion.

When this oscillation failed to restore conditions for Fordist accumulation, the policy debate moved beyond the national–international framework associated with the early stages of the Fordist crisis. There was an increasingly intense search for some other scale on which capital's structural contradictions and strategic dilemmas might again be reconciled for an extended period through an appropriate spatio-temporal fix and institutionalized compromise. This search process took different forms in different social formations, but there was also an increasingly significant international dimension to the restructuring of policy regimes and the reorientation of strategies. This also implies the search for a new state form. Despite the variety of criticisms and solutions, however, only a limited range of solutions is likely to be compatible with a successful transition to some form of post-Fordism. How they are combined and which predominates in particular societies will depend on the outcome of political and economic struggles on the terrain of different national regimes of accumulation and political regimes. These issues are discussed in later chapters.

6. The Discursive Mediation of Crisis

Crisis is never a purely objective phenomenon that automatically produces a particular response or outcome. Instead, a crisis emerges when established patterns of dealing with structural contradictions, their crisis-tendencies and dilemmas no longer work as expected and may even aggravate the situation. Crises are most acute when crisis-tendencies and tensions accumulate across several interrelated moments of the structure or system in question, limiting room for manoeuvre in regard to any particular problem. Changes in the balance of forces mobilized behind and across different types of struggle (see chapter 1) also have a key role here in intensifying crisis-tendencies and in weakening and/or resisting established modes of crisis-management (Offe 1984: 35–64). This creates a situation of more or less acute crisis, a potential moment of decisive transformation and an opportunity for decisive intervention. In this sense, there is an imbalance in a crisis situation: it is objectively over-determined but subjectively indeterminate (Debray 1973: 113). This creates the space for determined strategic interventions to significantly redirect the course of events as well as for attempts to 'muddle through' in the (perhaps hopeless) hope that the situation will resolve itself in time. These are, then, potentially path-shaping moments (on the dialectic of path-dependency and path-shaping, see Hausner et al. 1995).

We can see this situation emerging in relation to the crisis in/of the KWNS. Which of these alternative outcomes eventually emerges will be mediated in part through discursive struggles over the nature and significance of the crisis and what might follow from it. In periods of major social restructuring there is an intersection of diverse economic, political and sociocultural narratives that seek to give meaning to current problems by construing them in terms of past failures and future possibilities. Different social forces in the private and public domains propose new visions, projects, programmes and policies. The problems confronting the KWNS, for example, prompt competing narratives about whether it is in crisis, how deep the crisis is, how the crisis developed,

Table 2.2 Major symptoms in the perennial welfare state crisis

1950s	1960s	1970s–1980s	1990s
Inflationary and harms growth	Fails to produce equality Too bureaucratic	Stagflation Unemployment Postmaterialism Government overload	Globalization Unemployment Rigidities Inequalities Social exclusion Family instability
Rightist critique	Leftist critique	(OECD 1981)	(Less partisan) (OECD 1997)

Source: Based on Esping-Andersen 1997: 2

where it is likely to end and how it might be resolved. Indeed, as some cynics have correctly noted, the welfare state seems to have been 'in crisis' from the moment of its inception. It is only the nature of the crisis that seems to have been contested, with different readings being dominant at different times (see table 2.2; see also Esping-Andersen 1999: 2–4). As symptoms of crisis gather, however, a struggle for hegemony (or at least dominance) begins to establish new accumulation strategies, state projects or hegemonic projects. These economic and political conflicts concern not only the distribution of the costs of crisis-management but also the appropriate policies to escape from the crisis.

The plausibility of these narratives and their associated strategies and projects depends on their resonance (and hence capacity to reinterpret and mobilize) with the personal (including shared) narratives of significant classes, strata, social categories or groups that have been affected by the development of the postwar economic and political order. Moreover, given that there are always various plausible narratives, one must also consider the differential capacities of their narrators to get their messages across and secure support for the specific lessons they entail. This will depend heavily on the organization and operation of the mass media and the role of intellectuals in public life. The plausibility of competing narratives is also shaped by the structural biases and strategically selective operations of various public and private apparatuses of economic, political and ideological domination. Narratives do not compete for influence on an even playing field, but are subject to discursive and structural selectivities[17] as well as the need to establish some resonance with personal narratives. Such concerns take us well beyond a concern for narrativity, of course, into the many extradiscursive conditions of narrative appeal. Finally, the plausibility of specific narratives depends on a broader web of interlocution (Somers 1994: 614) comprising meta-narratives that reveal linkages between a wide range of interactions, organizations and institutions and/or help to make sense of whole epochs. That these institutional and metanarratives have powerful reso-nance does not mean that they should be taken at face value. All narra-tives are selective, appropriate some arguments and combine them in specific ways. In this sense, then, one must consider what is left unstated or silent, what is repressed or suppressed in official discourse.

Interpretations of the crisis in/of the KWNS were (and are) manifold. They have included romantic rejection of the welfare state (evident in the work of critics such as Ivan Illich 1979, 1981); calls for an alternative, communitarian welfare state and/or one addressed to the problems of patriarchal as well as class domination; social democratic arguments for the reorganization and retrenchment of the KWNS for a temporary period of economic austerity before it is resurrected in more or less the same form; the New Right's demands for the privatization of welfare services and/or the introduction of commercial criteria into the welfare state; and many others. As we shall see, a radical neoliberal regime shift is by no means the only outcome.

Such interpretations are related to debates and reflections on the state. Initially it was claimed that the national state was no longer func-tioning as it had done in the boom years. Whether due to the excessive demands placed upon it, a scarcity of resources to meet them, a deficit in state capacities to pursue objectives, a loss of political cohesion, declin-ing faith in the legitimacy of government or simple overload, the national state was said to be in crisis. Such assertions had a specific political resonance and, although politically contentious, served to orient the actions of a wide range of political forces. In particular, they fed into the proposals for managing or resolving the crises that were typical of the second stage of debate. One common suggestion was that state func-tions should now be shared with non-state bodies to reduce the overload on an overextended state apparatus. Another was that there should be a return to the liberal, nightwatchman state so that it could concentrate on more effective performance of its remaining, minimal functions. Later still it was recognized that changes in the national state could not be limited to a simple redistribution or reduction of otherwise unchanging functions and so attention turned to the search to develop a historically new type of state and politics. What would replace the KWNS therefore came to depend on the changing balance of political forces mobilized for and against competing interpretations of the crisis in/of the postwar mode of economic growth, its mode of regulation and the appropriate solutions to any problems identified in these narratives.

3

The Schumpeterian
Competition State

This chapter is mainly concerned with the changing economic functions of the state in advanced capitalist societies following the crisis in/of Atlantic Fordism. Changes in the state's institutional form and effectiveness are considered mainly in chapters 5 and 6 after the discussion of changing social functions in the next chapter. I relate the changing pattern of economic intervention to economic crisis-tendencies in Atlantic Fordism and to the emergent features of post-Fordism as well as to political crisis-tendencies in the KWNS and problems rooted in Fordist mass society more generally. As economic, political and social forces have responded to these crisis-tendencies, we can discern the tendential crystallization of a distinctive form of state concerned to promote economic and extra-economic conditions deemed appropriate to the emerging post-Fordist accumulation regime. This new type of state can be usefully described as a Schumpeterian competition state, and I will describe its form and functions and justify this description in this and later chapters. Its distinctive form and functions are clearly linked to the new configuration of contradictions and dilemmas that have emerged in the wake of the crisis of Fordism and to new techno-economic paradigms associated with the emergence of a new long wave of economic growth. But this link is far from automatic and mechanical. It derives from a trial-and-error search to make sense of the crisis-tendencies of Atlantic Fordism and its mode of regulation and to develop some strategic guidelines and sense of direction in response to initial failures to overcome the structural crises and moderate social conflict through normal routines of crisis-management. Indeed, in significant respects, the new state form (considered as a form-determined, strategically selective condensation of the changing balance of political forces) is playing a major role in the material and discursive constitution of the globalizing, networked, knowledge-based economy that its activities are seeking to govern.

'Competition state' is used here to characterize a state that aims to secure economic growth within its borders and/or to secure competitive advantages for capitals based in its borders, even where they operate abroad, by promoting the economic and extra-economic conditions that are currently deemed vital for success in competition with economic actors and spaces located in other states. Paradoxically, offshore economies can be an element in this struggle insofar as they are sponsored (or tolerated) by onshore states to secure competitive advantages for domestic or international capitals based in their own territories (Hudson 2000; Palan 1998). More generally, as we shall see, an important aspect of the activities of competition states concerns their attempts either alone or in conjunction with other forces (including other states) to project power beyond their political frontiers to shape cross-border or external economic spaces relevant to capital accumulation and social reproduction. Although the competition state's strategies may be targeted on specific places, spaces and scales and directed against specific competitors, they are always mediated through the operation of the world market as a whole – especially as efforts are made to widen and deepen the latter through strategies of neoliberal globalization. As such, the competition state prioritizes the pursuit of strategies intended to create, restructure or reinforce – as far as it is economically and politically feasible to do so – the competitive advantages of its territory, population, built environment, social institutions and economic agents.[1] Just as there are different forms of competition, so too are there different forms of competition state. In relation to its economic policy role, the dominant type that is currently emerging can be described as a Schumpeterian competition state, because of its concern with technological change, innovation and enterprise and its attempt to develop new techniques of government and governance to these ends. Although social and economic policy are more tightly coupled in the competition state than in the KWNS, I consider the nature and forms of this coupling in chapter 4 rather than here.

1. Post-Fordism and the Knowledge-based Economy

There has been an extensive and often heated scholarly discussion – now somewhat diminished – about whether the concept of post-Fordism is the most appropriate entry point for studying recent changes in capital accumulation and its implications for economic and social policy. Three issues are relevant here: (1) the general theoretical adequacy of the concept of post-Fordism; (2) the extent to which this concept is suitable for describing the full range of changes since the mid-1970s; and (3) the role of post-Fordism and associated notions in economic and political discourses deployed to justify recent changes in economic and social policy. I deal with these questions in turn.

First, it may be better for some purposes to characterize the emerging accumulation regime through a substantive concept that is analogous to Fordism, such as Toyotism, Sonyism, Gatesism or Wintelism. These refer to new techno-economic paradigms in established or emerging manufacturing sectors and/or to new forms of enterprise and competition deemed superior to the archetypal Fordist forms. These paradigms lack the pervasive resonance that the Fordist paradigm enjoyed as the Fordist accumulation regime came to be consolidated. But they are certainly more fruitful than the more formal concept of post-Fordism, which relies on a chronological prefix to distinguish it from Fordism. The same problem holds for the 'new economy' paradigm, with its simplistic and overdrawn contrast between old and new. Accordingly, I will refer instead to the 'knowledge-based economy' (or KBE). This paradigm has gradually become hegemonic as a rationale and strategic guide for economic, political and social restructuring, resonates across many different systems and the lifeworld, and reflects the general importance attributed, rightly or wrongly, to knowledge as a 'factor of production' in the post-Fordist labour process, accumulation regime and mode of regulation (see pp. 128–31). The notion of post-Fordism can also be applied productively, however, as long as attention is paid to continuities and discontinuities. For without continuities, the new labour process, accumulation regime or mode of regulation would not be post-*Fordist* but merely non-Fordist; without discontinuities, however, it would not be *post*-Fordist but merely another phase of Fordism – high Fordist, late Fordist, neo-Fordist, or whatever. Thus this and subsequent chapters also explore the importance of the conservation-dissolution effects entailed in the emerging accumulation regime and its dialectic of path-dependency and path-shaping.

Second, this said, it is clear that many key aspects of the contemporary labour process, accumulation regime and mode of regulation have little to do with the golden age of Fordism. These must be considered in their own right as well as in terms of their position within the emerging regime and its mode of regulation. And, third, whether the notion of post-Fordism is currently theoretically justified as an analytical concept or not, discourses more or less explicitly referring to post-Fordism or flexible specialization were important in the initial mediation of economic, political and social change during the crisis in/of Atlantic Fordism. The main substantive features of a feasible emerging accumulation regime and mode of regulation have since been outlined and integrated into accumulation strategies, state projects and hegemonic visions. In particular, under the rubric of the KBE, they are guiding and reinforcing activities that are intended to consolidate the emerging post-Fordist economy.

An adequate account of the emerging post-Fordist, knowledge-based regime must treat it like Fordism – discussing its different sites and levels and also considering the sort of spatio-temporal fix (or fixes) that might secure some structural coherence across these levels. In this spirit, then, *as a distinctive type of labour process*, post-Fordism could be said to involve flexible production based on the operation of flexible machines and flexible systems that are combined to secure economies of scope and/or networks. Economies of scope derive from the diversity of products that can be produced from a given technical and social organization of production rather than from the diminishing unit cost of long production runs of standardized commodities that generate the economies of scale typical of mass production. Economies of networks derive mainly from the positive production and consumption externalities associated with infrastructure networks (such as transport, utility and communication networks) and/or with the joint operation of complementary *and compatible* assets controlled by different organizations (Economides 1996; Shy 2001). The new information and communication technologies (hereafter ICTs) are significant for both sorts of network economies at all stages in the circuit of capital and from both their production and consumption sides. For example, new ICT networks often involve almost exponentially increasing returns to network size as 'each additional [consuming] member increases the network's value, which in turn attracts more members, initiating a spiral of benefits' (Kelly 1998: 25). Similarly, ICT-enabled forms of collaborative network enterprise, vertical disintegration, strategic alliances, outsourcing, and so forth, especially when they operate in real time, also generate positive externalities. The post-Fordist labour process also requires an appropriately flexible workforce that often combines multiskilled and unskilled workers in flexible ways in contrast to the dominant role of relatively inflexible semi-skilled labour in Fordist mass production. Not all forms of flexibility are positive for workers, however, as they range from reliance on flexi-waged, flexi-time, hire-and-fire, and outsourced jobs through self-employed or subcontracted skilled labour to the multiskilling of core workers enjoying job rotation, job enrichment and teamwork. Flexibilization can likewise take many forms, some meaner and leaner than others. Thus there are significant differences in the strategies and consequences of attempts to flexibilize the labour process.

The crucial hardware for the post-Fordist labour process – and the hardware that justifies its description at least chronologically as post-Fordist – is microelectronics-based ICTs. The Internet has an increasingly important role here, especially in intra-firm, business-to-business (B2B) and government-to-business (G2B) transactions.[2] The post-Fordist labour process also relies increasingly on intelligent software based on operating codes and codified knowledge as well as knowledgeable 'wetware' (intellectual labour-power possessing as yet uncodified or tacit knowledge).[3] Indeed, another description of post-Fordism – as informationalism – emphasizes precisely the reflexive application of knowledge to the production of knowledge (Castells 1996, 2000b). Flexible production based on flexible machines or systems operated by flexible labour is not confined to areas previously dominated by mass production, where it results in flexible mass production in large factories and/or concentrated control over decentralized production networks. It can also be applied to small-batch and flexibly specialized production conducted by extended producer networks and/or by small and medium-sized firms. Likewise, some of its process innovations can enhance productivity in cases of diversified quality production. Moreover, beyond the manufacturing field, it can also be applied to the production of many types of services in the private, public and so-called 'third' sectors. This is important for two reasons. The first of these is the trend towards deindustrialization in the Atlantic Fordist economies, as a result of growing productivity in domestic manufacturing industry, the relocation of such industry to foreign sites, and competition from more efficient foreign producers. The second is the scope that flexibilization offers to overcome the alleged problems involved in raising productivity in services relative to manufacturing – problems that are often characterized as the Baumol effect, which refers to continuing increases in the price of production of services relative to manufactured goods. This effect is often invoked to explain the fiscal crisis of the welfare state, but it is better seen as a socially and technologically conditioned tendency rather than as an iron law of service provision. It follows that the scope for post-Fordist technologies and labour processes to influence the dynamic of any emerging economic system is much greater than was the case for the Fordist labour process in relation to Atlantic Fordism. In this sense, the knowledge-based economy does appear to have genuine potential to initiate a new long wave of economic expansion.

As a stable mode of macroeconomic growth, post-Fordism would be flexible and permanently innovative. In ideal-typical terms and in contrast to Fordism, its virtuous circle would be based on flexible and networked production; growing productivity based on some combination of economies of scope, economies of networks and process innovations; rising incomes for skilled manual and intellectual workers (often jointly reclassified as 'knowledge workers'); increased demand for differentiated goods and non-exportable (and hence also non-importable) services favoured by the growing discretionary element in these incomes; increased profits based on technological and other innovation rents and the full utilization of flexible capacity; reinvestment in more flexible production equipment and techniques and/or new sets of products; and a further boost to productivity owing to a new round of creatively destructive innovation, economies of scope and economies of networks. While it is easy enough to posit such a virtuous cycle, it is hard, given the combination of increasing openness and decreasing structured coherence in some national economies, to identify the scale on which a stable and coherent pattern of production and consumption might be realized. This is one aspect of the current relativization of scale with its associated struggle to establish alternative scales as the new primary scale for a spatio-temporal fix suited to post-Fordism (pp. 179–81). Moreover, given that the post-Fordist growth dynamic need not generalize the rising incomes of core workers to peripheral workers or the economically inactive, a post-Fordist accumulation regime could lead to greater income polarization and social exclusion than Atlantic Fordism (see chapter 4). This is especially evident in neoliberal post-Fordist regimes.

As a mode of economic regulation, post-Fordism involves commitment to supply-side innovation and flexibility in the main structural forms of regulation. There is a shift from the predominance of bureaucratic forms of corporate structure towards flatter, leaner, more decentralized and more flexible forms of organization that emphasize the strategic management of interdependencies around core competencies; towards networked forms of organization based on increased integration through the Internet and other e-based forms of communication, coordination, control and intelligence; or towards 'virtual firms' that outsource most of the activities necessary to deliver their goods or, more commonly, services and, in extreme cases, exist only on the Net. This involves extending and deepening digital networks to improve the organization of B2B as well as business-to-consumer (B2C) relations. This may also be associated with economies of networks and first-mover advantages. The new predominant forms of competition are based on improved quality and performance for individual products as well as the capacities to engineer flexible production systems (or to design flexible service delivery systems) and to accelerate process and product innovation based on knowledge applied to the production of knowledge. In this context, engineering innovation and improved productivity in setting up manufacturing systems rather than manufacturing productivity within any given system are crucial within industry. ICTs, especially Internet use for B2B e-commerce, are important here. Systems innovation is also vital in the financial and commercial sectors. This is reflected in the fact that competition now depends heavily on a search for technological rents based on continuous innovation, de facto monopolies in advanced technologies or intellectual property rights; and economies of scope, agglomeration and/or networks (rather than the economies of scale typical of Fordism). In short, the post-Fordist enterprise is less concerned with competing through economies of scale in the production of standardized goods and services using dedicated production systems than it is with competing through economies of scope, network economies and knowledge-intensive processes and products based on increasing flexibility in all stages of production and distribution as long as this is compatible with continuing valorization.

The wage relation is modified to reflect changing market conditions (flexi-wage and hire-and-fire and/or responsibility wages and regular reskilling) and the social wage and collective consumption are given key roles in enhancing flexibility (see chapter 4). Industrial relations focus on integrating core workers into the enterprise through new wage systems, new forms of involvement, new human resources management strategies, and so on. And, in pursuit of an enhanced flexibility, collective bargaining tends to be decentralized from the national to sectoral and regional or even company and plant levels. This also serves to limit the role of connective or pattern bargaining in generalizing wage increases as a source of demand. The money form is dominated by private, rootless bank credit that circulates internationally and by proliferation of financial products, derivatives and other forms of liquid assets; and the expansion of state credit is subject to limits set by the logic of international currency markets and/or new international benchmarks and agreements. Commercial capital is reorganized to create and serve increasingly segmented markets and, especially in neoliberal regimes, to provide cheap mass consumer goods to the socially excluded and new poor. Finally, state intervention and international regimes are being reorganized in ways to be detailed in this and succeeding chapters.

As yet, there is no obvious predominant post-Fordist *mode of societalization* directly analogous to the urban, industrial mass society aspiring to the American dream in Atlantic Fordism. In part, this reflects the many uncertainties in the 1980s and 1990s about what would eventually replace the Fordist labour process as the driving force in economic expansion and about how the structured coherence of a post-Fordist accumulation regime could (or would) be secured. Indeed, there were heated debates over the relative superiority of competing national, regional and urban models of production, consumption and societalization. For example, America, Japan and Germany proved to be major contestants among national models; Silicon Valley, the Third Italy and Baden-Württemberg were among many alternative regional models; and there were disputes over whether the future of cities lay with global cities, entrepreneurial cities or postmodern cities. Indeed, different forces in different countries as well as a growing number of international or supranational bodies competed to define accumulation strategies, state projects and hegemonic visions to remake social life in one or another image. These uncertainties were reinforced by mounting problems facing each main alternative on its home ground during the 1980s and, for Germany and Japan, the 1990s. Interest in varieties of capitalism and their respective strengths and weaknesses still continues, of course, with increasing recognition of mutual complementarities and rivalries and, indeed, of possible evolutionary and adaptive benefits in maintaining institutional diversity. Nonetheless, American hegemony has been more or less successfully reasserted in the form of the global neoliberal project because of US advances in the crucial sectors of the knowledge-based economy, American dominance in the international regimes involved in the globalizing economy, and renewed American military supremacy based on informationalism and new forms of 'intelligent' networked warfare. Japan has been effectively sidelined in this regard in global terms, even though it remains a major regional hegemon, with only China as a serious potential challenger; and, although the recent consolidation of 'Euroland' provides alternative models of regulation and societaliza- tion, it does not yet threaten American dominance within the overall global economy. More generally, patterns of societalization are marked by the rise of more complex, hybrid forms of social organization and crises of national identity and social cohesion. In particular, at the cost of focusing one-sidedly on the privileged classes and strata in the north, we can note that lifestyle and consumption have become more impor- tant bases of stratification in advanced economies, the rise of the politics of identity, and the significance of new social movements in postmodern politics. This can be linked to the argument that we are living in a post- modern society, provided that one does not use the possible develop- ment of postmodern modes of societalization to justify postmodernism as a distinctive theoretical approach.

The contrast between Fordism and post-Fordism served (and can still serve) to contextualize responses to the crisis of the KWNS – especially at the discursive or paradigmatic level. But this crude contrast obscures the real complexity of the changes subsumed (and, indeed, mystified) under what has too often been treated in terms of a radical break. More- over, as regulationists have now emphasized for more than twenty years, the transition from Fordism to a stable post-Fordism is not guaranteed. Instead, it depends on complex trial-and-error search processes, on the development of new accumulation strategies, state projects and hegemonic visions, on major institutional innovation, and on the consolidation of new spatio-temporal fixes. This puts many difficulties in the way of finding anything like a comprehensive and transferable solution to the question of how best to manage such a transition.

2. Old and New Contradictions in Post-Fordism

Chapter 2 identified some economic crisis-tendencies in Atlantic Fordism that contributed to its crisis and that of the KWNS. This chapter addresses the emerging traits of the post-Fordist KBE and their implications for economic policy in new accumulation regimes, modes of regulation and spatio-temporal fixes. Later chapters consider their implications for the other dimensions of the capitalist type of state. Three cautions are appropriate here. First, raising these issues does not imply that states can always develop (let alone that they already possess) the ability to reorganize themselves and successfully perform new functions. Second, it does not mean that a post-Fordist accumulation regime with an appropriate mode of social regulation could ever be introduced without resistance and conflict and/or would remain trouble-free once it had been consolidated. On the contrary, the following discussion aims to highlight the magnitude of the task facing states in these new conditions as they undertake a trial-and-error search to solve old and new problems in their economic and social policy activities. And, third, as I have already argued, the post-Fordist economy does not first emerge through the spontaneous operation of market forces and then get regulated from outside by the various mechanisms and agents of an appropriate mode of regulation. On the contrary, struggles to define that economy as an imagined object of regulation and to formulate appropriate accumulation strategies and modes of regulation are themselves co-constitutive forces in the eventual emergence of post-Fordism. This calls for special attention to changing techno-economic paradigms, economic theories and discourses, and techniques of governance, as well as to the adequacy of the strategic capacities of the state as the primary extra-economic mechanism for economic regularization and governance.

For all the hype and irrational exuberance in current accounts of the flexible, globalizing, knowledge-based 'new economy', post-Fordism does not suspend the contradictions, dilemmas or conflicts of capitalism. Indeed, the expansion of the economic logic of capitalism and economic competitiveness to include more and more factors previously regarded as 'extra-economic' actually serves to extend the scope for these contradictions, dilemmas and conflicts to become more fully imprinted on social relations more generally. This is another aspect of the increasing ecological dominance of capital accumulation on a global scale as a principle of societalization. For the problem of re-regulating accumulation after the Fordist crisis involves more than finding new ways to manage the old pattern of contradictions and to do so within the same spatio-temporal fix. This is not just because of a reversal of the primary and secondary aspects of the two principal structural forms in the Atlantic Fordist mode of regulation, namely, the wage relation and money form. It also arises because other contradictions and their associated dilemmas have become more important and because the spatio-temporal contexts in which these contradictions are expressed have become more complex. This makes it hard to relocate the spatio-temporal fix of Fordism onto another scale – either lower or higher than the national – even if state structures and other relevant regularizing forms could be readily recreated on that scale. This indicates the need for a new spatio-temporal fix as well as new means of regulation and governance.

There are five significant contradictions linked to the crisis of Fordism and the transition to post-Fordism. Two involve simple inversions of the primary and secondary aspects of the principal contradictions in the Fordist mode of regulation and a decline in the overall importance of these two contradictions, at least on the national scale in the post-Fordist mode of regulation. The other three involve increased salience of contradictions that had had a secondary significance for the KWNS, as well as a reweighting of their different aspects.

First, there has been a transposition of the primary and secondary aspects of the wage form considered as cost of production and source of demand. Second, there has been a transposition of the primary and secondary aspects of the money form considered as national money and international currency (or stateless money). Third, the contradiction between the exchange- and use-value moments in productive capital has become more significant owing to a growing dissociation between abstract flows in space and concrete valorization in place compared to the heyday of Atlantic Fordism. This is particularly associated with the hypermobility of some fractions of financial capital, but affects other, relatively mobile actors and processes in the circuit of capital too. Fourth, the articulation between the economic and extra-economic conditions for capital accumulation (that is, between its commodified, fictitiously commodified, and non-commodified preconditions) has become more problematic. In particular, growing short-termism in economic calculation, associated with the dominance of the money concept of capital, is coming into serious conflict with the increasing dependence of valorization on a growing range of extra-economic factors that take a long time to produce. Fifth, the basic contradiction between the growing socialization of forces of production and continuing private control in the relations of production and appropriation of surplus gains a new force and significance in the network economy. Sixth, and in addition, although it is not a structural contradiction in itself, serious conflicts have arisen over the appropriate horizons of action for the spatio-temporal fix, if any, within which the principal (but now less important) contradictions of Atlantic Fordism and the newly important contradictions of the current period might prove manageable.

First, in Atlantic Fordism and the KWNS, the wage was treated primarily as a source of demand. Thus growth in wages served the interests of productive capital in attaining full capacity utilization in a relatively closed economy dominated by mass production as well as commercial capital's interests in the spread of mass consumption. The growing internationalization of capital accompanying the final stages of Fordism transformed this situation: wages were increasingly seen primarily as a cost of production and only secondarily as a source of national demand.[4] This holds both for individual wages and the social wage (on the latter, see chapter 4). This threatened the national institutionalized class compromise between organized labour and domestic industrial capital and, in conjunction with the inversion of the primary and secondary aspects of the money form, tends to shift the balance of power in this compromise from organized labour to productive capital. It also tends to strengthen money capital vis-à-vis productive capital. This may encourage capital in specific sectors or even the majority of capitals operating in a given national economic space to seek to overturn that compromise. This has occurred in those liberal economies that have witnessed a neoliberal regime shift that has been facilitated by the relatively uncoordinated nature of industry–finance–labour relations and by the capacity of their central states to pursue radical programmes without the need for much consultation or concertation. Elsewhere, however, this inversion may simply lead to a renegotiation of the terms of the compromise and, perhaps, a narrowing of the parties to that compromise. This is most likely where capital and/or the state regard the cooperation of workers and trade unions as essential for successfully addressing other structural contradictions in the emerging post-Fordist economy. This in turn will depend on the extent to which capital and/or the state regard labour-power as a locus of skills, creativity and knowledge rather than as just one substitutable factor of production among others. It will also depend on the more general features of the state (see chapter 1) and the prevailing political situation.

In short, how radical a break with the postwar compromise is possible depends on the precise features of the wage relation and on which fractions of capital, if any, are actually interested in breaking the compromise even though the underlying structural balance of forces on this front has shifted against labour. This is reflected in different national solutions to resolving the new problems. Thus, where labour-power is seen as a fixed cost (for example, core workforces in Japan or Germany) and/or labour unions are well established organizationally and legally at local level (for example, Belgium, Germany, Sweden), there has been a resort to innovation and reskilling in order to sustain a high-wage, high-tech, high-growth accumulation strategy. In cases such as Germany, Sweden and Belgium, this is reflected in productivity pacts that may also receive state backing. Conversely, where labour-power is seen as a variable cost (as in the differently organized British and American cases) and/or where local unions are weak, capital may attack unions at all levels and adopt a hire-and-fire approach in the hope that neoliberal flexibility would reinforce competitiveness (Hancké 1996). Social pacts have also developed in Southern Europe, albeit for somewhat different reasons (see below and chapter 4).

Second, whereas money in the KWNS functioned primarily as national money and its circulation in the national economy was controlled by the national state, the subsequent collapse of the regulated postwar regime of credit money opened up a Pandora's box. This can be seen in the development of financial deregulation in and among national economies and the expansion of 'offshore' finance capital. The movement to international market determination of credit terms and currency prices – sometimes, of course, with the connivance of national states themselves, especially by the USA – has weakened the KWNS as a distinctive state form. Increasing cross-border flows of financial capital (including trade in derivatives) have had a negative impact on monetary control by national states. Thus, as Alan Hudson notes '[t]he development of stateless monies reshaped the regulatory landscape, undermining the geography – a spatial organization of power and social relations – of fixed, mutually exclusive, territorial states' (2000: 277). One measure of this shift in primacy can be found in the expansion of international financial markets from the 1970s onwards. Between 1963 and 1995, the size of the total funds raised on international markets increased at an average annual growth rate of 24.3 per cent compared to a 5.5 per cent annual growth rate in world trade and 3.2 per cent growth in global production. Even more significant are short-term financial flows. Around 1.5 trillion US dollars (or their equivalent in other currencies) are exchanged daily on foreign exchange markets, only 5 per cent of which is directly related to payments for traded goods and services. These flows of stateless monies are essentially deterritorialized, possessing a logic and dynamic at odds with the national-centric order of the postwar international financial regime (Leyshon and Tickell 1994). The crisis of national money added significantly to the crisis of the KWNS, and finding an adequate response to the threat of massive and volatile currency movements will be crucial to any emerging mode of regulation at the national, regional and international levels. This has repercussions for the redirection of economic policy as well as for its institutional architecture. In particular, if the relative strength of the national money on international currency markets increasingly depends on the competitive strength of the national economy (or its most competitive firms, cities and regions), pressures will grow for state intervention to focus on supply-side developments. Likewise, if the impact of volatility is to be reduced, new measures are required to manage the demand and supply of bank credit, especially in so-called emerging market economies, to improve the absorptive capacities of economies in receipt of inward investment, and to limit the risks of regional and global contagion from particular financial crises.

The increased salience of money as international currency and/or stateless money has also modified investment priorities and altered the relationship between productive and financial capital (Guttman 2002). Moreover, linked to the changing roles of the money and wage forms in post-Fordism is the shift in concern from managing inflation in consumer goods prices and wages (linked to business cycles) to worries about boom-and-bust cycles in financial assets. Stock and property markets are especially important here, particularly when linked to other shifts, such as privatization of state-owned industries, the movement from pay-as-you-go pensions towards funded pensions and the outsourcing of collective consumption (see chapter 4). This requires new responses from central banks as well as cooperation among central banks within the context of a broader reshaping of the international financial architecture. The Internet and dot.com bubble is one example of this; the risks associated with so-called financial contagion provide another example.

Third, the contradiction between the exchange- and use-value moments in productive capital has become more significant owing to a growing dissociation between abstract flows in space and concrete valorization in place compared to the heyday of Atlantic Fordism. This is closely related to two sets of changes in the organization of capital accumulation: the resurgence of cross-border transactions (often labelled internationalization or globalization, although generally confined within relatively integrated triad regions rather than being global in scope) and the rise of the virtual economy. Short-term international financial transactions and the growth of mobile portfolio investments in an increasingly integrated world market tend to dissociate monetary flows from the need for the finance capitals directly involved to valorize specific assets in specific times and places.[5] This has been reinforced by the development of cyberspace as a sphere of economic transactions. As Kelly notes, 'the new economy operates in a "space" rather than a place, and over time more and more economic transactions will migrate to this new space' (1998: 94). Economic cyberspace is a non-propinquitous, multidimensional space, with complex dynamics rooted in the possibilities offered by cyberspace for the simultaneous co-location of myriad entities and relationships. It involves new forms of disembedding of economic activities and poses new problems for their re-embedding, regularization and governance. Rather than being a neutral, third space between capital and labour, market and state, public and private, cyberspace is a new terrain on which conflicts between these forces, institutions and domains can be fought out.

Together, these developments intensify the potential conflict between space and place. The most commonly cited expression of this is the institutional separation of hypermobile financial capital from industrial capital – the former moving in an abstract space of flows, the latter still needing to be valorized in place. Even those commentators who are most sceptical about the significance of contemporary forms of globalization concede that something has changed in relation to financial flows (for example, Hirst and Thompson 1999). Moreover, in the light of the Asian Crisis, if not before, international and national financial regulators have also come to recognize the problems this poses. But similar conflicts also appear in the circuits of financial, industrial and commercial capital considered severally as well as in their interconnections. For, however much capital migrates into cyberspace, it still requires some territorial roots. In the case of global finance capital, of course, these roots are found in the grid of global cities (Sassen 1994). E-commerce needs an infrastructure too. This is especially obvious in the case of the physical production and distribution of material goods and services linked to B2B or B2C transactions on the Internet; but virtual transactions require some form of infrastructure, even if this is no more than a 'celestial jukebox' sending digitized music on demand and an electronic payments system. In the case of industrial capital, the roots are found in innovation milieus, industrial districts, learning regions, etc., as well as physical infrastructure (Harvey 1982; Scott 1998; Storper 1997). Thus, the globalizing knowledge-based economy has not transcended spatial barriers but effects 'new and more complex articulations of the dynamics of mobility and fixity' (Robins and Gillespie 1992: 149).

A fourth source of problems in the reregularization of capitalism after Fordism is the paradox that the economic competitiveness of the most advanced economies increasingly depends on extra-economic factors. This occurs because of the growing importance that is attached to structural or systemic competitiveness and to cultivating the knowledge-base as a critical source of dynamic competitive advantage. Discourses and strategies of structural or systemic competitiveness emphasize not only firm- and sectoral-level factors but also the role of an extended range of extra-economic institutional contexts and sociocultural conditions in which economic actors compete.[6] They are linked to the rapid expansion of (competing!) benchmarking exercises and services concerned to construct league tables and offer recommendations on how to enhance such competitiveness. This extends economic competition to a virtual competition between entire social formations mediated through the audit of the world market and increases pressures to (develop the capacity) to valorize a wide range of extra-economic institutions and relations. This is reinforced by the growing importance attached to the knowledge-base in post-Fordism and thus to knowledge production and transfer throughout the social formation. These changed discourses and strategies mean in turn that hard economic calculation increasingly rests on the mobilization of soft social resources, which are irreducible to the economic and resistant to such calculation (Veltz 1996: 11–12). The competitiveness of cities and regions, for example, is now said to depend not only on narrow economic determinants but also on localized untraded interdependencies, knowledge assets, regional competencies, institutional thickness, social capital, trust and capacities for collective learning, as well as distinctive and attractive local amenities and culture (Amin and Thrift 1995; Maskell et al. 1998; Storper 1997). Similarly, there is also growing emphasis on improving the interface between business, universities and the state to promote the knowledge-based economy (Etzkowitz and Leydesdorff 1997). Overall, this involves redrawing the boundaries between the economic and the extra-economic such that more of the latter are drawn directly into the process of the valorization of capital. This can be expressed in terms of the increasing dominance of accumulation as a principle of societalization and is reflected in the colonization of extra-economic systems and the lifeworld by the logic of capital accumulation (see chapter 1). This is one aspect of the increasing ecological dominance of capitalism.

The development of this paradox is associated with major new contradictions and potential sites of conflict in contemporary capitalism that affect both its spatial and temporal organization. In temporal terms, there is increasing conflict between short-term economic calculation (especially in financial flows) and the long-term dynamic of real competition rooted in resources (skills, trust, collective mastery of techniques, economies of agglomeration and size) that may take years to create, stabilize and reproduce. The increasing emphasis on reflexivity and learning in the knowledge-based economy reinforces this contradiction. For, precisely because it takes time to create collective learning capacities and a strong entrepreneurial culture, '[t]hose firms, sectors, regions and nations which can learn faster or better (higher quality or cheaper for a given quality) become competitive because their knowledge is scarce and cannot be immediately imitated by new entrants or transferred, via codified and formal channels, to competitor firms, regions or nations' (Storper 1997: 250). Likewise, in spatial terms, capitalism always involves a potential contradiction between the formal market economy considered as a pure space of flows and the substantively instituted economy considered as a territorially and/or socially embedded system of extra-economic as well as economic resources and competencies. This contradiction has been recently reinforced by three developments: (1) growth of new technologies based on more complex transnational, national and regional systems of innovation; (2) the paradigm shift from Fordism, with its emphasis on productivity growth rooted in economies of scale, to post-Fordism, with its emphasis on agglomeration and network economies as well as on mobilizing social as well as economic sources of flexibility and entrepreneurialism; and (3) the more general attempts to penetrate microsocial relations in the interests of valorization. The intensification of this contradiction is reflected in turn in the increasing emphasis given to social capital, trust and communities of learning and to the importance of enhancing competitiveness based on entrepreneurial cities, learning regions, an enterprise culture and enterprising subjects. The latter strategic reorientation is linked to many concepts that are emerging to describe the knowledge-based economy, which is itself a specific construct linked to the new techno-economic paradigm. These concepts include national, regional and local systems of innovation, innovative milieus, systemic or structural competitiveness, learning regions, social capital, trust, learning-by-doing, speed-based competition, etc. This poses new dilemmas for actors seeking to stabilize the capital relation over an expanding range of scales and over increasingly compressed as well as extended temporal horizons of action.

Fifth, in the post-Fordist (or, at least, the post-industrial) accumulation regime, the inherent capitalist contradiction between the socialization of the productive forces and the private appropriation of profit acquires a new expression in the tension between knowledge as intellectual commons and knowledge as intellectual property. This is hardly surprising. For this basic contradiction has distinctive forms in different times and places that generate fundamental problems of collective action as well as more or less acute dilemmas for individual economic or political actors. In its most general form, it can be expressed in terms of the conflicting developmental implications of prioritizing the information economy or the information society (cf. Bell 1973 on the conflict between economizing and sociologizing logics in the post-industrial society). The basic form of the contradiction concerns the private appropriation of knowledge in the form of intellectual property rights (IPRs) so that it can become the basis for monopoly rents and national competitiveness (and thereby becomes subject to many of the tendencies towards market failure long recognized in the academic subdiscipline of the economics of information) and the widening of public access to knowledge as a source of personal empowerment and the expansion of the public sphere. But this contradiction is also replicated in the information economy itself in the form of intellectual property right versus access to the intellectual commons; and, from the viewpoint of the information society, in the form of rights to individual privacy and the claims of official secrecy versus the widening and deepening of public knowledge.

These contradictions and dilemmas obviously have a long and contested history. But they have acquired greater material and discursive significance through the development of the new ICTs and the increased importance of knowledge creation as a driving force in economic expansion on both the exchange- and use-value dimensions. Indeed, the importance of economies of agglomeration and economies of networks in knowledge-based economies heightens the contradiction from both sides. Thus, on the side of the productive forces, the increasing socialization of knowledge production in networked economies makes it hard to distinguish legally between the intellectual property of different firms as a basis for allocating the returns to innovation (Kundnani 1998–9: 56). This is even more obviously the case for the contributions of individual 'knowledge workers' to the overall social system of innovation. This in turn leads to a search for new forms of enterprise that can capture the rents from such network economies without destroying any broader network(s) involved in generating them. 'Virtual' firms, networked firms, and strategic alliances are one form in which this occurs (Catells 1996: 151–200); another form is more territorial, involving innovation milieus, learning regions, etc., where network economies can be captured in the form of club goods (classically, Silicon Valley). It also encourages attempts to protect vulnerable *monopolies in knowledge or information* by embedding them in technology, market-generated standards, tacit knowledge or legally entrenched intellectual property rights. These solutions serve to intensify the contradictions on the side of the social relations of production, however, unless the resulting networks embrace all those involved in producing the network economies. For, whereas every capital wants free access to information, knowledge and expertise, it also wants to charge for the information, knowledge and expertise that it itself can supply. This tension generates systematic asymmetries of interest within the information economy depending on actors' differing positions in the production, circulation and consumption of knowledge. The IPR regime is currently of overwhelming benefit, of course, to the US economy.

A sixth site of problems concerns the appropriate horizons of action for the spatio-temporal fix, if any, within which the old principal contradictions of Atlantic Fordism and the newly important contradictions of the current period might prove manageable. This is closely related to a new complexity of time–space in informational capitalism due to the interaction of new forms of time–space distantiation and time–space compression. Time–space distantiation stretches social relations over time and space so that they can be controlled or coordinated over longer periods of time (including into the ever more distant future) and over longer distances, greater areas or more scales of activity. In this regard, then, globalization results from increasing spatial distantiation reflected in the growing spatial reach of divisions of labour in different fields; and it is enabled by new material and social technologies of transportation, communication, command, control and intelligence. Conversely, time–space compression involves the intensification of 'discrete' events in real time[7] and/or increased velocity of material and immaterial flows over a given distance.[8] This is linked to changing material and social technologies enabling more precise control over ever-shorter periods of action as well as 'the conquest of space by time'. Differential abilities to stretch and/or compress time and space help to shape power and resistance in the emerging global order. Thus the power of hypermobile forms of finance capital depends on their unique capacity to compress their own decision-making time (at the extreme, for example, through split-second computerized trading), whilst continuing to extend and consolidate their global reach. It is the differential combination of time–space distantiation and time–space compression that was facilitated by new ICTs and enthusiastically embraced by some fractions of capital (and some states) that contributed to the erosion of the spatio-temporal fix of Atlantic Fordism.

At least as compared with the boom years of Atlantic Fordism, this phenomenon can usefully be described as the relativization of scale (Collinge 1996, 1999; chapter 5). The current period involves a proliferation of spatial scales (whether terrestrial, territorial or telematic: see Luke 1994), their relative dissociation in complex tangled hierarchies (rather than a simple nesting of scales) and an increasingly convoluted mix of scale strategies as economic and political forces seek the most favourable conditions for insertion into a changing international order. The national scale has lost the taken-for-granted primacy it held in the economic and political organization of Atlantic Fordism; but this does not mean that some other scale of economic and political organization (whether the global or the local, the urban or the triadic) has acquired a similar primacy. Indeed, there is intense competition among different economic and political spaces to become the primary anchorpoint of capital accumulation. As yet, the new politics of scale is unresolved – although I suspect that triads will eventually replace the nation as the primary scale for managing, displacing and deferring the contradictions and dilemmas of a globalizing, knowledge-based economy (for further discussion of the political economy of scale, see chapter 5). This relativization of scale is a further factor contributing to the growing heterogeneity and disarticulation of national power blocs and, a fortiori, to the apparent loss of power by national states.

3. The Impact of Globalization

This re-articulation of some basic contradictions of capitalist social formations is rooted in competition as the driving force behind capital accumulation. This creates pressures not only for technological innovation but also for innovation in many other areas that bear directly or indirectly on the rate of profit. For market-mediated competition increases pressures on firms, regions or production systems to stay ahead of their competitors so that ever-renewed technological rents and increasing market share can alleviate the normal tendency for superprofits to be competed away. Changing forms of scalar articulation and new scalar strategies are an important aspect of such competition, and these in turn affect the forms of appearance of structural contradictions and strategic dilemmas and the viability of the spatio-temporal fixes that from time to time come to be institutionalized as a means of stabilizing accumulation in some social spaces at the expense of displacing and deferring problems elsewhere. It is in this context that I propose to discuss the complex question of globalization, its nature and its alleged impact on accumulation regimes, modes of regulation and the state.

Globalization is a polyvalent, promiscuous, controversial word that often obscures more than it reveals about recent economic, political, social and cultural changes. It is best used to denote a supercomplex series of multicentric, multiscalar, multitemporal, multiform and multicausal processes. It is *multicentric* because it emerges from activities in many places rather than from a single centre – although some centres are more important than others as motors of transformation. It is *multiscalar* because it emerges from actions on many scales – which can no longer be seen as nested in a neat hierarchy like so many Russian dolls, but as coexisting and interpenetrating in a tangled and confused manner – and it develops and deepens the scalar as well as the spatial division of labour. Thus what could be described from one vantage point as globalization might be redescribed (and, perhaps, more fruitfully) in other terms from other scalar viewpoints: for example, as internationalization, triadization, regional bloc formation, global city network-building, cross-border region formation, international localization, glocalization, glurbanization or transnationalization (see pp. 181–3 and 189–90).[9] It is *multitemporal* because it involves an ever more complex restructuring and rearticulation of temporalities and time horizons. This aspect is captured in the notions of time–space distantiation and time–space compression as defined above (see p. 112). Globalization is clearly *multi-causal* because it results from the complex, contingent interaction of many different causal processes. And it is also *multiform*. It assumes different forms in different contexts and can be realized through different strategies – neoliberal globalization being but one (Ruigrok and van Tulder 1995).

Taken together, these features mean that, far from globalization being a unitary causal mechanism, it should be understood as the complex, emergent product of many different forces operating on many scales. Indeed, in some ways, the global is little more than '*a hugely extended network of localities*' (Czarniawska and Sevón 1996: 22; italics in original). Hence nothing can be explained in terms of the causal powers of globalization – let alone in terms of causal powers that are inevitable and irreversible and that are actualized on some intangible stage behind our backs and/or on some intangible plane above our heads. Instead it is globalization*s* themselves that need explaining in all their manifold spatio-temporal complexity and it is only when its different aspects are disentangled and their associated tendencies and countertendencies have been identified that we can begin to assess the implications of globalization for economic, political and social relations.

Thus seen, globalization has structural and strategic moments. Structurally, it involves the processes whereby increasing global interdependence is created among actions, organizations and institutions within (but not necessarily across) different functional subsystems (economy, law, politics, education, science, sport, etc.) and in different spheres of the lifeworld. These processes occur on various spatial scales, operate differently in each functional subsystem, involve complex and tangled causal hierarchies rather than a simple, unilinear, bottom-up or top-down movement, and often display an eccentric 'nesting' of the different scales of social organization. While globalization obviously develops unevenly in both space and time, it can be said to increase insofar as the covariation of relevant activities is spatially more extensive and/or occurs more rapidly. Indeed, a major element in the novelty of recent globalization trends is the speed at which such covariation occurs as well as its expanding spatial reach. The superior capacities of capital to engage in time–space distantiation and time–space compression are a major factor in the growing ecological dominance of accumulation on a global scale.

Globalization also poses serious problems for global governance insofar as this must be tackled across a range of potentially contradictory temporal and spatial horizons. This brings us to the strategic dimension of globalization.

Strategically, globalization refers to various actors' attempts to globally coordinate their activities in (but not necessarily across) different functional subsystems and/or the lifeworld. This does not require that the actors involved are physically present at all points in the globe, of course; all it requires is that they attempt to coordinate their activities with others in order to produce global effects. The latter can range from metasteering (constitutional or institutional design) for a more or less comprehensive global order to the pursuit of specific economic-corporate interests within such a metaframework. Among the most ambitious global projects one could include projects for world government, global governance or a New World Order. There is clearly scope for wide variation in such projects, as evidenced by the neoliberal, market-led globalization favoured by the World Bank, the horizontal global governance favoured by proponents – especially non-governmental organizations (NGOs) – of international regimes, and plans for more top-down inter-statal government. Less ambitious, but still global, projects might range from attempts to establish international regimes to govern particular fields of action on a global scale through strategic alliances orchestrated by transnational enterprises (alliances that may include more local or regionally based firms as well as non-profit-oriented organizations) or cooperation among global cities to consolidate their dominance in the hierarchy of global cities down to the efforts of individual firms to consolidate a dominant or even a niche position within the international division of labour and/or circulation of goods and services.

Thus viewed, what is generally labelled nowadays as economic globalization rarely, if ever, involves full structural integration and strategic coordination across the globe. Processes included under this rubric actually include: (1) internationalization of national economic spaces through growing penetration (inward flows) and extraversion (outward flows); (2) formation of regional economic blocs embracing several national economies – including, most notably, the formation of various formally organized blocs in the triadic regions of North America, Europe and East Asia – and the development of formal links between these blocs – notably through the Asia–Pacific Economic Cooperation forum, the New Transatlantic Agenda, and the Asia–Europe Meetings; (3) growth of more 'local internationalization' or 'virtual regions' through the development of economic ties between contiguous or non-contiguous local and regional authorities in different national economies – ties that often bypass the level of the national state but may also be sponsored by the latter; (4) extension and deepening of multinationalization as multi-national companies, transnational banks and international producer services firms move from limited economic activities abroad to more comprehensive and worldwide strategies, sometimes extending to 'global localization', whereby firms pursue a global strategy based on exploiting and/or adjusting to local differences; (5) widening and deepening of international regimes covering economic and economically relevant issues; and (6) emergence of globalization proper through the introduction and acceptance of global norms and standards, the adoption of global benchmarking, the development of globally integrated markets together with globally oriented strategies, and 'deracinated' firms with no evident national operational base. In each case these processes could be said to be contributing in however mediated and indirect a way to the structural integration and strategic coordination of the capitalist economy on a global scale. In this way these processes are also contributing in their interconnection to the formation of an integrated world market as the space within which the law of value operates. This in turn is associated with the increased ecological dominance of the capitalist economy and its contradictory dynamic. But these processes are achieving this in a dispersed, fragmented, and partial manner, and they are far from creating an homogenized world economy marked by the absence of uneven spatio-temporal development.

In short, what globalization involves both structurally and strategically is the creation and/or restructuring of scale as a social relation and as a site of social relations. This is evident in the continuing (if often transformed) significance of smaller scales (notably the urban, the cross-border, the national and macroregional) as substantive sites of real economic activities; in economic strategies oriented to the articulation of other scales into the global; and in new social movements based on localism, various tribalisms or resurgent nationalism, and resistant in different ways to globalization. This implies in turn that a global strategy should be sensitive to other scales than the 'purely' global – especially as the latter has social meaning only in relation to lesser scales. Indeed, the global more often serves as the ultimate horizon of action rather than the actual site of action. Or, in other words, as an ultimate horizon of action, it serves as a means to orient actions on lesser scales. This is not an insignificant role. For failure to take strategic account of the global, even if actions remain confined to other scales, could well lead to a more or less rapid loss of competitiveness.

Globalization is part of a proliferation of scales as institutionalized, narrated objects of action, regularization and governance. The number of discrete scales of action that can be distinguished is potentially infinite, but far fewer scales actually come to be institutionalized as explicit objects of regularization and governance. For this depends on the avail-ability of specific technologies of power – material, social and spatio-temporal – that transform potential scales of action into actual sites of action. In addition to logistical means (distantiation, compression, virtual communication), attention also needs to be given to modes of gover-nance, organizational technologies and institutional architectures. In this context I suggest that economically and politically significant institu-tionalized scales of action have proliferated as a result of the develop-ment of new technologies, organizations and institutions with new spatio-temporal horizons of action. Moreover, as new scales emerge and/or existing scales gain in institutional thickness, new mechanisms to link or coordinate them also tend to emerge. This in turn often prompts efforts to coordinate these new coordination mechanisms. Thus, as the triad regions begin to acquire institutional form and regional identity, new forums have developed for coordinating bilateral relations between them.

A similar process is at work regarding temporal horizons of action. New information, communication, and logistical and organizational technologies have enhanced the capacities of some actors to engage in time–space compression, and this has helped to transform power rela-tions within and across different systems and the lifeworld. Time–space compression contributes to globalization through the increased capac-ities it offers for time–space distantiation. It also reinforces the ecologi-cal dominance of the market economy by enhancing the opportunities for some economic agents to intensify the exchange-value moment of the capital relation at the expense of the use-value moment; and for others to respond to this by moving to just-in-time production and fast service to their markets (Sum 1999). Trends towards time–space com-pression are also accompanied by growing recognition of longer-term temporal horizons up to the *longue durée* of environmental damage – although globalization is also associated with its acceleration. These developments pose problems of intertemporal comparisons and calcu-lation as well as intertemporal coordination; and they call for more complex forms of organization and coordination – which thereby increase the complexity of the system as a whole.

Thus, far from producing homogenized global economic space, the many and varied processes involved in globalization actually involve the reordering – across a wide range of economic spaces on different spatial scales – of differences and complementarities as the basis for dynamic competitive advantages. This has structural aspects linked to the struc-tural coupling and co-evolution of different spaces within an emerging global division of labour and its eccentric, nested, subscales; and strategic aspects, with different actors looking for the best means of inserting themselves into the spatial, scalar and temporal divisions of labour. Not all actors are (or could hope to be) major global players in the world market, but an increasing number still need to attend to the global as a horizon of action, to the implications of changing scalar divisions, and to the differential impact of time–space distantiation and compression on their identities, interests and strategies. These structural and strategic dimensions of globalization and its role in reinforcing the operation of the capitalist law of value (see chapter 1) highlights the importance of producing, appropriating, organizing, restructuring and controlling social space as part of accumulation strategies and their regulation (Lefebvre 1991) as well as the ability to transform and control the multiple temporalities of economic, political and social action and their interaction with place, space, and scale.

These contradictions and conflicts are especially clear in the currently dominant neoliberal form of globalization. Current neoliberal trends in globalization reinforce the abstract-formal moments of exchange-value in the various structural forms of the capital relation at the expense of the substantive-material moments of use-value (see table 1.1 in chapter 1). For it is capital in these abstract moments that is most easily disembedded from specific places and thereby freed to 'flow' freely through space and time.[10] However, in each of its more concrete moments, capital has its own particular productive and reproductive requirements. These can often be materialized only in specific types of spatio-temporal location. This leads to a general tension between neoliberal demands to accelerate the flow of abstract (money) capital through an increasingly disembedded space and the need for the more concrete forms of capital to be 'fixed' in time and place as well as embedded in specific social relations as a condition for their valorization. This applies not only to the relation between different fractions of capital but also to the question of how to regard labour-power and the individual and social wage. Thus the neoliberal approach of finance capital tends to regard labour-power as one abstract, substitutable factor of production among others, to be sought around the globe wherever it can be purchased most cheaply; conversely, the more productivist approach of industrial capital still tends to regard labour-power as embodying concrete skills and knowledge that can be applied in specific production conditions in specific places. Different varieties of capitalism and scalar strategies are associated with different ways of attempting to manage this tension and to defer and displace its consequences. Chapter 1 already referred to the possibilities of different approaches to this tension on different scales (see also Gough and Eisenschitz 1996) and states on different scales will typically play a key role in managing this tension within any particular individual spatio-temporal fix (see section 6 below).

4. Schumpeterian Policies and Competitiveness

The changing forms of articulation of the economic and extra-economic, the relativization of scale that accompanies globalization (as defined above), and the growing complexities of time–space distantiation and compression have contributed to – and have also been affected in turn by – changes in the forms of competition and bases of competitiveness. There are many types of competitive advantage, many modalities of competition, many sites of competition, and different bases of each.[11] Nonetheless, the primary discourses of competitiveness, metastrategies to enhance competitive capacities, and strategies and tactics in competition have changed significantly since the heyday of Atlantic Fordism. A useful distinction here is that between static comparative and dynamic competitive advantages. Whilst the former refer to a superior position in control over so-called natural[12] factor endowments relative to potential trading partners or competitors, the latter are somewhat more obviously socially created, can be socially transformed and may well become objects of strategic intervention.[13] If competitiveness is understood purely in terms of comparative advantages, what matters is the overall efficiency of resource allocation, especially in producing traded goods and services. This approach is often said to be most relevant to nations, regions or cities that produce primary products and standardized manufactured goods. But factor-based advantages are usually hard to sustain – especially given the standardization of many technologies and capital goods (permitting their relatively quick and easy adoption if the necessary finance and skills are available), the increasing availability (or 'ubiquitification') of factors favourable to competition, the increasing mobility of international capital (reflected in access to mobile money capital as well as productive capital's search for lower production costs), and the shift of comparative advantages over the product cycle (which puts increasing emphasis on production costs as markets mature) (Porter 1990; Warr 1994). This suggests that longer-term competitiveness would be better based on developing and maintaining dynamic competitive advantages. This holds not only for firms but also for industrial or central business districts, cities, regions, nations and any other spaces able to create spatialized competitive advantages. The more broadly the latter are understood, the more one can talk of structural or systemic competitiveness (on structural competitiveness, see Chesnais 1986; on systemic competitiveness, Esser et al. 1996; Messner 1998; and, on other broad-ranging benchmarks, IMD 2001; and Porter et al. 2000).

The basis of competitive strategies is always and necessarily an 'imagined' economy. For the real economy is so unstructured and complex in its operation that it cannot be an object of management, governance or guidance. Instead, economic management, governance and guidance are always oriented to specific subsets of economic relations that have been discursively and institutionally fixed as objects of such intervention. These are always selectively defined and typically exclude elements that are essential to the overall performance of the subset of economic (and extra-economic) relations that have been identified. The link to spatio-temporal fixes should be obvious here. For the constitution of an economy involves its discursive construction as a 'natural' (commonsensical, taken for granted) unit of analysis, management, regulation, governance, conquest or other practices, which has definite boundaries, economic and extra-economic conditions of existence, typical economic agents and extra-economic stakeholders, and an overall spatio-temporal dynamic. The struggles to constitute specific economies as subjects, sites and stakes of competition typically involve manipulation of power and knowledge in order to establish recognition of their boundaries, geometries and tem-poralities. And this in turn involves the development of new institutional forms that help to institutionalize these boundaries, geometries and tem-poralities in a specific spatio-temporal fix, and thereby help to displace and/or defer some of the contradictions and crisis-tendencies with which the management of capital as a social relation is inevitably associated.

Once we consider the social creation of competitive advantage, the work of List and Schumpeter becomes relevant (for a brief discussion of Ricardian, Listian, Schumpeterian and Keynesian understandings of competitiveness, see box 3.1).[14] Schumpeter has a key role here as an emblematic thinker in shaping, directly or indirectly, the new under-standing of competitiveness and linking it to long waves of technologi-cal innovation and capital accumulation. Moreover, as commodification and market mechanisms are extended to more spheres of social activity and structural and systemic competitiveness gain in importance, the scope for economic entrepreneurialism proper also expands. The dis-tinctive function of the entrepreneur is *innovation* rather than technical *invention* (however original this may be), the routine *management* of cap-italist activities, or the bearing of risk. Entrepreneurship in its strict, strong or Schumpeterian sense, involves the devising and realization of new ways of doing things to generate above average profits (that is, 'rents' or, in Marxist terminology as applied to production, relative surplus-value and superprofits) from capitalist competition. Entrepre-neurship can be exercised at any moment in the overall circuit of capital and the articulation of these moments. Moreover, although it is common to equate the entrepreneur with the individual business dynamo, the function(s) of entrepreneurship can be exercised through various types of agency. Indeed, its forms will vary with the nature of combinations, the forms of competition and the objects of entrepreneurial governance.

Box 3.1   *Forms of competitiveness*

The idea of competitiveness is conceptually ambiguous and politically controversial. There are many ways to define and measure it; and current policy debates indicate the political issues at stake. These points are related. For competitiveness is a discursively constructed notion with obvious strategic implications both economically and politically: different notions entail different forms of political action with different effects on the competitive positioning of firms, sectors, regions and nations, as well as on the balance of political forces within and beyond the state.

The *Ricardian* account, named after David Ricardo, an early English political economist, stresses the importance of static comparative advantages and/or relative prices. Thus competitiveness depends on exploiting the most abundant and cheapest factors of production in a given economy (e.g., land, raw materials, labour, capital, enterprise) and exchanging products embodying these factors for products from other spaces with different factor endowments. Ricardian competitiveness depends on static efficiency in the allocation of resources to minimize production costs with a given technical division of labour and on the assumption that current economic conditions will continue.

The *Listian* account is named after Friedrich List, a nineteenth-century German political economist. It suggests that a national state can develop infant industries or services that are not based on abundant or cheap factors of production provided that it rejects free trade in favour of protection, state support and state guidance of the economy. This implies that international competitiveness depends on growth efficiency in allocating resources among *already available* processes and products in terms of the likely impact of their (re-)allocation on economic growth and on the ability to protect infant industries from premature competition from more advanced firms or economies.

The *Schumpeterian* account is named after Joseph Schumpeter, a twentieth-century Austrian political economist. It suggests that competitiveness depends on developing the individual and collective capacities to engage in permanent innovation – whether in sourcing, technologies, products, organization or marketing. These capacities extend beyond the narrow economy to include a wide range of extra-economic factors. Thus Schumpeterian competitiveness depends on dynamic efficiency in allocating resources to promote *innovations* that will alter the pace and direction of economic growth and enable the economy to compete more effectively.

The *Keynesian* approach is less concerned with international competitiveness, as it assumes a relatively closed national economy. It does imply that full employment of resources (including labour) will help efficiency by reducing unit costs of production, facilitating economies of scale and reducing the welfare costs of maintaining underemployed labour power. Moreover, if full capacity utilization leads to inflation, its effects can be compensated by devaluation.

Schumpeter listed several ways in which entrepreneurial innovation can occur:

> (1) The introduction of a new good – that is one with which consumers are not yet familiar – or a new quality of a good. (2) The introduction of a new method of production, that is one not yet tested by experience in the branch of manufacture concerned, which need by no means be founded upon a discovery scientifically new, and can also exist in a new way of handling a commodity commercially. (3) The opening of a new market, that is a market into which the particular branch of manufacture of the country in question has not previously entered, whether or not this market has existed before. (4) The conquest of a new source of supply of raw materials or half-manufactured goods, again irrespective of whether this source already exists or whether it has first to be created. (5) The carrying out of the new organization of any industry, like the creation of a monopoly position (for example through trustification) or the breaking up of a monopoly position. (Lim 1990: 215, summarizing Schumpeter 1934: 129–35)

Although the phrasing of Schumpeter's list of 'new combinations' bears the imprint of commercial and industrial capitalism, nothing limits it to these fields. It can clearly be applied to innovations in other fields, such as new forms of finance; and it also embraces the specifically spatial and/or temporal dimensions of commercial, industrial, financial or other forms of economic activity. It is worth emphasizing the potential scope of a Schumpeterian analysis because of the increased significance of services, the increased importance of space and time in dynamic competitive advantages and the more general redefinition of the 'economic sphere'.

There is a typical economic dynamic to entrepreneurial activities. As an integral element in competition, they are inseparable from its attendant risks and uncertainties. Although a successful innovation will initially generate surplus profits (or 'rents'), these tend to decline and eventually disappear as the innovation is either adopted (or superseded) as 'best practice' by other competitors and/or as less efficient competitors (are forced to) leave the market. Unless an effective (practical or legal) monopoly position can be established, this will tend to return profits to normal levels.[15] Moreover, once an innovation is generalized, the cost of production and the search for new markets begin to matter, changing the balance of competitive advantages within the product cycle. Whilst this emphasis on costs leads to the competing away of initial advantages, it also prepares the ground for the next wave of innovation and entrepreneurship – either by the initial pioneers or perhaps by latecomers who can exploit their competitive position in a later stage of the product cycle to build a resource base for subsequent innovations. This problem is intensified by reflexive accumulation. For 'the conditions which a firm, region or production system must now satisfy in order to win are manufactured and remanufactured more thoroughly and more rapidly than ever before, creating a moving target for success and a shifting minefield of risks of failure' (Storper 1997: 249–50).

5. Building the Competition State as a Response

I now review the principal form of political response to the challenges *and opportunities* posed by the ongoing decomposition of Atlantic Fordism and the emerging economic and extra-economic tendencies described above. Some of the economic responses at the level of firms and clusters have already been indicated in my stylized account of the distinctive features of post-Fordism as a globalizing, knowledge-based economy and, insofar as these already existed in piecemeal form in the heyday of Fordism, they can also be considered to have contributed to the crisis of Fordism as an accumulation regime. The actions of some states have also contributed, as we shall shortly see, to these challenges to the dynamic of Atlantic Fordism and the KWNS. Overall, the principal political response can be summarized briefly as the attempt by state managers, officials, economic and other forces to transform the Keynesian full employment state into a Schumpeterian competition state, to rescale and rearticulate its activities, and to develop new forms of government and governance to address the emerging problems of state as well as market failure. Describing the restructuring and strategic reorientation of the KWNS in these terms does not imply that the various social forces involved in promoting or resisting this transformation are all consciously concerned with an explicit project to construct a competition state. This is merely a convenient label to characterize current trends. It should also be emphasized that there is nothing automatic or mechanical about this transformation. Instead, it involves a trial-and-error search process, struggles to mobilize support behind alternative accumulation strategies, state projects and hegemonic visions, a good deal of monitoring of developments elsewhere, and more or less coordinated attempts at policy transfer where this is deemed appropriate. In this sense, it is critically mediated through discourses about the changed economic situation and hence through the outcome of struggles to define the nature of the crisis in/of the Keynesian state; and, for the same reasons, it is also crucially dependent on the specific, path-dependent forms of the state that are associated with different accumulation regimes and their strategic selectivities in regard to political representation, policy formation and intervention.

The tendential emergence of the Schumpeterian competition state can be seen on many different scales – from the emergence of entrepreneurial localities, cities and regions through national competition states to growing efforts in all three triadic growth poles to promote their systemic or structural competitiveness on an international, panregional and/or supranational basis. The distinctive feature of these diverse competition states is their self-image as being proactive in promoting the competitiveness of their respective economic spaces in the face of intensified international (and also, for regions and cities, inter- and intra-regional) competition. This involves not only the economy in the narrow sense but the overall institutional redesign of the accumulation regime, its mode of regulation and its implications for societalization. I address these issues in five steps that move from self-evidently 'hard' economic forms to apparently 'softer' sets of social relations that nonetheless have major implications for the reorganization of the economy in its integral sense. Thus I discuss in turn: the wage and money forms; managing internationalization; new forms of competition; the mobilization of knowledge both as intellectual commons and intellectual property to promote the development of the knowledge-based economy; and the subordination of extra-economic systems and the lifeworld to the discursively construed needs of competitiveness in the current period of capitalist development. This discussion cannot possibly exhaust the full range of objects of intervention and their associated economic, political and sociocultural measures. It is only intended to illustrate some key features of the emerging state functions and some of their implications for changes in state form, and for the same reason it neglects both the generic economic functions of the capitalist type of state and the extent to which distinctive economic functions of the KWNS have been modified through their integration into the changed modes of operation of the Schumpeterian competition state. Chapter 5 provides further comments on the scalar dimensions of these changing forms of intervention.

The wage and money forms

An emphasis on the wage as an international cost of production does not take full employment off the political agenda – but the latter is no longer regarded as an immediate objective of national state intervention. Job creation is now seen to depend heavily on the active management of the supply side and on the employability and flexibility of the labour force rather than to flow quasi-automatically from effective management of national demand. In certain respects, of course, small open economies already faced this problem in the period of Atlantic Fordism; and we can find prefigurative aspects of the Schumpetarian workfare postnational regime (SWPR), such as active labour market policies, in their operation. But even small open economies have been forced to adjust to the changed conditions of international competition and a far wider and deeper range of factors is now considered to bear on international competitiveness. Another response to the changed significance of the wage form is found in calls for international or at least European Keynesianism (see chapter 5). Other aspects of the post-Fordist wage relation are discussed in the next chapter.

There are also attempts to develop new forms of regulating the contradiction between money as national money and international currency. Among relevant measures pursued by national states have been jumping on the neoliberal bandwagon to float currencies, attempts to develop regional currency systems (most notably the euro in Europe and a yen-bloc in North-East Asia), and the adoption of dollar pegs or a straight-forward dollarization of the local economy either for foreign transactions or else for all major foreign and domestic transactions. There have also been increasing attempts to establish a new financial architecture, especially in the wake of the so-called Asian Crisis and subsequent rounds of financial crisis and contagion. These measures do not resolve the contradiction, but displace and defer its effects. For they greatly enhance the manoeuvrability of the American state and American TNBS and MNCs in the world market and increase the vulnerability of other economies to shifts in US policy, which was long ago reoriented from the collective economic good of the capitalist world market to more or less unilateral pursuit of US dominance. And, while this enables capital in its abstract-formal moments to disembed itself from the ties of specific places and temporalities, in each of its more concrete moments capital still has its own particular productive and reproductive requirements. These need to be addressed, often on new scales.

The relative opening of national economies

As states lose (or willingly abandon) control over the national economy as an object of Keynesian economic management, they get involved in guiding the process of internationalization itself and seeking to derive economic, political or social advantages therefrom. This has the paradoxical effect of further undermining national economic autonomy and vastly complicating the process of economic governance. This not only involves advancing the interests of home-based multinationals but also means creating conditions favourable to inward investment. In both cases regard is paid to the overall impact on the nation's technological and economic competitiveness and to possible repercussions on social cohesion. In addition, states get involved in redefining the international framework within which such economic processes occur. What is at stake today in international competition is the ability to switch quickly and easily among innovative products and processes with each new product offering better functional qualities and improved efficiency in production; analogous changes are discernible in relation to the culture industries and other knowledge-intensive sectors. It is in this context that the transition to the post-Fordist knowledge-based techno-economic paradigm began to prompt a reorientation of the state's principal economic functions. For the combination of the late Fordist trend towards internationalization and/or globalization and the post-Fordist stress on flexible, increasingly knowledge-based production encourages policy-makers to focus on supply-side aspects of international competitiveness and to attempt to subordinate social policy to the demands of flexibility, enterprise and innovation in a knowledge-based economy. Among many relevant economic policy objectives in this regard are: establishing new legal forms for cross-national cooperation and strategic alliances, re-regulating the international currency and credit systems, promoting technology transfer, managing trade disputes, defining a new international intellectual property regime, and developing new forms of regulation for labour migration. The political economy of scale is discussed in greater detail in chapter 5.

Innovation and entrepreneurship

The transition from Atlantic Fordism to post-Fordism is associated with a techno-economic paradigm shift that involves not only changes in the labour process but also in modes of growth, regulation, and societalization. Thus the need for innovation extends far beyond issues of technology and technology transfer to include social systems of innovation on different (and often interconnected) scales, the cultivation and promotion of an enterprise culture and enterprising subjects, and a wide range of organizational and institutional innovations that bear on the changing forms of competitiveness. Regarding the question of technological innovation and technology transfer, states have a key role in promoting innovative capacities, technical competence and technology transfer so that as many firms and sectors as possible benefit from the new technological opportunities created by R&D activities undertaken in specific parts of the economy (Archibugi et al. 1999; Chesnais 1986; Dunning 2000; Petit and Soete 1999; Sigurdson 1990). Indeed, even in relatively neoliberal economies, it is recognized that many high-growth sectors are so knowledge- and capital-intensive that their development demands extensive collaboration (especially at pre-competitive stages) among diverse interests (firms, higher education, public and private research laboratories, venture capital, public finance, etc.). This requirement is reinforced by the increasing spatial reach and speed of competition and puts the advanced capitalist economies under pressure to move up the technological hierarchy and specialize in the new core technologies if they are to maintain employment and growth. For, given the growing competitive pressures from newly industrializing countries (NICs) on low-cost, low-tech production and, indeed, in simple high-tech products, continued growth and employment in advanced economies depends on continued movement up the technological hierarchy. Newly industrializing economies in turn are under pressure to upgrade as even newer NICs emerge to challenge them. This is reflected in an overall intensification of competitive pressures on a global scale and, as indicated in chapter 1, an increasing ecological dominance of the logic of capital accumulation relative to other systems and the lifeworld.

The importance of innovation and entrepreneurship in post-Fordism is reflected in new state strategies. The competition state engages in technological intelligence gathering, helps to create independent technological capacities and promotes innovative capacities, technical competence and technology transfer so that as many firms as possible benefit from new technological opportunities created by R&D activities undertaken in specific parts of the economy. It develops, first, institutions and structures that directly support entrepreneurs, existing or potential; and, second, institutions and structures that sustain an entrepreneurial climate. These measures include venture capital provision, subsidies, business parks, technology transfer mechanisms and technical assistance, investment in knowledge production through public R&D or locally oriented R&D consortia, industry service centres, local and regional development funds and public procurement policies. Also relevant are policies that aim to increase the overall supply of entrepreneurs, develop enterprise skills/competencies in under-represented sectors (such as ethnic minorities or women), or promote new forms of enterprise (such as cooperative or community venture programmes). As well as specific areas of intervention or guidance to promote innovation, the state gets involved in promoting effective supranational, national, regional or local innovation systems.

This often involves refocusing economic strategies around the features of specific economic spaces and their role in the struggle to maintain international competitiveness and/or defend jobs, growth and welfare in the face of competitive pressures at home and abroad. In this context, political forces must mobilize not only ideological and political apparatuses but also forms of organizational intelligence and mechanisms for collective learning (Storper 1997; Willke 1992, 1997). The development of such metacapacities depends on the supply of relevant knowledge and organizational intelligence rather than capital; on shaping the institutional context in which firms operate rather than providing subsidies; on organizing place-specific advantages rather than an abstract space of flows; and on the (re-)territorialization of activities rather than their emancipation from spatial and temporal constraints. In this way dynamic competitive advantages can be targeted rather than being static comparative advantages with the attendant risk of a race to the bottom.

Finally, given the budgetary and fiscal pressures on states as national economies become more open, states tend to shift industrial support away from vain efforts to maintain declining sectors without transforming them towards attempts to promote 'infant' or 'sunrise' sectors and/or restructuring mature (apparently 'sunset') sectors so that they can apply new processes, upgrade existing products and launch new ones. In all cases the crucial point is that state action is required to guide the development of new core technologies as motive and carrier forces[16] of economic expansion and to widen their application to promote competitiveness. These technologies are creating whole new industrial sectors and, through their own cross-fertilization and/or their incorporation into traditional sectors, are helping to widen product ranges. Mastering them is critical to continued growth and structural competitiveness.

The knowledge-based economy

As the economy comes to be defined and naturalized as knowledge-based and/or knowledge-driven (an ongoing achievement that involves active and extensive discursive work), states are increasingly involved in promoting the production and diffusion of knowledge. Knowledge is a collectively generated resource and, even where specific forms and types of intellectual property are produced in capitalist conditions for profit, this depends on a far wider intellectual commons. The state has roles in both regards: it must promote the commodification of knowledge through its formal transformation from a collective resource (intellectual commons) into intellectual property (for example, in the form of patent, copyright and licences) as a basis for revenue generation; but it must also protect the intellectual commons as a basis for competitive advantage for the economy as a whole. It also gets involved in promoting the formal subsumption of knowledge production under exploitative class relations through the separation of intellectual and manual labour and the transformation of the former into wage-labour producing knowledge for the market. The transformation of universities, research institutes, etc., through market proxies and privatization is important here (on the first, see, for example, Aoki 1998 and Dawson 1998; on the second, see Schiller 1988: 33 and Sohn-Rethel 1978; on the third, see Kelly 1998: 77 and Menzies 1998: 92–3 and pp. 166–8).

First, states at all levels help in managing the contradictions rooted in the nature of knowledge as a fictitious commodity. For, on the one hand, '[t]he intellectual commons is fundamental to the production of knowledge' (Dawson 1998: 281); and, on the other, intellectual property is a key basis of accumulation in informational capitalism.[17] This contradiction was recognized in Bell's early claim that, since free circulation of knowledge offers no incentives to firms to produce, it must be created by some 'social unit, be it university or government' (1979: 174). With hindsight, Bell's proposal is clearly rooted in the logic of the Fordist mixed economy rather than the emerging logic of the networked economy. Nonetheless, one can accept his broad conclusion that states must produce 'a socially optimal policy of investment in knowledge' (ibid.: 175). Different states are, of course, situated differently in this regard. They tend to polarize, first, around interests in protecting or enclosing the commons (for example, North–South) and, second, around the most appropriate forms of intellectual property rights and regimes on different scales from global to local. Thus, some states are more active than others in promoting the primitive accumulation of intellectual property, in privatizing public knowledge and in commoditizing all forms of knowledge; others are more concerned to protect the intellectual commons, to promote the information society and to develop social capital. Given its competitive advantage in ICT products and the knowledge revolution, the American state has been especially important in promoting the neoliberal form of the knowledge revolution on a global scale. This is especially clear in its role in promoting the Trade-Related

Aspects of Intellectual Property Rights (TRIPS) agreement as a key element in the World Trade Organization (WTO) and in using bi- and multilateral trade agreements, conditionalities and other pressures to seek to enforce its interests in intellectual property rights.

Whatever their position on such issues, all states must try to resolve various contradictions and dilemmas in knowledge production whilst eschewing any direct, hierarchical control over it. For example, they 'must balance the need to protect and maintain the intellectual commons against the need to stimulate inventive activity' (Dawson 1998: 278). Likewise, in the latter context, they need to balance the protection of individual intellectual property and its associated revenue flows against the collective benefits that derive from the general diffusion of its applications 'by creating open systems, by moving key intellectual properties into the public domain, by releasing source code democratically' (Kelly 1998: 28). The latter task is often pursued through state promotion of innovation and diffusion systems (including social capital), broad forms of 'technological foresight', co-involvement and/or negotiated 'guidance' of the production of knowledge, and the development of suitable metagovernance structures (Messner 1998; Willke 1997). Thus states sponsor information infrastructures and social innovation systems on different scales; develop intellectual property rights regimes and new forms of governance and/or regulation for activities in cyberspace; promote movement away from national utility structures with universal supply obligations suited to an era of mass production and mass consumption to more flexible, differential, multiscalar structures suited to a post-Fordist era; and intervene to restructure research in universities to bring it more closely into alignment with the perceived needs of business and to encourage the management and exploitation of intellectual property through spin-offs, licensing, partnerships, science parks, technology parks, industry parks, and so on.

More particularly, some states are getting heavily involved in promoting the *primitive accumulation* of capital (in the form of intellectual property) through private expropriation of the collectively produced knowledge of past generations. This enclosure of knowledge takes several forms, including: (1) the appropriation of indigenous, tribal or peasant 'culture' in the form of undocumented, informal and collective knowledge, expertise and other intellectual resources, and its transformation without recompense into commodified knowledge (documented, formal, private) by commercial enterprises (Coombe 1998; Frow 1996: 96–7) – bio-piracy is the most notorious example; (2) divorcing intellectual labour from the means of production – embodying it in smart machines and expert systems – and thereby appropriating the knowledge of the collective labourer (Robins and Webster 1987); and (3) gradual extension of the limited nature of copyright into broader forms of property right with a consequent erosion of any residual public interest (Frow 1996: 104). States have a key role here in changing IPR laws and protecting domestic firms' appropriation of the intellectual commons at home and abroad.

States also promote the commoditization of knowledge and the integration of knowledge and intellectual labour into production. This is reflected in the increased emphasis on the training of knowledge workers and lifelong learning, including distance learning (see chapter 4), the introduction of ICTs into its own spheres of activity and the more general prosyletization of the knowledge-based economy and information society. It promotes these strategies in the private sphere and third sector. There is also increasing emphasis on flexibility in manufacturing and services (including the public sector) based on new technologies (especially microelectronics) and more flexible forms of organizing production. Hence it attempts to introduce post-Fordist labour practices into the state sector itself and into new public-private sector partnerships. New technologies actively promoted by the state include: information and communication technologies, manufacturing technology, nanotechnology, biotechnology, optoelectronics, genetic engineering, marine sciences and technology, new materials and biopharmaceuticals.

The state also heavily promotes the dynamics of *technological rents* generated by new knowledge as part of a more general promotion of innovation. This serves to intensify the self-defeating character of the informational revolution from the viewpoint of capital, insofar as each new round of innovation is prone to ever more rapid devalorization. But it nonetheless wins temporary advantages and technological rents for the economic spaces it controls and, insofar as there are sustainable first-mover advantages, it can consolidate longer-term advantages for a region, nation or triad. This strategy is an important and quite explicit element in the reassertion of US hegemony since the years of pessimism about the growing threat of the Japanese and East Asian economies, and helps to explain the American commitment to the consolidation of a robust IPR regime (cf. Lehman 1996; Schiller 1999). Moreover, if firms in the information economy are to maintain above-average profit rates despite the tendency for technological rents to be competed away, less technologically advanced sectors must secure below-average profits. This is another driving force behind globalization insofar as less profitable firms are forced to relocate or outsource to lower cost production sites, and it reinforces the tendencies towards unequal exchange and development associated with globalization. States also get involved in often contradictory ways in promoting and retarding the mobility of productive capital.

The extra-economic

The increased importance of structural and/or systemic competitiveness leads to a fundamental redefinition of the 'economic sphere', because many phenomena previously regarded as 'extra-economic' are now seen as directly economic and/or economically relevant. During the heyday of Atlantic Fordism the primary discourse around international competitiveness revolved around relative unit labour costs and the need to develop large markets and economies of scale. This reflected the relative closure of national economies, the primacy of the wage and money forms in economic management, and the role of mass production in generating productivity growth. More recently, competitiveness is seen to involve a far wider range of phenomena, many of which would have been regarded as extra-economic during the heyday of Fordism. In addition, the development of global benchmarking of international competitiveness on a wide array of economic and extra-economic factors serves to generalize neoliberal norms of competitiveness in management, government, the mass media and the academy.

This is prompting a generalized Schumpeterian orientation – that is, concern with innovation, competitiveness and entrepreneurship tied to long waves of growth and the more recent pressures for perpetual innovation. States engage in the pursuit of technological rents on behalf of capital. This leads in turn to the subordination of the totality of socio-economic fields to the accumulation process so that economic functions come to occupy the dominant place within the state. Other functions thereby gain direct economic significance for economic growth and competitiveness and this tends to politicize those formerly (or still formally) extra-economic domains that are now direct objects of state intervention. In this context, states also get involved in managing the conflicts between time horizons associated with time–space distantiation and compression – especially in regard to protecting the social capital embedded in communities, promoting longer-term economic orientations and designing institutions that sustain innovation. But this expanding field of intervention means that the state finds it harder to reconcile its responses to ever more insistent economic imperatives with the more general demands of securing general political legitimacy and social cohesion (Poulantzas 1978).

6. Discourse and Discursive Change

The rise of the competition state is reflected in, and reinforced by, changes in economic discourse, modes of calculation and strategic concepts. Such changes are important mediations between the structural changes in the global economy and the transformation of the national state. For discourses provide an interpretative framework to make sense of these structural changes, the crises that often accompany them and appropriate responses thereto. One major discursive-strategic shift in this regard is the demotion of 'productivity' and 'planning' in favour of an emphasis on 'flexibility' and 'entrepreneurialism'. Another is the shift from a discourse about entitlements to lifetime employment to one about obligations to engage in lifelong learning to ensure that workers are employable and flexible. A third major change is the emergence since the mid-/late 1980s of the discourse of globalization as signifying – rightly or wrongly – a fundamental shift in the dynamic of capital accumulation (and, indeed, the mode of societalization) compared with the previous forty years. A fourth shift, also increasingly important in recent years, is the emphasis on knowledge-based growth in the new economy. This is closely linked to emphasis on learning regions, lifelong learning, and so forth. A fifth shift is evident in the demotion of monetarism as an economic theory in favour of 'new growth theory', which emphasizes the virtues of state intervention to create conditions favourable to economic growth that had previously been regarded as exogenous to the operation of the economy (on new growth theory, see Cortright 2001; Nelson and Romer 1996). All five shifts are reflected in changing discourses about competitiveness. The articulation of these and related discursive-strategic shifts into new accumulation strategies, state projects and hegemonic projects, and their capacity to mobilize support are shaping the restructuring and reorientation of the contemporary state and helping to produce new regulatory regimes. And it is precisely the need for such mediation (as well as, for example, variability in state capacities) that ensures that successful consolidation of a competition state is far from automatic.

7. How this Corresponds to Post-Fordism

The general consistency of these shifts across a wide range of economic and political regimes suggests that more than mere happenstance and/or purely local economic and political conditions are involved. It indicates that these shifts are closely related and grounded in responses to the crisis of Atlantic Fordism and the discursively constituted features of an imagined post-Fordist economy. The initial 'post-Fordist' paradigm certainly helped to contextualize and shape the responses to the crisis of the KWNS. But it also obscured the real complexity of the changes grouped under the rubric of post-Fordism, as well as the problems faced in finding anything like a comprehensive solution to the crisis-tendencies of the preceding accumulation regime and its mode of regulation. This is evident in the successive and conflictual reinterpretations of the general nature of post-Fordism and alternative post-Fordist scenarios: from flexible specialization through lean production to the globalizing, knowledge-based economy and, perhaps, beyond. This is why particular attention must be paid to the full range of general and specific changes affecting particular Fordist economies and to the ways in which new contradictions as well as path-dependent legacies shape the transition to post-Fordism.

Nonetheless, the overall effect of these changing functions is a transformation in the economic role of the state. In Atlantic Fordism, this involves a shift from nationally specific versions of the KWNS to regionally, nationally and supranationally specific versions of the competition state, especially in a Schumpeterian form. In East Asia, it involves a shift from forms of a Listian workfare national state[18] to other versions of the competition state. Indeed, it was in part the apparent superiority of East Asian economies in catching up with the West and, especially, Japan's record of innovation in some knowledge-based industries that prompted the reorientation of Atlantic Fordist economies in a similar direction.

During the crisis of Fordism the unity of the KWNS tended to disintegrate (see chapter 2) and there was a transitional period when a trial-and-error search occurred to find new state forms and functions that might contribute to the discovery and consolidation of a new accumulation regime and mode of regulation. This is by no means an automatic process – especially as emerging modes of regulation themselves play a key role in constituting the eventual objects of regulation. The transitional period can be particularly confusing and disorienting, especially when it involves an attempt to introduce a radical regime shift rather than emerging from a series of more incremental changes. For it is associated with a complex array of tasks besides those that are typical of any capitalist type of state and this situation is reflected in an apparently contradictory set of political activities.

These tasks derive from its location at the intersection between a consolidated Fordism in decline and a putative post-Fordism in the ascendant. In this sense, the transitional regime is Janus-faced and must engage in creatively destructive interventions. It must both 'roll back the frontiers' of Fordist state intervention and 'roll forward' those for post-Fordist intervention. Thus, on the one hand, it will seek to roll back the exceptional, crisis-induced state forms and functions associated with Fordism in decline as well as to weaken the normal, routinized forms of intervention linked to the Keynesian welfare national state as a whole. And, on the other hand, a transitional regime must pursue exceptional measures to establish the conditions for a post-Fordist 'take-off' as well as begin to consolidate the 'normal' state forms and functions associated with post-Fordism. Neither the first nor the second set of tasks is ever structurally inscribed or strategically pre-scripted. On the contrary, they involve chance discoveries, search processes, policy transfers and social struggles. This indicates the need for *ex post* analyses of how post-Fordist states emerge rather than *ex ante* (and therefore teleological) accounts of the necessary transition to post-Fordism.

Since it is not yet evident that consolidated post-Fordist states have emerged, however, we must risk teleology. Thus I will now indicate some criteria for identifying an ideal-typical consolidated post-Fordist state. This may seem to be putting the post-Fordist cart before the transitional horse, but it has a heuristic value in assessing whether crises in/of Fordism are being resolved or perpetuated. Time alone will tell, however, whether or not I have judged the next step and its postulated state correctly. To establish whether the emerging Schumpeterian competition state is appropriate to post-Fordism or not, we must proceed in three steps. The first is to detail the key features of Fordism and its crisis-tendencies. The second is to identify the key features of a post-Fordist accumulation regime. And the third is to establish what structural forms and strategic capacities in the state and political system might correspond to this regime.

One might argue that it is still too soon to specify this state form, but I suggest that some initial clues can be gleaned from apparently fundamental tendencies in the current restructuring and their implications for state forms and functions. Moreover, since these arguments were first formulated in the early 1990s and expressed in terms of the tendential rise of a Schumpeterian workfare state (Jessop 1992c, 1993, 1994a,b), a reasonable period has passed to begin to judge whether the tendencies that this approach implies are being realized or not. There are at least three possible tests in this regard:

- showing that KWNS regimes were structurally coupled in major respects to the growth dynamic of Atlantic Fordism and that the transition to the SWPR helps directly or indirectly to resolve (or is held to do so) the principal crisis-tendencies of Atlantic Fordism and/or its associated KWNS regimes so that a new wave of accumulation becomes possible, based on a new virtuous circle and a new spatio-temporal fix;
- showing that the distinctive aspects of the emerging SWPR correspond in key respects to the emerging growth dynamic of the new global economy and contribute significantly to the overall shaping and consolidation of this dynamic considered from an integral

viewpoint – thereby encouraging the renewal and re-regulation of capitalism after its Fordist period; and
- showing that the most competitive economic spaces (even if they were not really Fordist themselves but existed as non-Fordist islands in a sea of Fordism) in this emerging order actually pioneered this form of state and have thereby gained a paradigmatic, exemplary status for restructuring and re-regulating efforts elsewhere.

A full evaluation of these tests must wait until the three other dimensions of the SWPR have been considered. Nonetheless, the Schumpeterian version of the competition state seems to satisfy to some extent all three potential criteria. I do not intend to argue that this type of state alone could ever resolve all the crisis-tendencies of Fordism, preside single-handedly over the rise and consolidation of post-Fordism, or totally exclude all other strategic paradigms. Indeed, the very concept of mode of regulation implies that changes would also be needed in the wage form, corporate organization, forms of competition, innovation systems, and so forth, to resolve fundamental crises in accumulation regimes. Likewise, regarding the strategic moment of restructuring and re-regulation, there are few limits to the operation of the economic and political imaginary. But attempts to restructure and reorient the state system do have a major role in shaping the transition from Fordism to post-Fordism both directly and through their repercussions on changes in other regulatory domains.

Before considering possible grounds for describing the competition state as post-Fordist, let us recapitulate relevant crisis-tendencies in Atlantic Fordism. These include the gradual (and always relative) exhaustion of the growth potential that came from extending mass production into new branches; the relative saturation of markets for mass consumer durables; a decline in profitability; the disruption of the virtuous circle of Fordist accumulation through internationalization; the growing incoherence and ineffectiveness of national economic management as national economies become more open; the stagflationary impact of the KWNS on the Fordist growth dynamic (especially where state economic intervention is too concerned with sustaining employment in sunset sectors); a growing fiscal crisis due to the ratchet-like growth of social consumption expenditure; and an emerging crisis of social security due to the expansion of part-time, temporary and discontinuous employment at the expense of a full-time Fordist norm.

An emerging post-Fordist accumulation regime could be said to respond to such crisis-tendencies in various ways. It transforms mass production and transcends it, segments old markets and opens new ones, offers opportunities to restore the rate of profit, is less constrained by national demand conditions but makes new demands upon regional and national innovation systems, replaces macroeconomic planning in autocentric economies with supply-side policies to promote innovation, flexibility and structural competitiveness in response to the enormous ramifications of new technologies. Likewise, its concern with structural and/or systemic competitiveness recognizes the changing terms and conditions of international competition as well as its increased significance. It offers new ways of regenerating old industries as well as replacing them, promises new ways of organizing social consumption to reduce costs and make it more functional for business, and is able to further exploit the fragmentation and polarization of the labour force consequent upon the crisis in Fordism. It goes beyond the mere retrenchment of social welfare to restructure and subordinate it to market forces. Its restructuring and reorientation of social reproduction towards flexibility and retrenchment signifies its awareness of the post-Fordist paradigm shift as well as the impact of internationalization on the primary functions of money and wages. It rescales these forms of intervention in economic and social reproduction to correspond to the more complex and multiscalar forms of accumulation in a globalizing economy that are reflected in the complex dialectic between globalization and regionalization. And it introduces new forms of strategic guidance and coordination that overcome the limits of top-down state intervention in the mixed economy. The Schumpeterian competition state could play a key role in several of these areas (see box 3.2). This approach must also rely largely on assertion for its persuasive effect until the effectiveness of specific SWPR regimes (and alternative modes of social regulation of the emerging global order) have been properly examined and their viability in specific conjunctures is assessed.

An alternative approach is more promising for present purposes, however, since its persuasive force depends on past performance rather than possible post-Fordist futures. It involves demonstrating that those economies that grew most rapidly during the global crisis in/of Fordism and that have become models for those in crisis are especially advanced in developing the Schumpeterian competition state. Among the most prominent examples today might be the USA, Germany, Finland and the Third Italy, as well as some of the most successful regional economies in otherwise crisis-prone economies. Japan and first-wave East Asian dragon economies once provided other exemplars, but Japan's stagnation and the Asian Crisis have cast doubt on their present and past relevance (for an alternative view on East Asia, see Weiss 1998; and on Japan, see Boyer and Yamada 2000). Even if it were wrong to categorize all these national and/or regional economies as literally post-Fordist (because they were never truly Fordist), their increasing role as exemplars of alternative (and

Box 3.2 *The Schumpeterian competition state and capital accumulation*

1. Changing regulatory frameworks to facilitate labour market flexibility and mobility within national economic space.

2. Liberalization and deregulation of foreign exchange movements and redesign of international financial architecture with the effect of internationalizing and accelerating capital flows.

3. Modifying institutional frameworks for international trade and foreign direct investment.
   - addressing the multiformity of economic globalization by engaging in the rivalrous and conflictual struggle to define the rules for harmonizing or standardizing technological, economic, juridicopolitical, sociocultural and environmental issues;
   - promoting the space of flows in this context by organizing conditions favourable to the international mobility of technologies, industrial and commercial capital, intellectual property and at least some types of labour-power.

4. Planning and subsidizing spatial fixes that support the activities of financial, industrial and commercial capital within and across borders.

5. Promoting their own national or regional capitalisms and appropriate conditions for their global spread.

6. Engaging in complementary forms of *Standortpolitik* and other forms of place-based competition in an attempt to fix mobile capital within the state's own economic spaces and to enhance the interurban, interregional or international competitiveness of its own place-bound capitals.

7. Seeking to manage the tension between (a) the interests of potentially mobile capital in reducing its place-dependency and/or freeing itself from temporal constraints and (b) the state's own interest in fixing (allegedly beneficial) capital in its territory and rendering capital's temporal horizons and rhythms compatible with its own political routines, temporalities and crisis-tendencies.

8. Promoting new temporal horizons of action and new forms of temporal flexibility.

- coping with the increased salience of multiple time zones (in commerce, diplomacy, security, etc.);
- recalibrating and managing the intersection of temporalities (e.g., regulating computer-programmed trading, promoting the 24-hour city as centre of consumption, managing environmental risk).

9. Socializing long-term conditions of production as short-term calculation becomes more dominant in marketized economic activities.

10. Articulating the interlinked processes of de- and reterritorialization and de- and retemporalization associated with new forms of time–space distantiation and time–space compression in the hope of creating a new spatio-temporal fix for managing the structural contradictions inherent in the capital relation.

Note: This list is incomplete and the activities partly overlap. Tables in other chapters will identify further activities. Each of these activities can be linked into different accumulation strategies and state projects (see especially chapter 7).

apparently successful) trajectories for Fordist regimes in crisis does mean that they have a paradigmatic post-Fordist status.

8. Concluding Remarks

To avoid a teleological analysis of the competition state as the functionally necessitated complement to an emergent post-Fordist labour process, accumulation regime or mode of regulation, the arguments presented above must be qualified by more concrete and complex analyses of Fordist modes of growth as well as by more substantive work on the crisis mechanisms of the KWNS considered as a distinctive state form and political regime (see chapter 5). A more detailed analysis of the competition state would need to show the structural coupling between each type of Fordism and the character of the national state and the problems this creates; the complexities of the capital relation in each regime type and its implications for the forms of economic and political struggle over crisis-resolution; the path-dependency of the trajectory out of crisis that emerges in and through such struggles; and, thus, the problems that arise when the state lacks the capacities to manage the transition.

4

Social Reproduction and the Workfare State

What is conventionally termed the welfare state is far from universal. It is not found in all industrial societies nor even in all advanced capitalist societies and it is by no means an irreversible evolutionary achievement. On the contrary, for some years there have been remarkable changes in economic and social policies, their discursive framing and legitimation, the speed and scale at which policy formation and reform occur in these areas, the institutional mechanisms and networks through which these policies are pursued, and their economic, political and social bases. These changes are related, as we have seen, to four sets of factors: (1) the reorganization of the labour process, accumulation regimes and modes of regulation in response to the basic crisis-tendencies of Atlantic Fordism and to the emergence of new primary contradictions in capitalism; (2) the emerging fisco-financial squeeze on the KWNS, the crisis in the catch-all party system with which it was linked, the institutionalized compromise on which it was based and the development of new social forces; (3) the re-emergence or resurgence of liberalism in the guise of neoliberalism as an alternative to corporatism and statism as modes of economic governance and state projects, and its active promotion by the USA as the hegemonic state in Atlantic Fordism and Britain as its junior partner; and (4) the rise of new economic and social problems and new social movements that challenged the prevailing mode of regulation and demanded new ways of dealing with old and new problems. The responses to these challenges have major implications for the politics of the welfare state, for its retrenchment and restructuring, and for attempts to move beyond the welfare state without losing critical electoral and more general political support or undermining the legitimacy of the national state.

This chapter examines the restructuring and strategic reorientation of the KWNS from the mid-1970s regarding the social reproduction of labour-power as a fictitious commodity. This requires us to consider changes in the forms and functions of collective consumption as well as in income transfers based on the contributory insurance principle, citizenship rights or, perhaps, residence privileges; and it also demands attention to the discursive and material construction of new forms and bases of social reproduction deemed appropriate to the transition to, and subsequent operation of, a globalizing, knowledge-based economy. Thus, alongside changes in social redistribution and income transfers, I also consider labour market policy and the restructuring of education. Albeit at different times and speeds and with different degrees of discontinuity, changes have occurred in these regards not only under neoliberal governments but also under more traditional social democratic, Christian democratic, and centre-left regimes.

1. Preliminary Considerations

With the development of formally free labour markets, market forces became the chief mode of coordination in regard to all economic activities in capitalism. But the invisible hand, with its formal monetary maximands, impersonal operation (working, as Marx put it, behind the backs of the producers), procedural rationality, and *post hoc* operation, has always been supplemented by other modes of coordination that introduce more substantive objectives, elements of interpersonal or interorganizational deliberation, orientation to collective goals, and *ex ante* concertation. This is where welfare regimes may help to secure some of the key conditions for capital accumulation. For they institutionalize substantive criteria for evaluating and correcting market outcomes, political and bureaucratic procedures for guiding the operation of market forces and addressing market failure. They also have a key role in establishing accumulation strategies and linking them to state projects and hegemonic visions, and in securing crucial preconditions for the operation of market forces. In this regard, they constitute an important interface between the economic and extra-economic conditions for capital accumulation. This has implications for the structural coupling and co-evolution of the economic, political, legal, educational, medical and other functional systems, as well as for the relationship between these systems and the lifeworld. In the latter respect, welfare regimes are heavily implicated in governing the economic, gender, ethnic, intergenerational and many other aspects of the division of labour throughout the social formation. Indeed, they also contribute to the 'labour of division' through their differential treatment of existing social identities and/or their creation of other social identities (Munro 1997). They thereby contribute to the classification and normalization of individuals, groups and other social forces as a basis for differential treatment in the division of labour and for social inclusion-exclusion within the context of specific spatio-temporal fixes (see also chapters 1 and 2).

The general and widespread nature of the changes involved in the tendential emergence of the SWPR suggests that the primary causes of this transition should be sought in general and widespread features of the postwar political economy since the 1970s and '80s. They are unlikely to be found just in factors that are specific to one or two special cases. Thus it is important to define the explanandum at a sufficiently high level of abstraction and simplicity to establish the basic tendencies involved whilst recognizing that the latter will be overdetermined at more concrete-complex levels of analysis. This will enable us to search for an appropriate macro-explanation and avoid redundant micro-causal explanations (Garfinkel 1981: 55, 59; Jessop 1982: 282–90; Manners 1998). Nonetheless, the wide variation in the timing and trajectories of transitions, their discourses and legitimacy, their social bases and outcomes, also requires careful attention to their proximate material causes, the discursive framing of any perceived crisis in and/or of the welfare state, links to historically specific balances of forces in particular conjunctures, institutional mediations and strategic selectivities, and issues of sequencing. Likewise, the actual outcomes of attempts to restructure and strategically reorient social reproduction will be linked to different modes of insertion into the world market and international political system. So our macro-explanation must be compatible with more micro-level analyses that explain the historical specificity of continuities and discontinuities in different welfare regimes.

I have already indicated part of the macro-explanation for changes in the welfare dimension of the KWNS in the preceding two chapters. Nonetheless, although the crisis of Atlantic Fordism did exclude continuation of the KWNS in its old form, it did not require that attempts be made to dismantle or destroy the welfare state rather than to reform it. Indeed, given my arguments about the necessity of extra-economic factors in the reproduction of labour-power as a fictitious commodity, it is improbable that a general and enduring rollback could be consolidated. Far more likely are attempts to redesign institutions and/or to reorient their role in social reproduction. In this sense, the various attempts to effect a major neoliberal regime shift found in the United States, the United Kingdom, New Zealand and, to a lesser extent, Australia and Canada constitute exceptions rather than the norm in welfare restructuring. Moreover, given the overall liberal nature of these regimes before the neoliberal turn, even these attempts to promote a neoliberal regime shift were less radical than the same attempts would have been in other welfare regimes. Even here, however, we should consider the contradictions and limitations both in their own terms and as models for other economic and political spaces.

2. Alternative Approaches to Welfare State Reform

Much of the existing literature on recent welfare reforms, important though it is, addresses issues that are tangential to the present chapter. A first problem for present purposes is that some studies are too concerned with austerity and retrenchment in response to the initial crisis in/of the welfare state and/or focus excessively on what often prove to be quite marginal quantitative fisco-financial variations. We certainly know far more now about changing tax mixes (the relative contribution of taxes on mobile and immobile economic agents as revenue sources), revenue mixes (the changing balance of taxation and borrowing) and budget mixes (the changing targets of expenditures). Unfortunately there are many complex and interacting factors that may affect the absolute figures, trends and ratios, and this makes simple analyses of quantitative variation hard to interpret in comparative analyses. Moreover, even in more neoliberal welfare regimes, welfare expenditure remains at high levels even two decades after the first serious and insistent calls for retrenchment (see pp. 150–2). This poses interesting questions about conservation-dissolution effects in social change as well as about possible qualitative shifts in the role of the welfare state.

In addition, these long-run time series studies tend to ignore the deliberate or providential use of short- to medium-term fluctuations in spending to provide the state with leverage in restructuring and reorienting collective consumption (for example, in education, health services and housing) and/or to recompose the labour force and modify incentives and attitudes in the public sector. Among other tactics, periods of underfunding may be followed by the selective release of additional monies conditional on compliance with new modes of working, new-blood posts in strategic areas, new performance targets, benchmarks, etc. Likewise, access to extra funds may be made to depend on ad hoc challenges, generalized competition or specific requirements that public funding be matched by the mobilization of private funds. In addition, a long-term squeeze on employment and wages in the public sector may be imposed in the face of more or less resistance in order to free revenues for other purposes – albeit at the expense of motivation, morale and recruitment at a later date. Cuts in capital spending may likewise be made in order to support the prevailing level of electorally more sensitive current spending – an effect that would not show up in studies that focus solely on income transfers or on current spending more generally. The resulting deterioration in the quality of collective consumption may also be significant enough to necessitate and/or legitimate the subsequent transfer of responsibility for its provision to public-private partnerships or private enterprise. This is most evident in the neoliberal cases. In all cases, this strategy could enable the state to release funds for various other purposes because of its reduced capital spending in these particular areas; to generate revenues from privatization proceeds that could be used to finance tax cuts and/or other state expenditures; to permit greater flexibility in the operation and provision of hitherto public services and/or in wages and working conditions in these sectors; to create opportunities for small and medium enterprises as well as larger service firms and/or to promote the internationalization of services; and to promote community involvement and citizen participation in social reproduction. Finally, returning to the issue of current spending, we should also note that targeting, means-testing and fiscal claw-back may have significant effects independently of whether current spending rises, falls or stays the same.

All of this indicates that a concern with quantitative variation and aggregate levels of spending can distract attention from what could prove to be far more important shifts in the qualitative forms and functions of social policy and social welfare in the context of a broader rearticulation and rescaling of the capitalist type of state and changing forms of governance. One of the functions of the fourfold approach to welfare regimes adopted here is precisely to facilitate the analysis of qualitative issues.

A second problem is that much of the literature assumes that welfare states in the circuits of Atlantic Fordism (if not outside) exist in the same time, i.e., have the same genealogy, rhythms, cycles, and so forth, and hence that one calendar year or decade has the same significance for any and all welfare states. This is reflected in the neglect of four interrelated problems. First, 'welfare states are always out of date' as a result of social and demographic developments and the emergence of new needs and risks. This is especially important in those 'historical periods when the very modes of integration which underpin welfare states are challenged' (Daly 1998: 130; cf. Pierson 2001a on the need to 'recalibrate' welfare regimes in the light of new risks, problems and challenges). Second, economic, political, social and cultural developments are often 'out of phase', especially when considered cross-nationally. Thus, whereas some KWNSs began to emerge in the interwar period and were consolidated in the 1950s and 1960s, others first emerged in the 1950s or 1960s and had not reached maturity before the onset of the crisis in/of Atlantic Fordism. In particular, the peripheral Fordist economies of Southern Europe (Spain, Portugal, Greece) began their postwar economic expansion later, began to develop a KWNS mainly after the collapse of their respective dictatorships, had faster economic growth rates than the EU average in the 1980s and 1990s (albeit with higher unemployment rates) and are still catching up with their northern neighbours in consolidating the welfare state at the same time as undertaking neoliberal policy adjustments. Likewise, first-wave East Asian newly industrializing economies are now facing problems of building a welfare state to replace their more Ricardian and/or familial workfare regimes, especially in response to economic volatility and growing insecurity even for core workers. Third, viewed on a smaller time scale and from the viewpoint of class and other social struggles, welfare regimes may be 'out of cycle' in relation to each other, thereby further complicating any comparison. For, as Kalecki (1943) anticipated and subsequent analysts observed, postwar economic expansion involved a political business cycle. Thus, after Keynesian-induced full employment strengthened the bargaining power of organized labour, employers and the state would provoke a recession in order to reduce wage pressures; but, as a national election neared, the government would reflate to garner votes from economic recovery. Likewise, as Piven and Cloward (1971, 1993) have shown, there is also a political cycle in welfare regimes as state managers and their allies seek alternately to dampen social protest and to restore the incentive to work. And, fourth, owing to differences in the timing and sequencing of economic and social reforms, it is also possible for time to be 'out of joint'. Thus the structural coupling and co-evolution of welfare regimes and the wider national and plurinational economic and political systems in which they are embedded come to be marked by specific patterns of unevenness and dislocation.

A third source of problems is an understandable tendency to fetishize Esping-Andersen's typologies (or their derivatives) in work on changes in welfare regimes. Thus much recent research has concerned issues of convergence or divergence within this pattern of welfare regimes. Interestingly, it is the liberal regime that now often serves as the empirical benchmark against which to assess changes even if social democracy is retained as the normative ideal. This can lead to neglect of other types of change within the three (four, or five) regimes and, more importantly, of alternative paths away from all of these regimes (including the liberal model) as they existed in the golden age of Atlantic Fordism. This is especially problematic, as Esping-Andersen's models capture only part of the state's role in social reproduction (see chapter 2) and thereby divert attention from other changes in current social reproduction.

Fourth, some studies have been too concerned with identifying and critically assessing the significance of globalization as a possible cause of changes in welfare regimes. This worthwhile interest reflects the discursive role of 'globalization' as an alibi for changes being made for other reasons, resulting in the claim that increasing international competition necessitates cuts in taxes and in the individual and social wage as well as in other aspects of economic and social policies. It also relates to the familiar claim, which can also serve as an alibi for politicians, that the electorate, public opinion and other significant social forces are in general opposed to taxes and public spending – even as particular groups of electors and pressure groups demand more spending (cf. Kitschelt 1994, 1997; Taylor-Gooby 1997, 2001a). And it corresponds to the more general impact of the global neoliberal project, which promotes privatization, commodification and market proxies in the public sector, as well as reduction and redistribution of tax burdens. However, while this renders research on the social policy impact of globalization intelligible, it also explains why it is often theoretically ill-considered and tends to muddle questions of causation. In particular, this research fails to note the multiscalar, multicentric, multitemporal nature of globalization (see chapter 3), to take account of the extent to which states on different scales (especially certain national states) have been actively involved in promoting globalization and to recognize that even those states that are 'more sinned against than sinning' in regard to globalization still have political choices in responding to globalization and its associated discourses. It also tends to ignore the fact that globalization, even in its own terms, is just one vector among several through which the contradictions and dilemmas inherent in the capital relation are currently being expressed. In this sense, too, the debate as to whether the pressures on the national state are primarily global or domestic in origin misses the point about the changing dynamic of capital accumulation (see, for example, Iversen 2001; Pierson 2001b; and Swank 2001, 2002).

In addition, the impact of globalization often involves a one-sided focus on the hypermobility of financial capital, the possibilities for the cross-border relocation of productive capital, the role of the individual and social wage as a cost of production, and labour-power as one substitutable factor of production among others. Its impact in this regard is certainly important. But it cannot be properly understood without considering the state's ability to reorganize state budgets and expenditure, the importance of the extra-economic and place-bound conditions of productive activities, the role of the individual and social wage as a source of demand and the significance of labour-power as a creative and knowledgeable source of added value that requires extra-economic cultivation. In short, many studies ignore the extent to which the manifold pressures of globalization as a multicentric, multiscalar, multitemporal, multiform and, of course, multicausal process express themselves differently in different labour processes, branches of production, regions, parts of the overall circuit of capital, accumulation regimes, modes of regulation, and so forth. I will expand on the contradictory implications of the (il)logic of globalization below (see also Jessop 1999c) and explain its significance for the restructuring, the rescaling and the reorientation of the welfare state. I will also refer to more recent work that has begun to address these issues in important and methodologically innovative ways.

Fifth, social policy has too often been considered in isolation from economic policy. For good or ill, making this connection was a major concern of early Marxist work on the functions of the welfare state in capitalism (for example, Gough 1979; O'Connor 1973; Offe 1984; and, for a critique of these three authors, Klein 1993). It was also explicitly thematized in the discourses that justified the development of the KWNS and the projects in and through which this initially occurred. Esping-Andersen also deals with this issue one-sidedly insofar as he emphasizes the role of the welfare state in decommodification without noting how, by virtue of the contradictory nature of labour-power as a *fictitious* commodity, such intervention could reinforce as well as weaken the logic of capital accumulation. This could well be linked to his emphasis on a class-theoretical approach at the expense of a capital-theoretical analysis. It is also paralleled by his neglect of the contradictory implications of the welfare state for women's dual burden in performing both paid and domestic labour, where the extension of welfare rights, child care provision, lone parent allowances and similar measures serves to facilitate the recommodification of women's labour-power and their further integration into the labour force.

Among a growing body of work that is re-examining these issues are three important exceptions to the neglect of the mutual implications of social and economic policy: the statistically sophisticated, institutionally rich study of Huber and Stephens (2001) and the collective projects presented in Hall and Soskice (2001) and Ebbinghaus and Manow (2001a). The last-named authors note that it is important to

> consider social protection provided by social security systems, collective bargaining practices and employment regimes. Our knowledge of modern welfare states, and especially the sources of their current crises, remains limited until we reconsider the economic foundation on which they stand. Moreover, the productive function of social protection has often been overlooked due to the focus on redistribution as the main goal of welfare state policies. Hence, we also believe that for a better understanding of modern capitalism we ought to take into account the important impact of the welfare state on employment, skill acquisition, wage setting and investment. (Ebbinghaus and Manow 2001b: 2)

Nonetheless, even the best recent work on this and other aspects of welfare reform fails to consider the fourfold linkages between changes in economic and social policy, the rescaling of the capitalist state, and the changing forms of governance. Raising the question of these linkages (without claiming to have fully resolved them) is the main aim of the present work. So, whilst this chapter can and must be parasitic upon the best recent work for its analytical insights and empirical detail, its principal aim is not to repeat or critique that work but to contextualize the changes that are identified therein. Thus I will give more weight to the structural imperatives and changes in the balance of economic and political forces and the resulting qualitative shifts in the economic and social priorities of the welfare state that are bound up with the transition to post-Fordism. It is this set of qualitative shifts that I seek to capture with my concept of the SWPR.

3. The Specificity of the Welfare State in Atlantic Fordism

Welfare regimes deliver welfare through a complex mix of mechanisms. These involve changing mixes of occupational benefits, direct state financial redistribution, fiscal measures, state-funded and/or state-provided collective consumption, household redistribution, intra- and intergenerational solidarity within extended families, and charitable activities. Alongside the social reproduction of labour-power is a regime of 'welfare for capital' that also involves a complex mix of mechanisms (fiscal welfare, direct state subsidies, infrastructural provision, asymmetrical private-public partnerships, etc.) which direct state revenues to the benefit of particular capitals or capital in general and/or forgo revenue through tax expenditures (tax reliefs) to the same ends. Such welfare regimes have quite different distributive consequences in class, gender, ethnic and spatial terms according to the mix of private, public and 'third' sectors. This very same selectivity also makes the struggle over welfare mixes a key issue in debates over the restructuring of welfare states. In this context, ideas about social partnership, stakeholding, the role of informal networks and governance, etc., provide some interesting new sites of struggle.

There are three main forms of welfare delivery: (1) collectively organized social insurance leading to financial entitlements in the case of certain contingencies, such as unemployment, sickness, pregnancy or retirement; (2) redistribution through the fisco-financial system, including not only transfer payments but also fiscal welfare and state-subsidized occupational welfare and state-subsidized private provision of goods such as housing and various other tax reliefs; and (3) collective consumption in the sense of public finance of public goods and services. These different but interconnected forms of welfare delivery have contrasting implications for class, gender, 'race', ethnic and regional (re)distribution and for the specific forms in which the crisis in/of the KWNS manifests itself. The politics that shapes the mix of welfare mechanisms is equally complex, depending not only on economic factors but also on the nature of the state and its articulation to civil society. Regardless of these complexities, however, it is useful to consider their role in securing the conditions for the self-valorization of capital and those for reproducing labour-power as a fictitious commodity.

The concept of collective consumption emerged during the 1950s and 1960s[1] as the KWNS was gradually consolidated in the economic space dominated by Atlantic Fordism. It had both a general and a particular significance. On the one hand, it highlighted the growing importance of state expenditure in lubricating and integrating the circuit of capital (thereby revealing the limitations of the idea of final household consumption); and, on the other hand, it identified the particular forms and functions of this expenditure in Atlantic Fordism. In the latter context it signified a major form of socialization of consumption that developed in tandem with the socialization of production in Atlantic Fordism. Thus, just as liberal markets and oligopolistic competition were displaced in favour of the mixed economy and indicative planning based on bi- or tripartite negotiation, liberal market forces and private households (or, at best, private, enterprise-level paternalism and civic philanthropy) came to play a smaller role in the reproduction of labour-power as the state became increasingly involved in the socialization of reproduction and consumption. National and/or local state involvement increased, with an emphasis on comprehensive, universal or near-universal redistributive measures that socialized individual risks over the life-course in what had become a mass, wage-earning society. This was combined with the provision of collectively financed and provided consumption in fields such as housing, education, health and, later, personal social services.

The collective nature of consumption was rooted in a specific articulation of three discursively as well as materially constituted divisions within contemporary capitalism: (1) 'private-public'; (2) 'market' and 'state'; and (3) 'national' space and its external environment. What made consumption 'collective' was its public organization by a distinctive form of national state in an economic space discursively construed and materially instituted to coincide broadly with that state's territorial boundaries. More recently, however, we have seen: (1) the rediscovery and active promotion of a third sector intermediate between private and public; (2) the growing recognition of the role of networks and self-organization as an alternative mode of governance allegedly capable of compensating for state as well as market failure; and (3) complex processes of de- and reterritorialization of economic and social spaces and a dialectic of globalization–regionalization. This has made it hard to continue collective consumption in its KWNS form – a situation worsened by neoliberal pressures to privatize state activities as far as possible.

In important respects the KWNS in Atlantic Fordism had already 'grown to limits' (Flora 1986–7) by the early 1980s. Although the transition from a social insurance or social security state (*Sozialstaat*) to more comprehensive welfare regimes had begun in the interwar period, it was during the years of postwar economic expansion that welfare states reached maturity (see chapter 2). As noted above, of course, some late developing welfare states still had room for growth. But it is generally true that the KWNS was comprehensive, being based primarily on past, present or future participation in the labour market and/or on national citizenship (hence tending to marginalize immigrant or non-national labour and treating them as second-class citizens, if at all). Likewise, the KWNS did generally cover most fields of everyday, lifetime and inter-generational social reproduction, offered universal or near-universal provision with high income replacement rates for the insured and, for citizens in its income transfer programmes, provided for a universal national education system and a more or less extensive socialization of basic medical care. Furthermore, it was generally sustained by high levels of taxation compared to the era of the liberal state.

However, while there were economic and political limits to further expansion of this type of welfare state in a capitalist society, especially as an instrument of economic and social redistribution, there are also three very important limits to welfare retrenchment. First, some form of extra-economic reproduction of labour-power as a fictitious commodity both individually and in the aggregate is essential to capital accumulation (see chapter 1). Moreover, whether or not the capitalist type of state is directly involved in its delivery in the first instance, it is nonetheless expected to serve as the social reproducer of labour-power in the last resort.[2] Thus, while the respective responsibilities and boundaries of market, state and civil society may shift, there is still an important steering role for the state. An interesting recent example of this is found in the competition between national states to recruit skilled workers from abroad to support their knowledge-based accumulation strategies – just as they had earlier sought to recruit unskilled workers from abroad to undertake work that was too physically demanding, dirty, oppressive in its working conditions, ill-paid, unsocial in its hours, or otherwise economically or socially unacceptable for their own citizens during the Fordist boom. Second, there are important institutional limits to welfare retrenchment through the effects of policy inheritance, programme inertia and the overall architecture of the state. These limits are reinforced by the potentially disruptive consequences of rapid and drastic cuts in welfare on the wider economy that would arise from the structural coupling and material interdependence of welfare states and market economies. For the past development of the welfare state produces a specific structure of economic organization reflecting its differential impact on opportunities for profit. Neoliberal discourse emphasizes the allegedly harmful 'crowding out' effects of public spending, however it is financed, as well as the unproductive nature of taxation and state borrowing. But sustained and consistent public spending also induces structural changes in supply and demand (e.g., social-industrial complexes linked to specific patterns of public sector welfare spending on capital projects, consumables and services) that would be more or less severely disrupted if radical cuts were made and the firms or sectors affected could not retool, restructure or redirect the resulting production in an acceptable time horizon.

Third, there are the political limits to welfare retrenchment that are rooted in the politics of representation (especially electoral dynamics and the mobilization of social movements), the internal organization of the state apparatus (vested departmental and ministerial interests, the multi-tiered nature of welfare delivery, the presence of the welfare professions, the rights of state employees, etc), and the politics of intervention (legally entrenched citizenship rights, social partnership dynamics, the residual power of 'policy-takers', etc.). This will inevitably be reflected in the balance of forces at any particular moment in a changing conjuncture and indicates the need for medium-term strategies to transform the structural constraints and mobilize new political alliances to counteract the institutional inertia and vested interests that favour maintenance of the status quo. In short, there is a strategic selectivity to welfare retrenchment in production and welfare regimes that interacts with the more general contradictions associated with the character of labour-power as a fictitious commodity:

> The broad social coalitions supporting the welfare state status quo prevent centrist and even right-wing parties from implementing, or even advocating, significant cuts in entitlements. Thus, to the extent that economic difficulties mean the agenda in most countries is not expansion but rather retrenchment, one should expect narrower partisan differences than in the past. The narrowing of differences is a result of constraints both on the right and the left. (Huber and Stephens 2001: 167)

Thus, while there is scope for some redesign of welfare delivery and the reallocation of the burdens of social welfare, these three sets of factors (among others) limit the economic and political scope for wholesale cuts in public provision without compensating changes elsewhere. For, whether performed in the private, public or the third sectors, social reproduction necessarily involves costs. Moreover, attention must be paid to the quality as well as the cost of securing such reproduction in one way or another. The case of privatized health care in the USA is particularly noteworthy, if not notorious, here; for it provides very unequal or non-existent coverage and is generally more expensive than European public health systems. There is much more scope, however, to refunctionalize welfare spending at or around the levels prevailing in particular regimes in response to changes in accumulation regimes, modes of regulation and their associated institutionalized compromises.

4. Towards the Workfare State

Changes have occurred in all three sites of KWNS welfare: insurance, fisco-financial redistribution and collective consumption. Across all three areas, we have been witnessing the increasing subordination of social policy to economic policy, although, of course, this remains far from total. This chapter identifies three related dimensions of welfare redesign, restructuring and reorientation. First, there are qualitative changes in social policy and its articulation to economic policy, with the latter being accorded greater primacy. Second, there is increasing downward pressure on the social wage considered as a cost of (international) production and/or as an electoral liability in the face of tax resistance – reflected in cost-cutting or, at least cost-containment, measures and the redesign of social transfers to make them more productive. And, third, changes are being made in the forms and functions of collective consumption. I illustrate these changes from policies for unemployed workers, the redesign of pension policy to reduce the long-run costs of pension provision and promote the financial services sector, and the restructuring of the education system in efforts to realign it with the alleged needs of a globalizing, knowledge-based economy. This choice is tied to the economic and political significance of unemployment, the fact that pensions constitute the largest item in the civilian budgets of most advanced capitalist states (with health typically the second biggest budget line), and education's key role in economic development and nation-building. A more extended treatment of welfare state restructuring in other fields of social policy, especially health, would be desirable in a longer work, but those chosen are sufficiently significant to identify the main trends.

The increasing subordination of social policy to economic policy

Globalization as defined in chapter 3 (and hence with a meaning far broader than that adopted in most recent studies of globalization and social policy) has two key features that affect the KWNS. First, it is linked with an economically expanded and sociologically enriched notion of competitiveness – even if neoliberal globalization projects sometimes fail to give this full public recognition. And, second, it enhances the opportunities for at least some capitals, especially financial capital providing transparent financial products, to move across borders. Combined with increasing inter-urban and interregional competition within national economies, this extends and reinforces capital's exit opportunities. Together these features tend to transform priorities in social policy, especially in relation to the latter's impact on competitiveness. However, since, as emphasized in chapter 3, there are different understandings of competitiveness, priorities can be reset in different ways. A Ricardian notion of competitiveness, for example, might indicate a need to cut social spending in increasingly open economies. For it suggests that such spending is a cost of production, is related more to populist demands and social engineering than to economic performance, is an unproductive deduction from revenues that could be better spent by individual economic agents in the market, and is a source of rigidities in the productive sector. Other accounts of competitiveness could lead in other directions. Thus an account oriented to systemic or structural competitiveness would give less emphasis to the absolute or relative cost of factors of production and more to their relative contribution to economic output; less to the economic and more to the extra-economic dimensions of competitiveness; less to the immediate tax costs of social spending and more to its long-term contribution to production; and less to the immediately unproductive nature of social expenditure and more to its role in compensating workers (and other adversely affected social forces) for the risks and disruptions involved in international trade. Focusing on these aspects of social spending would be less likely to generate demands for absolute welfare cuts as opposed to its redesign and reorientation. Inter alia, this suggests that, alongside their support for individual citizens and their dependants, social welfare could play a key role in socializing the costs of adjustment in open economies as these affect firms, cities or regions, and national economies. In both cases, however, growing internationalization, whether seen in terms of Ricardian or structural competitiveness, is linked to the subordination of social policy to the alleged demands of economic competitiveness. This is an important qualitative shift that is independent of any quantitative changes, and it represents a significant change in the nature of the welfare state and its role in social reproduction.

The resulting reordering of the relation between social and economic policy has passed through three main stages. In the initial crisis in/of Atlantic Fordism during the 1970s, welfare state activity and spending was increased. In part, this was a reflection of the automatic stabilizers built into the KWNS such that rising unemployment triggered increased welfare spending as well as lower tax revenues; and in part it was motivated by hopes of restoring the conditions for Fordist economic expansion. When this seemed to have failed to overcome stagflation, the welfare state was portrayed on the right as a source of rigidities in the labour market and as adding to costs of production. This prompted demands for changes in the welfare state to enhance labour market flexibility and to reduce costs. This is reflected from the 1980s onwards in the tightening of eligibility criteria for unemployment benefit and social assistance and in attempts to reduce entitlements and/or put time limits on them. The second period overlaps with the beginnings of a third stage that can be seen more clearly in the 1990s. This involves giving more emphasis to active labour market policies and increased coordination of unemployment benefits and 'in-work' benefits to demonstrate that 'work pays'.[3]

The second and third stages differ from the ideal-typical KWNS, especially in its liberal form, with its more passive approach to unemployment. For, while macroeconomic policy targeted full employment, unemployed workers received passive support until jobs became available again (cf. Mishra 1985). This support took two main forms. For those with sufficient labour market experience, unemployment and related benefits based on social insurance were paid; conversely, those who did not qualify for such benefits received social assistance. In contrast, the SWPR adopts a more active approach to labour market policy through a combination of measures to create the conditions for full employability in the labour market and of active preparation of some or all of the unemployed to help them back into work. Thus, one of the major features of recent changes in social reproduction is the roll-out of new regimes, rhetorics and routines of 'workfarist' regulation to replace the national framework of an allegedly crisis-prone welfare state or 'welfarist' regime (see Peck 2001). A basic feature of this new approach is its role in encouraging and/or enforcing work through active forms of social and employment policy and the development of transitional labour markets intended to smooth the path (or transition) from welfare into work. It has been advocated at all levels of policy formulation and implementation from the OECD (in its jobs study, OECD 1994) and the EU (for example in the 1993 White Paper, Growth, Competitiveness, Employment, or the 1995 EU report, Social Protection in Europe, as well as at a series of economic summits) through national states to the regional and local level (for general surveys of this shift from passive to active labour market policy, see Kalish et al. 1998; Peck 2001; Schmid 1996).

The activation approach is more or less universal in the economic space of Atlantic Fordism, but it can take different forms. First, in liberal welfare regimes, the emphasis has fallen on wage flexibility, reductions in insurance-based unemployment benefits and means-tested social assistance, and the abolition or reduction of minimum wages. The northern and antipodean liberal regimes, in part because of their state structures and in part because their welfare entitlements are less well entrenched, are better able to impose these changes from above without serious consultation. However, for the reasons noted above, this may not be the optimal solution economically in the medium- to long-term; and it could be damaging electorally because it exposes the responsible neoliberal governments politically should market failure re-emerge (Taylor-Gooby 2001b: 10–11). Second, social democratic welfare regimes have tended to intensify their past commitments to demand management and active labour market policies, but have given them a new workfarist inflection whilst maintaining relatively high levels of public welfare spending (see pp. 156, 158). A third pattern is found in the conservative-corporatist or Christian democratic regimes. These rely heavily on payroll taxes rather than on general taxation to finance social welfare, and their well-organized social partners tend to believe they have property rights in the welfare regime. These regimes therefore face a 'continental dilemma' (Scharpf 1997) that is generated by a 'scissors effect'. One blade of this involves growing inactivity rates that are largely due to rising levels of unemployment and (often early) retirement; the other blade involves increasing public expenditure based on entrenched insurance-based and corporatist-mediated entitlements. This has prompted negotiation between the different occupational estates and government with the aim of seeking ways to reduce the cost of the social wage for firms and transfer it to general taxation without triggering wage demands to enable employees to maintain their real disposable income after inflation and taxation (see also Taylor-Gooby 2001b).

Even where activation policies were already an important part of the KWNS system (e.g., in the Nordic economies), work obligations have become more explicit, stricter and mandatory in the 1990s. It is no longer a question of whether or not the jobless should participate in a programme, but rather of the programme into which they should be enrolled, willingly or not. It has become harder to refuse participation and the authorities have gained powers to sanction non-participation. In addition, the discourse has shifted from entitlements to obligations, especially as regards the young unemployed. Together with a restructuring of social services to target unemployment and social exclusion and to cut social assistance costs, this amounts to a general movement away from the social democratic tradition (Johansson 2001: 70–4).

There are four key aspects, for present purposes, in activation policies: (1) they aim to enhance the flexibility of labour markets; (2) they seek to enhance workers' employability and transform them into enter-prising subjects in a post-Fordist world where jobs for life can no longer be guaranteed and should no longer be expected; (3) rather than involv-ing standard national policies and measures, they rely far more on local agencies to design and manage policy in an experimental manner in the belief that this will produce solutions that meet local needs and that can mobilize local stakeholders, competencies and resources; and (4) they are being increasingly oriented to the knowledge-based economy, reskilling and lifelong learning. Thus unemployment benefits are linked to work, training or other programmes designed to help the unemployed move back into employment. Activation policy also extends into education and training and not just unemployment insurance and social security.[4] The methods adopted to activate workers may be more or less coercive or empowering (Peck 2001); the targets also vary within and across regimes and over time – including the registered unemployed, lone parents and the disabled (Robinson 1998: 87); and the cost and duration of pro-grammes can range from cheap and quick to quite costly and extended programmes based on retraining. This is evident in the contrast between coercive neoliberal job-search-focused welfare-to-work tactics through extended retraining and reskilling programmes to the still more com-prehensive Dutch 'flexicurity' approach and Danish job rotation and work leave schemes (Hemerijck and Manow 2001; Jørgensen 2002; Torfing 1999; Wilthagen 1998). In some cases the cheap and quick approach is combined with state subsidies to working households, espe-cially with children, so that their net incomes in employment can rise above the poverty line and the fiscal poverty trap can be reduced. This tends to subsidize employers paying low wages as well as to involve fiscal redistribution to the poor in a new guise (see Robinson 2000). Nonethe-less, in general, the overall effect of activation programmes is one of explicit or implicit disentitlement – in the former case through direct cuts, in the latter through shifts in work patterns when benefits remain tied to standard life-work cycles (Rhodes and Mény 1998: 11).

More generally, activation policies can be placed on a continuum running from *flexploitation* to *flexicurity*. Flexploitation refers to 'the anti-worker aspects of flexibility' (Gray 1998: 3), especially the combi-nation of increased coercion on the unemployed to find work and increased insecurity for those in work. Flexploitation is particularly asso-ciated with neoliberal workfare measures and tends to increase social exclusion (Cook et al. 2001; Glyn and Wood 2001; Haughton et al. 2000; Hyde et al. 1999; Jones and Gray 2001; Peck and Theodore 2000). In con-trast, flexicurity, although an English word, was coined by the Dutch in 1995 to refer to a new range of policies intended to make labour markets more flexible at the same time as providing greater social and employment security for those in or out of work, and improving social inclusion for all labour market participants (see Wilthagen 1998: 21). Dutch flexicurity aims to provide the security of a job (but not security in a job) for core workers as well as contingent, atypical or flexible workers, and to support this through a correspondingly flexible system of social security and activation policies. It is particularly concerned to establish good transitional labour markets to smooth the path of the unemployed into work. Thus it is committed to the 'empowerment of workers, organizational cooperation (in networks and private-public partnership), dynamic efficiency, leading to effective employment promotion, and sustainable employment (rather than "dead end jobs")' (Wilthagen 1998: 1). More generally, flexicurity tends to be associated with neo-corporatist bargaining and social pacts on a number of scales (for a general review of 'flexicurity'-type active labour market arrangements in Europe, see Schmid 1996).

Downward pressure on the social wage

Despite the crisis that began to emerge in the late 1970s, state budgets remained high in the 1980s and continued to rise in the 1990s (Garrett 1998, 2001; Garrett and Mitchell 2001; Huber and Stephens 2001). Demands for cuts in state spending on the grounds that it blocked economic growth had already begun to attract wide attention in the mid-1970s and the OECD soon joined the chorus for cuts in 1981 (OECD 1981). This reflects the view that the social wage represented by welfare spending is a cost of production like the individual wage and that taxation is always a disincentive to effort, savings and investment. This is associated in turn with a public burden model of welfare, which has been defined by Wilding as 'the view that much traditional welfare expenditure is an unproductive burden on the productive side of the economy and should therefore be reviewed and reduced' (1997: 417). This can be contrasted with an alternative view that taxes are the price of admission to a civilized society (Hutton 2002). Notwithstanding such demands, however, the crisis led to higher rather than lower spending. Indeed, the 1980s saw a more marked mean annual increase in public expenditure across all welfare regimes than had occurred during the 1970s, the period when the KWNS had reached its peak and began to display crisis symptoms (Huber and Stephens 2001: 207). This continuing increase prompted the OECD in the early 1980s to ask quite logically whether this trend reflected the temporary costs of managing the transition or implied that the state welfare budget would always remain at these levels. Its officials were optimistic enough at that time to maintain that 'it should be possible to maintain the gains in security and services which were reached in the 1960s and 1970s, and to improve them in line with the rate of economic growth, but not faster' (OECD 1985). It soon became less sanguine, however, and, together with the IMF, recommended the redesign of social policy around three goals: (1) increased efficiency in the delivery of government goods and services and in programme efficiency; (2) a review of spending priorities and programme objectives; and (3) the devolving of some public responsibilities to the private sector (Oxley and Martin 1991). And more recently still, whilst maintaining this line and the demand for continued downward pressure on spending commitments (for example, in the area of pensions, on which see below), it has also begun to put more emphasis on the need for a human capital approach to the residual welfare state (OECD 1994, 1999).

These trends in public spending outcomes are best interpreted in conjunction with state revenues. Thus, whereas expenditure increased faster than revenue in the 1970s, revenue grew faster than spending in the 1980s, indicating an attempt to reduce deficits even as expenditure continued to increase. This pattern continued into the 1990s, as governments sought to increase revenues and rein back spending (Huber and Stephens 2001: 207). There is also evidence that the higher spending welfare states have moved closer to the trend line of 'expected' spending than those that underspend relative to their type of regime (Alber and Standing 2000). A further indication of the struggle to reduce spending is the reduced significance of partisan control and accumulated partisan incumbency over government spending from the 1970s through to the 1990s, suggesting that external constraints are limiting room for manoeuvre (Huber et al. 1999: 190–2).

Moreover, when one turns to the wood rather than the trees, we find that '[e]verywhere programmes of benefit curtailment and retrenchment are on the agenda; and the differences are of degree and of the vigour with which these policies are pushed home' (Taylor-Gooby 1996: 214). Or, as Bonoli et al. claim in regard to Europe welfare regimes:

> There is now general agreement that the bulk of the social legislation introduced in recent years is intended to reduce the role of the state in welfare. Policies that lead in the opposite direction play a subordinate role. . . . This mass of restrictive social legislation consisted of several overlapping types. Some new policies have reduced the level of cash benefits, restricted entitlement and reduced the period for which the benefits can be paid. Other legislation increased the payments made by users of the health, education and social care services. Still other legislation made the provision or the administration of some of the cash benefits the responsibility of employers or other bodies or introduced market principles in the management of services. Finally, legislation privatized parts of the social services or many public utilities in their entirety. (Bonoli et al. 2000: 1)

There are many ways in which this downward pressure is expressed. I have already noted the role of cuts in unemployment benefit and their articulation with activation policies and 'work pays' strategies. There is also a general extension of means-testing for marginal workers, unemployed and lone parents – this response is especially common in liberal regimes. There are attempts to transfer risk and uncertainty to individuals through increased emphasis on private provision and civil society rather than on state guarantees (e.g., through variation in pension fund performance and annuity rates upon retirement). The overall result is increasing dependence on the market for an income adequate to sustain the socially accepted levels of consumption or, in other words, an increasing administrative recommodification of labour-power (Bonoli et al. 2000; Offe 1984; Pierson 2001a). And, indeed, where neoliberal policies have reinforced segmented and dualistic labour markets, the resulting flexploitation will also lead to increased impoverishment and social exclusion.

More generally, insurance has been partially privatized or placed in the third sector. This approach is sometimes linked to promotion of 'popular capitalism', a property-owning democracy, and wider share ownership; but elsewhere it is linked to wider community participation, a stakeholding society, and public-private partnership involving NGOs. There were precedents for this in the old corporatist welfare regimes and tripartite social democratic regimes, where trade unions had a key role in insurance. Fisco-financial redistribution tends to become more selective and targeted as a means of containing costs. And, in the context of Schumpeterian policies for competitiveness, fisco-financial redistribution is also linked to promoting rather than to moderating inequalities. This is reflected in the tendency for 'welfare for capital' to expand at the same time as 'welfare for labour' contracts, as well as more general forms of welfare restructuring and retrenchment. It is also linked to the neoliberal Schumpeterian tendency to promote uneven regional development rather than to compensate for it.

Pensions

A useful case study in this regard is the development of pensions. This is an important field of public expenditure because pensions became the most costly single item in governments' social budgets in the 1990s and should therefore have become a major target for retrenchment, especially as there is rapid ageing of the population (including the health-care-intensive population aged 75 years or older).[5] Indeed, the OECD had already identified this as a major problem for welfare states in the 1980s; and the World Bank has recently been pushing for a system of private defined contribution pensions to reduce the burden of pensions on state budgets. Pension reform is also interesting because it contrasts with the case of unemployment benefit, which represents a smaller proportion of state budgets even when it is relatively high. Whereas unemployment benefit has been cut as part of a package of active reintegration of the unemployed into the labour market, pensions have been subject to greater downward pressure.

These demographic pressures are common to all industrial countries and this is reflected in the fact that almost all states have acted to reduce state expenditure on retirement pensions or, at least, to reduce its rate of increase and to finance it in different ways. Thus, as Bonoli et al. note: 'In the 1980s, and even more so in the 1990s, the direction of change in pension policy has reverted from overall expansion to retrenchment. As a result, in the current situation, the term "pension reform" is increasingly used as a synonym for cuts in old age pensions' (2000: 30). This claim is confirmed by data for eighteen OECD countries provided by Huber and Stephens, who further show that liberal welfare regimes are the most likely to cut and social democratic regimes the most immune from cuts (2001: 208–9). Yet it is the Christian democratic conservative-corporatist regimes that are most vulnerable to these demographic pressures by virtue of the greater increase in their dependency ratio of pensioners to wage earners and the nature of their pension systems.

In general, all governments have preferred low visibility reforms, which can be seen as part of a 'strategy of obfuscation' to disguise the extent and impact of changes over time (Pierson 1995: 19–22). Among the measures used to disguise the extent of cuts are:

1   A shift in indexation of pensions to prices rather than wages. This contrasts with the position in Atlantic Fordism, where pensions were linked to wages and the latter were linked in turn to productivity and inflation. Coupled with an extension of qualifying years requirements and a reduction in early retirement incentives, this will steadily reduce the level of individual pensions relative to average earned incomes.

2   A shift from pay-as-you-go pensions systems (effectively a collective intergenerational redistribution from the active labour force to the retired that is financed from general taxation) to pre-funded systems (effectively a means of redistributing income over the lifecycle by boosting savings). This poses transitional problems, as those currently in the labour force must pay general taxes to finance the pensions of the currently retired at the same time as they are obliged (or incentivized) to contribute to their own future pensions. Unsurprisingly, this approach has provoked significant resistance to pension reform.

3 A shift from defined benefit to defined contribution schemes in public pension provision, with various actuarial allowances being made for increasing life expectancy, wage growth, returns on capital, etc. The intended net effect of these allowances is to reduce the pension bill.
4 A push to move from public-defined benefit to private-defined contribution schemes. This would not only privatize risks relative to the state system, it would also redistribute risk from employers, governments and pension funds to future pensioners. Although strongly pushed by international bodies such as the World Bank and by national states, there are doubts whether private systems can actually match the risk diversification and profile of public systems (Froud et al. 2001; Orszag and Stiglitz 2001). There are also concerns about the high costs of private pension schemes (including marketing costs, management charges, regulatory and compliance costs, and adverse selection effects) and the extent to which pension privatization serves as an indirect state subsidy to the financial services sector at the expense of the insured and citizens.
5 The promotion of multi-tiered systems in which a minimal public pension is supplemented by means-tested assistance and/or an occupational pension or individual portable personal pension tied to stock market performance.
6 Measures to make pensions more 'portable' so that they correspond better to more flexible and mobile labour markets.

There are differences among welfare regimes here too. Liberal regimes are most associated with a steady downward pressure on pensions, with strong reliance on de-indexing pensions from wage increases to link them only to price inflation, and strong encouragement to private savings – which has the additional benefit in a market-coordinated and money-capital dominated economy of boosting demand for financial services. In social democratic regimes there are measures to prevent early retirement (previously used to deal with deindustrialization, to disguise unemployment and to enable a greater targeting of unemployment measures on the young unemployed and the reskilling of those in middle age) and/or to provide strong incentives to delay retirement so that the pension will be higher. Social democratic regimes have also acted to remove public sector employment privileges and to claw back or means-test the national pension where the retired also have occupational pensions. There has also been a tightening of residence requirements and other eligibility measures. In conservative-corporativist systems we find an extended qualifying period for pensions coupled with a family-friendly shift because child care years can now count as active years (Taylor-Gooby 2001b: 7).

5. Collective Consumption and the Competition State

There has also been a retreat from collective consumption provided by the state in the mixed economy to more market- and/or third sector solutions to the socialization of consumption. This is reflected in five main sets of changes in the form and functions of collective consumption. First, whereas collective consumption in the KWNS involved public provision and public finance, this relationship has since been dis- and rearticulated to produce a more complex 'mixed economy of welfare'. At one extreme we find the total privatization of some sectors (involving private payment as well as private provision); then come various types of private and third sector provision combined with continuing public payment; less radical still is the introduction of market proxies into what remains of public provision financed by the state; and, at the other extreme, we find measures such as modest user changes, means-testing, co-payment by the state and private insurers (for example, in medical treatment for victims of automobile accidents), and so forth. Second, collective consumption has been rescaled as part of a more general denationalization of the state (see chapter 5). With a decentralization and deconcentration of state services, there is now greater scope for local and regional variations and for experimentation compared with the heyday of the KWNS. Third, there is a shift in the governance of collective consumption with increased reliance on public-private partnerships, multi-agency cooperation, and participation of the third sector. Fourth, the production process and the wage relation have been reorganized in line with prevailing post-Fordist norms. Thus we can observe more flexible labour markets, more flexible working conditions, more differentiated products and services, more performance targets, more benchmarking, and so forth. And, fifth, there is a trend towards using collective consumption to promote the transition to a globalizing, knowledge-based economy. This is seen in changing public procurement policies, use of ICTs – including the Internet – for demonstration as well as efficiency purposes, the promotion of best practice, and so on. In this way collective consumption is explicitly used to promote systemic and/or structural competitiveness.

I will now illustrate these changes from the field of education. While education obviously and necessarily had a key economic role in reproducing the labour force in the period of Atlantic Fordism and the KWNS, it also had major parallel roles in the development and expansion of a mass welfare state based on national citizenship. In stylized terms that were never fully matched in reality, we can say that education was expected to promote equality of access and opportunity, to create the basis for a talented and just 'meritocracy' that would undermine inherited class and status structures, to create, codify and disseminate a shared national identity and culture appropriate to a universal and solidaristic welfare state, and to develop knowledgeable and critical citizens able and willing to participate in an expanding public sphere as well as a mass plebiscitary democracy. This was reflected in the prolongation of the period that children and young people spent in compulsory education and in the development (accelerating in the 1960s and 1970s) of state-sponsored and state-funded mass further and higher education. Whilst the growth of mass higher education was clearly related to the task of training the technical and professional labour forces deemed appropriate to a Fordist economy, KWNS and mass society, it was also justified in terms of the right to continue one's education in the field of one's choice to the highest level one could attain. Adult education in this period was likewise still strongly linked to a wider democratic project to promote citizenship and solidarity rather than to develop human capital. The expansion of mass education was also intended to compensate for economic, social and regional inequalities and hence had a role in social redistribution. In short, education played a key role in the institutionalized compromise underpinning Atlantic Fordism. Moreover, where the actual development and operation of education did not fully match this model, its failure to do so was strongly criticized in terms of the hegemonic KWNS values of economic growth, equality of opportunity and national integration.

The economic, political and social crises in/of Atlantic Fordism (see chapter 3) were reflected in the education system too. On the one side, there was an increasing disquiet in business and state circles about the failure of pupils, teachers and schools, the growing 'mismatch' between educational outputs and the changing needs of industry and the wider economy, the failures of 'big science', the inadequate return on public investment in education and the growth of graduate unemployment as unemployment more generally increased.[6] And, on the other side, faculty members began to turn from a professional ethos to a more trade union mentality and student movements protested against the corporate 'education factory' as well as against more general features of Fordist mass society. The crisis in education was eventually resolved discursively through a growing hegemony of accounts that cast educational reform in terms of economic imperatives such as the need for more technical and vocational education, for enhanced skills, creativity, flexibility and enterprise on the part of students, and for greater attention to the new demands of international competition and the knowledge-based economy on the part of university administrators, teachers and researchers. The contributions of education to social welfare and national citizenship roles were increasingly subordinated to the purported functions of education in preparing the bearers of human capital to participate in a lifelong learning society as well as in renewing intellectual capital (or the knowledge base) for the knowledge-based economy. The democratic function of education in the KWNS has likewise been transformed into one of reducing social exclusion to increase employability and mobilize scarce skills. Both aspects of this recasting of the functions of education emphasize the economic returns to public investment in education ('human resource development') and the need for efficiency, value for money and public accountability. In the words of the UK's Department for Education and Employment (since renamed as the Department for Education and Skills), 'learning is the key to prosperity' (DfEE 1998).

Green summarizes the changes well in identifying two trends:

> Firstly, it was increasingly the case that where education was identified with the national interest, as it has been repeatedly in the rhetoric of all western governments in the 1980s and 1990s, this was in terms of the national economy and economic competitiveness, and not in terms of citizenship and national cohesion. Secondly, among some of the older nation states, there was a sense in which education was no longer so explicitly part of the cultural process of nation-building. . . . As western countries, somewhat reluctantly, began to acknowledge the growing diversity and cultural pluralism of their populations, they found themselves uncertain of what their nationality meant and what kind of citizens should be produced by their schools. (1997: 142, 143; cf. Marginson 1999: 27)

This transformation can also be periodized. The initial crisis in/of Fordism prompted a critique of education as failing to meet the needs of a changing economy and redefined labour market. This was associated with an increased emphasis on inculcating flexibility and adaptability as a short-term response to the vagaries of the business cycle and greater volatility in the labour market (Robins and Webster 1989). Flexibility and flexible learning were also linked to organizational change, especially with the rise of open and distance learning enabled by new ICTs and new methods of context-situated and problem-oriented teaching and learning. Later, there was a broader emphasis on the role of education in promoting the globalizing, knowledge-based economy through the development of human capital. This is linked to growing emphasis on the certification of transferable as well as specific skills in schools, post-compulsory education and on-the-job training. Training and lifelong learning are now a central component of economic as well as social policy in all advanced capitalist economies and are tied to the growing consensus that successful competition depends on building the knowledge base and human capital.

These trends are evident at all levels of education from schools through further and higher education to on-the-job training and career-linked lifelong learning and thence to 'universities of the third age' for older people. A cross-national survey of general discourses and proposals for educational reform has identified a new orthodoxy based on:

> (1) improving national economies by tightening the connection between schooling, employment, productivity, and trade; (2) enhancing student outcomes in employment-related skills and competencies; (3) attaining more direct control over curriculum content and assessment; (4) reducing the costs to government of education; and (5) increasing community input to education by more direct involvement in school decision-making and pressure of market choice. (Carter and O'Neill 1995, summarized by Ball 1998: 122)

Schools are now expected to enable children to become enterprising subjects and develop their personal skills and capacity for teamworking. They are also expected to provide the basis for the transition to work and to forge closer links with future employers. This is reflected in a proliferation of programmes to integrate education and work through more vocational training, partnerships, work experience, training credits, and so on. Linked to this is the extension of the new managerialism and audit culture into schools (as well as universities) with its emphasis on quasi-markets, internal cost centres, performativity, targets, benchmarking, staff appraisal, etc. (Clarke and Newman 1997; Power 1997).

The tightened connection between schooling, employment, productivity and trade is reflected in a cross-national reorientation of the notion of skill, with increasing emphasis on key skills, lifelong learning and employability, as technology, corporate restructuring and volatile markets are believed to have ended the Fordist fantasy of jobs for life (Lauder et al. 2001). Education has become integrated into the workfarist project that downgrades the Keynesian state's commitment to full employment and now emphasizes its contribution to creating conditions for full employability. Thus responsibility for becoming employable is devolved to individual members of the labour force, who should acquire the individual skills, competencies, flexibility, adaptability and personal dispositions to enable them to compete for jobs in national and global labour markets. They may be largely responsible for this as enterprising individuals investing in their own human capital or as equal citizens entitled to support from the state and social partners to improve their skills. In all cases there is increasing cooperation between colleges, universities and other learning providers and the world of work. Thus employers and practitioners are involved in curriculum development, managers are drawn into educational governance and agenda-setting, mobility between the academy and non-academic worlds is encouraged, and colleges and universities deliver lifelong learning through advanced professional programmes, continuing professional development, part-time, evening, and distance teaching, remedial and second-chance courses, and so on (Teichler 1999: 85).

Notwithstanding this cross-national policy discourse convergence, there are still marked differences in take-up and implementation. Lauder, et al. (2001) report, for example, that, where economies were dominated by a belief that the future lay in a post-industrial service economy, there was a polarization between education and training for high-skilled elites and for a flexible, low-skilled service sector. The latter sector also had relatively low investment and generated output more through long working hours than increasing productivity. Conversely, where manufacturing was still accorded a key role in accumulation strategies, the state emphasized intermediate skills and the need for education and training to link industry and services. This was coupled with high capital investment to harness skills for a high productivity economy. The USA and UK exemplify the first model; the second is illustrated by Germany.[7]

Turning more directly to further and higher education, there has been a great emphasis on shifting university teaching and research from its ivory-towered intellectual isolation back into continuous contact with the economy, the state and the community as vital co-producers and con-sumers of useful knowledge. This is especially clear in technology, the sciences and medicine, and has also penetrated the social sciences, so that it is not merely graduates but faculty members themselves who are expected to develop extensive links with users in industry, business, the professions, government and local communities. There is growing emphasis on external fund-raising, patenting, technology transfer, research parks, commercial spin-offs, science and technology parks, incubators, consultancy services – amounting to the emergence of a veritable 'academic capitalism' in liberal economies that encourages entrepreneurial universities and transforms faculty members into enterprising bearers of intellectual capital (Slaughter and Leslie 1997). This change was encouraged in the USA (the principal cheerleader for the knowledge-based economy) through changes in federal funding for research, enabling universities to keep the intellectual property in their discoveries, as well as through the more general extension of the scope and duration of intellectual property rights. Universities are also encouraged to commercialize their research. This was intended to encourage academic entrepreneurialism, to subsidize corporate R&D, and to facilitate regional economic development. Similar patterns can be found in other university systems.

Overall, in the words of Etzkowitz, a leading researcher on the 'triple helix' interface between university, business and the state:

> Virtually every country that has a university, whether it was founded for reasons of education or prestige, is now attempting to organize knowledge-based economic development. . . . As the university becomes more dependent upon industry and government, so have industry and government become more dependent upon the university. In the course of the 'second academic revolution' a new social contract is being drawn up between the university and the wider society, in which public funding for the university is made contingent upon a more direct contribution to the economy. (Etzkowitz 1994: 149, 151)

Two apparently contrary but complementary strategies are being adopted here. On the one hand, the state is asserting the importance of education in the realization of national economic interests; and, on the other hand, it is conceding greater autonomy to educational institutions in how they serve these interests (Marginson 1999). But this autonomy is being exercised in the context of the hegemony of the knowledge-based accumulation strategy, the increasing participation of the bearers of this strategy in the shaping of education mission statements and the increasing financial dependence of further and higher education on third-party revenues deriving neither from the state nor from students. The first strategy 'involves a reaffirmation of the state functions of education as a "public good", while the second subjects education to the disciplines of the market and the methods and values of business and redefines it as a competitive private good' (Marginson 1999: 122). Together, these strategies serve to reinforce the ecological dominance of accumulation over the educational system.

Again, there are different routes to this reconfiguration. In the USA, universities have long been encouraged to operate as business firms and to be entrepreneurial. Pressures in this direction have nonetheless been reinforced from the 1980s onwards with the result that many universities have reoriented their activities from teaching towards research to generate patents and royalties. Moreover, because they must still teach, this prompts them to cut costs and boost efficiency by standardizing and commoditizing education, casualizing and flexibilizing intellectual labour, and merchandizing on-line lecture courses. In Europe, the European Round Table is promoting a neoliberal agenda that sees education and training as 'strategic investments vital for the future success of industry' and has proposed measures to strengthen the comparatively weak influence of business on the curriculum and adapt it to the needs of industry through the development of private-public partnerships

(Levidow 2001). This is encouraged by the EU itself in the hope of increasing the international market share of EU education (European Union 1999).

6. Concluding Remarks

I now highlight six broad preliminary conclusions about the political economy of welfare restructuring – conclusions that will need to be revisited after I have considered the rescaling of economic and social policy and changes in its governance. First, state intervention in relation to social reproduction displays two major changes compared with the period of the KWNS: (1) the use of social policy to enhance the flexibility of labour markets and to create flexible, enterprising workers suited to a globalizing, knowledge-based economy; and (2) the redesign and reorganization of social policy to put downward pressure on the social wage, which is now regarded more as a cost of international production than as a source of domestic demand. The first tendency has been pursued fairly systematically, especially when the social wage is seen as an investment in the collective labourer, i.e., in a pool of skilled, knowledgeable and creative workers who can jointly contribute to the intellectual commons, rather than as an investment in individual human capital, where it is in individuals' rational self-interest to invest in education and training to maximize their future earnings. The second tendency has been limited by the material, institutional and political limits to retrenchment and, short of total privatization, which is largely confined to societies where a neoliberal regime shift has occurred, the emphasis has been on cost containment rather than radical cuts.

Second, there is significant variation in the emerging welfare–workfare mix and the forms in which it is delivered from case to case. In part, this reflects real path-dependent differences in political traditions and institutional structures that affect welfare regimes and in the resulting challenges that now face them. In part, it reflects the results of trial-and-error experimentation and/or the willingness of state managers to import policy models from other levels of an increasingly multi-tiered political system and/or from abroad. It also reflects, of course, different balances of forces. Nonetheless, it is worthwhile attempting to identify broad policy sets linked to different accumulation regimes and specify the policy mix associated with a given state.

Third, it would be premature to take the ascendancy and prevalence of neoliberalism in the early 1990s as evidence of the long-term reproducibility of neoliberal workfare. For this ascendancy reflected a specific conjuncture in which three different types of change – neoliberal system

Table 4.1   Forms of neoliberalism

Neoliberal policy adjustments	Modulation of policies to improve performance of an accumulation regime and mode of regulation
Neoliberal regime shift	Paradigm shift in accumulation and regulation, introducing new economic and political principles
Neoliberalism as radical system transformation	Neo-liberalism as strategy for moving from state socialism to capitalist social formation

transformation in post-socialist societies, the neoliberal regime shift in the anglophone democracies and neoliberal policy adjustments in 'modernizing' corporatist and statist regimes – combined to lend some credence to wild neoliberal triumphalist fantasies (see table 4.1). This conjuncture is already on the wane as a result of disillusion with the post-socialist experience and the short-term nature of policy adjustments in other regimes. Moreover, even during this highpoint of the neoliberal phase, there was a greater rupture in rhetoric than in practice. The contradictions of the neoliberal policy are now being exposed as they lose the protective and mystifying penumbra of other forms of neoliberalism. This is being reflected in the reversal of some elements of neoliberalism even in neoliberal regimes – although this does not eliminate the path-dependent legacies of neoliberal errors. In addition, the absence of concerted opposition to the most radical forms of neoliberal workfare is no guarantee of its overall functionality for the capitalist economy, as opposed to its efficacy in destabilizing political opposition to the overall neoliberal project. This is linked to the need to analyse the contradictory functions of the welfare state, since the need to balance different functions in a spatio-temporal fix limits the variations that are possible in the longer term. For the needs of capital in general reassert themselves through the contradictions and oscillations of economic and social policy as well as through the adjustment of corporate strategies.

Fourth, among the preconditions for reproducing a welfare/workfare regime is a specific institutional fix that resolves, within a given spatio-temporal fix, the contradictions and strategic dilemmas involved in regularizing capital as a social relation and managing its always problematic connections with the state and the wider political system. Whereas the primary scale of regulation in the KWNS was the national, there is a relativization of scale in the emerging SWPR – especially in its neoliberal guise. Indeed, so problematic is this, that it is unlikely that a pure neoliberal workfare regime could ever become 'stable'. At least two issues are at stake here. First, there are doubts about such a regime's capacity to institutionalize a 'scalar selectivity' in which resistance to workfare measures is marginalized from the core decision-making sites and becomes so fragmented and dispersed as to be largely ineffective. Even the absence of resistance does not as such guarantee success. Workfare involves more than simply making the poor work; it is also about making flexible labour markets work. The latter task requires coordinated action across different scales deploying a range of market and non-market measures. Second, despite its internal contradictions, neoliberal workfare threatens other approaches to workfare. Thus, as well as local resistance in the societies most committed to the neoliberal project, there is also national and supranational resistance to neoliberalism among states committed to other models as they try to avoid the regulatory race to the bottom linked to the neoliberal project.

Fifth, the neoliberal approach to workfare prioritizes just one moment of the contradictions and dilemmas associated with capital as a social relation (see chapter 1). It regards wages primarily as a cost of production and neglects the issue of demand. It regards labour-power primarily as one substitutable factor of production among others and neglects the critical role of labour-power as a source of added value and creativity. It regards money primarily from the viewpoint of international currency flows and neglects the continuing contributions that control over capital flows can play in economic management. It regards capital primarily in terms of mobile investment capital in a space of flows rather than as a set of concrete invested assets to be valorized in particular places. And it adopts a short-term mode of economic calculation to the detriment of longer-term aspects of the economy in its integral sense. Whereas the KWNS managed for some time to balance these different moments through a distinctive pattern of scalar coordination based on the national economy and national state, the neoliberal workfare regime finds it hard to reconcile these different moments on any scale. This is another illustration of neoliberalism's counterproductive nature in its attempts to destroy the institutional embeddedness and spatial-institutional fixes associated with the KWNS and in its optimistic belief in the spontaneous regenerative powers of disembedded market forces free to operate on a world scale. In particular, by dismantling key organizational and institutional supports of the KWNS, this approach denies its advocates access to potential flanking and complementary measures that could serve to stabilize a neoliberal regime. In the complex dialectic of 'conservation-dissolution effects', neoliberalism loses the opportunity to transform the functions of conserved organizations and institutions within the new logic of a market-driven approach. It is hardly surprising, therefore, that, outside the framework of social formations characterized by a neoliberal regime shift, there is far greater emphasis on redesigned forms of social partnership, a continuing role for the state in managing the new collective action problems involved in promoting capital accumulation and reconciling it with the demands of political legitimacy, and a greater concern to recalibrate existing institutions to deal with new problems rather than to believe that the market can solve them.

Sixth, and finally, in the search for a new spatial-institutional fix, neoliberals risk depriving themselves of an Archimedean point from which to coordinate the different scales of economic, social and political actions and to develop compensatory and flanking measures on other scales in response to changes pursued on other levels. This is already complicated by the relativization of scale, which makes the contradictions and dilemmas of an after-Fordist capitalism harder to manage because they are also more dispersed over time and space. In other economies, however, there is stronger commitment to a key role for the national state in this regard. This too is reflected in the limited diffusion of the neoliberal model beyond uncoordinated market economies and the continued importance, subject to conservation-dissolution effects, of older welfare regime and production patterns.

5

The Political Economy of State Rescaling

The continuing restructuring of the capitalist type of state can also be related to the overall primacy of the national scale in the era of Atlantic Fordism and the current relativization of scale associated with the after-Fordist period.[1] The absence of any primary scale on which the structured coherence of capital accumulation and social reproduction can currently be secured explains the continued crisis-tendencies of the capitalist societies in which the welfare state was embedded. It is also reflected in controversies and struggles around other scales of economic, political and social organization; and attempts to establish appropriate forms of governance for these scales in all their tangled complexity. This chapter argues that a postnational order is emerging that is more explicitly multiscalar, multicentric and multitemporal than the postwar Atlantic Fordist regime. Particular attention is paid to the resurgence of entrepreneurial cities and regions, the development of supranational triadic regimes, the growth of cross-border regions, the attempt to develop multilevel governance and the claim that a global (or at least western) state is emerging. In examining the predominantly neoliberal form of this postnational order on a global scale, I also discuss the illogic of globalization in its neoliberal form. I relate this to the continuing search for a new scale on which the postnational order could be reregularized and new economic and social problems resolved. I conclude that a central political role remains for the national state and note how this differs from that in the period of Atlantic Fordism.

Table 5.1 Typology of imagined political communities linked to nation-states

Type of nation	Simple national community	Basis of community membership	Multiplex form of community	Form taken by nation when decomposed
Volksnation	Ethnos	Blood ties or naturalization	Multiethnic	'Melting-pot society'
Kulturnation	Shared culture	Assimilation, acculturation	Multicultural	Postmodern play of identities
Staatsnation	Constitutional patriotism	Test of political loyalty	Nested political loyalties to multi-tiered government	'Dual state' in given territory or transnational diasporas

1. The National State

We must distinguish between the nation-state and the national state in order to avoid the confusions that arise from references to the nation-state in general work on the future of the state. First, 'territorial delimitation antedated the policy of nation-formation, and the latter, as a blanket principle, has as yet not been fully realized, whereas the principle of territorial statehood has established itself world-wide' (Brock and Albert 1996: 6). Second, as Benedict Anderson (1991) has argued, the nation is an 'imagined community'. It emerges from the mutual recognition of large numbers of persons unknown to each other on the basis of supposedly shared attributes that qualify them for membership of the same nation and, it should be added, that distinguish them from other persons who are thereby excluded from such membership. These shared attributes may establish the imagined identity of a *Volksnation* in an ethnonational state (for example, Germany) and there are many routes to such ethnic nationhood and self-determination (Balibar 1990; Brubaker 1992; Gellner 1993; MacLaughlin 2001). But there are also stable (and unstable) territorial states with two or more ethnic nations (so-called multinational states).

In addition to ethnic nationhood, there are at least two other forms of nationhood that are linked to state formation and have proved compatible with the existence of more than one ethnic group or nation within a national state (see table 5.1). These are a cultural nation (*Kulturnation*), based on a shared national culture that may well be defined and actively promoted by the state itself (for example, France); and a civic nation (*Staatsnation*), based on patriotic commitment to the constitution and belief in the legitimacy of representative government (for example, the USA). These three forms of nationhood can reinforce each other (for example, Denmark), be combined to produce relatively stable hybrid forms of national state (for example, mainland Britain) or provoke conflicts over the proper basis of the nation-state (for example, Canada, New Zealand). Pressures may also develop to grant significant autonomy to regionally based national minorities within the existing territorial boundaries of a national state (for example, Spain, mainland Britain) or to establish 'consociational' forms of government in which different nations are guaranteed adequate (or even proportional) representation in the exercise of state power (for example, Belgium, New Zealand). Even in stable cases, however, nationhood provides the basis for displacing contradictions and institutionalizing social exclusion within the boundaries of a spatio-temporal fix organized around the national state as well as beyond its territorial boundaries (cf. Tölölyan 1991).[2] Of particular importance here are the multiform patterns of gendering nations and 'racializing' national differences.

Regardless of their corresponding form of nationhood and the extent to which this has proved stable or conflictual, the states of interest in this study can all be described as national states – that is, as formally sovereign territorial states presiding over 'national' territories. Moreover, insofar as they were included in the primary circuits of Atlantic Fordism, they can also be characterized as Keynesian welfare national states. In this regard, they were all subject to similar pressures for change as a result of the emerging dynamic of globalization and regionalization in different functional domains. Thus, concentrating solely on the future of ethnically based nation-states (whenever they developed) or, alternatively, treating all national states as if they were ethnically based nation-states would divert attention from the more general and important issue of the future of postwar national states, ethnonational or not. It is this issue that concerns us here. Forms of nationhood could then be introduced later as a secondary variable when attention turned to more detailed analyses of the institutional legacies and path-shaping possibilities of specific production and/or welfare regimes.

2. Crisis in the National Character of the KWNS

I now show how the features of the KWNS, as noted in chapter 2, came to be (seen as) crisis-prone in the late 1960s and 1970s. As the distinctiveness of the KWNS as a particular type of state often went unrecognized, however, these crises and crisis-tendencies were often attributed to a generic modern or capitalist state. After noting the crisis-tendencies associated with each of its features, I indicate how they were sometimes condensed into a more fundamental organic crisis affecting the KWNS as a whole.

1   The centrality of the sovereign state itself was called into question with the development of allegedly overloaded 'big government', which led to a legitimacy crisis as the state no longer seemed able to guarantee full employment and economic growth, and to an emerging fisco-financial crisis that threatened to undermine the welfare state. These crisis-tendencies were aggravated by growing conflicts between local states and central government, and by the crisis of the international regimes organized under American hegemony, such that they were less able to secure the conditions for effective economic and political performance by national states. The crisis of the postwar international regimes organized under American hegemony also undermined their capacity to facilitate the effective economic and political performance of national states. More generally, the various forms of national state were challenged by increasing migration, especially into the core national states of Atlantic Fordism. This has affected all three forms of nationhood. First, it has contributed to declining ethnic homogeneity, as inward migration from other ethnic communities led to multiethnic or 'melting-pot' societies and/or as outward migration created durable transnational diasporas. Second, cultural homogeneity has declined because of a growing plurality of ethnic and cultural groups, leading to informal or even official multiculturalism (especially in large cities) and/or to the rise of spaces and places for a postmodern play of social identities. And, third, civic commitment to the national state may decline either through the development of multi-tiered political loyalties to units above and below the national state or through identification with transnational social movements.

2   The legitimacy of the national state has also declined to the extent that it is seen to disappoint the economic and social expectations generated by Atlantic Fordism and the KWNS. Furthermore it has failed to mobilize support for alternative accumulation strategies, state projects or hegemonic visions. It became harder to achieve such official national economic objectives as full employment, stable prices, economic growth and a manageable balance of payments. This contributed to a loss of the national economy's taken-for-grantedness as the primary object of economic management. This was sometimes associated with a resurgence of protectionism to defend the national

economy (or, at least, so-called 'sunset' sectors and their associated jobs) and/or with attempts to establish a wider economic space within which the expanded reproduction of accumulation could be renewed. The latter attempts could occur through formal political means (such as the European Community and European Union) or through more open economic borders.

3   Regional and local economies were increasingly recognized to have their own specific problems that could not be resolved either through national macroeconomic policies or through uniformly imposed meso- or microeconomic policies. This prompted demands for specifically tailored and targeted urban and regional policies to be implemented from below.

4   There was a growing contradiction in the field of social reproduction with encouragement to those who wanted to immigrate for economic purposes being accompanied by an increasing concern in the policing of the boundaries of national citizenship and its associated welfare rights. While the core European states of Atlantic Fordism had previously been seen largely as countries of emigration and/or, in the wake of postwar decolonization, the return of nationals to their homelands, in the 1970s immigration was construed as a threat to national cohesion, full employment and the welfare state (Bieling 1993; cf. Kofman 1995; Leitner 1995; Soysal 1994; see also Joppke 1998). Indeed, 'migration illustrates both the logically closed character of the welfare state and the difficulty with which that closure is maintained' (Freeman 1986: 63; cf. Kearney 1991). Additional destabilizing demographic factors were the decline of the stable two-parent family, the feminization of the paid labour force and long-term unemployment.

5   There was a crisis of forms of political representation that were based on 'governing parties', 'business unionism' and capitalist associations. This was evident in growing electoral volatility and disaffection with the major parties and, in some quarters, in militant rejection of the terms of the postwar capital–labour compromise. New social movements also developed to challenge the industrial logic of Atlantic Fordism and the statist logic of Keynesian welfarism in favour of alternative forms of economic and political organization and an antibureaucratic, autonomous, politicized civil society (cf. Offe 1985b; Hirsch and Roth 1986).

6   The 'national-popular' dimension of hegemonic struggles shifted away from expanding prosperity and welfare rights towards a more nationalist, populist and authoritarian discourse and/or towards a more cosmopolitan, neoliberal demand for 'more market, less state' in a more open economy. Whilst both these latter trends continue,

the hegemony of Keynesian welfarism has been superseded by hegemonic struggles around how best to enhance competitiveness as the route to prosperity.

The overall effect of these changes was to erode the KWNS and, in the worst cases, to produce an *organic crisis* of this type of state (on this concept, see Gramsci 1971; Poulantzas 1974a). There are several symptoms of an organic crisis. These include a progressive loss of state unity, declining effectiveness, representational crises and a legitimacy crisis. The loss of state unity was reflected in the declining structural and operational coherence among different branches, apparatuses and tiers of government in securing the state activities tied to specific accumulation strategies, state projects and hegemonic projects. In other words, there was an *internal disarticulation* (institutional crisis) of state apparatuses in terms of their vertical coherence across different organizational levels and their capacity to engage in horizontal coordination of different domains of activity. This was associated with *declining effectiveness* in attaining declared state objectives linked to the prevailing economic, political and hegemonic projects. A further consequence in cases of organic crisis was the disorganization and strategic disorientation of the power bloc (or 'establishment') and its associated state managers and/or the decomposition of the social bases of support for the state and its projects. This could lead in turn to a *representational crisis* of the state in regard both to its broad 'national-popular' social basis – reflected in growing volatility or even absolute loss of support for the governing political parties and other mainstream mass organizations – and to the growing instability or even disintegration of institutionalized compromise in the establishment. Another manifestation of crisis was the state's *legitimation crisis*, that is, a loss of faith in this particular type of state's claims to political legitimacy, including, notably, its claim to be able to deliver economic growth and generalized prosperity (for a comparison of the organic crisis of the British state that led to Thatcherism with the more limited economic and political crises in West Germany in the 1970s and 1980s and the more limited German *Wende*, or 'turn', see Jessop 1989).

3. The Political Economy of Scale

The effects of this crisis in the national state for the changing forms and functions of economic and social policy have been discussed in the last two chapters. This chapter is concerned with the rescaling of the postwar national state and its contribution to the restructuring and strategic reorientation of state intervention. Analyses of the political economy of scale concern the strategic selectivity of the interscalar division of labour and attempts to shape this selectivity in particular ways. It has major implications for the manner and extent to which contradictions and dilemmas can be displaced and deferred in specific spatio-temporal fixes. A useful approach in this regard is suggested by Swyngedouw, who argues that scale is:

> the arena and moment, both discursively and materially, where socio-spatial power relations are contested and compromises are negotiated and regulated. Scale, therefore, is both the result and the outcome of social struggle for power and control . . . [By implication] theoretical and political priority . . . never resides in a particular geographical scale, but rather *in the process* through which particular scales become (re)constituted. (1997: 140–1; emphasis added)

In the 'thirty glorious years' of postwar economic growth in Atlantic Fordism, the dominant scale was the national. It was primarily on this scale that socio-spatial power relations were contested and compromises were negotiated and regulated. This occurred within the framework of international regimes that reinforced national states while local states acted as relays or micro-level adjustment mechanisms for policies determined at national level. National economies were the taken-for-granted objects of economic management in Atlantic Fordism, the trading nations of East Asia and those Latin American economies pursuing import-substitution strategies. This taken-for-grantedness actually depended on quite specific material and ideological foundations that could not be taken for granted themselves. The naturalization of the structural congruence (or spatio-temporal coincidence) of national economies, national states and national societies was grounded in postwar reconstruction in Europe, in the national security state in East Asia and in critiques of dependency in Latin America. In each case, this national framework was supported by various (typically asymmetrical) international regimes and alliances that had to be put in place. Reproduction of these forms of structured complementarity depended in turn on the trial-and-error discovery of forms of economic management, regularization and governance that could provide a spatio-temporal fix within which to resolve at least partially capitalism's contradictions and dilemmas.

Nonetheless, as the contradictory dynamic of accumulation and its resulting conflicts and struggles always tend to escape attempts to fix them within any given spatio-temporally anchored institutional framework, all such solutions are unstable and provisional. This is particularly evident in the case of the national scale that predominated in the organization of postwar economic expansion. For this has since been undermined in many different ways, including the various multiscalar, multitemporal processes that contribute to globalization.

The relativization of scale

The decreasing structured coherence among national economy, national state and national society that characterized the heyday of the postwar boom has relativized scale. For, although the national scale has lost the taken-for-granted primacy it held in postwar Atlantic Fordist regimes, no other scale of economic and political organization (whether the global or local, urban or triadic) has yet acquired a similar primacy in the current phase of the after-Fordist period. There is no new privileged scale around which other levels are now being organized to ensure structured coherence within and across scales. Instead, there are continuing struggles over which spatial scale should become primary and how scales should be articulated, and this is reflected in a more complex nesting and interweaving of different scales as they become rearticulated (Amin and Robins 1990; Boyer and Hollingsworth 1997; Collinge 1996, 1999). Indeed, views of naturalness seem to have branched from the national towards the global economy, the triad economies and different types of subnational or cross-border economy, without the national having disappeared from view. This can be seen in the rediscovery of 'always-already-there' local, urban and regional economies as sites and objects of economic and political intervention as well as in the development of new discourses about the emerging significance of the global as the natural scale of economic and political organization. Arguments about triads are also sometimes presented as if they are a natural development and extension of the regional scale and/or the product of natural fusion among economically interdependent nations. Subsequent material and social developments have complicated this position, moreover, with the emergence of cyberspace as a virtual arena of action that appears to be everywhere and nowhere.[3] For cyberspace provides both a means to escape from the fetters and frictions of territorial borders into a functional space and a means to connect territories and localities in new ways (see chapter 3).

The new political economy of scale does not involve a pregiven set of places, spaces or scales that are merely being reordered. Instead, new places are emerging, new spaces are being created, new scales of organization are being developed and new horizons of action are being imagined – all in the light of new forms of (understanding) competition and competitiveness. In particular, the global, about which we hear so much today, is only one of many scales on which attempts to restabilize capitalism are being imagined and pursued. Indeed, globalization, whether viewed from a structural or strategic viewpoint, is often linked closely and in complex ways to processes on other spatial scales. It is best seen as part of a proliferation of scales and temporalities as narrated, institutionalized objects of action, regularization and governance. The number of scales and temporalities of action that can be distinguished is immense[4] but far fewer ever get explicitly institutionalized. How far this happens depends on the prevailing technologies of power – material, social and spatio-temporal – that enable the identification and institutionalization of specific scales of action and temporalities. It is the development of new logistical means (of distantiation, compression, communication), organizational technologies, institutions with new spatio-temporal horizons of action, broader institutional architectures, new global standards (including world time) and modes of governance that helps to explain this proliferation of economically and politically significant institutionalized scales and temporalities.

Moreover, as new scales emerge and/or existing scales gain in institutional thickness, social forces also tend to develop mechanisms to link or coordinate them. This generates increasing complexity as different scales of action come to be linked in various hybrid combinations of vertical, horizontal, diagonal, centripetal, centrifugal and vortical ways. This complexity cannot be captured in terms of simple contrasts, such as global–national or global–local, or catch-all hybrid concepts such as glocalization or the transversal. Instead, there is a proliferation of discursively constituted and institutionally materialized and embedded spatial scales (whether terrestrial, territorial or telematic), which are related in increasingly complex tangled hierarchies rather than being simply nested one within the other, with different temporalities as well as spatialities.

This means, among other effects, that there is a greater eccentricity of spatial scales relative to the early and boom years of Atlantic Fordism.[5] Larger territorial units have come to contain a decreasing proportion of the economic, political and social linkages of smaller units in their borders compared to the heyday of Atlantic Fordism. This means that smaller units can no longer be so readily regarded as nested within the former like Russian dolls. This is particularly clear in the emerging network of global cities, which, as a network, is not contained within any given state-regulated territorial space. This contrasts with the nineteenth century when world cities functioned mainly as the capital cities of empires and state-organized plurinational trading blocs (Hall 1998; Knox and Taylor 1995). Another example of the eccentricity of new spaces is the growth of cross-border regions, many of which are deliberately promoted by their respective national states or, in the case of the European Union, a supranational political body (for further discussion of cross-border regions from this perspective, see Jessop 2002d). In addition, there are processes of debordering, that is, 'changes resulting in the emergence of new political spaces that transcend territorially defined spaces without leading to new territorial demarcations (in other words, to a simple shift in borders)' (Brock and Albert 1995: 171). In short, past scalar fixes, as well as past spatial fixes, are decomposing under economic and political pressure and being actively reworked through a wide range of often-conflictual scalar strategies.

The present relativization of scale clearly involves very different opportunities and threats for economic, political, and social forces compared to the period when the national scale was constructed and taken for granted as primary. It is associated with actions both to exploit and resist the processes producing globalization. While the world market and the triads have become the most significant *spaces of competition*, however, the most important *spaces of competitiveness* are more often national, regional or local (Brenner 2000: 321). In other words, whereas the capitalist law of value increasingly operates on a global scale, subjecting all economic and economically relevant activities to the audit of the world market, the pursuit of place-specific competitive advantages by firms, states and other actors is still rooted in local, regional or national specificities. This shapes the forms of competition and strategies to build competitiveness (see chapter 3 and pp. 187–93). It also shapes the forms in which economic, political and social forces more generally seek to protect themselves from global competition and the most feasible strategies to this end. The following paragraphs comment briefly on the range of different scales *below the level of the global* on which the search for new spatio-temporal fixes for accumulation and regulation is being pursued. I discuss the global level later as an effect of different scalar strategies as well as an object of governance in its own right.

Triad power

As the global economic hierarchy is redefined, we find increased emphasis on three supranational growth poles that exclude significant areas of the globe. These are based on the regional hegemonies or, at least, dominance of the USA, Germany and Japan respectively and are reflected in the creation of the North American Free Trade Agreement (and more recent efforts to extend it into Latin America on a hemispheric basis), attempts to widen and deepen a 'European Economic Space' that extends beyond the current borders of the European Union, and recent efforts to develop a regional financial as well as regional production system in East Asia. Each of these supranational or triadic growth poles has its own spatial and scalar divisions of labour and its own associated tangled hierarchies of space and place. There is already a material basis to these triadic developments, of course, with a growing intensity of intrabloc trade (most marked in the European Union but also growing in the other two triads), a further deepening of the inter-regional division of labour within each bloc, and attempts to develop appropriate forms of governance. This development may eventually come to provide a new scale on which to seek to reregularize capital accumulation and construct a new spatio-temporal fix that will limit the disruptive impact of neoliberal forms of globalization. This is most likely to occur in the short- to medium-term in the European Union. For the triads more generally to become the complementary nodal points of a reregularization of the continuing global–local disorder, however, the dominance of neoliberalism in two of the three triads (America and, to a lesser extent, Europe) and the political paralysis of the Japanese state in the third triad must be reversed.

Recent celebration of triads should not blind us to three other impor-tant tendencies: (1) the growing interpenetration of the triads themselves as efforts are made to develop and deepen their overall complementar-ities and as multinationals headquartered in one triad form strategic alliances with partners in others; (2) shifts in the spatial hierarchies within each triad due to uneven development – reflected not only in shifts among 'national economies' but also in the rise and fall of regions, new forms of 'north–south' divide, and so forth; and (3) the re-emergence of regional and local economies within some national economies or, in some cases, cross-cutting national borders – whether such resurgence is part of the overall globalization process and/or develops in reaction to it. All of these changes have their own material and/or strategic bases and thus contribute to the complex ongoing rearticulation of global–regional–national–local economies.

Regional blocs and cross-border regions

In addition to the triadic macroregions, two of which are emerging within the economic space previously dominated by Atlantic Fordism, there are proposals for other kinds of regional blocs or systems that fragment, transcend or cross-cut national space. Some theorists explain these alternative proposals as rooted in 'natural economic territories' (NETs), which have been allowed to re-emerge or develop with the decline of the national state as an economic as well as political power container. It is certainly remarkable how older, cross-border trading blocs and link-ages have re-emerged after the Iron Curtain collapsed in 1989–90. But NETs have been discursively naturalized as well as economically and politically constructed. Whether any given space is seen as natural or not depends, for example, on views about the dominant modes of economic competition and the various economic and extra-economic factors that might promote systemic or structural competitiveness. Thus, as we saw in chapter 3, a Ricardian interpretation (based on factor-driven growth in open economies) would lead one to identify different NETs and economic strategies from those implied in a Listian account (based on protectionist catch-up investment dynamics promoted by a national state concerned with its economic and politico-military security). Likewise, a Keynesian reading (based on securing the interdependent conditions for mass production economies of scale and mass consumption) would imply different NETs and economic strategies from a Schumpeterian one (based on securing the conditions for systemic competitiveness and permanent innovation).

The erosion of the relative closure of Atlantic Fordism, the end of the Cold War, the decomposition of the Soviet Bloc and the 'opening' of China to foreign capital have reinforced the relativization of scale and created space for new economic and political strategies on the part of firms and states alike. These changes are reflected in a proliferation of scales on which attempts are now being made to restructure economic, political and social relations – ranging from economic globalization, global governance and global culture to the promotion of local economies, neighbourhood democracy and 'tribal' identities. At one extreme is whole-hearted adoption of free trade and the unconditional integration of economic spaces as quickly as possible into the world economy. Historically, advocacy of free trade is associated with economically dominant powers, that is, powers that have a lead in new technologies, a predominant role in production and trade, and control of a hegemonic or master currency. It is not usually willingly embraced in weak economies, however, where free trade is likely to generate declining economic coherence or disintegration of the economy and its subordination to external influences – whether through growing technological dependence, import penetration at the expense of local enterprise (with little chance to adjust structurally), currency depreciation and inflation in cases where the currency floats, or else recession, in cases where the national currency is pegged to a stronger one (such as the US dollar). Nonetheless, elements of this neoliberal strategy were initially advocated in several post-socialist economies (reinforced, of course, by neoliberally inclined international agencies, the USA and Thatcherite Britain); they are also included in the conditionalities attached to structural adjustment programmes proposed by the World Bank for crisis-ridden African and Latin American economies; and they have also been recommended for several of the post-crisis economies in East Asia (again encouraged by the usual international suspects). On more local scales, neoliberalism is also evident in the massive expansion of free economic zones, open market enclaves, free trade zones, and so forth.

Second, at the opposite end of the spectrum, the crisis of national economies has been associated with various plans for protectionism, if not autarky. Such plans involve selective, if not complete, withdrawal from the world economy to develop a strong national economic base before being exposed to international competition. This approach is sometimes linked to infant industry-style arguments and/or referred to the import substitution phase of several East Asian NICs' growth trajectories before they turned to export-led development. It is also linked occasionally to geostrategic and security considerations (again as in the South Korean or Taiwanese cases). But a full-blown autarkic strategy is difficult where economies depend on imported raw materials, have foreign debts, or are already integrated into the international division of labour.

Third, building on the process of triad formation, there are attempts by other economies to extend and deepen their links to the neighbouring triad bloc. For example, integration into the EU or the European Free Trade Association was the most popular initial option among several Eastern and Central European economies, especially given the collapse in the Soviet-era Comecon bloc after 1989 (Bakos 1993). With due caution about the financial costs and economic impact on sensitive sectors, this strategy of enlargement has also been promoted by the leading EU economies for various economic and/or geopolitical reasons. This is reflected in a number of programmes to promote cross-border linkages and cooperation among non-contiguous regions, cities or localities. The same general strategy is found in East Asia. This has been articulated most clearly in Japan's so-called 'flying geese strategy' – that is, integration of first-, second- and third-tier East Asian NICs into a regional division of labour under Japanese hegemony. This strategy not only involves a new regional division of labour but also Japanese attempts to export its distinctive system of labour relations (Woodiwiss 1998) and to promote complementary forms of Ricardian workfare regime (Esping-Andersen 1997; Jones 1993; Kwon 1997). The increasingly complex forms of regional and cross-border integration in the American hemisphere, especially regarding the various nested and/or eccentric hierarchies of local and regional economies in Latin America, also provide a rich field of study here (Grugel and Hout 1999; Hettne et al. 2000; Schulz et al. 2001; Vellinga 2000).

Fourth, and conversely, there are proposals to establish neo-mercantilist trading blocs. This is well illustrated in the idea of resurrecting Comecon as a multilateral macroeconomic organization in the form of a Customs Union with common external customs regulations and/or a Central European Payments Union that would clear trade imbalances on a bi- or multilateral basis (Andreff and Andreff 1995; Smyslov 1992). On a lesser but still supranational scale, there were proposals for local economic integration among subsets of the former post-socialist economies. The best-known case (and one initially backed by western capitalist forces) aimed to establish a Central European Free Trade Association involving Hungary, Poland and Czechoslovakia, but it has been overshadowed by their candidacy for the European Union. Analogous proposals have been put forward for a yen-trading bloc in East Asia as a basis for deepening the regional division of labour, reducing overdependence on the American market (and, indeed, the US dollar), providing a space within which Confucian capitalism and/or Asian values can be consolidated in the face of a neoliberal offensive, and a means of reducing future exposure to volatile global forces (Frankel 1994; Gong 1999; Sum 2001; Vellinga 2000).

Fifth, there are various international proposals for cooperation between post-socialist and capitalist economies to create new regional economic formations. They include: (1) a Black Sea Economic Cooperation Project; (2) the Economic Cooperation Organization in Central Asia; (3) Baltic Sea cooperation; (4) a resurrected Danubian Confederation; and (5) the 'Japan Sea' Rim Economic Zone. Such proposals are intended to build on a history of regional exchanges, growing economic ties and the complementary strengths of different partners; and they also have a variety of geopolitical, ethnic, religious, cultural and other bases, which vary from case to case. The increased US role since the attacks on the World Trade Center and the Pentagon in the southern Turkic republics of the former Soviet Union provides a further illustration of this option.

Sixth, various cross-border regional partnerships have been proposed to link more than two subnational economies into new regional entities in the hope of deepening existing complementarities. These include proposals for post-socialist Europe and for EU/non-EU linkages (such as Interreg Greece, Interreg Viadrina, Interreg Italy-Slovenia, and many others) (see European Communities 1994, 2001; Perkmann 2000); and, again, outside the European sphere, in the Mutankiang delta, involving Siberia and the Far Eastern republics of the CIS, provinces in north-eastern China and North Korea, with Japanese backing (cf. European Communities 1992). In addition, there are virtual regions comprising economic networks connecting non-contiguous regions and/or cities. The most famous of these is the Four Motors Region in Europe that links four non-contiguous high-growth regions: namely, Baden-Württemberg, Rhône-Alpes, Lombardy and Catalonia; but there are several other such regions and/or formally organized European urban networks (Camhis and Fox 1992; Interreg 2001; Scott 2001; Vellinga 2000).

Cities

A further scale of action that is emerging (or, more accurately, re-emerging in new forms) also cuts across conventional geoeconomic and geopolitical hierarchies. This is the urban scale. There are three significant changes occurring here: (1) the vast expansion of the size and scale of leading cities within urban hierarchies so that they become larger metropolitan or regional entities with several centres (on extended metropolitan regions and urban corridors in Pacific Asia, see Forbes 1997); (2) an increasing structural integration and strategic orientation of cities' activities beyond national space – an orientation that creates potential conflicts with the national state as some cities become potential 'regional states' less oriented to their respective national hinterlands than to their ties with cities and economic spaces abroad (witness the increasing use of the 'gateway', 'hub' and 'network' metaphors); and, paradoxically, (3) the growing role of some leading cities (rather than, as hitherto, specific firms or sectors) as state-sponsored and state-protected national champions in the face of intensifying international competition.

Harding has defined the content of these entrepreneurial policies as involving growing concern with:

> the state of the local economy; the fortunes of locally-based businesses; the potential for attracting new companies and/or promoting growth within indigenous firms; the promotion of job-creation and training measures in response to growing urban unemployment; the modernization of the infrastructures and assets of urban regions (communications, cultural institutions, higher educational strengths and capacities) to attract investment and visitors and support existing economic activities; and the need to limit further suburbanization, retain population (particularly middle-to-upper income families) and workplaces and create compact, livable cities. (1995: 27)

Storper's analysis of the reflexive city claims that uncertainty and risk are changing in a period when market forces and the extra-economic environment for economic actors are becoming more turbulent, more influenced by the strategic calculation of other actors, and more open to influence on a wide range of spatial scales. But not all entrepreneurial cities target the same forms of competitiveness. In some cases policy innovations involve little more than attempts to secure largely static comparative advantages by attracting inward investment from mobile capital at the expense of other places through such measures as tax breaks, subsidies and regulatory undercutting and/or simple, civic boosterist image-building. In other cases, cities and regions introduce economic, political and social innovations to enhance productivity and other conditions affecting the structural and/or systemic competitiveness of both local and mobile capital. This would be reinforced to the extent that they possess a socially dense, institutionally thick space for economic reflexivity and the flexible pooling of risks and uncertainties in an increasingly turbulent national, regional and global environment (cf. Storper 1997; Veltz 1996).

Alliance strategies

These complexities point to the potential for alliance strategies among states on similar or different regional scales (for example, the EU, whether as an intergovernmental organization of nation-states or a 'Europe of the regions') to secure the basis for economic and political survival as the imperatives of structural competitiveness on a global scale make themselves felt. Other forms of protectionism have been proposed or organized on different scales as past regional and local modes of growth are disrupted (ranging from 'Fortress Europe' to 'new localisms', from the São Paulo Forum or the People's Plan for the Twenty-First Century to the informal economic self-organization of shanty towns). Nonetheless, in general terms, as noted by Mittelman, '[r]egionalism in the 1990s is not to be considered as a movement toward territorially based autarkies as it was during the 1930s. Rather, it represents con-centration of political and economic power competing in the global economy, with multiple interregional and intraregional flows' (1996: 190; see also Keating 1998).

4. Scales of Competition

The preceding analysis suggests that competition occurs not only be-tween economic actors (for example, firms, strategic alliances, networks) but also between political entities representing spaces and places (for example, cities, regions, nations, triads). It is justified to treat cities, regions and nations as 'units' or 'subjects' of competition insofar as com-petitiveness depends on extra-economic as well as economic conditions, capacities and competences. For this means that competition is mediated by more than pure market forces and raises the question whether the conditions of successful competition for a city, region or nation are analogous to those for a single firm. Can cities, regions or nations achieve competitiveness in similar ways to firms, and, if not, do they at least pursue economic competitiveness in the same way as each other? The answer clearly depends on how broadly one interprets competition, competitiveness and capacities for action (on nations, see IMD 2001; Porter 1990; Porter et al. 2000; Warr 1994; on cities and city-regions, see Brenner 2000; Ohmae 1991, 1995; Porter 1995; Scott 1998, 2001; Storper 1997). Competition is mediated through the invisible hand of the market and would occur whether or not actors explicitly oriented their economic activities to enhancing their competitiveness. In this sense, market forces allocate such activities among places and spaces whether or not attempts occur to attract (or repel) economic activities at levels above individual market agents. Cities, regions and nations can also compete on a more explicit, strategic and reflexive level, however, in developing and pursuing plans and projects to attract investment and jobs and to enhance their performance in competition with other places and spaces. If these competitive strategies are explicit and capable of being pursued, then it is clear that cities, regions and nations really are 'entrepreneurial' actors and are not just describing themselves as such. I now want to argue that an important distinguishing feature of post-Fordism, when compared with Fordism, is the increasing significance of the reflexive pursuit of entrepreneurial strategies by non-economic actors.

Drawing on Schumpeter's analysis of entrepreneurship (see chapter 3), it can be suggested that there are five fields of innovation that can be pursued by scalar actors on behalf of localities, cities, regions, nations or triadic blocs:[6]

1 The introduction of new types of place or space for living, working, producing, servicing, consuming, etc. Examples include multicultural cities, cities organized around integrated transport and sustainable development, and cross-border regional hubs or gateways.
2 New methods of space- or place-production to create location-specific advantages for producing goods/services or other urban activities. Examples include new physical, social and cybernetic infrastructures, promoting agglomeration economies, technopoles, regulatory undercutting and reskilling.
3 Opening new markets – whether by place-marketing specific localities, cities or regions in new areas and/or modifying the spatial division of consumption through enhancing the quality of life for residents, commuters or visitors (for example, culture, entertainment, spectacles, new cityscapes, gay quarters, gentrification).
4 Finding new sources of supply to enhance competitive advantages. Examples include new sources or patterns of immigration, changing the cultural mix of cities, finding new sources of funding from the central state (or, in the EU, European funds) or reskilling the workforce.

5 Refiguring or redefining local, urban or regional hierarchies and/or
   altering the place of a given economic space within them. Examples
   include the development of a world or global city position, regional
   gateways, cross-border regions and 'virtual regions' based on interregional cooperation among non-contiguous spaces.

There are obvious dangers in trivializing entrepreneurial activities by
reducing them to routine activities that are directly economic or economically relevant; and in treating an entrepreneurial self-image or
mere place-marketing as evidence of Schumpeterian entrepreneurship.
Some places may simply be administering or managing an existing
business-friendly climate efficiently rather than being actively engaged
in innovation. That this may suffice to maintain certain extra-economic
conditions for capital accumulation does not mean that a place is
entrepreneurial. Nor does routine place-marketing make a city, region,
nation or triad entrepreneurial. What is really essential, from a structural
viewpoint, is that an 'entrepreneurial' locality has institutional and
organizational features that can sustain a flow of innovations. What is
involved here is a spatialized complex of institutions, norms, conventions, networks, organizations, procedures and modes of economic and
social calculation that encourage entrepreneurship. Viewed strategically, an 'entrepreneurial' locality is one that has developed the capacity to act entrepreneurially. It may then itself directly target one or more
of the five fields of innovation as an economic entrepreneur in its own
right and/or actively promote institutional and organizational conditions favourable to economic entrepreneurship on the part of other
forces. These forces may include all manner of local, locally dependent
and interested outside parties who support a given entrepreneurial
endeavour.
   With the increasing interest in dynamic competitive advantages
and the bases of structural and/or systemic competitiveness, the extra-
economic features of places and spaces have come to be increasingly
significant in the design and pursuit of entrepreneurial strategies. Thus,
so-called natural economic factor endowments become less important
(despite the path-dependent aspects of the positioning of places in urban
hierarchies); and socially constructed, socially regularized and socially
embedded factors become more important for competitiveness. Entrepreneurial cities (or other localities), therefore, must not only position
themselves economically but also in the extra-economic spheres that are
so important nowadays to effective structural or systemic competition.
We can refer to 'glurbanization' here as a trend analogous to 'glocalization' (see table 5.2). While the latter term refers to firms' strategies to
build global advantage by exploiting local differences, the former refers

Table 5.2   Glurbanization vs glocalization

	Glurbanization	*Glocalization*
Strategic actors	Cities (perhaps as national champions)	Firms (perhaps in strategic alliances)
Strategies	Place- and space-based strategies	Firm- or sector-based strategies
New scales of activities and temporalities	Create local differences to capture flows and embed mobile capital	Develop new forms of scalar and/or spatial division of labour
Chronotopic governance	Rearticulate time and space for structural or system competitive advantages	Rearticulate global and local for dynamic competitive advantages

Source: Jessop and Sum 2000

to a local, regional or national state's strategies to build global advantage by restructuring urban spaces to enhance their international competitiveness. This may also reproduce local differences and/or ubiquities that enable MNCs to pursue their own 'glocalization' strategies. Analogous strategies can be found on other scales, such as the subregional and cross-border.

There are strong as well as weak forms of glurbanization strategies. Whereas the former are typical of the leading cities or regions in urban and regional hierarchies, the latter are more often pursued by 'ordinary cities' and 'ordinary regions' (Amin and Graham 1997). Strategies differ in at least three respects: their respective concepts and discourses of competitiveness, the spatial horizons over which they are meant to operate and their association with different local contexts and positions in prevailing scalar hierarchies. What they share is the key role of political authorities in their overall framing and promulgation. At the level of cities and regions we can distinguish seven main options:[7]

1   The first option is to widen or deepen the scalar division of labour within an integrated, vertically nested set of scales. This involves pursuit of some form of 'structured complementarity' by building favourable linkages to the wider economy in an expanding set of wider scales of economic and political action. Such strategies may be promoted from above and/or emerge from below. Discursively, this is reflected in attempts 'to position places centrally on "stages" of

various spatial scales: regional, national, international, global' (Hall and Hubbard 1996: 163–4). Practically, it generally involves promoting economic development on any given scale by exploiting growth dynamics at progressively ascending spatial scales from the local through the regional and national to the supranational.

2   The second option is to build horizontal linkages on the same scale within an integrated, vertically nested set of scales. There is a wide range of such strategies ranging from the local to the triadic scale. Many cross-border regions exemplify this strategy, as do translocal alliances and virtual regions. The latter are developed to link non-contiguous locales with shared or complementary interests – such as the cooperation among the so-called European Four Motors Region, comprising Baden-Württemberg, Rhône-Alpes, Lombardy and Catalonia, each of which is a dynamic city-region associated with a major non-capital city. In general, this strategy builds on common territorial interests and identities and seeks to exploit joint or complementary resources and capacities. The aim is either to develop a critical mass through simple agglomeration economies or to develop a division of labour at the same scale rather than across scales. This horizontal strategy could be developed locally from below and/or be promoted by bodies on lower and/or higher tiers or scales. Thus cross-border regions in Europe are promoted by local communes as well as the European Union.

3   The third option involves building what one might call 'transversal' linkages – that is, bypassing one or more immediately neighbouring scale(s) to seek closer integration with processes on various other scales. This is especially significant where foreign direct investment (FDI) and production for export are involved, with the result that links to an immediate hinterland or even the national economy may prove far less important than the connection between local and supranational scales. Some cross-border regions in Asia are good examples of this strategy – namely, growth triangles and growth polygons (Parsonage 1992; Smith 1997; Thant et al. 1998). Other examples include export-processing zones, free ports and regional gateways – although these tend to be located within one national territory and to be oriented outwards (cf. Chen 1995 on the evolution of cross-national growth zones; Ohmae 1995 on contemporary region states).

4   Resource procurement is another economic development strategy that is common in weak or marginal localities, such as inner cities, declining industrial or coastal regions, and so on. This is an understandable response in inner cities, for example, which suffer from urban deprivation, poor housing, a weak fiscal base, a lack of land for

property development schemes and political and institutional fragmentation. Local authorities in Europe may turn to the EU for funds (for example, the various structural funds); and in multi-tier federal states, they may turn to the federal authority as well as to states. However, successful bids under a resource-procurement strategy typically come with strings attached. This constrains the range of economic initiatives that can be pursued and threatens the coherence of an overall economic development plan (Hay 1994).

5 Localities may also pursue place-marketing via regulatory undercutting, international 'beauty contests' for inward investment and international 'ugly sister contests' for structural funds and other restructuring or compensatory funds for declining regions. The two obvious targets for such activities are mobile capital and funding agencies; central states often aid and abet local and regional authorities in pursuing inward investment and restructuring funds. Regulatory undercutting is a counterproductive strategy, however, for generating jobs in areas of economic decline and can promote a regulatory race to the bottom. Strong competitive strategies are generally far better from this viewpoint, but even their resulting competitive advantages can be competed away (see chapter 3).

6 A sixth option is to seek an escape from scalar or place-bound constraints by locating one's activities in a borderless space of flows or moving into 'cyberspace'. But this does not obviate the need for some sort of spatial fix (offshore islands, tax havens, etc.) (see Hudson 2000; Leyshon and Thrift 1999; Palan 1998).

7 A seventh option is a partial or complete decoupling of a given scale from the wider division of labour and world market and is most likely to be linked with anti-capitalist economic, political and societalization projects (see chapter 1).

An important aspect of most of these different spatial scale strategies is their concern to limit competition within the region (structured coherence) through market-oriented cooperation as the basis of more effective competition beyond the relevant spatial scale. The spatial scale on which these compromises will be struck is shaped in part by the nature of commodity chains and economic clusters, by associated spatial externalities (including district, proximity and synergy aspects of agglomeration economies) and by the existing forms of social embeddedness of economic relations and learning processes (Camagni 1995; Messner 1998; cf. Porter 1990; Smith 1988).

The existence of such entrepreneurial projects is no guarantee, of course, that real economic spaces with 'structured coherence' and sustainable competitive advantages will be consolidated. There are many difficulties in launching and consolidating entrepreneurial strategies not only because of the inherent uncertainty of competition as a continuing process, but also because of the difficulties of economic and extra-economic coordination within the economic spaces identified as the objects of entrepreneurial strategies. Nor is there any reason to expect that all the factors needed for a successful regional or local strategy will be found within the borders of the economic space that provides its primary location.

5. Trends in the State

Changes in the state's role in capital accumulation and social reproduction involve changes in the formal articulation and operational autonomy of national states. This is sometimes discussed in terms of the decline of the national state in the face of globalization. But this is highly misleading. For we are not witnessing a *singular emergent globalizing flow-based economy* evolving in a zero-sum relationship with a *plurality of traditional national territorial states*. To adopt such a view would involve treating the current, partly globalization-induced crisis of the territorial national state – whether in its postwar Atlantic Fordist form, developmental statist, national security state, or other forms – as signifying the present and future impossibility of any other institutional form(s) for the territorialization of political power. Instead, the approach developed here suggests that attempts will be made to reconstitute the national territorial state in response to globalization and/or to establish new territorial scales as dominant and/or nodal points in the institutionalization of political power. This expectation is reinforced if we note that the Westphalian state was never as rigid or as complete as 'the fetishization of space in the service of the [national] state' might suggest (Lefebvre 1978; cf. 1991: 280–2; cf. Osiander 2001). Moreover, once we accept that the delimitation of the state as an institutional ensemble is both internal to the political system and contingent, we can also assess whether non-territorialized forms of government-governance might acquire increased significance in the exercise of political power. These points are reinforced when we recall the constitutive incompleteness of the capitalist economy and its dependence on extra-economic factors. For this suggests that economic globalization will require significant shifts in the institutional forms, principal activities, and primary scales in and through which its extra-economic supports are secured.

To consider the scope for de- and re-territorialization of forms of state power and/or for the substitution of non-territorial forms of political power, we must reconsider the alleged challenge to national states posed by globalization. The scope for increased ecological dominance of the globalizing economy depends on the capacities of leading economic forces to distantiate and/or compress time–space in ways that escape the control capacities of most state-based and state-oriented political forces. For there are few, if any, individual states with an effective global reach and an ability to compress their routines to match the time–space of fast hypermobile capital. This creates a growing disjunction between the latter's spatio-temporal horizons and routines and those of most con-temporary states and, through their impact on the overall dynamic of the capitalist economy, a growing disjunction between a potentially global space of flows and the place-boundedness of a territorially segmented political system. Temporally, this limits the typical state's ability to react according to its own routines and modes of calculation – which is why many state managers feel the pressures of globalization and believe they have lost operational autonomy. Likewise, spatially, given the porosity of borders to many different kinds of flow and the growing mobility of capital over a range of transnational scales, states find it increasingly hard, should they want to, to contain economic, political and social processes within their borders or control flows across these borders. These changes are related in turn to a growing fragmentation of the Westphalian state system to the extent, indeed, that some commentators suggest it is being replaced by a neo-medieval system (e.g., Anderson 1996; Cerny 2000; Ruggie 1993). However, while there are observable trends towards fragmentation in relation to specific fields, this does not necessarily challenge the more general role of the national state as a crucial nodal point within interscalar articulation (see pp. 201–2).

It is nonetheless quite clear that the changes associated with the glob-alizing knowledge-based economy do have major repercussions on forms of representation, intervention, internal hierarchies, social bases and state projects across all levels of state organization. In part, this involves major changes in relations on the same organizational level. For example, apart from shifts in the relative power of the executive, legis-lature and judiciary, there are also shifts in the relative weight of finan-cial, educational, technological, environmental, social security and other organs. But reorganization also extends to the reordering of relations among different political tiers, the articulation of government and gov-ernance and the rebordering of political systems. These aspects of reor-ganization can be summarized in terms of three sets of changes or broad trends in the organization of the state and politics. Each broad trend is also associated with a countertrend that both qualifies and transforms its significance for political class domination and accumulation and, more specifically, for the form of the state and its economic and social policies. These countertrends can be interpreted in the first instance as specific reactions to the new trends rather than survivals of earlier patterns. This is why they are better seen as countertrends to the trends, rather than vice versa. Thus, I first present the trends and then discuss their respective countertrends.

Before moving on to this discussion of trends and countertrends, however, it is necessary to caution against treating states as if they were identical units. For the formal sovereignty accorded to national territorial states in the Westphalian system does not imply any substantive identity or equality among them in terms of their capacities for exercising power internally and/or internationally. They will be presented with different problems by the multiscalar, multitemporal, multicentric processes that generate globalization; and they will have different capacities to address these problems and reorganize themselves in response. Moreover, whereas the form-determined condensation of forces in some states leads state managers to resist globalization, other states are clearly heavily committed to promoting it in one form or another. I have already commented above on different scalar strategies in this regard and will not repeat these comments. Suffice to say that leading states are associated with different globalization projects and that less powerful states will often seek to position their economic spaces and actors more favourably within more specific local, regional or functional niches within the emerging global division of labour. In so doing, some states will reinforce their hegemony or dominance within the inter-state system, others will fall further down the inter-state hierarchy. In particular, after worries were expressed about its declining hegemony in the wake of the crisis of Atlantic Fordism, the USA has clearly gained in global influence in recent years through its identification with and promotion of globalization in its own image.

The denationalization of the state

The first trend is the denationalization of the state (or, better, statehood). This is reflected empirically in the 'hollowing out' of the national state apparatus with old and new state capacities being reorganized territorially and functionally on supranational, national, subnational and translocal levels as attempts are made by state managers on different territorial scales to enhance their respective operational autonomies and strategic capacities. Thus some of the particular technical-economic, more narrowly political and ideological functions of the national state are being relocated to panregionally, plurinationally or internationally scaled state or intergovernmental bodies; others are devolved to the regional or local level inside the national state; and yet others are undertaken by emerging horizontal networks of power – regional and/or local – which bypass

central states and link regions or localities in several societies and may give rise to the development of so-called 'intermestic'[8] (or interlocal but transnationalized) policy-making regimes. The sideways shift involves relatively autonomous cross-national alliances among local states with complementary interests and is particularly associated with the Europeanization of local government and associated forms of partnership (Andersen and Eliassen 2001; Benington 1995, Benington and Harvey 1994; Jönsson et al. 2000; Keil 1998; Tömmel 1992, 1994, 1998).

First, the role of supranational state systems is expanding. Such international, transnational and panregional bodies are not new in themselves: they have a long history. What is significant today is the sheer increase in their number, the growth in their territorial scope and their acquisition of important new functions. This reflects the steady emergence of a world society rooted in a growing number of global functional systems (economic, scientific, legal, political, military, etc.) and in wider recognition of the global reach of old and new risks. One of the major areas for this functional expansion is the concern of supranational bodies with structural or systemic competitiveness within the territories that they seek to govern. This goes well beyond concern with managing international monetary relations, foreign investment or trade to encompass a wide range of supply-side factors, both economic and extra-economic in nature.

The upwards shift is particularly associated with the delegation of powers to supranational bodies and the resurgence of a reinvigorated and relatively unchallenged American 'superstate' with revitalized capacities to project its power on a global scale (Shaw 2000). As we shall see below, this creates a tension between unicity and particularism in these supranational bodies, with the USA above all oscillating between attempts to unify such bodies under its hegemony and attempts to use them to impose its currently prevailing perception of its own immediate interests. The same upwards shift, on a lesser scale and with different dynamics, is also reflected in the EU. Hooghe and Marks, updating calculations by Schmitter, show that there was an increase in the transfer of powers upwards to the EU level in twenty-eight different policy areas between 1950 and 2000. This has been most marked in the field of economic policy, followed by international relations and external security/economic policy. It is least marked in social and industrial policy, with legal-constitutional policy also scoring relatively low on this measure (Hooghe and Marks 2001: 47–8; cf. Wessels 2000; see also section 8 below).

Such movements do not, however, amount to the rise of a 'global state' – at least if the concept of the state is to retain its core meaning of the territorialization of a centralized political authority – such that a global state would become equivalent to a single 'world state'. Normally, what one finds, as Poulantzas (1974b, 1975) remarks, is a partial and conditional delegation of such functions in order to improve economic policy coordination across different states as part and parcel of each national state's new responsibilities for managing the process of internationalization. Moreover, even were a world state to be established, it would inevitably be subject to a tension between its juridico-political claim to unicity (sovereignty) and the harsh reality of plurality (particularistic competition among states on other scales for influence in its counsels and deliberately selective implementation of its decisions). This tension between unicity and plurality is precisely what we find in the European case, which is further complicated by its multi-tiered character. It is for this reason that interstate politics on a global scale is often marked by the international hegemony of a national state that seeks to develop a hegemonic political strategy for the global system – with that hegemony armoured, of course, by various forms of sanction and resting on a complex articulation of governmental powers and other forms of governance. This is evident in the postwar period in the changing forms of the continuing hegemony of the USA within the capitalist bloc and applies with particular force following the end of the Second Cold War, when the USA became the sole superpower and began to extend its influence into the former Soviet bloc and the Soviet sphere of influence. Even in this later period, however, we must be careful to distinguish the extent to which the American writ shapes different policy fields (contrasting military policy, for example, with social policy). More generally, the tension between unicity and pluralism is also evident in the growing disputes between US multilateralism and unilateralism respectively in a wide range of international regimes.

Second, in tandem with the rise of international state apparatuses, we find a stronger role for regional and/or local states. During the Fordist era, local states operated as extensions of the KWNS and regional policy was mainly oriented to (re)locating industry in the interests of spreading full employment and reducing inflationary pressures that had arisen as a result of localized overheating. Such states provided local infrastructure to support Fordist mass production, promoted collective consumption and local welfare state policies and, in some cases (especially as the crisis of Fordism unfolded), engaged in competitive subsidies to attract new jobs or prevent the loss of established jobs. In the wake of the Fordist crisis, however, local economic activities involve greater emphasis on economic regeneration and competitiveness. The central concern has become how state institutions can improve the competitiveness of regional and local economies in the emerging world economy. There is growing interest in regional labour market policies, education and training, technology transfer, local venture capital, innovation centres, science parks, and so on (see chapter 3). The declining ineffectiveness and legitimacy of the national state in the face of Fordist crisis had already led in the late 1970s to enhanced roles for regional and local states as new activities were adopted both to compensate for the crisis and to seek new ways out (Moulaert et al. 1988; van Hoogstraten 1983). This is even clearer today. Indeed, as national and international states retreat from some key economic functions, we find more interventionist policies at the regional, urban and local levels (Brenner 1998, 1999b, 2000; Gough and Eisenschitz 1996) as well as an increasing resort by capital itself to networking and other forms of partnership to secure these requirements. This transfer of powers downwards is not confined to economic intervention but affects a wide range of other policy areas. For example, Hooghe and Marks (2001) report that no EU member state has become more centralized after 1980 and that many have decentralized authority to a regional tier of government.

Third, closely connected to the first two changes, there are growing links among local states. This trend is reinforced by the central state's inability to pursue sufficiently differentiated and sensitive programmes to tackle the specific problems of particular localities. It therefore devolves such tasks to local states and provides the latter with general support and resources. Indeed, 'one of the most interesting political developments since the 1970s has been the erratic but gradual shift of ever more local authorities from an identification of their role in purely national terms towards a new interest in transnational relationships' (Dyson 1989: 1). In Europe this involves both vertical links with EU institutions, especially the European Commission, and direct links among local and regional authorities in member states. The search for cross-border support is strengthened to the extent that the central state pursues a more neoliberal strategy, but it can be found in other countries too (Jönsson et al. 2000; Perkmann and Sum 2002). Similar trends are discernible in East Asia (notably in links between Hong Kong, Macao and Guangdong, and in the so-called growth triangle formed by Singapore, Johore and Riau). This third trend is also developing in North America, with striking examples in the expansion of transborder cooperation of linked cities along the US–Mexican boundary, the promotion of Cascadia as a multistate/province cross-border region involving a corridor in the Northwest American coast stretching from Vancouver to Seattle and Portland, and a more general integration of cities and regions along the US–Canadian border (Blatter 2001; Sparkes 2002). This general phenomenon has led Duchacek (1990) to talk of the spread of 'perforated sovereignty' as nations become more open to transsovereign contacts at both local and regional level.

The destatization of the political system

There is also a trend towards the destatization of the political system. While denationalization concerns the territorial dispersion of the national state's activities (hence de- and reterritorialization), destatization involves redrawing the public–private divide, reallocating tasks, and rearticulating the relationship between organizations and tasks across this divide on whatever territorial scale(s) the state in question acts. In other words, some of the particular technical-economic, narrowly political and ideological functions previously or newly performed by states (on any level) have been transferred entirely to, or shared with, other (that is, parastatal, non-governmental, private or commercial) actors, institutional arrangements or regimes. At stake here is the increased importance of quite varied forms (and levels) of partnership between official, parastatal and NGOs in managing economic and social relations in which the state is often only first among equals. This leads to a blurring of the division between public and private, to conscious deployment of the principle of subsidiarity, to an increased role for the informal sector as well as private enterprise (especially in the delivery of welfare and collective consumption) and to increased reliance on mechanisms such as 'regulated self-regulation' and officially approved 'private interest government' (Streeck and Schmitter 1985). It is also linked to the state's growing involvement in decentred societal guidance strategies rather than the exercise of its sovereign powers of centralized imperative coordination (Matzner 1994; Willke 1992). In this sense it involves growing recognition of interdependence, the division of knowledge, and the need for mutual learning, reflexivity and negotiated coordination. This trend occurs on various territorial scales and across various functional domains and has often been summarized as the shift from government to governance (see chapter 6).

Governments have always relied on other agencies to aid them in realizing state objectives or projecting state power beyond the formal state apparatus. There is nothing new about parallel power networks that cross-cut and unify the state apparatus and connect it to other social forces. But this reliance has been reordered and increased. The relative weight of governance has increased on all levels – including not only at the supranational and local or regional levels but also in the transterritorial and interlocal fields. This need not entail a loss in the power of government, however, as if power were a zero-sum resource rather than a social relation. Thus resort to governance could enhance the state's capacity to project its influence and secure its objectives by mobilizing knowledge and power resources from influential non-governmental partners or stakeholders. Moreover, in the light of shifts in the balance of class forces, the turn to governance could also be part of a more complex power struggle to protect key decisions from popular-democratic control (cf. Poulantzas 1978) and/or to socialize risks in favour of private capital.

This strategic reorientation from govern*ment* to govern*ance* is especially noticeable in the case of the EU and is reflected in a common concept that captures both this and the preceding trend, namely, multi-level governance. It is difficulties in European state-building as much as changes in the European economy that have prompted this reorientation. Thus the current development of supranational European governance involves far more than the emergence of a federal, confederal or intergovernmental apparatus. It also involves the active constitution of other supranationally organized and/or oriented economic and social partners – whether functional or territorial – and their integration into loosely coupled, flexible policy-making networks through specific communication, negotiation and decision-making channels (see Tömmel 1994: 14). Indeed, 'the European Commission places a major emphasis on the formation of networks as a means of encouraging the achievement of the difficult goal of European integration and . . . cohesion' (Cooke and Morgan 1993: 554). Especially interesting here is the commitment to multi-tiered networks involving both territorial and functional actors.

The same trend towards governance is found on the national, regional-local and translocal (or 'intermestic') levels. Having made the case in general terms and illustrated it from the European level, however, I simply refer to the large literature on regional and local governance and its role in promoting the 'joint product' of endogenous economic development based on enhanced structural competitiveness (see also pp. 189–90 on cities). The strengthening of local and regional governance is linked with the reorganization of the local state as new forms of local partnership emerge to guide and promote the development of local resources. For example, local unions, local chambers of commerce, local venture capital, local education bodies, local research centres and local states may enter into arrangements to regenerate the local economy.

The internationalization of policy regimes

A third trend in the organization of the state and politics is a complex one that leans towards the internationalization of policy regimes. The international context of domestic state action (whether national, regional or local) has expanded to include a widening range of extraterritorial or transnational factors and processes; and it has also become more significant strategically for domestic policy. The key players in policy regimes have also expanded to include foreign agents and institutions as sources of policy ideas, policy design and implementation (cf. Gourevitch 1978;

Doern et al. 1996). This trend is reflected in economic and social policies as the state becomes more concerned with international competitiveness in the widest sense. And it affects local and regional states below the national level as well as the development of supranational state formations and the development of international regimes. It is also evident in the development of the interregional and cross-border linkages connecting local and regional authorities and governance regimes in different national formations. Finally, this trend is reflected in a new field of enquiry that

> embraces not only the advice offered to national governments by supranational agencies, but also the capacity of those agencies to regulate economic activity in the interests of social protection; to redistribute resources from one country to another to achieve welfare objectives; and, in certain cases, to provide for social needs at a supranational level. (Deacon and Hulse 1997: 44)

While Deacon and Hulse refer only to the field of social policy, the same arguments also obtain for many other policy fields.

6. Countertrends in the State

These trends have been deliberately presented in a one-sided and undialectical manner. This involves more than a simple reference to what Poulantzas described as the complex 'conservation-dissolution' effects associated with successive stages in the development of capitalism. Such effects certainly exist insofar as past forms and functions of the state are conserved and/or dissolved as the state is transformed. The tendential emergence of the SWPR, for example, is linked with varying 'conservation-dissolution' effects on the KWNS across different spheres of state intervention as well as across different national societies (see pp. 255–9). We have already noted several of these effects in previous chapters. But let me now briefly present these countertrends (see box 5.1).

Countering the denationalization of statehood are the attempts of national states to retain control over the articulation of different spatial scales. Whilst it might be thought that there is a simple continuity of function in this regard, I would argue that a major discontinuity has been introduced through the current relativization of scale. Nonetheless, in the absence of a supranational state with equivalent powers to those of the national state, the denationalization of statehood is linked to attempts on the part of national states to reclaim power by managing the relationship among different scales of economic and political organization. Thus loss of autonomy engenders both the need for supranational

Box 5.1   *Trends and countertrends in state restructuring*

Trends
- denationalization of the state;
- destatization of politics;
- internationalization of policy regimes.

Countertrends
- increased scope for state in interscalar articulation;
- increased role for state in metagovernance;
- contesting the forms and implementation of international regimes.

coordination and the space for subnational resurgence, but it also extends thereby the scope for the national state itself to mediate between the increasing number of significant supra- and the subnational scales of action. In this context, using a distinction introduced by Collinge (1999) between dominant and nodal scales of organization, we can say that, while supranational institutions may have become more comprehensive and inclusive in the range of activities that they undertake and/or seek to influence, and while an increasing range of state activities may be delegated downwards and/or sideways, any tendency towards increasing *dominance* of the supranational level need not detract from the *nodal* role of the national state in the expanding web of state powers. In short, while the national state may have lost some formal sovereignty, it could well retain a key role in interscalar articulation.

Countering the shift towards governance is government's increased role in metagovernance. This is especially evident in the operation of the EU and in attempts to overcome decision traps and institutional gridlock owing to disagreements between member states. This indicates the extent to which governance operates in the shadow of government. Governments (on various scales) are becoming more involved in organizing the self-organization of partnerships, networks and governance regimes (on metagovernance, see chapter 6). This should not be confused with the survival of state sovereignty as the highest instance of government nor with the emergence of some form of 'megapartnership' to which all other partnerships are somehow subordinated. Instead, it involves a shift from the top-down hierarchical political organization characteristic of sovereign states to an emphasis on steering multiple agencies, institutions and systems that are both operationally autonomous from one another and structurally coupled through various forms of reciprocal interdependence. It falls to the state to facilitate collective learning about functional linkages and material interdependencies among different sites and spheres of action. And it falls to politicians – local as well as national – to participate in developing the shared visions that can link complementary forms of governance and maximize their effectiveness. Such tasks are conducted by states not only in terms of their contribution to particular state functions, but also in terms of their implications for political class domination and social cohesion.

The tendential shift from government to governance need not weaken the state apparatus as a whole or undermine its capacity to pursue specific state projects. Much will depend on the ways in which new governance mechanisms are linked to the pursuit of changed state goals in new contexts and to the state's capacities to project its power into the wider society. This is reflected ideologically in the neoliberal claim that an overextended state is a weak state – which implies that only by confining its activities to those which the state apparatus alone can (and must) do can it be sure to perform even these effectively. In both respects it is important to resist the idealistic and erroneous impression that expansion of non-governmental regimes implies that the state is no longer necessary. Indeed, the state retains an important role precisely because of the development of such regimes. For it is not only an important actor in many individual governance mechanisms, but also retains responsibility for their oversight in the light of the overall balance of class forces and the maintenance of social cohesion.

Somewhat ambiguously countering yet reinforcing the internationalization of policy regimes is the growing importance of national states in struggles to shape the development of international policy regimes and the manner in which they operate in the interests of their respective national capitals and electorates. This needs recognizing because of the extent to which the national state previously managed the insertion of national economic space into the wider economy. Nonetheless, one should not minimize the real discontinuities in the state's current concerns for the structural competitiveness of nationally based capitals at home and abroad that are due to the new forms of regionalization-globalization. Indeed, small open economies in this plurinational system were committed to maintaining the structured coherence of their national economies despite their dependence on exports. They appeared to have managed their national economies and secured the unity of the power bloc and people despite levels of internationalization that would now be said to imply a loss of sovereignty. This suggests that the power of the national state in the face of internationalization depends critically on the cohesion of the political establishment or power bloc. This said, state power in this regard will also be shaped, of course, by the dynamics of economic hegemony, economic domination and ecological dominance noted in chapter 1.

This brief general discussion of the three trends and countertrends has disregarded their individual and combined realization from case to case. Thus, my comments on denationalization ignore important differences between federal states, with clear constitutional powers allotted to national and regional levels of state organization, and unitary states, such as Britain, where the local state exercises only such powers as are currently required or permitted by the central state. Similarly, in dealing with the shift from government to governance, I neglect the extent to which some KWNS regimes had tripartite macroeconomic governance based on state, business and unions and/or adopted forms of regulated self-regulation for delivering social welfare. Nonetheless I maintain that, here too, the role of governance has been strengthened at the same time as the range of partners has changed (see chapter 6). Nor do I consider the differential importance of various governance mechanisms (for example, the contrast between the strengthening of the neocorporatist 'negotiated economy' in Denmark and the rise of neoliberal parastatal organizations in Britain). Finally, in dealing with internationalization, I ignore differences among SWPRs, the extent to which they can be described as 'postnational', their combination in specific cases, and the extent to which different states are more or less hegemonic and/or dominant in defining international policy regimes. Obviously more detailed studies of the restructuring and reorientation of the national state would need to look at each trend in more concrete and complex terms. It should be evident too that, if each of these three trends can vary, the manner and extent of their interaction must be even more varied. This said, it is important to consider all three trends in their interaction rather than to focus on just one or consider each in isolation.

7. Rescaling and the KWNS: The Case of Europe

Each of these trends is reflected in the restructuring of the KWNS. Thus economic and social policies are now increasingly defined and pursued at several levels rather than being primarily shaped by the national state (witness the social as well as the economic dimension of the EU, the importance of regional policies, and transnational cooperation); there is an increased emphasis on public-private partnerships, care in the community, self-help, cooperation, etc.; and there is an intensified international struggle to shape welfare regimes (see the activities of the OECD, EU, World Bank, IMF, WTO, etc., as well as international charities and philanthropic organizations). This argument can be illustrated from the

EU as the currently most advanced form of multilevel state formation and/or multilevel governance.

First, it is quite clear that the EU's overall economic policy has been reoriented in the direction of a Schumpeterian competition strategy from an earlier period when it was more suited to Atlantic Fordism. The origins of European integration can be found in postwar reconstruction that prepared the ground for Atlantic Fordism in Europe (for details, see van der Pijl 1984). Thus, in addition to their initial postwar role in restructuring iron, steel and coal in this context, the European communities also emphasized the creation of an integrated market so that industrial enterprises could realize optimal economies of scale. This involved an essentially liberal *Ordnungspolitik* to create a single market and was an important supplement to the pursuit of national Keynesian policies – especially as the Treaty of Rome left official responsibility for employment policy at the national level. Indeed, as Sbragia notes, the EU's basic constitutional framework structurally privileges liberal economic strategies: 'the norm of economic liberalization, embedded in the Treaty of Rome, was reinforced and elaborated in the Single European Act and the Treaty of Maastricht' (2000: 224). Thus even when the EU, under Delors' presidency (1985–95), began to develop a more active employment policy and to plan for a Social Europe and then attempted to institutionalize these twin responsibilities for the first time in the Maastricht Treaty (1991), this occurred in an institutional context that was already biased in favour of liberalism and in an ideological climate that was dominated by neoliberalism (see pp. 168–9).

It is worth noting here that the six initial members of the EEC – as it was then called – had modes of growth and modes of regulation belonging to one or other of the regulated or coordinated varieties of capitalism and either had one or other form of conservative-corporativist welfare regime or, in Italy's case, had a clientelist Mediterranean welfare regime (cf. Hantrais 2000; Ruigrok and van Tulder 1996). This suggests that the institutionalized commitment to economic liberalism might initially have provided the basis for the integration and consolidation of regulated capitalism on a wider scale rather than serve as the means to push through a far-reaching liberal programme. The situation changed, however, as new members with different modes of growth, modes of regulation and welfare regimes joined the European Community. This introduced greater economic and social heterogeneity into the European economy and helped to shift the balance of forces in a neoliberal direction. It has been correspondingly more difficult to establish the conditions for rescaling state planning from the national to the European level or to establish Euro-corporatism (on Euro-corporatism, see Falkner 1998 and Vobruba 1995; on its limits, Streeck 1995). Likewise, rather than seeing a rescaling of the welfare state upwards to the EU, social policy within the Union largely takes the form of social regulation. For, as Majone notes:

> [M]easures proposed by the Commission in the social field must be compatible with the 'economic constitution' of the Community, that is, with the principle of a liberal economic order. This requirement creates an ideological climate quite unlike that which made possible the development of the welfare state in the Member States. . . . The economic liberalism that pervades the Founding Treaty and its subsequent revisions gives priority to the allocation of public policy over distributional objectives. Hence the best rationale for social initiatives at Community level is one that stresses the efficiency-improving aspects of the proposed measures. (1993: 156)

These difficulties have been reinforced through the manner in which the European Monetary Union (EMU) has been instituted. The convergence criteria established under the Maastricht Treaty have made it more difficult for member states to break out of the neoliberal framework, and the limited EU budget prevents it from financing a major expansion of a European welfare regime. Indeed, in certain respects, the EMU serves as a new 'gold standard', requiring conformity to relatively rigid norms of economic and political conduct favourable to a liberal (money) conception of economic stability and growth. In particular, compliance with the Maastricht criteria has required public spending cuts or constraints, social security and welfare reforms, and more or less significant privatization of state-owned enterprises and commercialization of public services. Nonetheless, even in this context, we can discern a growing concern with active involvement in promoting competitiveness, innovation and enterprise in line with Schumpeterian perspectives. Although the main thrust of this involvement accords well with neoliberal strategy, it is nonetheless flanked by neostatist and neocorporatist strategies, illustrated by key features of EU technology policies and social policy respectively (see pp. 261–3). A very interesting development in this area is, of course, the resurgence of corporatism in a new guise – social pacts oriented to wage restraint, social security reform, supply-side competitiveness and general conformity to the logic of the new monetary system (see Deppe et al. 2000; Regini 2000; Grote and Schmitter 1999; Rhodes 1998; see also chapter 6).

Second, welfare and social policy was retained as a national competence in the founding treaties of the EC, and policy-making at the European level in these fields has systematically lagged behind macroeconomic, industrial and technology policies. Thus, as Kuhnle, notes, '[t]here exists as of today no European social law on the basis of which individual citizens can claim benefits from Brussels; no direct taxation or social contributions to the EU which can finance social welfare; and there hardly exists any welfare bureaucracy in the EU' (Kuhnle 1999: 6). Nonetheless, there is increasing evidence of a complex and complicated reorientation of welfare policy at the European level. This involves two apparently contradictory tendencies. On the one hand, some welfare policies (such as equal pay, equal opportunities, portable welfare benefits, minimum standards for health and security at work and rules on working hours) have been gradually rescaled to the EU level to supplement the more traditional nationally scaled welfare measures; and some structural policies have also been rescaled at a European level to facilitate industrial restructuring, compensate for uneven regional development, support agriculture and help to regenerate declining communities. On the other hand, the emergence of social policy at the European level tends to assume a workfare rather than a welfare orientation. Thus 'the political point of reference [of such economic and social policy initiatives] is not so much social integration but rather the instrumentalization of policy as a resource for competition oriented structural change' (Deppe et al. 2000: 20). In short, there is a growing mix of welfare and workfare strategies at the European level; but they are unified around the concern to create the conditions for an effective single market in post-Fordist rather than Fordist conditions.

One of the earliest signs of this reorientation can be found in the European Commission's White Paper, *Growth, Competitiveness, Employment* (1993). This reviewed a wide range of factors affecting the competitiveness of the European economy and its capacity to generate good jobs and sustainable economic growth; and it recommended an equally wide range of trans-European macroeconomic, environmental, infrastructural, technological, educational, vocational and social policy initiatives that might address – rhetorically at least – the challenges of the coming century. In the field of labour market policy, for example, the Commission called for a broad 'advanced training offensive' and other measures to enhance labour market flexibility. This reorientation was taken further at the 1994 EU summit in Essen, when it was finally recognized that effective employment policies conducted exclusively at the national level could no longer be successfully managed under the conditions of globalization and European integration (Hoffman and Hoffman 1997: 22). The Treaty of Amsterdam finally embedded a commitment to full employment as a 'matter of common concern' for the EU, translated this into the goal of reaching a 'high level of employment' without undermining competitiveness and established an Employment Committee to discuss appropriate policy in this area and to monitor progress. In line with the EU penchant for metagovernance rather than direct top-down intervention, however, the Union's responsibility in this area is to complement the activities of member states by developing a 'coordinated strategy', to formulate common guidelines, to establish benchmarks and 'best practice' and to monitor the pursuit of national action plans for employment.

Examining the emerging practice in this area since 1999 to the time of writing reveals both the extent to which the workfarist reorientation of social policy has penetrated to the EU level and also how far it is linked with the expansion of the domain of the 'economic' into areas previously regarded as non-economic. One aspect of this, as noted by Deppe et al. (2000: 15–16), is that, for the first time, the breadth of the EU labour market guidelines has forced the ministries of economy, culture, finance, welfare and labour to present a joint plan and to relate the separate policies to each other. This can be interpreted as the extension of the logic of commodification or, at least, of capitalist economic calculation into the wider society. Such pressures are also incremental, building up ratchet-fashion, with each successive cycle of national employment pacts.

Third, almost by definition, European economic and social policy illustrate the postnational nature of the emerging welfare regimes. Before considering the EU's role, however, we should note that it is itself part of a more complex internationalization of economic and social policy. Its policies are evolving within a broader framework of growing involvement in agenda-setting and policy-making by international institutions, supranational apparatuses, intergovernmental organizations and forums, transnational think-tanks, and transnational interest groups and social movements (cf. Deacon 1996; on policy transfer, see Dolowitz and Marsh 1996; Peck and Theodore 2001; and Stella 2000). It is important to recognize, with Deacon (1996: 45–58), that there is some real disagreement among these different bodies on policy recommendations; but this should not be exaggerated, since the bodies aligned with the 'Washington consensus' have tended to be the most influential in the internationalization of economic and social policy. Thus Deacon and Hulse (1997: 47) note some convergence between EU and OECD policies as the EU has discovered the adverse impact on competitiveness of KWNS social policy and the OECD's Directorate of Education, Employment, Labour and Social Affairs has come to recognize the economic benefits of expanded income-support programmes. This development, mediated through an increasingly dense web of parallel power networks, reflects the increased formation of a transnational capitalist class concerned to secure the conditions for capital accumulation on a global scale. This is associated with a 'new constitutionalism' (Gill 1995, 2001), that is, an attempt to establish a new articulation between the economic and the political on a global rather than merely a national scale. But it is also associated, as noted above, with attempts to rearticulate the relationship between the economic and the extra-economic conditions for capital accumulation in a globalizing, post-Fordist, knowledge-based economy.

The EU has a key role in this new constitutional settlement. Unsurprisingly, therefore, its still emerging character as a political arena-entity is subject to pressures from well beyond its borders (especially from the USA); and it is also becoming involved in international forums on various scales to restabilize the conditions for economic growth and stability in the wake of the crisis of the primacy of the national scale in the postwar 'embedded liberal' international settlement. At the same time, the tendential Europeanization of economic and social policy is also closely linked, in accordance with the principle of subsidiarity, to the increased role of subnational and cross-national agencies, territorial and/or functional in form, in its formulation and implementation. In this regard there is an interesting scalar division of labour between the EU, national states and subnational tiers of government. For, whereas national states retain significant powers in the traditional spheres of the sovereign state (military, police) and in welfare policy (where the limited EU budget blocks a major role in general social redistribution even if it acquired this competence), the EU has acquired increasing influence over economic policy.

Fourth, although the EU has never acquired the characteristics of a supranational sovereign state, or even a confederation of states, and so cannot be said to have undergone a shift from supranational govern*ment* to supranational govern*ance*, it has developed an increasingly wide and deep array of both governance and metagovernance capacities that enable it to influence economic and social policy in most areas and on most scales. Four specific features of the EU give it special influence here: the role of judges and litigation (which enables the EU to override national laws and to 'constitutionalize' the treaties); its location at the heart of information flows (which gives it a relative monopoly in organizational intelligence); its fiscal poverty (which limits its vulnerability to claims on public spending and thereby circumscribes the political agenda; see Sbragia 2000); and the increasing adoption of European projects and guidelines that entitle the EU to monitor national and regional state activities and partnerships across an increasingly interconnected set of policy areas – thereby giving it a means to steer national policy and endow it with greater coherence (Deppe et al. 2000; Majone 1993; Wallace 2000). The distinctive form of metagovernance in the EU, which invalidates attempts to judge its role in terms of traditional criteria associated with the sovereign national state, is well expressed by Sbragia as follows:

> The European Union governs in the sense of 'steering' because it is
> structurally designed [to keep] certain questions off the table while
> insisting that others be kept on the table. The use of treaties rather than a
> constitution, the institutionalization of the norm of economic libera-
> lization in those treaties, the creation of a powerful court, its unusual
> access to information, and the lack of public funds all help the Union steer.
> (2000: 236)

Likewise, Tömmel, having noted the key role of regional and local
authorities and various public-private partnerships in performing governmental roles in a complex web of cooperative networks organized in
tangled (or, more paradoxically yet, dehierarchized) hierarchies, suggests
that the Europe of regions is becoming

> an indispensable element of an emergent, new open and flexible system,
> in which the EC – or the Union as a whole – will stimulate competitive
> and cooperative behaviour and performance of decentralized – public and
> private – agents and institutions, by using open, market-oriented steering
> mechanisms and by institutionalizing more complex procedures in
> decision-making and consensus-building. (Tömmel 1998: 75).

In short, metasteering is one of the most significant areas in which the
EU is involved in restructuring, reorienting and rescaling welfare. The
very fact that these activities do not conform to the traditional notion of
the exercise of state power has made it hard to see their significance
for the overall dynamic of state formation at the European level. But
they have, nonetheless, played a key role in the gradual rise of an EU
workfare programme to promote full employment via enhancing the
flexibility and employability of workers in the interests of greater competitiveness and enterprise in the transition to post-Fordism. This still
leaves scope for different national or regional interpretations of flexibility and employability – ranging from the neoliberal model promoted
by Thatcherism and retained under New Labour through the neostatist
model found in France, to more neocorporatist patterns associated with
the Scandinavian and other Rhenish economies. The European Employment Strategy is a particularly good example of this and, as Leibfried
and Pierson note, it has become a key element in 'Europe's emerging
multitiered system of social policy' (2000: 288).

8. Is There Still a Role for the National State?

Do the trends and countertrends considered above imply the erosion
of the national state? My short answer, based both on theoretical

considerations and an analysis of the European Union, is 'no'. The rearticulation of the state involves neither a gradual withering away of the national state nor simple displacement based on 'more market, less state'. Instead, it is the KWNS that has been eroded. But the erosion of one form of national state should not be mistaken for its general retreat. On the contrary, as the frontiers of the KWNS (especially those which had been extended during crisis management) are rolled back, the boundaries of the national state are rolling forward in other respects and/or other forms of politics are becoming more significant.

Thus, despite the three general trends noted above (denationalization, destatization and internationalization), the national state retains a key role. This suggestion can be clarified through the distinction between particular state functions and the state's generic (or 'global') function. Poulantzas (1973) identified three particular sets of activities: techno-economic functions regarding the forces and relations of production; political functions (for example, taxation, policing, defence, legislation, official audit) concerned with the self-maintenance of the state's core military, police and administrative activities; and ideological functions (for example, education, patriotic and national rituals, mass communication). It is not necessary to accept this classification of particular functions to agree with the general point. Poulantzas also defined the generic (or 'global') function of the capitalist type of state as 'securing the social cohesion of a society divided into classes'. We should add a further clause to this statement of the generic function, of course, namely, 'and riven by other social cleavages, divisions and conflicts' (see chapter 1). In these terms, what we are witnessing is the erosion of key 'particular' functions associated with the KWNS state project, and their replacement by key 'particular' functions linked to an emerging postnational competition state that is pursuing Schumpeterian workfare functions. This reorganization does not end the national state's key role in exercising its generic political function. For *the national state remains the primary site for this crucial generic function* and, indeed, national state managers jealously guard this role even as they concede more specific functions. In this sense 'denationalization' should be seen as a partial and uneven process that leaves a rearticulated 'national state' still exercising the generic function of the capitalist type of state. It certainly does not imply that a fully fledged 'supranational' state has already emerged to maintain institutional integration and social cohesion in an extended, class-divided supranational social formation.

Thus the national state is still the most significant site of struggle among competing global, triadic, supranational, national, regional and local forces. This is the point behind the hollowing out metaphor, which is intentionally reminiscent of 'hollow corporations' – that is, transnationals headquartered in one country whose operations are mostly pursued elsewhere. The hollow corporation nonetheless retains its core command, control, communication and intelligence functions within the home economy even as it transfers various production activities abroad. By analogy, the 'hollow state' metaphor indicates two trends: first, that the national state retains many of its 'headquarters' (or crucial political) functions – including the trappings of central executive authority and national sovereignty as well as the discourses that sustain them and the overall responsibility for maintaining social cohesion; and, second, that its capacities to translate this authority and sovereignty into effective control are becoming limited by a complex displacement of powers upwards, downwards, and outwards. This does not mean that the national state loses all importance: far from it. Indeed, it remains crucial as an institutional site and discursive framework for political struggles; and it even keeps much of its sovereignty – albeit primarily as a juridical fiction reproduced through mutual recognition in the international political community. But there is still some loss of national states' formal legal sovereignty as rule- and/or decision-making powers are transferred upwards to supranational bodies and the resulting rules and decisions come to bind national states. It has a continuing role in managing the political linkages across different territorial scales, and its legitimacy depends precisely on doing so in the perceived interests of its social base (Kazancigil 1993: 128). Moreover, just as multinational firms' command, control, communication and intelligence functions are continually transformed by the development of new information and communication technologies and new forms of networking, bargaining and negotiation, so, too, as new possibilities emerge, are there changes in how 'hollowed out' states exercise and project their power.

Ziebura (1992) notes the continued importance of the generic political function of the national state. He argues that the tendencies towards globalization and transnational regionalization provoke a countertendency in a popular search for transparency, democratic accountability and proximity. He adds that the desire for local, regional or (at most) national identity reflects powerful drives, especially in small national states, to compensate for threats from powerful neighbouring states and/or the rise of supranational institutions that lack any real democratic accountability. National states are generally still better placed than their respective sub-national states to deal with social conflicts. In addition, whereas supranational bodies seem preoccupied with the internationalization of capital and promoting the structural competitiveness of macroregions and their constituent national and regional economies, they are often less interested in social conflicts and redistributive policies. These concerns are still mainly confined within national frameworks and it is national states that have the potential fiscal base to change them significantly in this regard. Indeed, without central government support, it is hard for most local or regional states to achieve much here. This explains the national state's dilemma that (a) it must become actively engaged in managing the process of internationalization and (b) it is the only political instance with much chance of halting a growing divergence between global market dynamics and conditions for institutional integration and social cohesion.

In short, there remains a central political role for the national state. But this role is redefined because of the more general rearticulation of the local, regional, national and supranational levels of economic and political organization. Unless or until supranational political organization acquires not only governmental powers but also some measure of popular-democratic legitimacy, the national state will remain a key political factor as the highest instance of formal democratic political accountability. How it fulfils this role does not depend only on the changing institutional matrix and the shifts in the balance of forces, as globalization, triadization, regionalization and the resurgence of local governance proceed apace.

9. Concluding Remarks

Even adopting an economic viewpoint that paid due attention to the social embeddedness and social regularization of capital accumulation, it would be wrong to explain these general trends in terms of economic changes. For they must first be translated through struggles into political problems for state action and their solution is then mediated through the specific, structurally inscribed, strategically selective nature of the state. Likewise, from a more state-centric viewpoint, it would be wrong to suggest that these trends are attributable solely to (politically mediated) economic changes. For there could also be *sui generis* political reasons prompting state actors and other political forces to engage in institutional redesign and strategic reorientation (cf. Jessop 1994b).

There are two main conclusions from this discussion. First, regarding the rescaling of accumulation, regulation and the state, we are seeing a reshaping of the hierarchy of regions on all spatial scales from world regions (triads) through international regions and nation-states to cross-border or virtual regions and on to intrastate regions and localities (Taylor 1991: 185). Transnational firms and banks are major players in this reshaping process, but, as noted above, they are often aided and abetted in this regard by national states. As these complex and contradictory processes unfold, however, states must also tackle the many domestic repercussions of global restructuring (for a summary of the changing state activities in regard to rescaling, see box 5.2). This requires the repositioning of states in the hierarchy of scales (that is, the rescaling of the state, politics and policy) as well as the restructuring and strategic reorientation of state agencies at any given scale. This is also associated with alliance strategies among states on different scales to provide the basis for economic and political survival as the imperatives of structural competitiveness make themselves felt. The nature of these alliances will vary with the position of the economies concerned in the international hierarchy.

Box 5.2   Rescaling and state intervention

1. Establishing new scales of activity (and dismantling others), thereby rescaling and rearticulating various state powers, institutional forms, and regulatory capacities and creating possibility for themselves and other actors to 'jump scales'.

2. Engaging in complementary forms of *Standortpolitik* and other forms of place-based competition in attempt to fix mobile capital in their own economic spaces and to enhance inter-urban, interregional or international competitiveness of their own place-bound capitals.

3. Promoting uneven development through policies for inter-urban, interregional and international competition – and seeking to compensate for this.

4. Cooperating in the rebordering and rescaling of state functions – including decentralization and cross-border region formation, regional bloc formation, and participating in forums for inter-triad negotiation.

Second, regarding the continued primacy of the national state, the extended reproduction of capitalism and social classes in the erstwhile economic space of Atlantic Fordism is no longer linked politically to the KWNS with its local relays, corporatist bias and international supports. It has been relocated in a more internationalized and localized SWPR. The latter's particular functions have been dispersed among several institutional levels of territorial organization and are shared with an extended range of functionally relevant (and politically and ideologically defined) stakeholders. Yet the generic political function of maintaining social cohesion is still exercised at the level of the national state within this restructured and reoriented political ensemble. Hence, the typical features and generic functions of this national state are quite different from those of the KWNS, and the strategic context in which it operates has also been significantly transformed.

6

From Mixed Economy to Metagovernance

This chapter builds on the preceding arguments about destatization to explore responses to the crisis of the mixed economy, which had played a key role in the Atlantic Fordist mode of regulation. It also builds on the earlier discussion of exchange, hierarchy and networks as forms of governance and suggests that their relative weights in capitalist social formations have changed in two respects. First, in the capitalist economy narrowly conceived, while hierarchical forms of organization have lost weight, network forms have become more significant compared to the heyday of Atlantic Fordism. This does not mean that networks were absent or unimportant in Fordism, of course, or that they could not have played important roles in the period before Fordism. And, second, regarding the conditions for capital accumulation in its integral or inclusive sense, networks have also acquired a greater role in securing the expanding range of extra-economic conditions central to continuing capital accumulation and, significantly, in correcting for market failures.

This double shift clearly affects the state's twin roles in securing the conditions for the profitable accumulation of private capital and reproducing labour-power as a fictitious commodity. This is reflected in a rearticulation of the state's role in governing capital accumulation and its more general role in securing the conditions for social cohesion within the wider social formation. We can describe this rearticulation in terms of a trend and a countertrend (see chapter 5). The former is associated with the increasing inability of the KWNS, as the crises in/of Atlantic Fordism intensified, to intervene successfully from above and/or in concertation with its social partners in order to correct for market failures. This lent credence to the neoliberal call for 'more market, less state' and a more general belief that the redesign of market institutions was a better response to market failure than increasing state intervention. Those presiding over neoliberal policy adjustments and neoliberal regime shifts discovered sooner or later, however, not only that familiar forms of market failure began to reassert themselves but also that yet other forms of market failure became evident with the primacy of other contradictions in the emerging post-Fordist accumulation regime. This prompted a wide range of social forces to search for alternatives to market and state alike in the coordination of increasingly complex societies. This search process generated a widespread turn to old and new forms of governance without government – a turn that has been encapsulated in the now familiar claim that there has been a generalized shift from government to governance over the last two decades. However, as I noted in the preceding chapter, this general trend has been countered by another trend that also complements it. This is the increased salience of the state in organizing the conditions for self-organization so that it can compensate for planning and market failures alike in an increasingly networked society. Or, to rephrase it in line with the tendential shift from government to governance, there has been a tendential shift from government to metagovernance. This chapter is mainly concerned to elaborate this apparently paradoxical development and to illustrate it from the evolution of the KWNS. But first it develops the categories for the study of governance that were introduced in chapter 1.

1. The Material Bases of Governance Mechanisms

We have already seen in earlier chapters that markets, hierarchies (especially bureaucratically organized firms and top-down imperative coordination by the state) and networking (both formal and informal) are the three primary poles around which economic, political and social governance are organized in social formations marked by high levels of economic, political and social complexity. This does not exclude a secondary role for community (or the solidarities of 'imagined communities') in supplementing these forms of governance and/or in organizing social relations in the lifeworld. Indeed, while markets, hierarchies and networks may often be undermined by the survival of these solidarities, they can also derive additional surplus or leverage in undertaking complex coordination from being embedded in such social relations. For the moment, however, I ignore issues of interpersonal relations and social embedding to focus on the significance of markets, hierarchies and networks in the political economy of capitalism.

It is surely no accident that references to markets, hierarchies and networks occur so systematically in discussions of contemporary capitalist societies. This is evident, for example, in the recurrent attempts to distinguish variants of capitalism through concepts such as uncoordinated liberal market capitalism; the developmental state and state-led, dirigiste, or governed capitalism; and corporatism, coordinated capitalism or the negotiated economy. Likewise, as we have seen in chapter 2, many students of welfare regimes distinguish between liberal, social democratic and conservative-corporatist regimes. Theorists of public administration and policy-making tend in turn to distinguish market, bureaucratic and participatory modes of policy-making and delivery. The recurrence of such tropes could be interpreted simply in terms of an intellectual residue of the Enlightenment conceptual triplet of market, state and civil society, and it is certainly interesting how far this trio of concepts has travelled in organizing research on Asian societies where its relevance is by no means self-evident.[1] But one might also explain their recurrence in terms of certain features of the organization of capitalist social formations. If this is so, then we should also ask why their relative weights vary across types of capitalism and over time. Does the overall matrix of the capitalist mode of production provide a partial answer to both problems?

Market exchange and liberalism

Liberalism emphasizes the role of market exchange as a coordination mechanism. Economically, liberalism endorses the expansion of the market economy through the generalization of the commodity form to all factors of production (including labour-power and knowledge) and the spreading of formally free, monetized exchange to as many spheres of social relations as possible. Politically, it implies that collective decision-making should involve: (1) a constitutional state with limited substantive powers of economic and social intervention; and (2) a commitment to maximizing the formal freedom of contracting parties in the economy and the substantive freedom of legally recognized subjects in the public sphere. The latter sphere is based in turn on spontaneous freedom of association of individuals to pursue any social activities that are not forbidden by constitutionally valid laws. Ideologically, liberalism claims that economic, political and social relations are best organized through the formally free[2] choices of formally free and rational actors who seek to advance their own material or ideal interests in an institutional framework that, by accident or design, maximizes the scope for formally free choice. These three principles may well conflict over the scope of anarchic market relations, collective decision-making and spontaneous self-organization, as well as over the formal and substantive freedoms available to economic, legal and civil subjects. As

Marx noted, however, 'between equal rights, force decides' (1996: 243). In other words, within the matrix of liberal principles, the relative balance of economic, political and civic liberalism depends on the changing balance of forces within an institutionalized (but changeable) compromise.

The resurgence of liberalism in the form of neoliberalism is often attributed to a successful hegemonic project voicing the interests of financial and/or transnational capital. Its recent hegemony in neoliberal regimes undoubtedly depends on the successful exercise of political, intellectual and moral leadership in elaborating a response to the crises of Atlantic Fordism. And it is also clearly related to the increased importance of the money concept of capital (see chapters 2 and 3). But its resonance is also rooted more deeply in the general nature of capitalist social formations. For liberalism can be seen as a more or less 'spontaneous philosophy' within capitalist societies insofar as it is a seemingly natural, almost self-evident economic, political and social imaginary that corresponds to general features of a bourgeois society. It is, in particular, consistent with four such features.

The first of these is the institution of private property – that is, the juridical fiction of autonomous private ownership and control of the factors of production. This encourages individual property owners and those who dispose over fictitious commodities such as labour-power, natural resources and, especially in the past two decades or so, intellectual property, to see themselves as entitled to use or alienate their property as they think fit without due regard to the substantive interdependence of activities in a market economy and market society. In this realm, 'rule Freedom, Equality, Property and Bentham, because both buyer and seller of a commodity, say of labour-power, are constrained only by their own free will' (Marx 1996: 186). Second, and relatedly, there is the appearance of 'free choice' in consumption, where those with sufficient money may choose what to buy and how to dispose of it. Third, the institutional separation and operational autonomies of the economy and state make the latter's interventions appear as external intrusions into the activities of otherwise free economic agents. Initially, this may be an unwelcome but necessary extra-economic condition for orderly free markets. However, if pushed beyond prevailing social definitions of this acceptable minimum nightwatchman role, it appears as an obstacle to free markets and/or as direct political oppression. This is even more the case, of course, where state intervention that does not transgress this socially accepted minimum harms immediate particular interests. And, fourth, there is the closely related institutional separation of civil society and the state. This encourages the belief that state intervention is an intrusion into the formally free choices of particular members of civil society once the conditions for social order have been established.

However, opposition to liberalism may also emerge 'spontaneously' on the basis of four other features of capitalist social relations. First, growing socialization of the forces of production, despite continued private ownership of the means of production, suggests the need for *ex ante* collaboration among producer groups to limit market anarchy, whether through top-down planning and/or various forms of self-organization. Second, there are the strategic dilemmas posed by the shared interests of producers (including wage earners) in maximizing total revenues through cooperation and their divided and potentially conflictual interests over how these revenues are distributed. Various non-market governance mechanisms may have a role here helping to balance cooperation and conflict. Third, there are contradictions and conflicts posed by the mutual dependence of the institutionally separate economic and political systems. This leads to different logics of economic and political action at the same time as it generates a need to consult on the economic impact of state policies and/or the political repercussions of private economic decision-making. And, fourth, there are problems generated by the nature of civil society or the lifeworld as a sphere of particular interests opposed to the state's supposed embodiment of universal interests. This indicates the need for some institutional means of mediating the particular and universal and, since this is impossible in the abstract, for some hegemonic definition of the 'general interest' (on the always imperfect, strategically selective nature of such reconciliations, see Jessop 1990b).

This suggests that, if liberalism can be interpreted as a more or less 'spontaneous philosophy' rooted in capitalist social relations, one should also recognize that it is prone to 'spontaneous combustion' due to tensions inherent in these same relations. This was noted in Polanyi's (1944) critique of late nineteenth-century liberalism, which argued that, in response to crisis-tendencies in laissez-faire capitalism, many social forces struggled to re-embed and re-regulate the market. The eventual compromise solution was a *market economy* embedded in and sustained by a *market society*. The same point applies to neoliberal capitalism. Thus, after the efforts of 'roll-back neoliberalism' to free the neoliberal market economy from its various corporatist and statist impediments, attempts are now being made to secure its medium-term viability by embedding it in a neoliberal market society (cf. Peck and Tickell 2002). This involves measures to displace or defer contradictions and conflicts beyond the spatio-temporal horizons of a given regime as well as supplementary measures to flank, support and sustain the continued dominance of the neoliberal project within these horizons (Jessop 2002c).

The division of labour and corporatism

This line of argument should not be restricted to liberalism and neoliberalism. The two other modes of governance typical of modern social formations are also deeply rooted in the economic, political and social organization of capitalism. And they are also contradictory and tension-ridden. Let us now briefly consider corporatism as an economic and political expression within capitalism of the more general pattern of heterarchic governance (see p. 52 and below). Corporatism is a form of functional representation that involves an interconnected system of representation, policy formation and policy implementation based on the alleged (socially defined) function in the division of labour of the various forces involved. This definition fixes the generic features of corporatism. It ignores the specificity of particular instances that derives from the secondary features of corporatism in different circumstances. These features include its ideological justification, its political legitimation, its functional bases and precise organizational forms of representation, the various levels at which corporatist structures are organized, the actual scope, purposes and mode of policy-making, the particular forms of implementation and the place (if any) of corporatism in the wider configuration of economic, political and social orders.

Corporatism first emerged in modern Europe as a reactionary and utopian politico-ideological critique of liberal capitalism with strong organicist overtones. The second main version of corporatism was linked to 'organized capitalism' in the late nineteenth and early twentieth centuries. This version was not opposed to capitalism as such (which was now consolidated and had begun to develop monopolistic and imperialistic tendencies), but was more concerned about the revolutionary threat represented by organized labour. These two versions played a major role in the emergence of conservative-corporatist welfare regimes (see chapter 2). A third phase of corporatism saw the emergence of tripartism in the context of postwar Atlantic Fordism and its associated KWNSs. Emerging during postwar reconstruction in Europe as an alternative to fascism and to liberal capitalism, it was supported by Christian democrats and 'One Nation' Conservatives as well as by social democrats. It was revived again in some Atlantic Fordist economies in the 1960s and 1970s in the hope of moderating emerging stagflationary tendencies (see chapter 2). The fourth variant of corporatism became prominent in the 1980s and 1990s and is likely to expand further in the coming decade. It is less often explicitly discussed in corporatist terms (in part due to the latter's negative association with the crises of the 1970s and with trade unions) although there is now increasing recognition of corporatist social pacts in a number of European welfare regimes on various scales. More often, it is discussed in such terms as networking, public-private partnerships, strategic alliances, inter-organizational collaboration, regulated self-regulation, stakeholding, productive solidarities, productivity coalitions, learning regions, the social economy and associational democracy.

This recurrence of corporatism, albeit in quite varied guises, is due, like the recurrence of liberalism, to certain material features of capitalist formations. These are the same features that tend to generate limits to a purely market-based form of capitalist organization, and were listed above. In brief, to avoid unnecessary repetition, they comprise: (1) the growing socialization of the forces of production despite continued private ownership of the means of production; (2) the dilemmas posed by the shared interest of producer classes and groups in maximizing total revenues and the conflict over their allocation; (3) the need for consultation among operationally and organizationally distinct but functionally interdependent forces about the economic impact of state policies and the political repercussions of private economic decision-making; and (4) the problems generated by the nature of civil society as a sphere of particular interests. Each of these four bases is inherently contradictory and each prompts instabilities in the very corporatist tendencies that it helps to generate. This is an important part of the explanation for the recurrent cycles of the rise of corporatism, its fall and its return in a new guise. This pattern can be seen in corporatist policy cycles within given stages of capitalism and in the rise of new types of corporatism associated with different stages of capitalism.

Institutional separation and statism

Imperative coordination is the third mode of governance to be considered here. It plays an important part in the governance of the economy in its narrow sense through the development of the firm and other hierarchical forms. But its role is even more evident in the activities of that inclusive hierarchical organization that is not itself subject to control by a superordinate organization, namely, the sovereign state form that is typical of capitalist social formations. This is reflected in Weber's classic definition of the modern state in terms of its distinctive means of political control and in the postulate of the realist theory of international relations that the relation between sovereign states is one of pure anarchy. Weber analysed the modern state as a compulsory association that has successfully monopolized the legitimate use of physical force as a means of domination within a given territory. Its defining features were an administrative staff, means of organized coercion, an effective claim to the legitimate exercise of that coercion, a distinct territory within which this coercion was exercised and subjects over whom it was exercised (Weber 1948). This definition is consistent with the idea of the state as an apparatus that makes decisions that are collectively binding on members of a given society and justified in the name of the public interest or common good (see chapter 1) but it could well lead to overemphasis on the role of force in the state's routine operations at the expense of other modes of state intervention. For, as noted in chapter 1, the capitalist type of state may intervene not only through the exercise of legitimate organized coercion and through legislation enacted according to the rule of law, but also through its command over fiscal and monetary resources (linked to its monopoly of organized taxation grounded in its monopoly of coercion and to its control over legal tender and the central bank), through a relative monopoly of organized intelligence, and through its powers of moral suasion rooted in the articulation of hegemonic accumulation strategies, state projects and hegemonic visions. The scope of state powers is especially problematic for many of the distinctive economic and social policies pursued by the ideal-typical KWNS and SWPR as opposed to the generic functions of the modern state (or capitalist type of state) in capitalist societies.

More generally, it is clear, as Weber took pains to emphasize, that there is considerable variation in the weight of imperative coordination in the overall pattern of state intervention. Regarding the conditions for capital accumulation, which is by no means all there is to the state's activities, for example, the role of imperative coordination tends to be most significant in establishing the initial conditions for capital accumulation (the first round of primitive accumulation)[3] and reproducing its general external conditions (such as the enforcement of property rights and contracts). Reliance on imperative coordination (or top-down state intervention) also tends to increase when the forms of private ownership block the growing socialization of the forces of production, when class conflict and/or conflict among owners of different entitlements to revenue threatens accumulation, when the logic of economic action conflicts with important political goals and when the pursuit of particular interests threatens the realization of the particular accumulation strategies, state projects and hegemonic projects with which the state is from time to time associated. And the resort to organized coercion rather than law is at its most significant, of course, in the initial stages of exceptional periods when the sovereign state declares states of emergency and suspends the formal democratic principles on which the normal bourgeois democratic form of the constitutional state is based. Such situations are not so relevant to the countries of direct concern in the present work, but they have played a key role in states and regions beyond the borders of the spatio-temporal fix associated with Atlantic Fordism (for example, in the military dictatorships in the oil-producing states on which the Atlantic Fordist economies depend so heavily).

The paradox of governance

There are strange complementarities in the oscillation and recurrence of different modes of governing the capital relation. For example, while liberalism tends to regenerate itself 'spontaneously' on the basis of key features of capitalist societies, this regeneration meets obstacles from some of their other key features. And, while the latter provide the basis for the resurgence of other discourses, strategies and organizational paradigms, such as corporatism or statism, their realization tends to be fettered in turn by the very features that generate liberalism. Overall, these mutually related tendencies and countertendencies produce oscillations in the relative weight of different kinds of coordination and modes of policy-making. This said, different principles of governance seem more or less well suited to different stages of capitalism and/or its contemporary variants. Thus liberalism was probably more suited to the pioneering forms of competitive capitalism than to later forms – though Polanyi and others would note that it has clear limitations even for competitive capitalism; and it is more suited to uncoordinated than coordinated market economies, for which statism and corporatism are better (see Coates 2000; Hall and Soskice 2001b; Hollingsworth and Boyer 1997b; Huber and Stephens 2001). Thus different stages and forms of capitalism may have distinctive institutional attractors (or centres of gravity) around which oscillation occurs. In addition, different variants of these forms and stages are also likely to have different patterns of governance that are structurally coupled to their specific patterns of specialization and their growth dynamics. This is a rich field of research that has already been well ploughed and cannot detain us here.

2. Market and State Failure

The previous section has considered three basic forms of governance and indicated in quite abstract and simple terms how they are rooted in general features of capitalist social formations and how these features also tend to undermine them. This provides a general explanation for the possibility of cycles in which the relative weight of different modes of governance rises, falls, and rises again. In this section I consider sources of failure internal to each of these mechanisms that reinforce these general tendencies and also help to explain some of the more concrete-complex aspects of variation in patterns of governance. I begin once more with the dominant coordination mechanism in capitalist social relations, namely, the market mechanism.

Market failure

Many orthodox economists tend to assume that the 'procedural rationality' of perfect markets guarantees market success. Failure occurs when economic exchanges do not produce what a perfect (hence 'imaginary') market would deliver. Since market rationality depends on free and equal exchange rather than on the purposes of economic transactions, success or failure cannot, on most accounts, be judged through substantive criteria such as market forces' uneven impact on wealth, income, lifechances or regional imbalance. For, provided that inequalities derive from (or are consistent with) the operation of perfect markets, they must be judged as rational and fair. At best, one could see such problems as market 'inadequacies' rather than genuine market failures. There is no shortage of claims about such inadequacies, however, nor about the need to remedy them as well as market failures through social and political action of various kinds.

In a market-rational framework, state and market are strictly demarcated. The state should stay at arms-length from market forces, merely establishing and defending the framework for market institutions. The latter can then allocate goods and services in the most efficient way. The market also functions as a learning mechanism. Thus Hayek argues that market failure is an essentially 'trial-and-error' discovery mechanism whereby markets prompt economic agents to learn and innovate. In the long run, on this view, the market provides the most flexible and least disastrous coordinating and adaptive mechanism in the face of complex interdependence and turbulent environments. Moreover, for neoclassical and Austrian theorists alike, the initial response to market failure is 'more market, not less' – even if this often requires, in the short term, yet further state intervention. But it is debatable, to say the least, whether even perfect markets could eliminate all forms of market failure. Even neoclassical economists recognize the extent to which markets may not 'suitably capture the full social benefits or levy the full social costs of market activity' (Wolf 1979: 138).

This approach is clearly inconsistent with that advocated here. For, as I have argued in chapter 1, it is not markets as such that are distinctive of capitalism but their extension to labour-power as a fictitious commodity. It is not the inherent efficiency of markets that drives 'wealth creation' or 'economic growth'. Instead, this is achieved through the market-mediated exploitation of wage-labour and the competitive (and creatively destructive) search for above-average profits; and both of these processes involve struggles to accumulate structural power in order to shape the operation of market forces and control the conditions for the valorization and realization of capital. Moreover, as I have also argued in chapter 1, the capital relation considered as a purely economic (or market-mediated) relation is constitutively incomplete. Its continued reproduction depends, in an unstable and contradictory way, on changing extra-economic conditions. Thus, while markets may mediate the search for added value, they cannot produce it. In addition, as commodification and fictitious commodification widen and deepen their penetration of social relations, they generate contradictions that cannot be fully resolved through the market mechanism, but only deferred and displaced (chapters 1–5). In this sense, much of what passes as market failure or market inadequacies is actually an expression of the underlying contradictions of capitalism. Thus, while markets may mediate contradictions and modify their forms of appearance, they cannot transcend them. Similarly, although the state may intervene in response to market failure, it typically only modifies the forms or sites of these contradictions – introducing class struggles into the state and/or generating tendencies towards fiscal crisis, legitimacy crisis, rationality crisis, etc. – or else displaces and defers them beyond the spatio-temporal boundaries associated with that particular state.

State failure

The rationale for state activity is not procedural (as with the market) but substantive. This rationale is expressed through imperative coordination (or hierarchy) rather than the anarchy of market forces. In pure form it is found in the definition and enforcement of collectively binding decisions made in the name of the public interest or general will. But it can also be seen in the definition of collective projects that are pursued through top-down planning and coordination. State failure is judged according to this substantive rationality: it refers to the failure to realize the state's own political project(s) within the terms of its own operating rules and procedures. In democratic regimes these rules and procedures include respect for legality and the regular renewal of popular mandates for action. Thus the primary criterion for identifying state failures is not allocative efficiency (as defined in terms of the procedural rationality of the market). Instead, it is the effectiveness (as often symbolic as material) with which specific state projects are realized. It is certainly possible, however, for efficiency to count among the criteria for the success of specific projects. Thus 'value-for-money' is one objective of the neoliberal state project.

Moreover, just as market failure can be related to substantive factors that block the realization of its procedural rationality, so state failure can be linked to specific procedural factors that block effective policy-making and implementation. Thus various commentators have suggested that planning, bureaucracy, participation, reliance on professional expertise, etc., may each fail in different ways to generate adequate policies and/or to secure their effective realization. The resulting tendencies towards implementation and fiscal crises can lead in turn to problems of political legitimacy if there is a widespread perception that the state's public purposes are not being achieved. One response to this within the state is a constant cycling through these different modes of policy-making and implementation in the attempt to compensate for their respective tendencies to failure (Offe 1975).

Just as neoclassical economists make unrealistic assumptions about markets, welfare economists make implausible claims about states. They assume that states not only have all the information necessary to maximize social welfare, but also that they have both the internal organizational capacities and the powers of external intervention needed to achieve their public objectives. Yet it is widely recognized that state managers (especially elected politicians) have short-term time horizons and are vulnerable to lobbying; that states are subject to bounded rationality (limited information, uncertainty and time pressures) when acting; that they often pursue multiple, contrary and even contradictory goals – many of which are also inherently infeasible; that state capacities are limited both by 'internalities' (calculations of private costs and benefits which differ from public goals) and external resistance; that non-market outputs are usually hard to define in principle, ill-defined in practice and difficult to measure; and that state intervention may prompt rent-seeking behaviour among policy-takers that merely redistributes rather than creates resources (Offe 1975; Wolf 1979).

There are different responses to state failure. Liberal critics see market forces as a self-correcting learning mechanism and the state as inherently incorrigible and ineducable. They do not ask whether state failure could be corrected in similar ways to market failure, but seek to replace it with the market. But other critics allow both for self-correcting policy cycles and/or institutional redesign in the state. Relevant measures in the latter regard to improve policy coordination and implementation can include redefining the division of labour in the state and wider political system, increasing state autonomy so that it is less vulnerable to particularistic lobbying, boosting reflexivity (including through auditing and the contract culture) and reorienting time horizons in favour of longer-term policy-making and policy-taking.

Heterarchy as a response to market and state failure

Discussions of market and state failure often appear to rest on dia-metrically opposed theoretical and politico-ideological positions. Yet they share some core assumptions. Both presume a dichotomistic public–private distinction and a zero-sum conception of the respective spheres of the market and state. Thus, on the one hand, critics of state failure see the economy as the site of mutually advantageous, voluntary exchange among formally free, equal and autonomous economic agents; and, on the other hand, they regard the state as premised on organized coercion that intrudes on the private liberties of citizens (especially in their capacity as economic agents). Conversely, critics of market failure see the state as a sovereign authority empowered to pursue the public interest against the particularistic, egoistic short-term interests of citizens (especially those of property owners). In both cases, the more there is of the state, the less there is of the market; what varies is the positive or negative evaluation of this ratio. Similarly, whereas those who believe in the beneficence of market forces regard state failure as normal and market failure as exceptional, those who believe in the rationality of the state and its embodiment of the public interest typically consider market failure as inevitable and state failure as something which, if not excep-tional, is at least conjunctural – and can therefore be overcome through improved institutional design, knowledge or political practice.

A third way between the anarchy of the market and the hierarchy of imperative coordination is found in 'heterarchy', which comprises horizontal self-organization among mutually interdependent actors. Amongst its forms are interpersonal networking, interorganizational negotiation and decentred intersystemic context steering (*dezentrierte Kontextsteuerung*). The first two of these forms of governance should be familiar to readers; the last requires some comment. It comprises efforts to steer (guide) the development of different systems by taking account both of their own operating codes and rationalities and of their various substantive, social and spatio-temporal interdependencies. This is fa-cilitated by communication oriented to intersystemic 'noise reduction' (mutual understanding), negotiation, negative coordination and co-operation in shared projects. And it is reflected in the use of symbolic media of communication such as money, law or knowledge to modify the structural and strategic contexts in which different systems function so that compliance with shared projects follows from their own operating codes rather than from imperative coordination (see Glagow and Willke 1987; Willke 1992, 1997).

The rationality of governance is neither procedural nor substantive: it is best described as 'reflexive'. The procedural rationality of the capitalist market is essentially formal in nature, prioritizing an endless 'economizing' pursuit of profit maximization; the substantive rationality of government is goal-oriented, prioritizing 'effective' pursuit of successive policy goals. Heterarchic governance institutes negotiation around a long-term consensual project as the basis for both negative and positive coordination among interdependent actors. The key to its success is continued commitment to dialogue to generate and exchange more information (thereby reducing, without ever eliminating, the problem of bounded rationality); to weaken opportunism by locking partners into a range of interdependent decisions over short-, medium- and long-term time horizons; and to build on the interdependencies and risks associated with 'asset specificity' by encouraging solidarity among those involved. The rationality of governance is dialogic rather than monologic, pluralistic rather than monolithic, heterarchic rather than either hierarchic or anarchic. In turn, this suggests that there is no one best governance mechanism.

There has been a remarkable increase in resort to heterarchy in the last two decades in many different systems and spheres of the lifeworld. This is most evident in the explosion of references to networking (for example, the networked enterprise, the network state, the network society, network-centric warfare) and in the growing interest in negotiation, multi-agency cooperation, partnership, stakeholding, and so on. This represents a secular response to a dramatic intensification of societal complexity. This has several sources: (1) increased functional differentiation combined with increased interdependence; (2) the increased fuzziness of some institutional boundaries, for example, concerning what counts as 'economic' in an era of increased systemic or structural competitiveness; (3) the multiplication and rescaling of spatial horizons; (4) the increasing complexity of temporal horizons of action; (5) the multiplication of identities; and (6) the increased importance of knowledge and organized learning. Such complexity is reflected in worries about the governability of economic, political and social life in the face of globalization and conflicting identities. It implies that important new problems have emerged that cannot be managed or resolved readily, if at all, through top-down state planning or market-mediated anarchy. This has promoted a shift in the institutional centre of gravity (or institutional attractor) around which policy-makers choose among possible modes of coordination.

The conditions for successful pursuit of reflexive rationality are just as complex as are those for well-functioning markets or state planning. Interpersonal networking, interorganizational negotiation and intersystemic steering pose different problems in this regard. Specific objects of governance also affect the likelihood of success. For example, governing the global economy, human rights regimes, transnational crime and transnational social movements clearly involve very different prob-

Table 6.1   Modalities of governance

	Exchange	*Command*	*Dialogue*
Rationality	Formal and procedural	Substantive and goal-oriented	Reflexive and procedural
Criterion of success	Efficient allocation	Effective goal-attainment	Negotiated consent
Typical example	Market	State	Network
Stylized mode of calculation	*Homo economicus*	*Homo hierarchicus*	*Homo politicus*
Spatio-temporal horizons	World market, reversible time	National territory, planning horizons	Rescaling and path-shaping
Primary criterion of failure	Economic inefficiency	Ineffectiveness	'Noise', 'talking shop'
Secondary criterion of failure	Market inadequacies	Bureaucratism, red tape	

lems. Turbulent environments pose different governance problems from those that are relatively stable – especially as time is required for self-organization to operate consensually. Governance mechanisms must provide a framework in which relevant actors can reach agreement over (albeit possibly differential) spatial and temporal horizons of action vis-à-vis their environment. They must also stabilize the cognitive and normative expectations of these actors by shaping and promoting a common 'world-view' as well as developing adequate solutions to sequencing problems. In this way they can produce a predictable ordering of various actions, policies or processes over time, especially where they have different temporal logics. At stake here is establishing secure bases of coordination with their own structurally inscribed strategic selectivity. There can certainly be no guarantees of success in the pursuit of collective goals through self-organization – any more than there can be through reliance on the invisible hand of the market or the iron fist (perhaps in a velvet glove) of imperative coordination. Nonetheless, when faced with continuing evidence of market and state failure, networking and self-organization can prove attractive (for a summary account of the three modes of coordination, see table 6.1).

3. The Governance of Atlantic Fordism and Beyond

In the light of these preliminary remarks I will now consider the changing forms of economic and social coordination since the 1980s. There are three interrelated issues worth pursuing here: the changing definitions of the objects of economic and social governance; the changing institutions and governance mechanisms responsible for its delivery; and the practices in and through which economic and social policies are delivered. These issues are closely linked. For governance practices (mediated by institutions) attempt to delimit, unify, stabilize and reproduce their objects of governance as the precondition as well as the effect of governing them. Moreover, governance practices also typically aim to create and reproduce the subjects needed for governance to operate effectively (Barry et al. 1996; Hunt and Wickham 1994). Thus, as the objects and modes of governance change, institutional mechanisms and actual practices change too – and so do the typical forms of governance failure. In this sense we should see economic and social policy regimes as constitutive of their objects of governance and not just as responses to pre-given economic and social problems. Indeed, this is one of the bases on which the welfare state has often been criticized – that it generates the problems it addresses. This also suggests that it will be self-expanding – always finding new problems to solve – and, perhaps, ultimately self-defeating as it becomes more complex, overloads itself with tasks, and eventually produces a crisis of ungovernability (for example, Crozier et al. 1975; Luhmann 1990).

Whether or not one subscribes to such criticisms, it was the purported failure of the KWNS as a mode of economic and social governance that prompted the search for new forms of governance. Its alleged crisis affected not only the modes of 'governance-government-governing' in the KWNS but also the latter's objects and subjects of social and economic governance. The KWNS began to fail as a mode of governance when its coherence as an institutional ensemble became inconsistent with the objects it was governing, the practices being deployed to govern them, and the identities and interests of the active agents and/or 'passive' subjects of the KWNS regime. Thus, taking its four dimensions in turn, the following crisis-tendencies can be identified.

First, the primary object of economic governance in the KWNS was the national economy. The emergence and consolidation of Keynesian practices had helped to delimit and reproduce the national economy (Tomlinson 1985). They provided the means of measuring national economic performance, controlling economic flows across national borders, setting economic aggregates such as inflation, employment and growth as goals of national economic management, and creating the infrastructure for national economic development. But Keynesian economic management became increasingly problematic and generated stagflationary tendencies that fuelled the emerging crisis of the Atlantic Fordist economies that Keynesian state intervention (as broadly defined in chapter 2) was supposed to have the capacity to manage. Economic internationalization exacerbated these problems. It undermined the national economy as an object of economic management and led to quite different conceptions of the economy and, a fortiori, its mechanisms of economic and social governance. As we saw in chapter 3, replacing the national economy as the primary object of economic governance is the knowledge-based economy in an era of globalization. As with the national economy that was discursively imagined and materially consti-tuted as an object of economic governance out of a far more complex and inherently unmanageable ensemble of economic relations, the knowledge-based economy first has to be imagined as an object of eco-nomic governance before it gains a sufficiently solid material and insti-tutional form to become potentially governable through the political technologies of an emerging SWPR. I have already indicated the massive efforts on the part of many different social forces operating in many dif-ferent domains and on many different scales to establish the globalizing, knowledge-based economy as the more or less widely taken-for-granted focal point of accumulation strategies, state projects and hegemonic visions. Whether or not it proves any more manageable in the long term than the national economy did in the Atlantic Fordist era is another ques-tion entirely (see chapter 1). Nonetheless, at present, the growth dynamic of the knowledge-based economy is held to depend on how effectively the economic space in which it is anchored – not necessarily a national economy – is inserted into (or, better perhaps, networked into) the changing global division of labour, and can survive the audit of the world market. This in turn has prompted growing concern with international economic competitiveness (if only through international benchmarking to establish best practice) and with supply-side intervention – the latter initially to supplement national demand management, subsequently as the primary objective and means of economic intervention. Moreover, because of the relativization of scale noted in chapters 3 and 5, attempts to stabilize the knowledge-based economy and/or to benefit from such stabilization are being pursued on many more scales.

The imagined scope and inclusiveness of the economy that needs gov-erning have also expanded. This is no longer interpreted in narrow terms but has been extended to include many additional factors, deemed 'non-economic' under the KWNS regime, that affect economic performance. This expansion is reflected in concepts such as structural competitiveness or systemic competitiveness – concepts that highlight the combined impact of diverse societal factors on competitiveness. State managers therefore intervene in a growing range of economically relevant prac- tices, institutions, functional systems and domains of the lifeworld to enhance competitiveness. This has two interesting and paradoxical effects on the state. First, whilst it expands the potential scope of state intervention for economic purposes, the resulting complexity renders the sorts of top-down intervention typical of the postwar KWNS less effec- tive – requiring that the state retreat from some areas of intervention and reinvent itself as a condition for more effective intervention in others (Messner 1998). And, second, whilst it increases the range of stakehold- ers whose cooperation is required for successful state intervention, it also increases pressures within the state to create new subjects to act as its partners. Thus states are now trying to transform the identities, interests, capacities, rights and responsibilities of economic and social forces so that they become more flexible, capable and reliable agents of the state's new economic strategies – whether in partnership with the state and/or with each other or as autonomous entrepreneurial subjects in the new knowledge-based economy (Barry et al. 1996; Deakin and Edwards 1993; Finer 1997).

This is also reflected in the transfer of techno-economic paradigms from the firm to broader fields of governance. This occurs in at least two ways: through the simple extension of techno-economic paradigms from the private sector to public and third sector organizations and through the respecification of the best institutional arrangements and most appropriate tasks of the state (cf. Hoggett 1987; Goodwin and Painter 1996). In organizational terms the Fordist period was one of large scale, hierarchical structures that operated in a bureaucratic, top-down man- ner, and this model was allegedly extended to the local state and its eco- nomic and welfare roles (cf. Hoggett 1987; and below). Post-Fordism is associated with the network firm and a new 'network paradigm' (Capello 1996; Cooke and Morgan 1993). The former has been described in the following terms:

> The traditional models of the large, vertically integrated firm of the 1960s, and of the small autonomous, single-phase firm of the 1970s and part of the 1980s, are replaced by a new type of large networked firm, with strongly centralized strategic functions extending in several directions, and by a new type of small enterprise, integrated into a multi-company local network. Across the network, a system of constantly evolving power relationships governs both the dynamics of innovation and the appropriability of returns to the partners involved. The network firm is attracted towards diversified mass production and the competitive factor of the single firm is the control of complementary assets in the hands of its potential partners. (Capello 1996: 490)

The rise of the network paradigm is reflected both in the institutional redesign of public sector governance, in the 'new territorial politics' (or new urban politics) with which new forms of governance are associated (cf. Cox 1993; Gough and Eisenschitz 1996) and in the increased importance attached to public-private partnerships of various kinds. Thus Parkinson and Harding have described the entrepreneurial city as 'one where key interest groups in the public, private and voluntary sectors develop a commitment to realizing a broadly consensual vision of urban development, devise appropriate structures for implementing this vision and mobilize both local and non-local resources to pursue it' (1995: 66–7).

Second, the generic object of social governance in the KWNS (as in other forms of national state) was a national population divided in the first instance into citizens of the national state and resident aliens. But this population was categorized and governed in distinctive ways suited to Atlantic Fordism and its mode of regulation. Above all, social policy was premised on conditions of full or near-full employment, lifelong employment – albeit not necessarily with the same employer – with a family wage for male workers, and the patriarchal nuclear family as the basic unit of civil society (Esping-Andersen 1994). The KWNS was also premised on a class compromise between organized labour and organized business in which responsible unionism and collective bargaining permitted managers to manage and workers to benefit from rising productivity as wage earners and welfare recipients. There were nonetheless some marginalized or overburdened social groups – most notably women as housewives, mothers and secondary participants in the labour force and also immigrants or other workers (and their families) who worked in disadvantaged segments of the labour market (Lewis 1998). This pattern was undermined both economically and socially. The crisis of Atlantic Fordism undermined the assumptions of full employment, the family wage and the gendered division of labour; and also led state managers to see the social wage increasingly as a cost of international production rather than as a source of domestic demand. The KWNS was also affected by a weakening of the national identity and solidarity that shaped it in its formative period and helped sustain the coalition behind it. This is reflected in changes in the values, social identities and interests associated with the welfare state (see chapter 2). These shifts have fragmented the KWNS coalition of forces, led to demands for more differentiated and flexible forms of economic and social policy, and led to concern with problems of social exclusion and ensuring life-time access to the benefits of a restructured welfare regime (for example, lifelong learning).

Third, the primacy of the national scale of economic and social governance depended on the coincidence of national economy, national state, national society and the survival of the national state as a sovereign body. This structured coherence has also been weakened. The national economy has been undermined by internationalization, the growth of multi-tiered global city networks, the formation of triad economies (such as the EU), and the re-emergence of regional and local economies in national states (see chapters 3 and 5). This complex articulation of global-regional-national-local economies is related to the 'hollowing out' of the national state, as its powers are delegated upwards to supraregional or international bodies, downwards to regional or local states, or outwards to relatively autonomous cross-national alliances among local metro-politan or regional states with complementary interests. There are also growing attempts to internationalize (or, at least, in Europe, to Euro-peanize) social policy. And the unity of the nation-state has been weak-ened by the (admittedly uneven) growth of multiethnic and multicultural societies and of divided political loyalties (with the resurgence of region-alism and nationalism as the rise of European identities, diasporic net-works, cosmopolitan patriotism, etc.). Thus we see a proliferation of scales on which economic and social policy are pursued as well as competing projects to reunify interscalar articulation around a new primary level – whether this be the industrial district, the city-region, wider subnational regions, cross-border regions, the triads or the global level.

Finally, the KWNS mixed economy model emerged in response to market failure and emphasized the state's role in correcting for market failures. The state's role in this regard nonetheless reflected the Fordist organizational paradigm. Large-scale, top-down hierarchical structures based on the belief in economies of scale spread easily to the state's eco-nomic and welfare roles as the primary means to correct for market failure. This was an era of big business, big unions and big government and 'organized capitalism' even in the more liberal forms of Atlantic Fordist regimes. This model was undermined by various factors. These include: growing political resistance to taxation and the emerging stagnation-inflation; crisis in postwar compromises between industrial capital and organized labour; new economic and social conditions and attendant problems that cannot be governed easily, if at all, through con-tinuing reliance on top-down state planning and/or simple market forces; growing resentment about the bureaucratism, inflexibility and cost of the welfare state as it continued to expand during the late 1960s and 1970s; and the rise of new social movements that did not fit easily into the postwar compromise (see chapter 2). These problems of the mixed economy model indicated that planning and other forms of top-down intervention by the Keynesian welfare state had their own distinctive crisis-tendencies and seemed to be increasingly prone to failure. After attempts to reinvigorate this state form through increased intervention on various scales, flanked in some cases by efforts to extend participation in decision-making, appeared to have failed in the 1970s, there were insistent calls from liberals and neoliberals for 'more market, less state'. Yet, after a few years' experimentation with neoliberalism, market forces also seemed to be less than perfect in several areas. In particular, while the Keynesian welfare forms of intervention may have been rolled back, privatization, deregulation and liberalization have also been seen to require new or enhanced forms of regulation, reregulation and competition policy. This has contributed to the more general trend towards increasing reliance on self-organization. Thus, despite the survival of market rhetoric in neoliberal regimes, the most significant trend in these, as well as in post-Fordist regimes where other types of governance predominate, is towards networking, governance, partnership and other forms of self-organization as the primary means of correcting for market failure. This is reflected, as we have seen, in the new 'network paradigm', with its emphasis on partnership, regulated self-regulation, the informal sector, the facilitation of self-organization and decentralized context-steering. Thus we can observe a tendential shift from imperative coordination by the sovereign state to an emphasis on interdependence, divisions of knowledge, reflexive negotiation and mutual learning.

4. Governance Failure?

Recognizing these major shifts in modes of governance compared to the Atlantic Fordist era, with its emphasis on the mixed economy, should not lead us to neglect the possibility of governance failure. Self-organization through networks need not prove more efficient procedurally than markets and states as means of economic or political coordination mechanism; and it is by no means guaranteed to produce more adequate outcomes. A commitment to continuing deliberation and negotiation does not exclude eventual governance failure. The criterion for such failure must nonetheless differ from that for markets or the state. There is no pre-given formal maximand or reference point to judge governance success, as there is with monetized profits in the economy and/or the (imaginary) perfect market outcome. Nor is there a contingent substantive criterion – the realization of specific political objectives connected to the (imagined) public interest – as there is with imperative coordination by the state. The primary point of governance is that goals will be modified in and through ongoing negotiation and reflection. This suggests that governance failure may comprise failure to redefine objectives in the face of continuing disagreement about whether they are still valid for the various partners.

But one can also apply procedural and substantive criteria to heterarchy and assess whether it produces more efficient long-term outcomes than market allocation and more effective long-term outcomes in realizing collective goals than imperative coordination by states. This requires comparative evaluation of all three modes of coordination in terms of all three of their respective rationalities. A very general claim about the superiority of networks has been proposed by Castells, the theorist of informational capitalism and the network society. He suggests that the traditional weakness of social networks is that 'they have considerable difficulty in coordinating functions, in focusing resources on specific goals, in managing the complexity of a given task beyond a certain size of the network' (2000a: 15). This is why, he continues, they were liable to be outperformed by organizations that relied on imperative coordination to mobilize resources around centrally defined goals and pursued them through rationalized, vertical chains of command and control. This disadvantage has now been definitively overcome, however, thanks to the spread of the new ICTs. For these enable networks to compress time and space, to negotiate and adjust their goals in real time and to decentralize responsibility for their execution. This in turn enables networks to share decision-making and to decentre performance (Castells 2000a: 15). One might well question this celebration of the miracle of ICT-enabled global networking in the light of the continued importance of vertical divisions of economic power and authority as well as of horizontal divisions of labour in economic networks and the networked state. But there can be little doubt that such marvelling at the performative power of self-organization is widely shared. This can be seen in the increasing interest in heterarchy (in all its forms) as a mechanism to reduce transaction costs in the economy in cases of bounded rationality, complex interdependence and asset specificity. It is also reflected in the state's increasing interest in heterarchy's potential for enhancing its capacity to secure political objectives by sharing power with forces beyond it and/or delegating responsibilities for specific objectives to partnerships (or other heterarchic arrangements). At the same time, however, we should not ignore the continuing advantages of the market and top-down command as means of coordination. After all, economic networks operate within the world market and continue to rely on it at all points in their economic activities; and economic networks typically involve the self-organization of organizations rather than of otherwise isolated individuals. And, *pace* Nozick's anarcho-capitalist fantasies, we have yet to see the state dissolve itself into a series of free-floating, self-organizing networks with no overarching coordination and no preservation of the right to recentralize control if the operations and/or results of networks do not fulfil the expectations of state managers, affected interests or public opinion.

Potential sources of governance failure

There are very good reasons for the failure of networks to completely displace markets and hierarchy as modes of coordination of complex interdependence. Here, given the concern of this book with the future of the capitalist state, I will concentrate on three main sets of factors which limit the success of the shift from government to governance for the purposes of economic and social policy. The first set affects all forms of economic and social coordination and is inscribed in the nature of capitalism itself. The latter has always depended on a contradictory balance between marketized and non-marketized organizational forms. Although this was previously understood mainly in terms of the balance between market and state (a distinction based on the institutional separation and operational autonomy of economics and politics), governance does not introduce a neutral third term but adds another site upon which the balance can be contested (for example, in terms of the leading role in private-public partnerships). One aspect of this is the scope that new forms of governance provide for a new meeting ground for the conflicting logics of accumulation and political mobilization. This is one of the reasons why the apparent promise of symmetry in reflexive self-organization is rarely realized when the governance of capital accumulation is at stake. For there are marked structural asymmetries in the capital–labour relation and in the forms of interdependence between the economic and the extra-economic conditions for capital accumulation. There are two further points to emphasize. We should recall that the logic of capital accumulation is itself inherently contradictory and dilemmatic and the turn to governance to compensate for market failure neither suspends these contradictions or dilemmas nor resolves them without displacing or deferring at least some of the costs of their provisional resolution elsewhere. And, in addition, we should recall that the state and politics are themselves riven by dilemmas and conflicts and this problematizes the scope and meaning of legitimation.

The second set concerns the contingent insertion of governance arrangements into the more general state system – which is itself an integral aspect of the structural asymmetries just mentioned but which also has its own specific structural biases. Of particular importance here is the relative primacy of different modes of coordination and access to institutional support and material resources to pursue reflexively arrived-at governance objectives. Among crucial issues here are the flanking and supporting measures that are taken by the state, the provision of material and symbolic support and the extent of any duplication or counteraction by other coordination mechanisms. For governance mechanisms are part of a much wider set of mechanisms that exist within the state in its integral sense, understood in this context as 'government + governance'.

There are three dimensions to this: (1) territorial scale; (2) temporalities; and (3) the technical division of labour and its relation to the state's general political role. First, as both governance and governance mechanisms exist on different scales (indeed one of their functions is to bridge scales), success at one scale may well depend on what occurs on other scales. Second, coordination mechanisms may also have different temporal horizons. One function of governance (as of quangos and corporatist arrangements beforehand) is to enable decisions with long-term implications to be divorced from short-term political (especially electoral) calculations. Corporatism once played this role, but the relativization of scale has worked to denationalize and disincorporate producer groups and to widen the range of 'stakeholders' whose participation might be relevant. But disjunctions may still arise between the temporalities of different governance and government mechanisms and this poses problems as to the ability of the state to address intertemporal problems and coordinate them – especially as these problems arise within the state apparatus itself as well as in other spheres. Third, although various governance mechanisms may acquire specific techno-economic, political and/or ideological functions, the state typically monitors their effects on its own capacity to secure social cohesion in divided societies. In this sense states attempt to retain control over the allocation of these different functions from the viewpoint of its general role and the continuing primacy of politics. They reserve to themselves the right to open, close, juggle and rearticulate governance from the viewpoint not only of its technical functions but also from the viewpoint of partisan and overall political advantage.

The third set of constraints is rooted in the nature of governance as self-organization. First, one of the causes for governance failure is the oversimplification of the conditions of action and/or deficient knowledge about causal connections affecting the object of governance. This is especially problematic when this object is an inherently unstructured but complex system, such as the insertion of the local into the global economy. Indeed, this leads to the more general 'governability' problem, namely, the question of whether the object of governance could ever be manageable, even with adequate knowledge (Mayntz 1993; Malpas and Wickham 1995). Second, coordination problems often arise on one or more of the interpersonal, interorganizational and intersystemic levels. These three levels are often related in complex ways. Thus interorganizational negotiation often depends on interpersonal trust; and decentred intersystemic steering involves the representation of system logics through interorganizational and/or interpersonal communication. Third, linked to this is the problematic relation between those engaged in communication (networking, negotiation, etc.) and those social forces whose interests and identities are being represented. Gaps inevitably open between these groups leading to representational and legitimacy crises and/or to problems in securing compliance. And, fourth, where there are various partnerships and other governance arrangements concerned with interdependent issues, there is a problem of coordination among them.

5. Metagovernance

Given the complexity of the social world, structural contradictions, strategic dilemmas and multiple or, at least ambivalent, goals, failure is a necessary outcome of attempts at coordination through the anarchy of the market forces, the hierarchy of state control, or the heterarchy of the self-organization of inter-organizational relations. It is worth emphasizing, *pace* Castells, that network and/or partnership forms of governance are not always procedurally more efficient than markets or states in solving problems of economic and/or political coordination, nor are they always more likely to produce outcomes that are acceptable in terms of substantive values. More generally, there is a clear paradox with regard to the failure of markets, states and governance as proposed solutions to the reduction and mastery of complexity – that failure itself leads to greater complexity as fresh attempts are made to govern and to deal with its consequences.

If markets, states and governance are each prone to failure, how is economic and political coordination for economic and social development ever possible and why is it often judged to have succeeded? In part, this can be explained through the multiplicity of satisficing criteria and the range of potential vested interests so that at least some aims are realized to a socially acceptable degree for at least some of those affected. A further explanation can be derived from the observation that 'governing and governance itself should be dynamic, complex and varied' (Kooiman 1993b: 36). This highlights the role of the 'metastructures' of inter-organizational coordination (Alexander 1995: 52) or, more generally, of metagovernance or, perhaps better, collibration – the governance of governance.

Metagovernance involves the organization of the conditions for governance in its broadest sense. Thus, corresponding to the three basic modes of governance distinguished above, we can distinguish four modes of metagovernance, one of which is an umbrella mode.

First, there is metaexchange. This involves the reflexive redesign of individual markets (for example, for land, labour, money, commodities, knowledge – or appropriate subdivisions thereof) and/or the reflexive reordering of relations among markets by modifying their operation and articulation. Market agents often resort to market redesign in response to failure and/or hire the services of those who claim some expertise in this field. Among the latter are management gurus, management consultants, human relations experts, corporate lawyers and accountants. More generally, there has long been interest in issues of the institutional redesign of the market mechanism, its embeddedness in non-market mechanisms, and the conditions for the maximum formal rationality of market forces. There are also markets in markets. This can lead to 'regime shopping', competitive deregulatory 'races to the bottom' or, in certain conditions, 'races to the top' to provide the most favourable conditions for strong competition (see chapter 3). Moreover, because markets function in the shadow of hierarchy and/or heterarchy, attempts are also made to modify markets, their institutional supports and their agents to improve their efficiency and/or compensate for market failures and inadequacies.

Second, there is metaorganization. This involves the reflexive redesign of organizations, the creation of intermediating organizations, the reordering of inter-organizational relations, and the management of organizational ecologies (in other words, the organization of the conditions of organizational evolution in conditions where many organizations coexist, compete, cooperate and co-evolve). Reflexive organizational managers can undertake such metaorganizational functions themselves (for example, through 'macro-management' and organizational innovation) and/or turn to alleged experts such as constitutional lawyers, public choice economists, theorists of public administration, think-tanks, advocates of reflexive planning, specialists in policy evaluation, etc. This is reflected in the continuing redesign, rescaling, and adaptation, sometimes more ruptural, sometimes more continuous, in the state apparatus and the manner in which it is embedded within the wider political system.

Third, there is metaheterarchy. This involves the organization of the conditions of self-organization by redefining the framework for heterarchy or reflexive self-organization. It has sometimes been called metagovernance (including, it must be admitted, in my own work) – a term that is better reserved for what Dunsire (1996) calls collibration and is best interpreted as the umbrella concept for the redesign of the relationship among different modes of governance. This can range from providing opportunities for spontaneous sociability (Fukuyama 1995; see also Putnam 2000) to introducing innovations to further 'institutional thickness' (Amin and Thrift 1995).

Fourth, and finally, there is metagovernance. This involves rearticulating and collibrating different modes of governance. The key issues for those involved in metagovernance are '(a) how to cope with other actors' self-referentiality; and (b) how to cope with their own self-referentiality' (Dunsire 1996: 320). Metagovernance involves managing the complexity, plurality and tangled hierarchies found in prevailing modes of co-ordination. It is the organization of the conditions for governance and involves the judicious mixing of market, hierarchy and networks to achieve the best possible outcomes from the viewpoint of those engaged in metagovernance. In this sense it also means the organization of the conditions of governance in terms of their structurally inscribed strategic selectivity, that is, in terms of their asymmetrical privileging of some outcomes over others. Unfortunately, since every practice is prone to failure, metagovernance and collibration are also likely to fail. This implies that there is no Archimedean point from which governance or collibration can be guaranteed to succeed.

Metagovernance should not be confused with some superordinate level of government in control of all governance arrangements nor with the imposition of a single, all-purpose mode of governance. Rather, it involves a containing process of 'muddling through'. It involves defining new boundary-spanning roles and functions, creating linkage devices, sponsoring new organizations, identifying appropriate lead organizations to coordinate other partners, designing institutions and generating visions to facilitate self-organization in different fields. It also involves providing mechanisms for collective feedback and learning about the functional linkages and the material interdependencies among different sites and spheres of action, and encouraging a relative coherence among diverse objectives, spatial and temporal horizons, actions and outcomes of governance arrangements. It involves the shaping of the context within which these arrangements can be forged rather than developing specific strategies and initiatives for them.

States play a major and increasing role in metagovernance. They provide the ground rules for governance and the regulatory order in and through which governance partners can pursue their aims; ensure the compatibility or coherence of different governance mechanisms and regimes; act as the primary organizer of the dialogue among policy communities; deploy a relative monopoly of organizational intelligence and information with which to shape cognitive expectations; serve as a 'court of appeal' for disputes arising within and over governance; seek to rebalance power differentials by strengthening weaker forces or systems in the interests of system integration and/or social cohesion; try to modify the self-understanding of identities, strategic capacities and interests of individual and collective actors in different strategic contexts, and hence alter their implications for preferred strategies and tactics; and also assume political responsibility in the event of governance failure. This emerging role means that networking, negotiation, noise reduction and negative as well as positive coordination occur 'in the shadow of hierarchy' (Scharpf 1994: 40). It also suggests the need for almost permanent institutional and organizational innovation to maintain the very possibility (however remote) of sustained economic growth.

Thus metagovernance does not eliminate other modes of coordination. Markets, hierarchies and heterarchies still exist; but they operate in a context of 'negotiated decision-making'. So, on the one hand, market competition will be balanced by cooperation and the invisible hand will be combined with a visible handshake. On the other hand, the state is no longer the sovereign authority. It becomes but one participant among others in the pluralistic guidance system and contributes its own distinctive resources to the negotiation process. As the range of networks, partnerships and other models of economic and political governance expand, official apparatuses remain at best *primus inter pares*. For, although public money and law would still be important in underpinning their operation, other resources (such as private money, knowledge or expertise) would also be critical to their success. The state's involvement would become less hierarchical, less centralized and less dirigiste in character. The exchange of information and moral suasion would become key sources of legitimation and the state's influence would depend as much on its role as a prime source and mediator of collective intelligence as on its command over economic resources or legitimate coercion (Willke 1992).

6. Metagovernance Failure

Recognizing possible contributions of reflexive metagovernance to economic and social coordination is no guarantee of success. It is certainly not a purely technical matter that can be resolved by experts in organizational design or public administration. For all the particular activities and functions of the state are conducted under the primacy of the political owing to its ultimate responsibility for maintaining social cohesion. This constraint plagues the liberal prescription of an arms-length relationship between the market and the nightwatchman state – since states are rarely strong enough to resist pressures to intervene when anticipated political advantage is at stake or it needs to respond to social unrest. More generally, we can safely assume that, *if every mode of governance fails, then so will metagovernance!* This is especially likely where the objects of governance and metagovernance are complicated and interconnected.[4]

Overall, this analysis leads to three conclusions, intellectual, practical and philosophical respectively. For, once the incompleteness of attempts at coordination (whether through the market, the state or heterarchy) is accepted as inevitable, it is necessary to adopt a satisficing approach which has at least three key dimensions.

First, it requires a reflexive orientation about what would be an acceptable outcome in the case of incomplete success, to compare the effects of failure/inadequacies in the market, government and governance, and regular reassessment of the extent to which current actions are producing desired outcomes. This involves a commitment not only to learning but also to learning about how to learn reflexively.

Second, it requires deliberate cultivation of a flexible repertoire (requisite variety) of responses to retain the ability flexibly to alter strategies and select those that are more successful. For, if every mode of economic and political coordination is failure-laden, relative success in coordination over time depends on the capacity to switch modes of coordination as the limits of any one mode become evident. This may well seem inefficient from an economizing viewpoint because it introduces slack or waste. But it also provides major sources of flexibility in the face of failure (cf. Grabher 1994). Moreover, because different periods and conjunctures require different kinds of policy mix, the balance in the repertoire will need to be varied. This provides the basis for displacing or postponing failures and crises.

It also suggests that the ideologically motivated destruction of alternative modes of coordination could prove counterproductive: for they may well need to be reinvented in one or another form. This dilemma is evident from the experience of the Thatcher (1979–90) and Major (1990–7) governments. The neoliberal hostility to the interventionist state, trade unionism and corporatism, municipal socialism and other features of the postwar settlement was reflected in continuing efforts to destroy, weaken or marginalize them. But, whilst this was perhaps necessary to change attitudes in the attempted modernization of the British economy, state and society, it also dissipated experience and knowledge that could still prove useful. And, whilst it removed specific institutional and organizational obstacles to the neoliberal project, it also deprived the central state in the short term of an adequate range of modes of coordination to deal with complex issues in an environment made more turbulent by the intended and unintended effects of its own radical policies. So the Thatcher and Major governments eventually found it necessary to relearn lessons about the limits of the market mechanism and to reinvent alternative modes of coordination to supplement, complement or compensate for the operation of market forces. This rediscovery was usually disguised behind changed names, innovative discourses, policy churning and institutional turnover. Nonetheless, the usual policy cycle of market, governance and state was repeated in central government policies for urban regeneration and many other policies.

Third, it requires self-reflexive 'irony' in the sense that the relevant social forces must recognize the likelihood of failure but proceed as if success were possible. The supreme irony in this context is that the need for irony holds not only for individual attempts at governance using individual governance mechanisms, but also for the practice of metagovernance using appropriate metagovernance mechanisms. More often, however, we find cynicism and fatalism. Cynics anticipate failure but seek to further their own interests if and when failure occurs (the behaviour of its directors as Enron collapsed is only the most egregious recent example of such behaviour). Fatalists anticipate failure and therefore either do nothing or carry on regardless (for further discussion of requisite reflexivity, requisite variety and requisite irony, see Jessop 2002b). All three dimensions of dealing with the prospects of metagovernance failure highlight once again, of course, the importance of agency for the course of economic, political and social development.

7. Concluding Remarks

The arguments in this chapter began with general reflections on the recurrence of liberalism, corporatism and statism as means of governing the complex material, social and temporal interdependences that characterize the always-problematic course of capital accumulation. I then supplemented this account with general reflections on the recurrence of failures in markets, concertation and planning as means of governing these same interdependences. On this basis I described the mutual constitution of the objects, subjects and modalities of governance of Atlantic Fordism on all four dimensions of the KWNS and sketched their crisis-tendencies and emerging failures. I identified the increased salience in discourse and in practice of various forms of self-organization in the governance of the globalizing, knowledge-based economy. Rather than join in the current celebration of governance as a superior mode of coordination to markets and the state, however, I offered a contrarian account of the general tendencies to governance failure. I reinforced this account by noting once again the contradictions and dilemmas inherent in the capital relation and the limitations to effective state intervention owing to the primacy of the political in the exercise of state power. In contrast to preceding chapters, however, I have not followed this general analysis with more detailed work on specific forms of governance and governance failure. The main reason for this is that there can be no general theory of governance because there is no general object of governance. This contrasts with the possibilities of constructing a general theory of capital accumulation on the basis of the specificities of the capital relation (for further discussion of this point, see Jessop 1995). Nonetheless, the analyses presented in earlier chapters should suffice to support the overall argument.

To conclude, whilst recognizing the inevitability of failure, we should also note that there is much that remains contingent. This includes the modalities, sites, forms, temporalities, spatialities and effects of failure; and, in addition, the capacities for recuperating or responding to failure. Interest in self-organization has grown in recent years in response to the experience of market and state failure and in response to the increasing complexity of the social world. But, as I have also argued, self-reflexive self-organization itself is prone to failure. There are different ways of coping with the inevitability of failure ranging from small-scale incremental adjustments based on trial-and-error learning to comprehensive attempts at constitutional and institutional redesign. Indeed, without learning *and forgetting*, social order, such as it is, would be impossible. Finally, in addressing the four main forms of metagovernance (concerned respectively with the reflexive reorganization of markets, hierarchies and networks and with the collibration of these different modes of governance), I have emphasized three general principles of governance in the face of complexity: these are the principles of requisite reflexivity, requisite variety and requisite irony. How these are applied, if at all, in the regulation and governance of capital accumulation is an issue still to be properly explored.

7

Towards Schumpeterian Workfare Postnational Regimes?

This chapter draws together the main threads of arguments spread over the last five chapters. It suggests that what is tendentially replacing the Keynesian welfare national state is a Schumpeterian workfare postnational regime. I first discuss this as an ideal-type and then, as with the KWNS, propose some variant forms. It is not my intention to offer an alternative to the SWPR as it is outlined here as a key element in the mode of regulation of contemporary capitalism, let alone to propose a detailed blueprint for an alternative to capitalism as a mode of production. There are three reasons for this reticence. First, this study has been mainly concerned to provide the theoretical basis for a radical re-examination of the dynamic of Atlantic Fordism and for an exploration of probable forms of economic and social policy in the post-Fordist period. Such a limited study cannot provide the basis for sketching an alternative, which would need to embrace the entire world market and lifeworld and thus look well beyond the confines of the spatio-temporal matrices with which this work is concerned. Second, although I have hinted at the ecological contradictions of capitalism, I have not really addressed these contradictions even for the economic spaces of Atlantic Fordism, let alone for the world as a whole. Any alternative would need to integrate the political economy of capitalism into a more encompassing critique of its political ecology. The same point needs to be made regarding the military dimensions of state power and its relationship to geo-politics and geo-economics. And, third, given my remarks on governance failure and the importance of collective reflexivity and romantic irony, any alternative to the globalizing, knowledge-based economy or the SWPR, let alone capitalism as a whole, would have to be developed and elaborated collectively and democratically and not pronounced *ex cathe-*

dra by an inveterate theorist. I hope that the modest remarks contained in this work will nonetheless contribute to the search for alternatives.

1. Trends and Claims

Chapter 2 presented a stylized account of the form of state that developed in the space of Atlantic Fordism. The next four chapters each elaborated emerging trends in advanced capitalism and its state form relative to one or another dimension of the KWNS. Specifically, they identified:

- a tendential shift from Keynesian full employment towards Schumpeterian economic intervention, which I summarized in terms of the rise of a specifically Schumpeterian version of the competition state;
- a tendential shift from a welfarist mode of social reproduction towards a workfarist mode, defined in terms of the increasing subordination of social policy and collective consumption to the discursively constructed needs of the economy;
- a tendential shift from the primacy of the national scale in determining the economic and social functions of the extra-economic towards a postnational relativization of scale; and
- a tendential shift from the primacy of state intervention to compensate for market failures in a mixed economy to an emphasis on public-private partnerships and other self-organizing governance mechanisms to compensate for both state and market failures in a networked economy.

So far these trends have largely been considered separately. This mode of presentation was adopted to simplify what would otherwise have become a very unwieldy analysis in which everything was being related to everything else and, moreover, at the same time. It has also enabled me to elaborate some of the more novel concepts and theoretical arguments at the most appropriate point in the overall development of the book rather than at their first mention in another context. Moreover, presentational concerns apart, it is worth treating the four trends separately because each of the trends has its own causal dynamic and has also developed in quite varied ways in the different Atlantic Fordist social formations. Only after we have considered the uneven development of the four trends individually could we hope to explore how they are combined, if at all, to create any overall trend towards a SWPR in any given social formation. This is particularly important because the current relativization of scale also affects the scalar articulation of economic and social policy in different ways and poses major problems in their governance.

Finally, whether taken individually or together, these changes are most certainly closely linked to the search for solutions to the objective crisis-tendencies and perceived crises of Atlantic Fordism. Thus the transition in advanced capitalist economies – in the context of the overall global division of labour and the world market – from Fordism to post-Fordism is an important part of the overall context for the move from some version of the KWNS to some version of the SWPR. Although the reasons for this shift are primarily grounded in responses to specific economic and social problems, such responses are always politically mediated. Thus national variations in the pace, direction and emerging patterns of the SWPR are often rooted in their respective initial starting points, differences in modes of growth and insertion into the global economy, and in the institutional specificities and distinctive balance of forces. This means that, even if certain general tendencies can be identified and grounded in the logic of contemporary capitalism, this does not justify a simple, 'one-size-fits-all' account of the restructuring of the capitalist type of state. Instead, proper comparative analyses are required to comprehend and explain variations as well as similarities across the advanced capitalist economies. Such studies have not been undertaken in the context of this particular work because it has been concerned to identify the more abstract tendencies associated with the ecological dominance of the capital relation in an increasingly integrated world market. The approach to economic determination adopted in this work excludes absolutely any claim that the logic of capital accumulation somehow determines every aspect of social formations. Instead, ecological dominance means that the course of capital accumulation creates more problems for other institutional orders and the lifeworld than they can cause for it. How these institutional orders and the lifeworld adapt to these problems cannot be determined at this level of analysis. This requires a more detailed analysis both of the distinctive path-dependent and strategically selective character of these institutional orders and of the changing balance of forces organized around different responses to the logic of capital accumulation.

The broad empirical trends presented in the preceding chapters have a wide range of causes, and each trend should be seen as 'the complex synthesis of multiple determinations' (Marx 1973: 100). It would certainly be wrong to treat any trend as a singular causal mechanism and neglect their essentially descriptive, synthetic and generalized nature.[1] This is why I have discussed some of the more abstract tendencies and counter-tendencies that have combined to produce these trends. For the same reason I considered possible empirical countertrends that might

qualify or limit the full realization of these trends – countertrends themselves produced through specific abstract tendencies and countertendencies. The expression of these trends also varies markedly across time
and space. Lastly, I have suggested how the four shifts involved in the
KWNS–SWPR transition are linked mainly – but not exclusively – to the
search for responses to the crisis of Atlantic Fordism. Distinguishing
cause and effect in this complex set of interrelations is clearly difficult
because so many features of the once taken-for-granted economic,
political, social and cultural landscape are changing at the same time.
This is why it is important at this level of abstraction to consider them
in terms of the structural coupling of economic and political transfor-
mations without attempting to judge the relative causal weight of economic and political factors in isolation. This is where the concept of
ecological dominance is especially useful heuristically and analytically.
For it highlights the interaction between the economic and the political
under the dominance of the logic of capital accumulation, which depends
on a close link between the economic and the extra-economic.

2. The Ideal-Typical SWPR

The ideal-typical SWPR can be described, at the risk of some repetition,
as follows (see also table 7.1). First, regarding its distinctive role in securing the conditions for the improbable continuation of profitable private
business from the viewpoint of particular capitals and capital in general,
the SWPR is Schumpeterian insofar as it tries to promote permanent
innovation and flexibility in relatively open economies by intervening on
the supply-side and to strengthen as far as possible the structural and/or
systemic competitiveness of the relevant economic spaces. The primary
organizing concept for the development of accumulation strategies, state
projects and hegemonic visions in this context is the knowledge-based
economy. This broad concept has the advantage in this regard that it is
relatively open-ended but nonetheless resonates with a wide range of
highly visible and interconnected changes in contemporary capitalist formations. As such, it can serve as the nodal point in a wide range of economic, political, social and cultural discourses and has implications for
the restructuring of entire social formations (on the narrative construction of crisis and the discursive reorientation of accumulation strategies,
state projects and hegemonic visions, see chapter 2). Complementing
these new strategic concerns in economic policy has been the rejection,
demotion or rearticulation of other, earlier policy objectives.

Second, regarding its distinctive functions in securing the conditions
for the problematic reproduction of labour-power as a fictitious com-

modity, the SWPR can be described (no doubt infelicitously and at the risk of misunderstanding) as a workfare regime insofar as it subordinates social policy to the demands of economic policy. Included under this latter rubric are the promotion of labour market flexibility and employ-ability, the development of the new globalizing, knowledge-based economy and the cultivation of structural and/or systemic competitive-ness. It is worth repeating here that the scope of economic policy has been massively widened and deepened because of the increased impor-tance for capital accumulation of what was previously regarded as being 'extra-economic'. Thus, whilst the KWNS tried to extend the social rights of its citizens, the SWPR is more concerned to provide welfare services that benefit business and thereby demotes individual needs to second place. This workfarist subordination of social to economic policy is most likely where these policies concern the present and future working population. This is why labour market policy, education and training have such a key role in the workfare strategy. Concern with training and labour market functioning has long been a feature of state involvement in the social reproduction of labour-power, of course, but the SWPR gives greater weight to flexibility and gives it new meaning (Ainley 1997), and also redefines the nature of the skills and competencies that education and training are intended to deliver. It is for these reasons that the state also attempts to (re-)make the subjects who are expected to serve as partners in the innovative, knowledge-driven, entrepreneurial, flexible economy and its accompanying self-reliant, autonomous, empowered workfare regime (for a recent illustration, see Blair and Schröder 1999).

Workfare is also associated with downward pressure on public spend-ing that is reflected in absolute or relative reductions in public spending and, failing that, in vigorous measures of cost containment. This is most likely where social spending concerns those who are not (potentially) active members of the labour force and/or have already left it. This is particularly evident in the recent treatment of pensions (the largest single item in welfare budgets) and involves an increasingly systematic assault on pension rights in both the public and the private sectors. It can also be discerned in the health service. Cuts in social expenditure are especially likely where the social wage is seen as a cost of produc-tion, as being related more to populist demands and social engineering than to economic performance, as an unproductive deduction from rev-enues that could be better spent by individual economic agents in the market and as a source of rigidities in the productive sector. It is less likely to occur where less emphasis is given to the absolute or relative cost of factors of production and more to their relative contribution to economic output; less to the economic and more to the extra-economic

Table 7.1   The Schumpeterian workfare postnational regime

Distinctive set of economic policies	Distinctive set of social policies	Primary scale (if any)	Primary means to compensate market failure
Focuses on innovation and competitiveness in open economies, with increasing stress on supply-side to to promote KBE	Subordinates social policy to an expanded notion of economic policy; downward pressure on the 'social wage' and attack on welfare rights	Relativization of scale at expense of national scale. Competition to establish a new primary scale but continued role of national state(s).	Increased role of self-organizing governance to correct both for market and state failures. But state gains greater role in the exercise of metagovernance.
Schumpeterian	Workfare	Postnational	Regime

dimensions of competitiveness; less to the immediate tax costs of social spending and more to its long-term contribution to production; and less to the immediately unproductive nature of social expenditure and more to its role in compensating workers (and other adversely affected social forces) for the risks and disruptions involved in international trade. Nonetheless, both accounts of social spending regard it in economic terms and both seek to put downward pressure on social spending as well as to reorient in line with their respective accounts of competitiveness.

Third, compared with the earlier primacy of the national scale in economic management and the provision of social policy, the SWPR is postnational. This trend is occasioned by the increased significance of other spatial scales and horizons of action, which make the national economy less susceptible to effective macroeconomic management and the national territory less important as a power container.[2] This does not mean the end of the national economic policy concerned with promoting international competitiveness, nor the end of the national state. It does signify the relativization of scale in economic and social policy compared to the Atlantic Fordist period. This is associated with the transfer of economic and social policy-making functions upwards, downwards and sideways. On a global level, this can be seen in the growing concern of a growing number of international agencies (such as the IMF, World Bank, OECD, and ILO) and intergovernmental forums (such as the G8) with the shaping of current social as well as economic policy agendas. In part, the EU acts as a relay for these agenda-shaping efforts and, in part, it has itself played an active role in developing its own agenda for countries outside its borders. This is most clear in the case of the post-socialist economies, especially those in the front ranks of new candidate member states; but it can also be seen in its interest in social as well as economic policy in associate member states and North Africa (cf. Deacon 1995, 1996, 2001; de Swaan 1992; Leibfried 1993; Wilding 1997). The EU level is also imposing more numerous and tighter restrictions on national economic and social governance, especially through the norms of the Single European Market (SEM), the Maastricht criteria for economic convergence, and the requirements of the EMU. This is reflected in the tendential Europeanization of labour market policies, in the transformation of national corporatist and bargaining arrangements and in the development of social pacts. What is emerging in this context is a series of multilevel government and/or governance regimes oriented to issues of the interscalar rearticulation of the economic and political – with the EU just one among many such emerging regimes (Poulantzas 1978; Jessop 2000). At the same time, there are tendencies to devolve some economic and social policy-making to the regional, urban and local levels on the grounds that policies intended to influence the micro-economic supply-side and social regeneration are best designed close to their sites of implementation. In some cases this also involves cross-border cooperation among regional, urban or local spaces. In all three regards regulation regimes have thus become more postnational. Yet, paradoxically, this can lead to an enhanced role for national states in controlling the interscalar transfer of these powers – suggesting a shift from sovereignty to a *primus inter pares* role in intergovernmental relations.

The postnational moment of economic and social policy restructuring is complex because of the proliferation of scales and the relativization of scale with which it is associated. There are clear differences among the triads here. NAFTA is primarily a continental trading system based on America's dominance as a quasi-continental economy (itself comprising many different regional economies with different levels of economic performance), with Canada and Mexico being increasingly obliged to internalize US production and consumption norms as well as to find their place as best they can within an emerging continental division of labour. The East Asian triad has developed an increasingly important regional division of labour organized primarily under Japanese regional hegemony, but it has no coherent institutional mechanisms to ensure effective coordination and is weakened by Japan's continuing inability to break out of its political impasse as well as by the residual bitterness felt by significant social forces in countries occupied by Japan in the 1930s and 1940s. The EU provides the only example among the three triad regions of a clear commitment to economic, political and social integration and, more ambivalently, to the development of supranational state structures. Nonetheless all three regions/triads are linked to internationalization of policy regimes not only in economic but also in juridical, political and social fields. This excludes any easy generalization from the EU case to the other two triads – or vice versa; this in itself is a sign that one should not push globalization too far as a general explanatory framework of recent changes.

Finally, regarding the mode of delivery of economic and social policies, the SWPR has become more regime-like relative to the statism of the KWNS. This is reflected in the increased importance of non-state mechanisms in compensating for market failures and inadequacies in the delivery of state-sponsored economic and social policies. This provides a second important aspect to the apparent (but deceptive) 'hollowing out' of national states, namely, the increased importance of private-public networks to state activities on all levels – from local partnerships to supranational neo-corporatist arrangements (e.g., Clarke and Gaile 1998; Falkner 1998). The often remarked shift from government towards governance (from imperative coordination to networking and other forms of self-organization) means that traditional forms of intervention now play a lesser role in economic and social policy. This does not mean that law and money have disappeared, of course; instead, active economic and social steering now tend to run more through soft regulation and reflexive law, additionality and private-public partnerships, organizational intelligence and information-sharing, etc. A key role is also played by metagovernance, that is, the organization of the institutional framework and rules for individual modes of governance and the rebalancing of different modes of governance (see Dunsire 1996; Jessop 1998, 2002b). This can be seen at the European level, where EU institutions typically operate less in the manner of an upscaled, supranational sovereign state apparatus than as a nodal point in an extensive web of metagovernance operations. Thus they have a central role in orchestrating economic and social policy in and across many different scales of action involving a wide range of official, quasi-official, private economic and civil interests (Ekengreen 1997; Sbragia 2000; Tömmel 1994, 1998; Willke 1992, 1997).

3. On the Use of Ideal Types

Like all ideal-types, the KWNS and SWPR have been formed through the one-sided accentuation of empirically observable features (in this case, those of Atlantic Fordist social formations) to construct a logically possible social phenomenon. This does not mean that they derive from a naïve, theoretically innocent observation of surface appearances – on the contrary, they derive from a reflexive, theoretically informed reconstruction of basic trends and countertrends and an attempt to ground them in underlying causal mechanisms.[3] They accentuate certain distinctive features of a phenomenon in order to identify what lends it structural coherence (including, perhaps, a patterned incoherence that comes from historically specific structural contradictions, strategic dilemmas and discursive paradoxes) and to highlight distinctive developmental tendencies. In this sense they are intended to serve as theoretically informed reference points in empirical analyses rather than as substitutes for such analyses and to enable connections to be made between such analyses and a critical realist analysis of the evolving political economy of capitalism. Such one-sided ideal types are never completely realized. Thus neither the ideal-typical KWNS nor its various subtypes were found in pure form in Atlantic Fordism. Likewise, constructing an ideal-type SWPR does not presuppose actually existing examples of the SWPR in pure form, nor does it imply that any movement along its different dimensions occurs evenly and at the same pace. Indeed there is major variation in the search for solutions to the problems of Atlantic Fordism and the KWNS. It involves neither a unidirectional movement nor a multilateral convergence across all national regimes. What do exist are path-dependent mixes of types (alloyed with incidental and accidental features) which must be considered in all their complexity rather than one-sidedly. Although the distinctive features of the SWPR emerge most clearly in this rather Eurocentric contrast with the KWNS, there are important East Asian examples of its having developed in the absence of any more or less crisis-prone KWNS. Indeed, these latter examples once served – before the so-called Asian Crisis – as models to solve crisis-tendencies in the West.

Four comments on the ideal-typical SWPR are appropriate here. First, the choice of this term for the emergent state form was intended to make the contrast with the KWNS as stark as possible. Thus the ideal-typical SWPR marks a clear break with the KWNS insofar as (1) domestic full employment is deprioritized in favour of international competitiveness; (2) redistributive welfare rights take second place to a productivist reordering of social policy; (3) the primacy of the national state is deprivileged in favour of particular state activities on other scales; and (4) governance in a negotiated, networked society is given more emphasis than government in a mixed economy. In practice, of course, the opposition will be less marked. Yet this contrast can be justified on both critical and heuristic grounds because of a continuing penchant among many commentators to suggest that international Keynesianism could restore the conditions for global expansion and/or that the welfare state is an irreversible historical achievement[4] and has not been much affected by globalization. My aim in developing this alternative concept is to show that, whilst the capitalist type of state is necessarily involved in securing the conditions for economic and social reproduction, this need not take a KWNS form. Indeed, the current restructuring for capital would actually seem to require a break with the KWNS. That some states may prove unable to effect the necessary changes would only undermine this claim if they could still compete successfully in the new global economy whilst retaining their earlier form.

Second, the two ideal types present the distinctive features of the KWNS and SWPR respectively as opposed to all their historically given, currently dominant or possible future features. For example, designating the postwar state form as 'Keynesian' and thereby emphasizing its demand-side role does not mean that the KWNS had no supply-side policies. As shown in chapter 2, it also promoted a uniform national infrastructure as a basis for generalizing Fordist norms of production and consumption and to diminish uneven national development. It also contributed to the supply of technological innovation through increased support for science, a massive expansion of higher education along Fordist lines and, sometimes, military support for R&D. But there are significant differences in the relation between demand- and supply-side policies in the KWNS and SWPR. Whereas KWNS supply-side policies were shaped by the Fordist paradigm with its emphasis on economies of scale, big science and productivity growth, SWPR supply-side policies are oriented to permanent innovation, to economies of scope, agglomeration and networks, to promoting the knowledge-based economy and to structural and systemic competitiveness. This puts a far greater premium on the explicit, strategically self-conscious management of the innovation systems and competition policy, on broad interpretations of the factors bearing on successful innovation and competitiveness in open economies and on the capacity for institutional learning than would have been typical of the Fordist KWNS. Conversely, whereas KWNS macroeconomic policies were concerned to create the conditions for full employment to suit the demands of domestic productive capital, SWPR macroeconomic policies are concerned with inflation (including asset inflation) and with prudent budgets to satisfy the demands of mobile money capital. Likewise, turning to social policy, whilst concern with training and labour market functioning has long been a feature of state involvement in the social reproduction of labour-power, the transition from Fordism, with its expectation of a job for life (if not the same job for life), to post-Fordism, with its emphasis on economic insecurity and constant change, leads to a different form of training and education. This analysis could be continued, but enough has been written, I hope, to bring out the importance of the discontinuities in apparently similar activities as well as the significance of new activities. More generally, of course, the SWPR will also express other concerns and perform many other functions typical of capitalist states, but it is the four features noted above, together with their implications for the dynamic of capitalism and the overall functioning of states, that differentiate it from other capitalist regimes. Together they become an integral part of its accumulation strategy and they are also reflected in the state and hegemonic projects with which this accumulation strategy is associated.

Third, four clarifications are needed to avoid misunderstanding the purport of the SWPR ideal type:

1   In referring to Schumpeterianism in the characterization of the state's new role in economic reproduction, I do not wish to suggest that Schumpeter himself advocated the SWPR in all its complexity and variety. Nor, of course, did Keynes provide a blueprint for all subsequent institutional and policy developments associated in whatever country with the KWNS. Neither Keynes nor Schumpeter can be seen as the legitimate founding fathers of regimes with which they have since been identified. Nonetheless, in referring to these economists I have identified emblematic thinkers whose ideas have come to be associated (rightly or wrongly) with the state's role in promoting capital accumulation in specific periods and/or economic regimes.[5] Keynes was often cited to justify the increasing concern with the state's possible role in securing full employment; Schumpeter has been rediscovered as a theorist of innovation as the motor force of long waves of economic expansion. There were analogues to Keynes in other economies, of course, such as Wicksell in Sweden, but Keynes has become the emblematic figure for macroeconomic management oriented to the demand side. Likewise, other economists have examined the dynamics of competition, innovation, entrepreneurship and long waves of economic growth, but none has done so as vividly and comprehensively as Schumpeter. In addition, Keynes and Keynesianism, with their emphasis on economic policy, provided a context within which the welfare state could develop: for, as we have subsequently observed, without full employment, a universalist welfare state would be hard to maintain. The role of a 'Keynesian epistemic community' (Ikenberry 1993) in establishing the foundations for the international postwar settlement associated with Atlantic Fordism is especially important even if there were different routes followed at different speeds to Keynesian full employment policies (on which, see the contributions in Hall 1989).

2   The contrast between the two economists is far more specific than
    would be implied in any simple contrast between concern with the
    demand- and supply-side. For Schumpeter's interest in the latter dif-
    fered markedly from that of economists such as Hayek, Friedman or
    Laffer. Thus Hayek was concerned with the economic and constitu-
    tional conditions for liberty, Milton Friedman with the money supply,
    and Laffer (who now remembers the laughable but politically con-
    venient Laffer?) with the supply-side impact of varying rates of taxa-
    tion. It is the supply of innovation that was central to Schumpeter's
    analysis of capitalist growth dynamics rather than the supply-side
    implications of liberty, money or taxation. And it is innovation-driven
    structural competitiveness that is becoming central to the successful
    performance of the economic functions of the contemporary capital-
    ist state.

3   In adopting 'workfare' to identify the social policy dimension of the
    SWPR, I am not claiming that a precondition of welfare support for
    the able-bodied is to work, retrain or prove a willingness to do so.
    Instead I want to highlight a major reorientation of social policy:
    away from redistributive concerns based on expanding welfare rights
    in a national state towards more productivist and cost-saving
    concerns in an open economy. The more usual meaning of 'work-
    fare' is merely a special, neoliberal example of the more general
    trend in the reorganization of the state's role in promoting social
    reproduction.

4   In adopting 'regime' to characterize the mode of governance, I am
    not claiming that the state has withered away. Instead, I am seeking
    to highlight the increased importance of various forms of self-
    organization to compensate for market failure. This is actually
    reflected in a dual shift from government to governance and from
    government to metagovernance that accompanies the other changes
    in the capitalist type of state that I have noted.

Finally, in suggesting that there is a tendential movement from one to
the other, I am not suggesting that a radical rupture has occurred that
has transformed everything. There are always variable path-dependent
'conservation-dissolution' effects (Poulantzas 1975). Change can
transform and refunctionalize earlier social relations, institutions or
discourses, conserving them in the new pattern; or, alternatively, can
dissolve them into elements that are selectively articulated into the new
relations, institutions or discourses and that thereby lose their earlier
integrity. Such effects are grounded in the polyvalence of all social phenomena, which means they can be articulated into different institutional
orders and/or discourses and will vary in significance with this articula-

tion. Failure to note these effects can easily lead to the misreading of the relative continuity or discontinuity across different periods.

4. Alternative SWPR Strategies

Because my analysis has operated mainly in terms of a global contrast between the KWNS and the SWPR, it could be argued that it subsumes too much under too dualistic a set of concepts. This is not my intention. I have already discussed variant forms of the KWNS and will now introduce variant forms of the SWPR. The various economic and political tendencies noted above can be (and often are) integrated and expressed in quite different discourses and are associated with contrasting strategic directions as different forces seek to make sense of the conflicting tendencies and countertendencies at work in the new global economy. There is extensive improvization and trial and error involved in the current changes and no clearly dominant pattern has yet emerged. For heuristic purposes, however, we can posit four ideal-typical forms: neoliberal, neocorporatist, neostatist and neocommunitarian (see box 7.1). In using the prefix 'neo' to identify them, I want to emphasize that the first three would embody important discontinuities with the liberal, corporatist and statist KWNS regimes linked to Fordism and that neocommunitarianism also has significant discontinuities compared to previous efforts to institutionalize communitarianism in capitalist social formations. The particular strategy mixes to be found in individual cases will depend on institutional legacies, the balance of political forces and the changing economic and political conjunctures in which different strategies are pursued.

Neoliberalism

This could well be described as the hegemonic strategy for economic globalization because of its support by leading international economic bodies (such as the OECD, IMF and World Bank), its primacy in the United States (the currently undisputed capitalist hegemon) and in other anglophone countries (notably England, Australia, New Zealand and Canada), and its formerly paradigmatic status for restructuring the post-socialist economies and integrating them into the global economy. It is also evident, but not hegemonic, in the neoliberal policy adjustments (even in the absence of a more radical neoliberal regime change) in most other advanced capitalist economies. Even where this strategy is not wholeheartedly embraced by the dominant economic and political forces in other economic and political spaces, the effects of the neoliberal global project continue to operate through their contribution to the increasing ecological dominance of capital accumulation and to the economic domination of those fractions of capital that benefit from this project.

Neoliberalism is concerned to promote a market-led transition towards the new economic and social regime. For the public sector, it involves privatization, liberalization and the imposition of commercial criteria in the residual state sector; for the private sector, it involves deregulation and a new legal and political framework to provide passive support for market solutions. This is reflected in government promotion of 'hire-and-fire', flexi-time and flexi-wage labour markets; growth of tax expenditures steered by private initiatives based on fiscal subsidies for favoured economic activities; measures to transform the welfare state into a means of supporting and subsidizing low wages as well as to enhance the disciplinary force of social security measures and programmes; and the more general reorientation of economic and social policy to the perceived needs of the private sector. Coupled with such measures is disavowal of social partnership in favour of managerial prerogatives, market forces and a strong state. Neoliberalism also involves a cosmopolitan approach that welcomes internationalization of domestic economic space in the form of both outward and inward investment and also calls for the liberalization of international trade and investment within regional blocs and more generally. Innovation is expected to follow spontaneously from the liberation of the animal spirits of individual entrepreneurs as they take advantage of incentives in the new market-led climate and from the more general government promotion of an enterprise culture. In turn, national competitiveness is understood as the aggregate effect of the microeconomic competitiveness of individual firms. Hence there is little state concern to maintain a sufficiently deep and coherent set of core economic competencies in the home economy and/or adequate national or regional innovation systems to provide the basis for structural competitiveness. In this context local and international state apparatuses are expected to act as relays for the market-led approach to innovation and workfare. Whilst neoliberalism is sometimes said to involve a return to the free market and the liberal state, neither is really feasible in current conditions. Instead, it typically involves the subordination of small and medium enterprises to new forms of monopolistic competition on a global scale. Likewise, even if national and local states adopt a laissez-faire role in the hope of generating an entrepreneurial culture, they must still prove strong enough both to dismantle and replace the old mode of social regulation and to resist subsequent political pressures for all manner of ad hoc interventions for short-term economic or political advantage. These are not easy tasks.

Neocorporatism

This strategy relies on institutionalization of a continuing, negotiated, concerted approach to the economic strategies, decisions and conduct of economic agents. Based on a self-reflexive understanding of the linkages between their own private economic interests and the importance of collective agreements to the stability of a socially embedded, socially regulated economy, the economic forces involved in neocorporatism strive to balance competition and cooperation. This system differs from Fordist corporatism based on the dominance of mass production and mass unions and on the primacy of full employment and stagflation as economic concerns. Thus the scope of neocorporatist arrangements reflects the diversity of policy communities and networks relevant to an innovation-driven mode of growth as well as the increasing heterogeneity of labour forces and labour markets. Neocorporatist arrangements in an emerging SWPR are also more directly and explicitly oriented to the crucial importance of innovation, the expansion of the knowledge-based economy, structural competitiveness, and activation rather than passive support in relation to labour markets. Neocorporatism extends beyond business associations and trade unions to include policy communities representing distinct functional systems (e.g., science, health, education, law); and policy implementation will become more flexible through the extension of 'regulated self-regulation' and private interest government so that there is less direct state involvement in managing the 'supply-side' and more emphasis on private industrial policies. Inherited corporatist arrangements may also become more selective (e.g., excluding some previously entrenched industrial interests and peripheral or marginal workers, integrating some 'sunrise' sectors and giving more weight to core workers); and, reflecting the greater flexibility and decentralization of key features of the post-Fordist economy, the centres of neocorporatist gravity will move towards the micro-level of firms and localities at the expense of centralized macroeconomic concertation. This is certainly not inconsistent with 'bottom-up' neocorporatist linkages connecting firms and/or localities in different national economic spaces and bypassing central government. Whether at local, national or supranational level, the state is just as involved in such neocorporatist strategies as it is in the neoliberal and neostatist approaches. Its resources and actions are used to back or support the decisions reached through corporatist negotiation, however, rather than to promote either neoliberal disengagement or autonomous, proactive, neostatist initiatives. And this in turn means that compliance with state policies is either voluntary or depends on actions taken by self-regulating corporatist organizations endowed with public status.

Box 7.1   *Strategies to promote or adjust to global neoliberalism*

Neoliberalism
1. Liberalization – promote free competition
2. Deregulation – reduce role of law and state
3. Privatization – sell off public sector
4. Market proxies in residual public sector
5. Internationalization – free inward and outward flows
6. Lower direct taxes – increase consumer choice

Neocorporatism
1. Rebalance competition and cooperation
2. Decentralized 'regulated self-regulation'
3. Widen range of private, public and other 'stakeholders'
4. Expand role of public-private partnerships
5. Protect core economic sectors in open economy
6. High taxation to finance social investment

Neostatism
1. From state control to regulated competition
2. Guide national strategy rather than plan top-down
3. Auditing performance of private and public sectors
4. Public-private partnerships under state guidance
5. Neo-mercantilist protection of core economy
6. Expanding role for new collective resources

Neocommunitarianism
1. Deliberalization – limit free competition
2. Empowerment – enhance role of third sector
3. Socialization – expand the social economy
4. Emphasis on social use-value and social cohesion
5. Fair trade not free trade; think Global, act Local
6. Redirect taxes – citizens' wage, carers' allowances

Neostatism

This involves a market-conforming but state-sponsored approach to economic reorganization in which the state intervenes to guide the development of market forces. It does so through deploying its own powers of imperative coordination, its own economic resources and activities, and its own knowledge bases and organizational intelligence. In deploying these various resources in support of an urban, regional, intermestic, national or supranational accumulation strategy, however, the state is still well aware of the changing nature and discourses of international competition and, indeed, is actively involved in promoting these discourses and corresponding economic and social policies. In this context neo-statism involves a mixture of decommodification, state-sponsored flexibility and other state activities aimed at securing the dynamic efficiency of a structurally coherent and institutionally thick productive core of economic activities. This is reflected in an active structural policy in which the state sets strategic targets relating to new technologies, technology transfer, innovation systems, infrastructure and other factors affecting the overall structural competitiveness of the emerging knowledge-based economy; and in an active territorial strategy in which efforts are made to promote the untraded interdependencies that underpin a successful learning region, innovation mileu, industrial cluster, entrepreneurial city, and so forth. It favours an active labour market policy to reskill the labour force and to encourage a flexi-skill rather than flexi-price labour market; it intervenes directly and openly with its own political and economic resources to restructure declining industries and to promote sunrise sectors; and it engages in a range of societal guidance strategies based on its own strategic intelligence and economic resources to promote specific objectives through concerted action with varied policy communities that embrace public, mixed and private interests. These activities aim to move the domestic economy (or other relevant economic space) up the technological hierarchy by creating and maintaining a coherent and competitive productive base and pursuing a strategy of flexible specialization in specific high-technology sectors. Whilst the central state retains a key strategic role in these areas, it also allows and encourages parallel and complementary activities at regional and/or local levels. In the terms introduced in chapter 6, neostatism involves a strong state role in decentred context steering. Nonetheless the state's desire to protect the core technological and economic competencies of its productive base and its innovation system may be associated with neomercantilism at the supranational level.

Neocommunitarianism

This variant promotes the social economy[6] as a challenge to the logic of capital accumulation in the economy, its extension to other spheres of social life and the struggle to establish bourgeois hegemony over society as a whole. Against this logic, especially its most abstract aspects rooted in the dominance of exchange-value, the social economy prioritizes social use-value. It seeks to re-embed the organization of the economy in specific spatio-temporal contexts oriented to the rhythms of social reproduction rather than the frenzied circulation of digitalized finance capital. Neocommunitarianism also opposes the extension of capitalist logic to other spheres of life such that education, health services, housing, politics, culture, sport, and so on are directly commodified or, at least, subject to quasi-market forces. Indeed, extending the social economy provides a basis for resisting capital's increasing hegemony over society as a whole. For it demonstrates the possibility of organizing economic and social life in terms that challenge capitalist 'common sense'.

Combining the strategies

These four strategies have also been formulated as ideal-types based on theoretically informed empirical observation and, as such, are nowhere to be found in pure form. Indeed, elements of these different strategies for effecting the transition to a globalizing, knowledge-based economy are typically combined in specific cases. This can be seen at all levels of political intervention. For example, while the leading international and supranational organizations in the redesign of the global economy are generally committed to the neoliberal strategy, there are still some differences between them as well as some fluctuation in the relative weight attached to different elements of the four strategies. For example, Deacon, who has been especially interested in the globalization of social policy, has noted that:

> there continue to be interesting shifts in the position of particular players within this debate. The IMF has taken the social dimension of globalization more seriously, considering whether some degree of equity is beneficial to economic growth. The Bank has articulated more clearly its risk management approach to social protection in the context of globalization. The OECD now warns that globalization may lead to the need for more, not less social expenditure. The ILO has begun to show signs of making concessions to the Bank's views on social security. More recently, the role of the World Trade Organization and its views on the desirability of fostering a global market in health and social services provision is assuming a prominence it did not have in the past. (2001: 60–1)

Likewise, in the EU, the single market strategy is premised on a neoliberal approach to competitiveness – creating an EU-wide market through liberalization, deregulation and internationalization – and the EMU is intended to entrench a neoliberal economic and social policy framework that would leave member states limited room for manoeuvre. Within this neoliberal framework there is also a neostatist strategy in and through which the EU coordinates networks linking different levels of government in different states as well as semi-public and private agencies ranging from educational institutions, research institutes, enterprises and banks in order to promote new technologies, technology transfer, etc., and to create a European innovation space. This is the most obviously Schumpeterian moment of EU economic strategy. Also within the neoliberal framework there is an emergent neocorporatist strategy oriented to a Social Charter which will prevent 'social dumping' and thereby underpin attempts to reskill and retrain workers in the interests of more flexible, responsible work (Falkner 1998; Grahl and Teague 1991; Perrin 1988). This is an important flanking measure for the neoliberal market-building strategy and, although not yet strongly institutionalized, may provide a basis for resisting further moves down the neoliberal road. And, finally, we find that the EU is actively engaged in promoting the social economy in smaller areas to combat social exclusion.

This sort of combination of approaches need not indicate eclecticism or incoherence. Indeed, the EC even argued (not without a hint of special pleading and political fudging) some ten years ago that the neoliberal elements of its strategy could be viewed as the catalysts of structural competitiveness and the neostatist elements as its accelerators. It also suggested that some aspects of the neocorporatist project could be seen as prerequisites of structural adjustment and enhanced competitiveness insofar as they promote economic and social cohesion (European Communities 1991: 23).[7] This account need not be taken at face value. It could be seen uncharitably, for example, as no more than a sign of confusion and muddling through. More plausibly it could be interpreted as an expression of the compromises that are inevitable in arriving at any accumulation strategy or state project. But there could also be a deeper structural coherence to this strategy when examined from the viewpoint of attempts to construct a new spatio-temporal fix around the primacy of European economic space. In this context the SEM is a neoliberal mechanism intended to institutionalize European economic space and to entrench the money concept of capital as the primary axis around which future accumulation strategies could be defined and pursued. This also serves to integrate the European triad into the emerging neoliberal world market that is being actively promoted by the USA and the international organizations in which it is hegemonic. In this sense the neoliberal project is one that serves to link the global economy, European economic space and the increasingly tangled web of economic spaces below the European level. Since the market mechanism is prone to failure, however, neoliberalism needs supplementing and flanking. The neostatist strategy is important for building the structural competitiveness of the European economy, especially given the many economic and extra-economic barriers to building European-wide cooperation to counteract the growing penetration of the European economy by American and East Asian capital and its resulting fragmentation and Balkanization among competing strategic alliances and national and transnational interests. Conversely, the neo-corporatist strategy is more important in the field of social policy. Although the EU lacks an official competence in this area, it can still attempt to promote a social policy for Europe through cooperation with the social partners (see Falkner 1998). Thus it is essential to establish new institutional arrangements and allocate specific roles and comple-mentary competencies across different spatial scales and/or types of actor and thereby ensure that the dominant strategic line is translated into effective action.

Different strategies are also found inside each European national state. While the policies of Thatcherism and, more recently, New Labour clearly involve the dominance of a neoliberal strategy, for example, other strategies have not been totally rejected. Thus, in the case of Thatcherism, central government programmes (admittedly on a small scale) were oriented to technology transfer and research into generic technologies; and, notwithstanding blanket hostility to tripartite corpo-ratism and national-level social partnership, it also promoted enterprise corporatism and a 'new realism' on the shop floor. Moreover, while central government was in retreat, local economic development initia-tives along SWPR lines proliferated. Under Labour-led local authorities these were often run on neocorporatist or neostatist lines; conversely, Conservative-led local authorities were more inclined to neoliberalism or favoured private-public partnerships without organized labour. New Labour under Blair has embraced most of the neoliberal legacy of Thatcherism and has extended it into new areas. It has also taken the first steps on the road to a routinization of neoliberalism. Thus more emphasis has been given to securing the operation of the emerging neoliberal regime through normal politics, to developing supporting poli-cies across a wide range of policy fields and to providing flanking mech-anisms to compensate for its negative economic, political and social consequences. All of these measures are being pursued, of course, in a context marked by continuing political worries about state unity and ter-ritorial unity, political legitimacy and re-election, as well as more general concerns with the future of social cohesion.

In short, while there are economic, political and intellectual forces that are closely identified with one or other mode of governance, these sub-types of the SWPR are best seen as poles around which different solu-tions have developed (and are developing) on different scales during more or less extended periods of conflict and experimentation. Cur-rently, the neoliberal form of SWPR is hegemonic on the international level, but important countercurrents exist in specific macroregional, national, subregional and cross-border regional contexts. The particular mix in individual cases will depend on institutional legacies, the balance of political forces and the changing economic and political conjunctures in which different strategies are pursued. They will also be overdetermined by factors beyond those included within this particular approach to the political economy of welfare. There is certainly no reason to expect a multilateral convergence of modes of regulation around one subtype of the SWPR – let alone a rapid convergence. Indeed, since there is a strong path-dependent structural coupling between different accumulation regimes, modes of regulation and modes of societalization, it is far more probable that there will be continuing divergence rooted in the continuing institutional fit between different production regimes and different strategies.

5. Post-Fordism and the SWPR

The KWNS was a key structural support of the long postwar boom and entered crisis along with its associated Atlantic Fordist accumulation regime. Indeed, these crises are related and feed into each other. As the crisis of the KWNS unfolded, and as efforts to restore the conditions for postwar growth through economic austerity and social retrenchment in an attempt to squeeze out inflation and reduce public spending failed, emphasis shifted to attempts to restructure and reorient the state in the light of changed perceptions of the conditions for economic expansion. Insofar as this restructuring and reorientation succeed, they will tend to produce one or another variant of the SWPR. This is by no means an automatic, mechanical transition but is mediated through changes in economic discourse, modes of calculation, new economic theories and strategic concepts. These are all-important mediating links between structural changes in the global economy and state transformation. For they provide a framework for making sense of these changes, the crises that often accompany them, and the responses that might be appropriate to them. It is the articulation of discursive-strategic shifts into new accumulation strategies, state projects and hegemonic projects, and their capacity to mobilize support and deliver effective state policies that help to shape the restructuring and reorientation of the contemporary state and produce different regulatory regimes. The eventual realization and consolidation of the globalizing, knowledge-based economy and the SWPR as a key element in its regulation, if this occurs, will therefore depend on the outcome of a wide range of struggles. These include class struggles proper; struggles to extend or resist the colonization of other systems and the lifeworld by profit-and-loss economic calculation;

struggles to limit the growing ecological dominance of political struggles; and struggles to mobilize support behind counter-hegemonic projects proposing alternatives to the globalizing, knowledge-based economy as the dominant principle of societalization (see chapter 1).

Nonetheless, in the spirit of continuing the thought-experiment that has motivated the preceding arguments, we could condense them into the single, audacious claim that a Schumpeterian workfare postnational regime will provide the best possible – but still imperfect and always pro-visional – spatio-temporal fix for a globalizing, knowledge-based, post-Fordist economy. This claim can be justified in two ways. Either the SWPR is a contingently realized form of the modern state shaped by the ecological dominance of a globalizing knowledge-based economy; or it is the naturally necessary form of the capitalist type of state in a global-izing knowledge-based economy.[8] In the former case, the state would be seen as *contingently* post-Fordist (if at all) due to the dominance of a globalizing informational capitalism in economic and social relations, with the result that the state tends to acquire the features of the SWPR through its social embeddedness in this more encompassing social for-mation. The key mechanism in this case would be structural coupling and co-evolution under the ecological dominance of the capitalist market economy. Thus, if the modern state were situated within an economic or societal system with different features, it would acquire different sec-ondary properties and perform marginally different functions. In the latter case, however, the state system would be inherently post-Fordist. It would have basic structural features that are congruent[9] with the glob-alizing, knowledge-based economy that I have identified above as the substantive form of the emerging post-Fordist accumulation regime and would thereby serve to sustain post-Fordism as an accumulation regime, mode of regulation and mode of societalization. The key mechanism in this case would be the critical role of the state in securing the extra-economic conditions for capital accumulation and hence in shaping and guiding the forms that capital accumulation can take. This is the inter-pretation that I have advanced in the preceding chapters.

In this context we can distinguish analytically between two different forms of post-Fordist state: a transitional regime and a normal, con-solidated state. A transitional regime performs definite functions in the transition but has an underdetermined form. This will depend on the institutional legacies of the Fordist era and the KWNS from case to case and on the specific forms of crisis and struggle associated with the tran-sition from Atlantic Fordism to the globalizing, knowledge-based economy.[10] The shift from Fordism to post-Fordism would certainly seem to involve any transitional regime in a complex array of tasks besides those typical of any capitalist type of state. These tasks derive from its location at the intersection between a consolidated Fordism in decline and a putative post-Fordism in the ascendant. In this sense the transitional regime is Janus-faced and must engage in creatively destructive interventions. It must both 'roll back the frontiers' of Atlantic Fordist state intervention and 'roll forward' those for post-Fordist intervention. The first set of activities not only involves ending the exceptional, crisis-induced state forms and functions associated with Atlantic Fordism in decline, but also weakening the normal, routinized forms of intervention associated with the KWNS more generally. The second set is just as complex, albeit for different reasons. For a transitional regime must pursue exceptional measures to establish the conditions for a post-Fordist 'take-off' as well as begin to consolidate the 'normal' state forms and functions associated with post-Fordism (see figure 7.1). Neither the first nor the second set of tasks is ever structurally inscribed or strategically pre-scripted. They both involve chance discoveries, search processes and social struggles. For the same reason this means that there can be many different routes to a post-Fordist state. We saw the same contingency in the development of the KWNS in the discussion of typologies of welfare regimes in chapter 2 as well as the eventual consolidation of some functional equivalence between different forms of welfare regime and Atlantic Fordism. This indicates the need for *ex post facto* analyses of how post-Fordist states emerge through structural coupling as well as attempts at strategic coordination rather than for *ex ante* (and therefore teleological) accounts of the necessary transition to post-Fordism.[11] It would clearly be worth exploring whether effective transitional regimes are as well-suited to preserving the fruits of a transition once it has occurred. I have already indicated some reasons for believing that the neoliberal form of transition is unstable and difficult to sustain without significant flanking and supporting measures.

Since these changes involve far more than a simple technical fix, it is easy to see why the transition from KWNS to SWPR is always politically mediated and often difficult. Thus, although my entry point for analysing the transition is inspired by the Marxist critique of political economy, a critique of politics is also required. This would serve not only to interpret the political mediations of the transition (as well as any 'conservation-dissolution' effects) but also the constitutive role of politics in defining the problems to which the transition is a response and redefining both the objects and subjects of governance. This in turn helps to explain why, despite a tendential denationalization of the state and a shift from government to governance, national states still have major roles in shaping how the economic and social reproduction requirements of capital are met. For they try to determine which functions go upwards, downwards and sideways, and the conditions on which they stay there;

State intervention

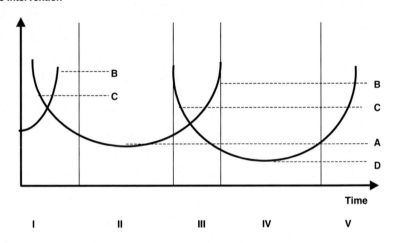

Forms and levels of state intervention
A = Normal level and form of intervention associated with current phase.

B = Exceptional crisis-induced level and forms of state intervention to reproduce current phase in face of its crisis.

C = Exceptional transitional level and forms of state intervention to roll back the normal and crisis-induced interventions from previous phase and to roll forward the normal forms of intervention associated with next phase.

D = Normal forms of intervention associated with emerging phase.

Phases
I, III, V = End phase of outgoing accumulation regime and its mode of regulation. High levels of state intervention derive from combination of crisis-induced measures to maintain dynamic of the current stage, measures to rollback both the normal and the crisis-induced phases of the current stage, and trial-and-error emergence of the normal forms of intervention that may be associated with the next phase.

II, IV = Normal forms of state intervention associated with the new phase after its consolidation and before its crisis-tendencies accumulate.

Figure 7.1   *Schematic representation of changing forms of state intervention according to periodization of capital accumulation*

and also seek both to design governance mechanisms and to politically organize self-organization.

With the new configuration of contradictions and the relativization of scale, however, we cannot yet be certain that a normal form of post-Fordist state has been consolidated. At best I have been able to note the most probable features of this form of the capitalist type of state insofar as it is involved in securing the conditions for the reproduction of capital accumulation (see box 7.2). But this cannot pretend to be an exhaustive analysis of the contemporary capitalist type of state even in the economic and political spaces of the former Atlantic Fordism. This would be a much larger task than could comfortably be contained within a work of this kind. Nonetheless, we have now developed the argument to a sufficient degree to offer a solution to Offe's paradox.

Box 7.2   Synopsis: the SWPR and the reproduction of capital

1. Securing the general external conditions for capital accumulation, such as a formally rationally legal order and protection of property rights. More reflexive and discretionary legal order and wider and deeper involvement in intellectual property rights.

2. Securing the fictitious commodification of land, money, labour-power and knowledge and modulating their subsequent de- and recommodification in the light of the changing forms of appearances of capital's structural contradictions and strategic dilemmas and of the changing balance of forces contesting the extent and consequences of such fictitious commodification.
    *   securing the fictitious commodification of the electromagnetic spectrum, cyberspace, the gene pool, and the body;
    *   modulating extended market-driven commodification of stateless money;
    *   stratification, regulation and governance of global pool of labour-power and modifying the relations between manual and mental labour;
    *   promoting primitive accumulation of intellectual capital and widening and deepening intellectual property rights.

3. Securing the rights and capacities of capital to control labour-power in the production process and regulating the terms and

conditions of the capital-labour relation in the labour market and labour process.

- changing regulatory frameworks to facilitate various forms of labour market flexibility and mobility within and between (postnational) economic spaces;
- subordinating social policy (*Sozialpolitik*) to economic policy through redesign, recalibration and reorientation in line with purported needs of flexible, competitive knowledge-based economy and/or through cost reduction or containment in regard to social wage and collective consumption regarded as cost of (international) production.

4. Defining the boundaries between the economic and extra-economic and modifying the links between the economic and extra-economic conditions of capital accumulation in the light of changes in the materially and discursively constituted forms of competition and in the light of resistance to the colonization of the extra-economic by the logic of capital.
   - promoting the notion of systemic or structural competitiveness, hence promoting increasing subordination of entire social formation to the purported needs of capital accumulation, and generalizing this notion through adoption of wide-ranging international benchmarking of competitiveness;
   - promotion of knowledge-based economy as primary object of economic governance;
   - coping with resistance to colonization of extra-economic systems and lifeworld by logic of accumulation on a world scale.

5. Promoting the provision of the general conditions of production, especially capital-intensive infrastructure with a long turnover time, appropriate to a given stage and/or variety of capitalism.
   - socializing long-term conditions of production as short-term calculation becomes more dominant in marketized economic activities;
   - promoting global, national and regional information infrastructures;
   - promoting social systems of innovation;
   - planning and subsidizing spatial fixes that support the activities of financial, industrial and commercial capital within and across borders;

- engaging in complementary forms of locational policy (*Standortpolitik*) and other forms of place-based competition in an attempt to fix mobile capital within the state's own economic spaces and to enhance the interurban, interregional, or international competitiveness of its own place-bound capitals.

6. Managing the fundamental contradiction between the increasingly social nature of productive forces and the continuing and private nature of the social relations of production and the appropriation of surplus labour.
   - liberalization and deregulation of foreign exchange movements and redesign of international financial architecture with the effect of internationalizing and accelerating capital flows;
   - modifying institutional frameworks for international trade and FDI;
   - promoting the space of flows in this context by organizing conditions favourable to the international mobility of technologies, industrial and commercial capital, intellectual property, and at least some types of labour-power;
   - addressing the multiformity of economic globalization by engaging in the rivalrous and conflictual struggle to define the rules for harmonizing or standardizing technological, economic, juridicopolitical, sociocultural and environmental issues;
   - addressing the ecological contradictions of capital accumulation generated by the dissociation between real transformation and appropriation of nature and its incomplete and partial monetized expression;
   - managing fundamental contradiction between socialization of productive forces and relations of production as expressed in general tension between information society and information economy.

7. Articulating the interlinked processes of de- and reterritorialization and de- and retemporalization associated with the remaking of the spatio-temporal fixes necessary for relatively stable periods of accumulation.
   - cooperating in defining and establishing new scales of activity (and dismantling others), thereby rescaling and rearticulating various state powers, institutional forms and regulatory capacities and creating the possibility for

themselves and other actors to 'jump scales'. This includes decentralization and cross-border region formation, regional bloc formation and participating in forums for inter-triad negotiation;

- deterritorializing some state functions by transferring them to private forms of functional authority (including international regimes) and/or to mobile market forces;
- attempting, conversely, to fit some non-territorial problems into an areal structure (e.g., making national states responsible for enforcing international agreements on global warming with national states);
- seeking to manage the tension between (a) the interests of potentially mobile capital in reducing its place-dependency and/or freeing itself from temporal constraints and (b) the state's own interest in fixing (allegedly beneficial) capital in its territory and rendering capital's temporal horizons and rhythms compatible with its own political routines, temporalities, and crisis-tendencies.
- promoting new temporal horizons of action and new forms of temporal flexibility;
- coping with the increased salience of multiple time zones (in commerce, diplomacy, security, etc.);
- recalibrating and managing the intersection of temporalities (e.g., regulating computer-programmed trading, promoting the 24-hour city as centre of consumption, managing environmental risk);
- promoting uneven development through policies for inter-urban, interregional, and international competition – and seeking to compensate for this.

8. Addressing the wider political and social repercussions of the changing forms of appearance of capitalist contradictions and dilemmas as these are mediated in and through specific forms of political organization and mobilization.
   - denationalization of state and increased role of state in interscalar articulation;
   - destatization of current state functions by transferring them to private-public partnerships or place-bound market forces and thereby linking them to market-oriented temporalities and seeking to organize this process through metagovernance;
   - shaping international policy regimes and modulating their implementation.

Note: This list is incomplete and the activities partly overlap. Each of these activities can be linked into different accumulation strategies and state projects.

6. Resolving Offe's Paradox: Capitalism and the Welfare State

As I noted in the Introduction, Claus Offe once suggested that 'while capitalism cannot coexist *with*, neither can it exist *without*, the welfare state' (1984: 153; italics in original). Some might dismiss this as a mere rhetorical flourish without theoretical meaning or empirical application. In fact, Offe did attempt to ground his argument in the nature of capitalism; he also noted some of its practical implications. Indeed, his analysis is generally compelling and still repays careful reading. Its main problem lies elsewhere. For, like much theorizing about the crisis of the welfare state in the 1970s and early 1980s, it was shaped by the economic and political horizons of its time.[12] Offe developed his analysis in the context of the KWNS in Europe, North America and Australasia and did not fully address the more general difficulties involved in capital accumulation. As the Atlantic Fordist system has continued to decline, however, we have a better understanding of its nature and limitations. It is also easier to distinguish between its particular features and those characterizing capitalism as a whole.

Thus we are now in a position to suggest a solution to 'Offe's paradox'. On the one hand, capitalism (at least in its Atlantic Fordist form) co-existed with the welfare state (in the form of the KWNS) for an extended period. This did not preclude the demise or weakening of firms or sectors that could not compete in the new Fordist-KWNS setting. Eventually, the Fordist accumulation regime and its KWNS mode of regulation became mutually contradictory. This prompted a move away from Atlantic Fordism to search for new economic and social bases for capital accumulation; and this has involved a partial dismantling (with due recognition of complex 'conservation-dissolution' effects) of the KWNS. In this sense the emerging post-Fordist accumulation regime cannot coexist with the KWNS. But, to complicate and clarify matters at one and the same time, the continuing search for new economic and social bases of capital accumulation also involves a search for new forms of state intervention that might help to secure the valorization of capital and the social reproduction of labour-power. One could perhaps call this a search for a new type of state to help to manage a new type of spatio-temporal fix or, to suit Offe's paradox, the search for a new type of welfare state. But this emphasis on the continuity of state involvement in economic and social reproduction is both disingenuous and misleading because, as argued above, the core organizational principles of the KWNS are being superseded in favour of those of the SWPR as a condition for the renewed coexistence of capitalism and the welfare state.

Nonetheless, there is a deeper truth in Offe's claim. There are indeed basic structural contradictions and strategic dilemmas in the capital relation that ensure that the relationship between market, civil society and state is always problematic. Capitalist growth depends essentially on the market-mediated exploitation of wage-labour – not on the inherent efficiency of unfettered markets. Markets mediate the search for added value but cannot themselves produce it; and the very process of commodification engendered by the spread of the market mechanism generates contradictions that cannot be resolved by that mechanism itself. This is evident in contradictions inscribed in the most basic forms of the capitalist market society. It was in managing, at least for a while, such contradictions and dilemmas within the spatio-temporal matrix of the national economy and the national state that the 'welfare mix' associated with the KWNS made its own contribution to the Atlantic Fordist regime. Nonetheless, much of what passed then as 'market failure' (i.e., was discursively constructed as such) and to which the KWNS was judged an appropriate response was actually an expression of deeper contradictions of capitalism. Thus KWNS intervention often only modified the forms or sites of these contradictions – introducing class struggles into the state and/or generating tendencies towards fiscal crisis, legitimacy crisis, rationality crisis, etc. And, as the capital relation developed in ways that undermined the national economy as an object of state management, the underlying contradictions re-emerged. Thus, if the state had failed to compensate for the failures of the market within the KWNS and, in addition, generated its own failures, it does not follow that a return to the market will put things right. The SWPR is the latest attempt to square this capital accumulation–social welfare (reproduction) circle. Like the KWNS, it may be consolidated for a while; but, like the SWPR, it is unlikely to prove permanent.

Notes

Chapter 1: Capitalism and the Capitalist Type of State

1   The distinction between system and lifeworld was introduced by Habermas (1975, 1987 and 1996). I extend systems well beyond his initial economy and juridico-political couplet to include any self-organizing (or autopoietic) system with its own instrumental rationality, institutional matrix and social agents who consciously orient their actions to that system's code. I also interpret the lifeworld more widely than Habermas initially did. Thus it is used here to refer to all those identities, interests, values and conventions that are not directly anchored in the logic of any particular system and that provide the substratum and background to social interaction in everyday life, including enmity and antagonism as well as intimacy and solidarity.

2   With the continuing development of productivity and hence 'wealth creation', social norms of consumption (as indicated in the quantity and quality of consumer goods and services) in the advanced capitalist economies will tend to rise well above any bare subsistence minimum. Whether the increase and transformation in these use-values also represent an increased share of total added value of production is another matter entirely and depends on the outcome of wide-ranging economic and political struggles within and beyond the advanced capitalist social formations (on the distinction between *wealth* and *value*, see Postone 1993). Moreover, whilst recognizing the trend towards increased wealth in advanced capitalist societies, one should not forget that it depends on an increasingly global division of labour that is also marked by highly unequal working conditions, wages and living standards.

3   Structural contradictions tend to arise under at least three different types of condition: first, when the overall logic of an institutional ensemble generates opposed developmental tendencies (for example, the growing socialization of productive forces versus continuing private control over the relations of production and surplus appropriation); second, when there is a

conflict or tension between the requirements of system reproduction and the logic of individual action (for example, capital in general versus particular capitals); and, third, when a social relation is so constituted that it tends to produce socially structured conflicts between inherently antagonistic interests (for example, capital versus labour).

4   A strategic dilemma exists when agents face choices such that, within given parameters and horizons of action, any action that they pursue (including inaction) will undermine some key condition(s) of their existence and/or their capacities to realize a broader set of interests. Dilemmas can be defined at different levels of individual and collective agency. Partial solutions may be possible if the parametric conditions and horizons of action are changed. This could occur, for example, through alternating between the horns of the dilemma, through strategic learning based on iteration, through deferring or displacing the adverse consequences of a given path of action, and so on.

5   The term 'exploitation' is used here in a morally neutral manner.

6   Such 'real subsumption' (to use Marx's term) has since been extended to non-manual work through the use of intelligent office machines that monitor and regulate non-manual work. But it is never sufficient in itself to secure the compliance of the labour force and is typically supplemented by other forms of discipline and control, including coercion, bureaucracy, performance-related pay and attempts to mould workers' subjectivity (see Marsden 1999).

7   Class relations are never defined purely at the level of economic relations but are overdetermined by the intervention of juridico-political and ideological structures and the articulation of class to other social categories. Moreover, from strategic and/or tactical viewpoints, workers, capitalists and other social forces may seek to organize labour markets and the labour process in terms of other interests and categories, leading to segmented labour markets and skewed divisions of labour.

8   Innovations that enable a given enterprise to produce commodities below the socially necessary labour time that is typical for such commodities and/or to keep realization costs below average will produce surplus profits until they become generalized and thus redefine what is socially necessary. In this sense, capitalist competition revolves around the average rate of profit.

9   These laws and tendencies include: (1) the growing concentration of capital, that is, the accumulation of capitalist assets by single firms through the reinvestment of past profits; (2) the increased importance of productivity gains ('relative surplus-value') as opposed to longer working hours and greater effort ('absolute surplus-value') in the creation of surplus; (3) the increasing urgency of overcoming the obstacles to capitalist expansion involved in the tendency of the rate of profit to fall – a general tendency that emerges insofar as all enterprises seek a competitive edge by substituting labour-saving machinery for wage-labour even though the latter is, according to Marx, the sole source of profit on the total capital advanced to buy capital goods and materials as well as labour-power; (4) the growing centralization of capital, that is, the management of assets owned by different individuals or firms by one enterprise (for example, through joint-stock companies or banks); (5) the growing separation of legal ownership and effective control

of the means of production through the development of joint-stock companies and related forms of business organization; (6) the growing importance
of credit in the functioning of the capitalist system; and so forth.

10 Labour-power as a fictitious commodity is unusual here because it is not
produced as an exchange-value; and, in addition, its use-value in capitalism
is its capacity to produce exchange-value.

11 Cf. Cleaver on the wage form: 'It is exactly because workers have needs (and
no means of producing what they need) that capital can sell those use-values
and realize the exchange-values it desires. It is exactly because labor-power
is a use-value for capital that it is an exchange-value for labor' (1979: 92).

12 The same principle applies where money circulates within plurinational
spaces, such as formal or informal empires, dominated by one state.

13 This argument about ecological dominance would also apply to other types
of social forces in other types of social ecology, such as organizations and
networks. Organizations and networks can also be more or less ecologically
dominant in their respective social worlds.

14 To avoid any misunderstanding, this statement does not entail that the state
and capital are fully autonomous entities and that the state is therefore able
to intervene from a position wholly outside what is an exclusively economic
circuit of capital to suspend the full realization of its purely economic laws of
motion. It is merely intended to emphasize that the reproduction of capitalism always depends on appropriate extra-economic conditions and that its
tendencies are only fully realized to the extent that 'accumulation for the sake
of accumulation' is established as the dominant principle of societalization.

15 This apt phrase comes from Blühdorn's commentary on Luhmann, even
though he does not acknowledge Luhmann's own contribution to the analysis of ecological dominance (2000: 351).

16 Accumulation strategies are formulated on many scales of economic activity from the different units of a firm through the branch or region to the
national or supranational bloc. Different types of actor play a leading role
in each case. For a discussion of dimensions of accumulation strategies at
the firm level, see Williams et al. 1983, and, at branch level, Ruigrok and van
Tulder 1995.

17 For a strategic-relational critique and reinterpretation of institutions and the
significance of institutionalism, see Jessop 2001c.

18 Max Weber distinguished several forms of capitalism (for example, booty
capitalism, political capitalism) that could certainly exist and, perhaps, thrive
in the absence of what I am calling here the capitalist type of state (see
Weber 1978; and, for a good discussion, Swedberg 1998).

19 On the earlier concept of structural selectivity, see Offe 1972 and Poulantzas
1978; on the more recent concept of strategic selectivity, developed on the
basis of Poulantzas's work, see Jessop 1985 and 1990b.

Chapter 2: The Keynesian Welfare National State

1 See Lipietz 1982. Lipietz also notes that the virtuous circle of Fordism also
requires that increased productivity in the capital goods sector should offset

a rising technical composition of capital (or capital intensity of production) if the capital/output ratio is not to grow and so depress profits.

2 All economies have specific properties, of course; but it is worth noting here that Germany is distinctive because of the importance of export-oriented capital goods industries in its overall growth dynamic. Nonetheless, Germany's overall economic performance and capacity to develop mass consumption at home depended on demand for these capital goods generated in large part by the overall dynamic of Atlantic Fordism.

3 Australia and Canada are described as small economies because, despite their massive territories, their population and output are relatively small.

4 Pitruzello (1999) subjected Esping-Andersen's typology to cluster analysis and, on this basis, developed a new fivefold schema. This repeats the now common distinction between the Antipodean and Anglo-American liberal market regimes and reclassifies the other cases into three sets: universalistic (Belgium, Denmark, Norway, Sweden), Bismarckian (Germany, Swizerland, the Netherlands), and a new subset within the conservative-corporatist regime (Austria, Finland, France, Italy, Japan).

5 Pitruzello (1999) provides a good overview of mainstream critiques; see also Abrahamson 1999 and, for feminist critiques, Bussemaker and van Kersbergen 1994 and Daly 1994.

6 OECD data indicate that public spending in Southern European welfare states, Japan and the USA is particularly biased towards the elderly and that Antipodean and social democratic welfare regimes are more biased towards children and working adults (OECD 1996).

7 These features are secondary in relation to the regulationist state-theoretical starting point for this analysis. However, if, for example, gender were one's primary analytical focus, other features would be deemed secondary.

8 On Germany, Britain, France and northern Italy in this regard, see Biernacki 1995.

9 For Soskice (1999: 102), a production regime comprises the financial, industrial relations, education and training, and intercompany systems.

10 The terminology of principal and secondary contradictions and of the primary and secondary aspects of contradictions derives from Mao Zhe-Dong (1967) and was revived in a different context by Louis Althusser (1977). My own flirtation with this language serves heuristic purposes. See also chapter 4.

11 Indeed, several studies indicate that such fine-tuning was more likely to have pro- than contra-cyclical effects.

12 In contrast, the new postwar international regimes established under American hegemony served broader interests in capital accumulation.

13 This squeeze was aggravated to the extent that the Second Cold War, which was not just a reflex of the crisis of Fordism but was linked to the Soviet invasion of Afghanistan and the rise of neoliberalism, led to increased military spending.

14 Capitalism also introduces new products, stimulates new wants and thereby creates new vested interests. Moreover, privatized consumerism may threaten valorization through wage claims and excess consumer credit

expansion just as much as collective consumption does via taxation and public debt.

15 Other relevant factors here are international migration, a trend towards multiculturalism and the emergence of significant diasporas. These have helped to undermine national identities based on, respectively, the *Volksnation*, the *Kulturnation* and the *Staatsnation*. On transnationalism, see Smith 2000.

16 Seen in terms of the overall Fordist dynamic, it is tempting to argue that even factors such as demographic change are actually integral elements or inevitable consequences of a Fordist social structure.

17 On discursive selectivity, see Hay 1996; on structural selectivity, see Jessop 1990b.

Chapter 3: The Schumpeterian Competition State

1 The concept of the competition state was first introduced by Cerny (1986) and, as *nationaler Wettbewerbstaat* (national competition state), by Hirsch (1995). My approach differs from both of these but is certainly closer to Hirsch.

2 One calculation suggests that Internet use in all sectors of the US economy should raise productivity there by 5 per cent during 2000–10 (Brookes and Wahhaj 2000).

3 On the distinction between hardware, software and wetware, see Nelson and Romer 1996.

4 Given the significance of intra-European trade, whether the wage could be a source of demand for a rescaled European Keynesianism is another issue.

5 In the longer run, returns on portfolio investment are tied to the valorization of capital in the production process; in the short run, this is not the case. Herein lie the roots of the debate over the short-termism of finance capital.

6 The OECD introduced the concept of structural competitiveness in 1986 and remains a key organizing principle in its policy work on competitiveness. It refers to 'the global efficiency of the national economy, proficient and flexible structure of industries, the rate and pattern of capital investment, its technical infrastructure and other factors determining the 'externalities', i.e. the economic, social and institutional frameworks and phenomena which can substantially stimulate or hamper both the productive and competitive thrust of domestic firms (Chesnais 1986: 86–7). Systemic competitiveness is equally comprehensive. Messner defines it in terms of 'the outcome of a pattern of complex and dynamic interaction between states, firms, intermediary institutions, and the organizational capacity of given societies' (1998: 10).

7 This can occur either by reducing the time a given 'event' takes to produce within a given spatial frame of action, or by increasing the ability to discriminate more steps in an 'event' and so enhancing opportunities to modify its course or outcome by intervening in the event as it happens.

8 Time–space compression refers here to actual processes rather than a sense of disorientation generated by spatio-temporal changes linked to globalization.

9　On glocalization, see Brenner 1998, 2000 and Swyngedouw 1997; on glur-banization, see Jessop and Sum 2000; on transnationalization, see Smith 2000.

10　The temporal dimension of flow is captured in the metaphors of 'liquidity' and 'stickiness'.

11　Different theories of international competitiveness are often linked to different typologies and disputes about the bases of competitive advantage. For a recent survey of eleven different usages of competitiveness in economics, see Bloch and Kenyon 2001. In practice, however, different types of advantage may be complementary.

12　The related Ricardian discourse tends to treat as 'natural' many factors of production that actually depend heavily on broader social conditions: an abundance of cheap wage-labour is an obvious example.

13　As Warr notes '[t]he classical theory of comparative advantage rested on some seriously simplified assumptions: international market prices were assumed to be known and stable; there was no uncertainty about the prices that would be obtained for export products, or paid for imports; there was no learning-by-doing; technology was known; constant returns to scale prevailed; resources were all fully employed; and the characteristics of commodities were fixed and known to everyone' (1994: 4).

14　In naming just four economic theorists here, I am not implying that these are the only relevant figures or that theirs are the only approaches to competitiveness. They are simply useful emblematic figures in this context.

15　Indeed, if speculative imitation goes too far, oversupply could reduce profits below normal levels.

16　As used in the neo-Schumpeterian approach to innovation and long waves, a motive force refers to the adoption of a major innovation in a dynamic sector with potential repercussions throughout the economy (e.g., the introduction of the microchip) and a carrier force is a vector for the diffusion of these effects (e.g., the adoption of microchip technologies in vehicle construction). For further discussion, see Freeman and Perez 1988.

17　Interestingly, Castells, who introduced the notion of informational capitalism, neglects the significance of intellectual property in its dynamic, focusing instead on knowledge as a factor of production (Castells 1996, 2000b).

18　The principal exception among the leading East Asian economies was the Ricardian workfare colonial regime in Hong Kong (Sum 1998).

Chapter 4: Social Reproduction and the Workfare State

1　The practice is much older, however; see, for example, de Swaan 1988.

2　This expectation is economic and political. The state is expected cognitively and normatively to compensate for market failure; and the labour force itself has a specific presence both within the state and at a distance from it.

3　The distinction between passive and active is often blurred in practice: 'The administration of unemployment-related benefits always involves checks on the eligibility of the recipient, including whether they are seeking work and are being reasonable about the type of work they are prepared to undertake. This activity quickly meshes with programmes designed to help individuals with their job search, or to enable them to consider a wider range of work, which in turn leads to consideration of other programmes designed to help individuals secure work.... [Thus] we can say that active labour-market policy blends into workfare when the emphasis on compulsion becomes an overwhelmingly important feature of the system' (Robinson 2000: 87).

4   This shift was reflected in Britain by the renaming and merger of the relevant ministries: what started in the postwar period as the Ministry of Labour, the Board of Trade and the Department of Education were eventually fused and renamed as the Department for Employment and Education (and subsequently renamed the Department for Education and Skills).

5   It does not follow from this that welfare states are for the elderly, however. There are major variations in the generational beneficiaries of transfers (with Italy being the supreme example of a pensioners' welfare state, while the USA favours children); and other benefits may also disproportionately benefit younger generations (e.g., housing) rather than the elderly (e.g., health care).

6   Paradoxically, part of the response was to continue expansion of higher education as one means of disguising youth unemployment.

7   Lauder et al. also discussed two further models from East Asia: Japan relied on highly diffused skills, medium capital investment relative to skill, and high labour intensity to generate high levels of productivity; Singapore and South Korea relied on a high-skills strategy based on skill diffusion and capital investment related to skill utilization in the context of rapid but uneven skills formation with high labour intensity to generate productivity.

Chapter 5: The Political Economy of State Rescaling

1   I use post-Fordism to refer to an ideal-typical after-Fordist regime that is characterized by structured coherence; and I use after-Fordism to refer to actually existing after-Fordist regimes that are marked by a continuing relative incoherence because a new accumulation regime and mode of regulation have not yet been established.

2   'In [the nation-state], differences are assimilated, destroyed, or assigned to ghettoes, to enclaves demarcated by boundaries so sharp that they enable the nation to acknowledge the apparently singular and clearly fenced-off differences within itself, while simultaneously reaffirming the privileged homogeneity of the rest, as well as the difference *between* itself and what lies over its frontiers' (Tölölyan 1991: 6).

3   Cyberspace is, in fact, far from evenly distributed or accessible and it does have roots in specific places.

4   Whitehead, cited by Harvey, argues that 'there are an indefinite number of discordant time-series and an indefinite number of distinct spaces'. Hence it is important to examine how 'multiple processes flow together to construct a single consistent, coherent, though multifaceted, time–space system' (Harvey 1996: 260).

5   This qualification is important because Atlantic Fordism involved a retreat from earlier levels of internationalization or globalization.

6 The following list is inspired in part by Harvey 1989: 9–10.

7 This discussion draws on an ESRC project undertaken in conjunction with Colin Hay, who contributed significantly to the initial fourfold typology from which the present sixfold typology has been developed (ESRC grant L311253032).

8 'Intermestic' is a term coined by Duchacek to refer to the expanding area of international connections between local authorities. See Duchacek et al. 1988.

Chapter 6: From Mixed Economy to Metagovernance

1 Thus there are three main explanatory approaches to the economic miracles that have occurred in East Asia: a liberal interpretation emphasizing the emancipation of market forces, a statist interpretation that focuses on the role of the developmental state, and a culturalist reading that emphasizes the specificities of Confucian capitalism. Despite their differences of interpretation, however, all three approaches adopt the market-state-civil society paradigm. They ignore the extent to which Asian societies lack the clear institutional separation of market and state said to be typical of modern western societies, lack a clear, hierarchically organized sovereign state, and lack a bourgeois civil society with strongly developed individualism. This means that such interpretations also ignore the networks of economic and political forces that cross-cut private-public boundaries and deploy both economic and political resources in pursuit of specific economic and political projects; and ignore the extent to which collective rather than individual identities shape orientations in the lifeworld.

2 The concept of 'formal freedom' is used here to draw an implicit contrast with the lack of full *substantive* freedom due to the multiple constraints that limit free choice. But the institutionalization of formal freedom is nonetheless a significant political accomplishment and a major element in liberal citizenship as well as a precondition for market economies.

3 Primitive accumulation is not a one-off process that ends once the conditions for the self-valorization of capital have been established, but one that has a continuing role thereafter in capital accumulation (see de Angelis 1999). Nonetheless, it also varies in importance – witness the recent upswing through the commodification of the intellectual commons.

4 '[S]ince every project is always a part of some more extensive assemblage, so every project is always enmeshed with other projective activities, and there can be no guarantee that such projects, though connected, will even be wholly consistent with one another' (Malpas and Wickham 1995: 46).

Chapter 7: Towards Schumpeterian Workfare Postnational Regimes?

1 In this sense nothing can be explained in terms of the tendential shift from the KWNS to the SWPR, the 'hollowing out' of the state, or the movement from government to governance. It is these shifts themselves that need explaining.

2 Another meaning of postnational is also relevant. This is the movement from a nation-state (whether *Volksnation*, *Kulturnation* or *Staatsnation*) towards a multiethnic, multicultural, and more 'diasporic' society within given national territorial borders (see chapter 5).

3 The use of ideal-types is often incorrectly dismissed as empiricist and hence as inconsistent with the type of critical realist approach adopted here. This does justice neither to Weber's own use of ideal types in his historical analyses nor to the nature of concept formation in Marxism. On Weber's ideal types, see Ringer 1997; and on concept formation in the regulation approach and state theory, Jessop 1982, 1990b, and 2001b.

4 Thus Therborn and Roebroek discuss variant forms of the welfare state and then declare it irreversible (under democratic conditions); their argument depends on a simple equation between major public spending programmes and the presence of the welfare state. See Therborn and Roebroek (1986). On international Keynesianism, see also Piore and Sabel 1985.

5 Thus I have discussed elsewhere the ideal-typical Listian workfare national state and the ideal-typical Ricardian workfare colonial regime in the East Asian NICs in terms of their primary goals in accumulation (see Jessop 1999c; and Sum 1998). A different typology could be based on how different forms of economic and social intervention contribute to specific state projects. Thus one might contrast the Bismarckian social imperialist *Sozialstaat* with the Beveridgean social democratic welfare state (see also chapter 2).

6 The following argument derives from Carpi (1997) but has been rephrased to fit with the more general approach developed in earlier parts of the chapter.

7 The labels attached to these elements are mine. The EC Bulletin cited here simply lists a range of policies and describes their respective roles.

8 This issue is a specific version of the general problem in Marxist state theory (Jessop 1990b): is it a state in capitalist societies or a capitalist state?

9 Congruence is best analysed in this context in terms of the 'strategic selectivity' of state structures, i.e., the extent to which specific structural forms and operations privilege the pursuit of policies favourable to Fordism.

10 It would be wrong to posit two distinct types of post-Fordist state that succeed one another: transitional and consolidated. This would be reminiscent of the awkward structuralist fallacy of positing a transitional mode of production between each normal mode of production, with the latter defined in terms of its structurally inscribed function of securing the transition from one normal mode to the next (cf. Cutler et al. 1977). It is for this reason that I refer to a transitional regime with an indeterminate form and a normal state with a determinate form. Even with regard to the latter, it will prove necessary to specify its variant forms.

11 For further discussion of *ex post facto* analyses and how they can be developed through work on the co-constitution of modes and objects of regulation, see Jessop 1990a, 1990b, and 2001b.

12 The same point applies to the work of Poulantzas on the future of the state in the mid-1970s, which was also limited by Atlantic Fordist horizons (see Jessop 2002a).

References

Note: The arguments developed above derive from a wide range of reading. This bibliography lists only material actually cited in the book.

Abrahamson, P. E. 1999: The welfare modelling business. *Social Policy and Administration*, 33 (4), 394–415.

Aglietta, M. 1982: World capitalism in the eighties. *New Left Review*, 136, 5–41.

Ainley, P. 1997: Toward a learning society or towards learningfare? *Social Policy Review*, 9, 50–68.

Alber, J. and Standing, G. 2000: Social dumping, catch-up or convergence? Europe in a comparative global context. *Journal of European Social Policy*, 10 (2), 99–119.

Alexander, E. R. 1995: *How Organizations Act Together: Interorganizational Coordination in Theory and Practice*, Amsterdam: Overseas Publishers Association.

Althusser, L. 1977: On the materialist dialectic. In idem, *For Marx*, London: Verso, 161–218.

Altvater, E. 1993: *The Future of the Market: On the Regulation of Money and Nature after the Collapse of 'Real Socialism'*, London: Verso.

Altvater, E. and Mahnkopf, B. 1999: *Die Grenzen der Globalisierung* (4th edition), Münster: Westfälisches Dampfboot.

Amin, A. (ed.) 1994: *Post-Fordism: A Reader*, Oxford: Blackwell.

Amin, A. and Graham, S. 1997: The ordinary city. *Transactions of the Institute of British Geographers*, 22, 411–29.

Amin, A. and Robins, K. 1990: The re-emergence of regional economies? The mythical geography of flexible accumulation. *Environment and Planning D: Society and Space*, 8 (1), 7–34.

Amin, A. and Thrift, N. 1995: Globalisation, institutional 'thickness' and the local economy. In P. Healey, S. Cameron, S. Davoudi, S. Graham and A. Madani-Pour (eds), *Managing Cities: the New Urban Context*, Chichester: John Wiley, 91–108.

Andersen, S. S. and Eliassen, K. A. (eds) 2001: *Making Policy in Europe: The Europeification of National Policy-Making*, London: Sage.

Anderson, B. 1991: *The Imagined Community* (2nd edition), London: Verso.

Anderson, J. 1996: The shifting stage of politics: new medieval and postmodern territorialities? *Environment and Planning D: Society and Space*, 16 (4), 133–53.

Andreff, W. and Andreff, M. 1995: Economic disintegration in Eastern Europe: towards a new integration? In B. Dallago and G. Pegoretti (eds), *Integration and Disintegration in European Economies*, Aldershot: Dartmonth, 113–41.

Aoki, K. 1998: Considering multiple and overlapping sovereignties: liberalism, libertarianism, national sovereignty, 'global' intellectual property, and the Internet. *Indiana Journal of Global Legal Studies*, 5 (2), 443–74.

Archibugi, D., Howells, J. and Michie, J. (eds) 1999: *Innovation Policy in a Global Economy*, Cambridge: Cambridge University Press.

Ashton, D. and Green, A. D. 1996: *Education, Training and the Global Economy*, Chelmsford: Edward Elgar.

Aumeeruddy, A. T., Lautier, B. and Tortajada, R. G. 1978: Labour power and the state. *Capital and Class*, 6, 42–66.

Bakos, G. 1993: After COMECON: a Free Trade Area in Central Europe. *Europe-Asia Studies*, 45 (6), 1025–44.

Balibar, E. 1990: The nation form: history and ideology. *Review*, 13 (3), 329–61.

Ball, S. J. 1998: Big policies/small world: an introduction to international perspectives in education policy. *Comparative Education*, 34 (2), 119–30.

Barnes, W. R. and Ledubur, L. C. 1991: Toward a new political economy of metropolitan regions. *Environment and Planning C: Government and Policy*, 9 (2), 127–41.

Barry, A., Osborne, T. and Rose, N. (eds) 1996: *Foucault and Political Reason: Liberalism, Neo-Liberalism and Rationalities of Government*, London: UCL Press.

Bell, D. 1973: *The Coming of Post-Industrial Society*, London: Heinemann.

Bell, D. 1979: The social framework of the information society. In M. L. Dertouzos and J. Moses (eds), *The Computer Age: A Twenty-Year View*, Cambridge, MA: MIT Press, 163–211.

Benington, J. 1995: *The Europeanization of Local Governance – The Significance of Transnational Networks*, Coventry: Warwick University Local Government Centre.

Benington, J. and Harvey, J. 1994: Spheres or tiers? The significance of transnational local authority networks. In P. Dunleavy and J. Stanyer (eds), *Contemporary Political Studies*, vol. 2, London: Political Studies Association, 943–61.

Bieling, H.-J. 1993: *Nationalstaat und Migration im Postfordismus – Gerwerkschaften vor der Zerreissprobe*, Marburg: Forschungsgruppe Europäische Gemeinschaften, FEG-Studie Nr. 2.

Biernacki, R. 1995: *The Fabrication of Labour: Germany and Britain, 1640–1914*, Berkeley: University of California Press.

Blair, T. and Schröder, G. 1999: Europe: The Third Way/Die Neue Mitte, *http://www.labour.org.uk/views/items/00000053.html*

Blatter, J. 2001: Debordering the world of states. Towards a multi-level system in Europe and a multi-polity system in North America? Insights from border regions. *European Journal of International Relations*, 7 (2), 175–210.

Bloch, H. and Kenyon, P. 2001: The meaning and measurement of international competitiveness. In idem (eds), *Creating an Internationally Competitive Economy*, Basingstoke: Palgrave, 16–35.

Blühdorn, I. 2000: An offer one might prefer to refuse: the systems theoretical legacy of Niklas Luhmann. *European Journal of Social Theory*, 3 (3), 339–54.

Bonoli, G., George, V. and Taylor-Gooby, P. 2000: *European Welfare Futures: Towards a Theory of Retrenchment*, Cambridge: Polity.

Boris, E. 1995: The racialized gendered state: constructions of citizenship in the United States. *Social Politics*, 2 (2), 160–80.

Bowles, S. and Edwards, R. 1985: *Contemporary Capitalism: Competition, Command, and Change in the U.S. Economy*, New York: Harper Row.

Boyer, R. 1990: *The Regulation School: A Critical Introduction*, New York: Columbia University Press.

Boyer, R. 1997: French statism at the crossroads. In W. Streeck and C. Crouch (eds), *Political Economy of Modern Capitalism*, London: Sage, 71–101.

Boyer, R. and Durand, J.-P. 1997: *After-Fordism*, Basingstoke: Macmillan.

Boyer, R. and Hollingsworth, R. J. 1997: From national embeddedness to spatial and institutional nestedness. In R. J. Hollingsworth and R. Boyer (eds), *Contemporary Capitalism: the Embeddedness of Capitalist Institutions*, Cambridge: Cambridge University Press, 433–84.

Boyer, R. and Saillard, Y. (eds) 2002: *Régulation Theory: The State of the Art*, London: Routledge.

Boyer, R. and Yamada, T. (eds) 2000: *Japanese Capitalism in Crisis: A 'Regulationist' Interpretation*, London: Routledge.

Braudel, F. 1984: *The Perspective of the World*, London: Collins.

Brennan, T. 1995: Why the time is out of joint. Marx's political economy without the subject, Part I. *Strategies: Journal of Theory, Culture and Politics*, 9–10, 18–37.

Brenner, N. 1998: Global cities, glocal states: global city formation and state territorial restructuring in contemporary Europe. *Review of International Political Economy*, 5 (1), 1–38.

Brenner, N. 1999a: Beyond state-centrism? Space, territoriality, and geographical scale in globalization studies. *Theory and Society*, 28 (1), 39–78.

Brenner, N. 1999b: Globalisation as reterritorialisation: the re-scaling of urban governance in the European Union. *Urban Studies*, 36 (3), 431–51.

Brenner, N. 2000: Building 'Euro-Regions'. Locational politics and the political geography of neoliberalism in post-unification Germany. *European Urban and Regional Studies*, 7 (4), 319–45.

Brock, L. and Albert, M. 1996: De-bordering the state: new spaces in international relations. *New Political Science*, 35, 69–107.

Brookes, M. and Wahhaj, Z. 2000: *The Shocking Business of B2B*, New York: Goldman Sachs.

Brubaker, R. 1992: *Citizenship and Nationhood in France and Germany*, Cambridge, MA: Harvard University Press.

de Brunhoff, S. 1978: *The State, Capital, and Economic Policy*, London: Pluto.

Bryan, R. 1995: *The Chase across the Globe. International Accumulation and the Contradictions of Nation States*, Boulder: Westview.

Bussemaker, J. and van Kersbergen, K. 1994: Gender and welfare states: some theoretical reflections. In D. Sainsbury (ed.), *Gendering Welfare States*, London: Sage, 8–25.

Camagni, R. 1995: The concept of innovative milieu and its relevance for public policies in European lagging regions. *Papers in Regional Science*, 74 (4), 317–40.

Camhis, M. and Fox, S. 1992: The European Community as a catalyst for European urban networks. *Ekistics*, 352–3, 4–6.

Capello, R. 1996: Industrial enterprises and economic space: the network paradigm. *European Planning Studies*, 4 (4), 485–98.

Carabine, J. 1996: A straight playing field or queering the pitch? *Feminist Review*, 56, 31–64.

Carpi, J. A. T. 1997: The prospects for the social economy in a changing world. *Annals of Public and Cooperative Economics*, 68 (2), 247–79.

Carter, D. S. G. and O'Neill, M. H. 1995: *International Perspectives on Educational Reform and Policy Implementation*, Brighton: Falmer Press.

Castells, M. 1996: *The Rise of the Network Society*, Oxford: Blackwell.

Castells, M. 2000a: Materials for an explanatory theory of the network society. *British Journal of Sociology*, 51 (1), 5–24.

Castells, M. 2000b: *The Rise of the Network Society* (2nd edition), Oxford: Blackwell.

Cerny, P. G. 2000: Globalization and the disarticulation of political power: towards a new middle ages? In H. Goverde, P. G. Cerny, G. Philip, M. Haugaard, and H. Lentner (eds), *Power in Contemporary Politics. Theories, Practices, Globalizations*, London: Sage, 170–86.

Chen, X. 1995: The evolution of free economic zones and the recent development of cross-national growth zones. *International Journal of Urban and Regional Research*, 19 (4), 593–621.

Chesnais, F. 1986: Science, technology and competitiveness. *STI Review*, 1 (Autumn), 86–129.

Clarke, J. and Newman, J. 1997: *The Managerial State*, London: Sage.

Clarke, S. 1977: Marxism, sociology, and Poulantzas's theory of the capitalist state. *Capital and Class*, 2, 1–31.

Clarke, S. E. and Gaile, G. L. 1998: *The Work of Cities*, Minneapolis: University of Minnesota Press.

Cleaver, H. 1979: *Reading Capital Politically*, Brighton: Harvester.

Coates, D. 2000: *Models of Capitalism: Growth and Stagnation in the Modern Era*, Cambridge: Polity.

Collinge, C. 1996: *Spatial Articulation of the State: Reworking Social Relations and Social Regulation Theory*, Birmingham: Centre for Urban and Regional Studies.

Collinge, C. 1999: Self-Organization of society by scale: a spatial reworking of regulation theory. *Environment and Planning D: Society and Space*, 17 (5), 557–74.

Cook, J., Roche, M., Williams, C. C. and Windebank, J. 2001: The evolution of active welfare policies as a solution to social exclusion in Britain. *Journal of European Area Studies*, 9 (1), 13–26.

Cooke, P. and Morgan, K. 1993: The network paradigm: new departures in corporate and regional development. *Environment and Planning D: Society and Space*, 11 (4), 543–64.

Coombe, R. J. 1998: *The Cultural Life of Intellectual Properties*, Durham, NC: Duke University Press.

Cortright, J. 2001: New growth theory, technology and learning: a practitioner's guide. *Reviews of Economic Development Literature and Practice*, No. 4. Washington DC: US Economic Development Administration.

Cox, K. R. 1993: The local and the global in the new urban politics. *Environment and Planning D: Society and Space*, 11 (3), 433–48.

Crouch, C. 1993: *Industrial Relations and European State Traditions*, Oxford: Oxford University Press.

Crozier, M., Huntington, S. P. and Watanuki, J. 1975: *The Crisis of Democracy. Report on the Governability of Democracies to the Trilateral Commission*, New York: New York University Press.

Cutler, A., Hindess, B., Hirst, P. Q. and Hussain, A. 1977: *Marx's 'Capital' and Capitalism Today*, London: Routledge.

Czarniawska, B. and Sevón, G. 1996: Introduction. In idem (eds), *Translating Organizational Change*, Berlin: de Gruyter, 1–13.

Daly, G. 1994: The discursive construction of economic space. *Economy and Society*, 20 (1), 79–102.

Daly, M. 1998: Welfare states under pressure: cash benefits in European welfare states over the last ten years. *Journal of European Social Policy*, 7 (2), 129–46.

Dawson, A. C. 1998: The intellectual commons: a rationale for regulation. *Prometheus*, 16 (3), 275–89.

De Angelis, M. 1999: Marx's theory of primitive accumulation: a suggested reinterpretation. http://homepages.uel.ac.uk/M.DeAngelis/PRIMACCA.htm, accessed 29.11.01.

Deacon, B. 1995: The globalisation of social policy and the socialisation of global politics. *Social Policy Review*, 7, 55–76.

Deacon, B. 1996: *The Globalization of Social Policy*, London: Sage.

Deacon, B. 2001: International organizations, the EU and global social policy. In R. Sykes, B. Palier and P. M. Prior (eds), *Globalization and European Welfare States*, Basingstoke: Palgrave, 59–76.

Deacon, B. and Hulse, M. 1997: The making of post-communist social policy: the role of international agencies. *Journal of Social Policy*, 26 (1), 43–62.

Deakin, N. and Edwards, J. 1993: *The Enterprise Culture and the Inner City*, London: Routledge.

Debray, R. 1973: Time and politics. In idem (eds), *Prison Writings*, London: Allen Lane, 87–160.

Deppe, F., Felder, M. and Tidow, S. 2000: Structuring the state – the case of European employment policy. Paper presented at the International Conference 'Linking EU and National Governance', Mannheim, June.

DfEE 1998: *Learning is the Key to Prosperity*, London: Department for Education and Employment.

Doern, G. B., Pal, L. A. and Tomlin, B. W. (eds) 1996: *Border Crossings: the Internationalization of Canadian Public Policy*, Oxford: Oxford University Press.

Dolowitz, D. and Marsh, D. 1996: Who learns what from whom? A review of the policy transfer literature. *Political Studies*, 44 (2), 343–57.

Duchacek, I. D. 1990: Perforated sovereignties: towards a typology of new actors in international relations. In H. J. Michelman and P. Soldatos (eds), *Federalism and International Relations: The Role of Subnational Units*, Oxford: Clarendon Press, 1–33.

Duchacek, I. D., Latouche, D. and Stevenson, G. (eds) 1988: *Perforated Sovereignties and International Relations: Trans-sovereign Contacts of Subnational Governments*, New York: Greenwood Press.

Duménil, G. and Lévy, D. 2001a: Costs and benefits of neoliberalism. A class analysis. *International Review of Political Economy*, 8 (4), 578–607.

Duménil, G. and Lévy, D. 2001b: The nature and contradictions of neoliberalism. In L. Panitch and C. Leys (eds), *Socialist Register 2002*, London: Merlin, 43–72.

Dunning, J. H. (ed.) 2000: *Regions, Globalization, and the Knowledge-Based Economy*, Oxford: Oxford University Press.

Dunsire, A. 1996: Tipping the balance: autopoiesis and governance. *Administration and Society*, 28 (3), 299–334.

Dyson, K. (ed.) 1989: *Local Authorities and New Technologies: The European Dimension*, London: Croom Helm.

Ebbinghaus, B. and Manow, P. (eds) 2001a: *Comparing Welfare Capitalisms. Social Policy and Political Economy in Europe, Japan and the USA*, London: Routledge.

Ebbinghaus, B. and Manow, P. 2001b: Introduction. In idem (eds), *Comparing Welfare Capitalisms. Social Policy and Political Economy in Europe, Japan and the USA*, London: Routledge, 1–24.

Economides, N. 1996: Economies of networks. *International Journal of Industrial Organization*, 14 (6), 673–99.

Ekengreen, M. 1997: The temporality of European governance. In K. E. Jorgensen (ed.), *Reflective Approaches to European Governance*, Basingstoke: Macmillan, 69–86.

Esping-Andersen, G. 1985: *Politics Against Markets*, Ithaca: Cornell University Press.

Esping-Andersen, G. 1990: *The Three Worlds of Welfare Capitalism*, Cambridge: Polity.

Esping-Andersen, G. 1994: Equality and work in the post-industrial life-cycle. In D. Miliband (ed.), *Reinventing the Left*, Cambridge: Polity, 167–85.

Esping-Andersen, G. 1997: Hybrid or unique? The distinctiveness of the Japanese welfare state. *Journal of European Social Policy*, 7 (3), 179–90.

Esping-Andersen, G. 1999: *The Social Foundations of Postindustrial Economies,* Oxford: Oxford University Press.

Esser, K., Hillebrand, W., Messner, D. and Meyer-Stamer, J. 1996: Systemic competitiveness: a new challenge for firms and for government. *Cepal Review,* 59, 39–52.

Estevez-Abe, M., Iversen, T. and Soskice, D. 2001: Social protection and the formation of skills: a reinterpretation of the welfare state. In P. Hall and D. Soskice (eds), *Varieties of Capitalism: The Institutional Foundations of Comparative Advantage,* Oxford: Oxford University Press, 145–83.

Etzkowitz, H. 1994: Academic–industry relations: a sociological paradigm for economic development. In L. Leydesdorff and P. van Desselaar (eds), *Evolutionary Economics and Chaos Theory,* London: Pinter, 139–51.

Etzkowitz, H. and Leydesdorff, L. (eds) 1997: *Universities and the Global Knowledge Economy. A Triple Helix of University–Industry–Government,* London: Pinter.

European Commission 1992: *Enlargement Document: Candidate Countries and Member States,* Brussels: European Commission.

European Commission 1994: *Expanding Links between the European Communities and East Asia,* Brussels: European Commission.

European Commission 2001: *Unity, Solidarity, Diversity for Europe, its People and its Territory,* Brussels: European Commission.

European Communities, Commission 1991: European industrial policy for the 1990s, *Bulletin of the European Communities,* Supplement 3/91.

European Communities, Commission 1992: *Economic Development and Regional Integration in Asian Regions: Current Status Analysis and Scenarios for Regional Co-operation,* Brussels: FAST Programme Prospective Dossier no. 3.

European Communities, Commission 1993: *Growth, Competitiveness, Employment – The Challenges and Ways Forward into the 21st Century (White Paper),* Luxemburg: Office for Official Publications of the European Communities.

European Communities, Commission 1994: *An Industrial Competitiveness Policy for the European Union,* COM (94) 319 FINAL, Brussels.

European Union 1999: *Joint Declaration of the European Ministers of Education Convened in Bologna on the 19th of June 1999. http://www.europedu.org.*

Evans, P. B., Rueschemeyer, D. and Skocpol, T. (eds) 1985: *Bringing the State Back In,* Cambridge: Cambridge University Press.

Fairclough, N. 1992: *Discourse and Social Change,* Cambridge: Polity.

Fairclough, N. 2000: *New Labour, New Language?* London: Routledge.

Falkner, G. 1998: *EU Social Policy in the 1990s: Towards a Corporatist Policy Community,* London: Routledge.

Finer, C. J. 1997: The new social policy in Britain. *Social Policy & Administration,* 31 (5), 154–70.

Flora, P. (ed.) 1986–7: *Growth to Limits: The Western European Welfare States since World War II,* Berlin: Walter De Gruyter (4 volumes).

Forbes, D. K. 1997: Metropolis and megaurban region in Pacific Asia. *Tijdschrift voor Economische en Sociale Geografie,* 88 (5), 457–68.

Frankel, J. 1994: Is Japan establishing a trade bloc in East Asia and the Pacific? In M. Okabe (ed.), *The Structure of the Japanese Economy*, Basingstoke: Macmillan, 387–415.

Fraser, N. 1987: Women, welfare, and the politics of need interpretation. *Hypatia*, 2 (1), 103–21.

Fraser, N. 1997: Equality, difference and democracy: recent feminist debates in the United States. In J. Dean (ed.), *Feminism and the New Democracy. Re-Siting the Political*, London: Sage, 98–109.

Freeman, C. and Perez, C. 1988: Structural crises of adjustment: business cycles and investment behaviour. In G. Dosi, C. Freeman, R. Nelson, G. Silverberg and L. Soete (eds), *Technical Change and Economic Theory*, London: Pinter, 38–66.

Freeman, G. P. 1986: Migration and the political economy of the welfare state. *Annals of the American Academy of Political and Social Science*, 485, 51–63.

Froud, J., Johal, S., Haslam, C. and Williams, K. 2001: Accumulation under conditions of inequality. *Review of International Political Economy*, 8 (1), 66–95.

Frow, J. 1996: Information as gift and commodity. *New Left Review*, 219, 89–108.

Fukuyama, F. 1995: *Trust: The Social Virtues and the Creation of Prosperity*, New York: Free Press.

Galbraith, J. K. 1967: *The New Industrial State*, Harmondsworth: Penguin.

Garfinkel, A. 1981: *Forms of Explanation: Rethinking the Questions in Social Theory*, New Haven: Yale University Press.

Garrett, G. 1998: *Partisan Politics in the Global Economy*, Cambridge: Cambridge University Press.

Garrett, G. 2001: Globalization and government spending around the world. *Studies in Comparative International Development*, 35 (4), 3–29.

Garrett, G. and Mitchell, D. 2001: Globalization, government spending and taxation in the OECD. *European Journal of Political Research*, 39 (3), 145–57.

Gellner, E. 1993: Nationalism and the development of European societies. In J. Iivonen (ed.), *The Future of the European Nation State in Europe*, Aldershot: Edward Elgar, 16–30.

Gill, S. 1995: Globalisation, market civilization and disciplinary neoliberalism. *Millennium*, 24 (3), 399–423.

Gill, S. 2001: Constitutionalising capital: EMU and disciplinary neo-liberalism. In A. Bieler and A. D. Morton (eds), *Social Forces in the Making of the New Europe. The Restructuring of European Social Relations in the Global Political Economy*, Basingstoke: Palgrave, 47–69.

Glagow, M. and Willke, H. (eds) 1987: *Dezentrale Gesellschaftssteuerung: Probleme der Integration polyzentristischer Gesellschaft*, Pfaffenweiler: Centaurus-Verlagsgesellschaft.

Glyn, A. and Wood, S. 2001: New Labour's economic policy: how social-democratic is the Blair Government? *Political Quarterly*, 72 (1), 39–49.

Gong, G. W. (ed.) 1999: *South East Asia's Changing Landscape*, Washington, DC: Center for Strategic and International Studies.

Goodin, R. E., Headey, B., Muffels, R. and Dirven, H.-J. 1999: *The Real Worlds of Welfare Capitalism*, Cambridge: Cambridge University Press.

Goodwin, M. and Painter, J. 1996: Local governance, the crises of Fordism and the changing geographies of regulation. *Transactions of Institute of British Geographers*, 21 (4), 635–48.

Gough, I. 1979: *The Political Economy of the Welfare State*, Basingstoke: Macmillan.

Gough, J. and Eisenschitz, A. 1996: The construction of mainstream local economic initiatives: mobility, socialization, and class relations. *Economic Geography*, 72 (2), 178–95.

Gourevitch, P. A. 1978: The second image reversed: the international sources of domestic politics. *International Organisation*, 32 (4), 881–911.

Grabher, G. 1994: *Lob der Verschwendung. Redundanz in der Regionalentwicklung: ein socioökonomisches Plädoyer*, Berlin: Edition Sigma.

Grahl, J. and Teague, P. 1991: *1992: The Big Market*, London: Lawrence & Wishart.

Grahl, J. and Teague, P. 1997: Is the European social model fragmenting? *New Political Economy*, 2 (3), 405–26.

Gramsci, A. 1971: *Selections from the Prison Notebooks*, London: Lawrence & Wishart.

Grande, E. 2000: Charisma und Komplexität. Verhandlungsdemokratie, Mediendemokratie und der Funktionswandel politischer Eliten. *Leviathan*, 38 (1), 122–41.

Gray, A. 1998: New Labour – new labour discipline. *Capital and Class*, 65, 1–8.

Gray, H. (ed.) 1999: *Universities and the Creation of Wealth*, Buckingham: Open University Press.

Green, A. D. 1997: *Education, Globalization and the Nation State*, Basingstoke: Macmillan.

Grote, J. R. and Schmitter, P. C. 1999: The renaissance of national corporatism: unintended side-effect of European Economic and Monetary Union or calculated response to the absence of European social policy? *Transfer: Quarterly of the European Trade Union Institute*, 5 (1–2), 34–63.

Grugel, J. and Hout, W. (eds) 1999: *Regionalism Across the North–South Divide: State Strategies and Globalization*, London: Routledge.

Guttman, R. 2002: Money and credit in *régulation* theory. In R. Boyer and Y. Saillard (eds), *Régulation Theory: The State of the Art*, London: Routledge, 57–63.

Habermas, J. 1975: *Legitimation Crisis*, Boston: Beacon Press.

Habermas, J. 1987: *The Theory of Communicative Action. Vol. 2, System and Lifeworld: A Critique of Functionalist Reason*, Boston: Beacon Press.

Habermas, J. 1996: *Between Fact and Value*, Cambridge: Polity.

Hall, P. A. (ed.) 1989: *The Political Power of Economic Ideas: Keynesianism across Nations*, Princeton: Princeton University Press.

Hall, P. 1998: *Cities and Civilization*, London: Weidenfeld & Nicolson.

Hall, P. A. and Soskice, D. (eds) 2001: *Varieties of Capitalism: The Institutional Foundations of Comparative Advantage*, Oxford: Oxford University Press.

Hall, T. and Hubbard, P. 1996: The entrepreneurial city: new urban politics, new urban geographies? *Progress in Human Geography*, 20 (2), 153–74.

Hancké, B. 1996: Labour unions, business coordination and economic adjustment in Western Europe, 1980–1990, Berlin: Wissenschaftszentrum zu Berlin, Working Paper, FS 1, 96–309.

Hantrais, L. 2000: *Social Policy in the European Union*, Basingstoke: Macmillan.

Harding, A. 1995: European city regimes? Inter-urban competition in the new Europe. Paper to the ESRC Local Governance Conference, Exeter, 19–20 September.

Harvey, D. 1982: *The Limits to Capital*, Oxford: Blackwell.

Harvey, D. 1989: From managerialism to entrepreneurialism: the transformation of urban governance in late capitalism. *Geografiska Annaler, series B: Human Geography*, 17 B, 1, 3–17.

Harvey, D. 1996: *Justice, Nature and the Geography of Difference*, Oxford: Blackwell.

Haughton, G., Jones, M., Peck, J., Tickell, A. and While, A. 2000: Labour Market policy as flexible welfare: prototype employment zones and the new workfarism. *Regional Studies*, 34 (7), 669–80.

Hausner, J., Jessop, B. and Nielsen, K. 1995: Institutional change in post-socialism. In idem (eds), *Strategic Choice and Path-Dependency in Post-Socialism*, Chelmsford: Edward Elgar, 3–45.

Hay, C. 1994: Moving or shaking or cowering and quaking? Dances to the tune of local economic development. Paper for ESRC Colloquium on Community Power and Urban Governance, London School of Economics, 19 December.

Hay, C. 1996: Narrating crisis: the discursive construction of the 'Winter of Discontent'. *Sociology*, 30 (2), 253–77.

Hemerijck, M. and Manow, P. 2001: The experience of negotiated reforms in the Dutch and German welfare states. In B. Ebbinghaus and P. Manow (eds), *Comparing Welfare Capitalisms. Social Policy and Political Economy in Europe, Japan and the USA*, London: Routledge, 217–38.

Hettne, B., Inotal, A. and Sunkel, O. (eds) 2000: *National Perspectives on the New Regionalism in the North*, Basingstoke: Macmillan.

Hicks, J. R. 1959: *Essays in World Economics*, Oxford: Clarendon Press.

Hirsch, J. 1976: Bermerkungen zum theoretischen Ansatz einer Analyse des bürgerlichen States. *Gesellschaft 8–9*, Suhrkamp, Frankfurt, 99–149.

Hirsch, J. 1977: Kapitalreproduktion, Klassenauseinandersetzungen und Widersprüche im Staatsapparat. In V. Brandes, J. Hoffmann, U. Jürgens and W. Semmler (eds), *Handbuch 5 (Staat)*, Frankfurt: EVA, 161–81.

Hirsch, J. 1995: *Der nationale Wettbewerbstaat. Staat, Demokratie und Politik im globalen Kapitalismus*, Berlin: Edition ID-Archiv.

Hirsch, J. and Roth, R. 1986: *Das neue Gesicht des Kapitalismus: vom Fordismus zum post-Fordismus*, Hamburg: VSA.

Hirst, P. Q. and Thompson, G. 1999: *Globalisation in Question: The Myths of the International Economy and the Possibilities of Governance* (2nd edition), Cambridge: Polity.

Hoffman, J. and Hoffman, R. 1997: *Globalization. Risks and opportunities for labour policy in Europe*. European Trade Union Institute.

Hoggett, P. 1987: A farewell to mass production? Decentralization as an emergent private and public sector paradigm. In P. Hoggett and R. Hambleton (eds), *Decentralization and Democracy*, Bristol: School of Advanced Urban Studies, 215–32.

Hollingsworth, R. J. and Boyer, R. (eds) 1997a: *Contemporary Capitalism: The Embeddedness of Capitalist Institutions*, Cambridge: Cambridge University Press.

Hollingsworth, R. J. and Boyer, R. 1997b: Coordination of economic actors and social systems of production. In idem (eds), *Contemporary Capitalism: The Embeddedness of Capitalist Institutions*, Cambridge: Cambridge University Press, 1–47.

Hooghe, L. and Marks, G. 2001: *Multi-Level Governance and European Integration*, Oxford: Rowman and Littlefield.

Huber, E. and Stephens, J. D. 2001: *Development And Crisis Of The Welfare State: Parties And Politics In Global Markets*, Chicago: University of Chicago Press.

Huber, E., Stephens, J. D. and Ray, L. 1999: The welfare state in hard times. In H. Kitschelt, P. Lange, G. Marks and J. D. Stephens (eds), *Continuity and Change in Contemporary Capitalism*, Cambridge: Cambridge University Press, 164–93.

Hudson, A. 2000: Offshoreness, globalization and sovereignty: a postmodern geo-political economy? *Transactions of the Institute of British Geographers*, 25 (3), 269–83.

Hunt, A. and Wickham, G. 1994: *Foucault and Law: Towards a Sociology of Governance*, London: Pluto Press.

Hutton, W. 2002: *The World We're In*, London: Little, Brown.

Hyde, M., Dixon, J. and Joyner, M. 1999: 'Work for those that can, security for those that cannot': the United Kingdom's New Social Security Reform Agenda. *International Social Security Review*, 52 (4), 69–86.

Ikenberry, J. G. 1993: A world economy restored: expert consensus and the Anglo-American powers. *International Organisation*, 46 (1), 289–322.

Illich, I. 1979: *Medical Nemesis: the Expropriation of Health*, Toronto: Bantam.

Illich, I. 1981: *Shadow Work*, Boston: Marion Boyars.

IMD (Institute of Management Development) 2001: *World Competitiveness Yearbook*, Lausanne: Institute of Management Development.

Interreg 2001: *Impact of Enlargement on Regions Bordering Candidate Countries – Community Action Plan*, Brussels: European Commission.

Iversen, T. 2001: The dynamics of welfare state expansion: trade openness, de-industrialization, and partisan politics. In P. Pierson (ed.), *The New Politics of the Welfare State*, Oxford: Oxford University Press, 45–79.

Jenson, J. 1986: Gender and reproduction: or babies and the state. *Studies in Political Economy*, 20, 9–46.

Jenson, J. 1997a: Die Reinstitutionalisierung der Staatsbürgerschaft. Klasse, Geschlecht und Gleichheit im Fordismus und Postfordismus. In S. Becker, T. Sablowski and W. Schumm (eds), *Jenseits der Nationalökonomie? Weltwirtschaft und Nationalstaat zwischen Gloabliserung und Regionalisierung*, Berlin: Argument Verlag, 232–47.

Jenson, J. 1997b: Who cares? Gender and welfare regimes. *Social Politics*, 4 (2), 182–7.

Jessop, B. 1982: *The Capitalist State: Marxist Theories and Methods*, Oxford: Martin Robertson.

Jessop, B. 1985: *Nicos Poulantzas: Marxist Theory and Political Strategy*, Basingstoke: Macmillan.

Jessop, B. 1989: Neo-conservative regimes and the transition to post-Fordism. In M. Gottdiener and N. Komninos (eds), *Capitalist Development and Crisis Theory Accumulation, Regulation, and Spatial Restructuring*, Basingstoke: Macmillan, 261–99.

Jessop B. 1990a: Regulation theory in retrospect and prospect. *Economy and Society*, 19 (2), 153–216.

Jessop, B. 1990b: *State Theory: Putting the Capitalist State in its Place*, Cambridge: Polity.

Jessop, B. 1992a: Fordism and post-Fordism: critique and reformulation. In A. J. Scott and M. J. Storper (eds), *Pathways to Regionalism and Industrial Development*, London: Routledge, 43–65.

Jessop, B. 1992b: From social democracy to Thatcherism. In N. Abercrombie and A. Warde (eds), *Social Change in Contemporary Britain*, Cambridge: Polity, 14–39.

Jessop, B. 1992c: Regulation und Politik: Integrale Okonomie und Integraler Staat. In A. Demirovic, H.-P. Krebs and T. Sablowski (eds), *Akkumulation, Hegemonie und Staat*, Münster: Westfälisches Dampfboot, 232–62.

Jessop, B. 1993: Towards a Schumpeterian workfare state? Preliminary remarks on post-Fordist political economy. *Studies in Political Economy*, 40, 7–39.

Jessop, B. 1994a: From the Keynesian welfare to the Schumpeterian workfare state. In R. Burrows and B. Loader (eds), *Towards a Post-Fordist Welfare State?* London: Routledge, 13–37.

Jessop, B. 1994b: Post-Fordism and the state. In A. Amin (ed.), *Post-Fordism*, Oxford: Blackwell, 251–79.

Jessop, B. 1995: The regulation approach and governance theory: alternative perspectives on economic and political change? *Economy and Society*, 24 (3), 307–33.

Jessop, B. 1997: Twenty years of the regulation approach: the paradox of success and failure at home and abroad. *New Political Economy*, 2 (3), 499–522.

Jessop, B. 1998: The rise of governance and the risks of failure: the case of economic development. *International Social Science Journal*, 155, 29–46.

Jessop, B. 1999a: The changing governance of welfare: recent trends in its primary functions, scale, and modes of coordination. *Social Policy and Administration*, 33 (4), 348–59.

Jessop, B. 1999b: Globalization, entrepreneurial cities, and the social economy. In P. Hamel, M. Lustiger-Thaler and M. Mayer (eds), *Urban Movements in a Global Environment*, New York: Sage, 81–100.

Jessop, B. 1999c: Reflections on the (il)logics of globalization. In K. Olds, P. Dicken, P. F. Kelly, L. Kong and H. W. C. Yeung (eds), *Globalization and the Asia Pacific: Contested Territories*, London: Routledge, 19–38.

Jessop, B. 2000: The crisis of the national spatio-temporal fix and the ecological dominance of globalizing capitalism. *International Journal of Urban and Regional Studies*, 24 (2), 323–60.

Jessop, B. 2001a: Bringing the state back in (yet again): reviews, revisions, rejections, and redirections. *International Review of Sociology*, 11 (2), 149–73.

Jessop, B. 2001b: Capitalism, the regulation approach, and critical realism. In

A. Brown, S. Fleetwood and J. Roberts (eds), *Critical Realism and Marxism*, London: Routledge, 88–115.

Jessop, B. 2001c: Institutional (re)turns and the strategic-relational approach. *Environment and Planning A*, 33 (7), 1213–37.

Jessop, B. 2002a: Globalization and the national state. In S. Aaronowitz and P. Bratsis (eds), *Rethinking the State: Miliband, Poulantzas, and State Theory*, Minneapolis: University of Minnesota Press.

Jessop, B. 2002b: Governance and meta-governance. On reflexivity, requisite variety, and requisite irony. In H. Bang (ed.), *Governance, Governmentality and Democracy*, Manchester: Manchester University Press.

Jessop, B. 2002c: Liberalism, Neoliberalism and Urban Governance: A State-Theoretical Perspective. *Antipode* (special issue), 34 (2), 452–72.

Jessop, B. 2002d: The political economy of scale. In M. Perkmann and N. L. Sum (eds), *Globalization, Regionalization, and Cross-Border Regions*, Basingstoke: Palgrave, 25–49.

Jessop, B. and Sum, N. L. 2000: An entrepreneurial city in action: Hong Kong's emerging strategies in and for (inter-)urban competition. *Urban Studies*, 37 (12), 2290–315.

Johansson, H. 2001: Activation policies in the Nordic countries: social democratic universalism under pressure. *Journal of European Area Studies*, 9 (1), 63–78.

Jones, C. 1993: The Pacific challenge. In idem (ed.), *New Perspectives on the Welfare State in Europe*, London: Routledge, 198–213.

Jones, M. and Gray, A. 2001: Social capital, or local workfarism? Reflections on employment zones. *Local Economy*, 2–10.

Jönsson, C., Tägil, S. and Tönqvist, G. 2000: *Organizing European Space*, London: Sage.

Joppke, C. (ed.) 1998: *Challenge to the Nation-State: Immigration in Western Europe and the United States*, Oxford: Clarendon.

Jørgensen, H. (ed.) 2002: *Consensus, Cooperation and Conflict: The Policy Making Process in Denmark*, Chelmsford: Edward Elgar.

Kalecki, M. 1943: Political aspects of full employment. *Political Quarterly*, 14 (4), 322–40.

Kalisch, D., Tetsuya, A. and Buchele, L. 1998: *Social and Health Policies in OECD Countries: A Survey of Current Programmes and Recent Developments*, Labour Market and Social Policy Occasional Paper 33, Paris: OECD.

Katzenstein, P. J. 1985: *Small States in World Markets*, Ithaca: Cornell University Press.

Kaufmann, F.-X. 2000: Der Begriff Sozialpolitik und seine wissenschaftliche Deutung. In U. Wengst (ed.), *Geschichte der Sozialpolitik in Deutschland seit 1945*, Baden-Baden: Nomos.

Kaufmann, F.-X. 2001: Towards a theory of the welfare state. In S. Leibfried (ed.), *Welfare State Futures*, Cambridge: Cambridge University Press, 15–36.

Kazancigil, A. 1993: A prospective view on the European nation state. In J. Iivonen (ed.), *The Future of the Nation State in Europe*, Cheltenham: Edward Elgar, 117–29.

Kearney, M. 1991: Borders and boundaries of state and self at the end of empire. *Journal of Historical Sociology*, 4 (1), 52–74.

Keating, M. 1998: *The New Regionalism in Western Europe: Territorial Restructuring and Political Change*, Chelmsford: Edward Elgar.

Keil, R. 1998: Globalization makes states: Perspectives of local governance in the age of the world city, *Review of International Political Economy*, 5 (4), 616–45.

Kelly, K. 1998: *New Rules for the New Economy*, London: Fourth Estate.

Keman, H., Paloheimo, H. and Whitely, P. F. (eds) 1987: *Coping with the Economic Crisis: Alternative Responses to Economic Recession in Advanced Industrial Societies*, London: Sage.

Kitschelt, H. 1991: Industrial governance structures, innovation strategies, and the case of Japan: sectoral or cross-national comparative analysis? *International Organization*, 45 (4), 453–94.

Kitschelt, H. 1994: *The Transformation of European Social Democracy*, Cambridge: Cambridge University Press.

Kitschelt, H. 1997: *The Radical Right in Western Europe: A Comparative Analysis*, Ann Arbor: University of Michigan Press.

Klein, R. 1993: O'Goffe's tale. In C. Jones (ed.), *New Perspectives on the Welfare State in Europe*, London: Routledge, 7–17.

Klein-Beekman, C. 1996: International migration and spatiality in the world economy: remapping economic space in an era of expanding transnational flows. *Alternatives*, 21 (4), 439–72.

Kleinman, M. 2002: *A European Welfare State? European Union Social Policy in Context*, Basingstoke: Palgrave.

Knox, P. and Taylor, P. J. (eds) 1995: *World Cities in the World System*, Cambridge: Cambridge University Press.

Kofman, E. 1995: Citizenship for some but not for others: spaces of citizenship in contemporary Europe. *Political Geography*, 15 (2), 121–38.

Kooiman, J. (ed.) 1993a: *Modern Governance: New Government–Society Interactions*, London: Sage.

Kooiman, J. 1993b: Governance and governability: using complexity, dynamics and diversity. In idem (ed.), *Modern Governance: New Government–Society Interactions*, London: Sage, 35–48.

Krätke, M. 1984: *Kritik der Staatsfinanzen: zur politischen Ökonomie des Steuerstaates*, Hamburg: VSA Verlag.

Kuhnle, S. 1999: *The New Social Europe*, London: Routledge.

Kundnani, A. 1998–9: Where do you want to go today? The rise of information capital. *Race and Class*, 40 (2–3), 49–72.

Kwon, H. J. 1997: Beyond European welfare regimes: comparative perspectives on East Asian welfare systems. *Journal of Social Policy*, 26 (4), 467–84.

Laclau, E. 1977: *Politics and Ideology in Marxist Theory: Capitalism; Fascism; Populism*, London: New Left Books.

Lange, S. and Schimank, U. 2000: Sociology for complex societies: Niklas Luhmann. In L. Nash and A. Scott (eds), *Blackwell Companion to Political Sociology*, Oxford: Blackwell, 60–70.

Lauder, H., Brown, P. and Green, A. D. 2001: *Education and Training for a High Skills Economy: A Comparative Study*, Swindon: Economic and Social Research Council.

Lefebvre, H. 1978: *L'État. Tome 4: les contradictions de l'État modern*. Paris: Union Générale des Éditions.

Lefebvre, H. 1991: *The Production of Space*, Oxford: Blackwell.

Le Galès, P. and Harding, A. 1998: Cities and states in Europe. *West European Politics*, 21 (3), 120–45.

Lehman, B. W. 1996: Intellectual property: America's competitive advantage in the 21st century. *Columbia Journal of World Business*, 31 (1), 6–16.

Leibfried, S. 1993: Toward a European welfare state. In C. Jones (ed.), *New Perspectives on the Welfare State in Europe*, London: Routledge, 133–56.

Leibfried, S. and Pierson, P. 2000: Social policy. In H. Wallace and W. Wallace (eds), *Policy-making in the European Union*, Oxford: Oxford University Press, 267–92.

Leitner, H. 1995: International migration and the politics of admission and exclusion in postwar Europe. *Political Geography*, 14 (3), 259–78.

Levidow, L. 2001: Marketizing higher education: neoliberal strategies and counter-strategies. *Education and Social Justice*, 3 (2), 12–23.

Lewis, J. 1992: Gender and the development of welfare regimes. *Journal of European Social Policy*, 2 (3), 159–73.

Lewis, G. 1998: 'Coming apart at the seams'. The crises of the welfare state. In G. Hughes and G. Lewis (eds), *Unsettling Welfare: The Reconstruction of Social Policy*, London: Routledge, 39–79.

Leyshon, A. and Tickell, A. 1994: Money Order? The discursive construction of Bretton Woods and the making and breaking of regulatory space. *Environment and Planning A*, 26 (12), 1861–90.

Leyshon, A. and Thrift, N. 1997: *Money/Space: Geographies of Monetary Transformation*, London: Routledge.

Lim, C. Y. 1990: The Schumpeterian road to affluence and communism. *Malaysian Journal of Economic Studies*, 27 (1–2), 213–23.

Lindner, G. 1973: Die Krise als Steuerungsmittel. *Leviathan* 3 (4), 342–82.

Lipietz, A. 1982: Towards global Fordism. *New Left Review*, 132, 33–47.

Lipietz, A. 1985: *The Enchanted World: Inflation, Credit and the World Crisis*, London: Verso.

Lipietz, A. 1988: Accumulation, crises, and ways out: some methodological reflections on the concept of 'regulation', *International Journal of Political Economy*, 18 (2), 10–43.

Lipietz, A. 1996: *La société en sablier: le partage du travail contre la déchirure sociale*, Paris: La Découverte.

Luhmann, N. 1990: *Political Theory in the Welfare State*, Berlin: de Gruyter.

Luhmann, N. 1995: *Social Systems*, Stanford: Stanford University Press.

Luke, T. W. 1994: Placing power/siting space: the politics of the global and the local in the new world order. *Environment and Planning D: Society and Space*, 12 (4), 613–28.

Lundvall, B.-A. (ed.), 1992: *National Systems of Innovation: Towards a Theory of Innovation and Interactive Learning*, London: Pinter.

MacLaughlin, J. 2001: *Re-Imagining the State. The Contested Terrain of Nation-Building*, London: Pluto.

Maier, C. S. 1978: The politics of productivity: foundations of American economic policy after World War II. In P. J. Katzenstein (ed.), *Between Power and Plenty*, Madison: University of Wisconsin Press, 23–50.

Majone, G. 1993: The European Community between social policy and social regulation. *Journal of Common Market Studies*, 31 (2), 153–70.

Majone, G. 1994: The rise of the regulatory state in Europe. *West European Politics*, 17 (1), 77–101.

Malecki, E. J. 1997: *Technology and Economic Development: The Dynamics of Local, Regional, and National Change*, Harlow: Longman.

Malecki, E. J. 2002: Hard and soft networks for competitiveness. *Urban Studies*, 39 (5–6), 929–46.

Malpas, J. and Wickham, G. 1995: Governance and failure: on the limits of sociology. *Australian and New Zealand Journal of Sociology*, 31 (3), 37–50.

Malpass, P. 1994: Policy making and local governance: how Bristol failed to secure City Challenge funding (twice). *Policy and Politics*, 22 (4), 301–17.

Mandel, E. 1970: *Late Capitalism*, London: Verso.

Manners, J. 1998: Marxism and meaning: towards an immaculate conception of determination. *Studies in Marxism*, 5, 37–54.

Mao, Z. 1967: On contradiction. In idem, *Collected Works of Mao Tse-Tung*, vol. IV, Beijing: People's Publishing House, 311–47.

Marginson, S. 1999: After globalization: emerging politics of education, *Journal of Education Policy*, 14 (1), 19–31.

Marglin, S. A. and Schor, J. B. (eds) 1990: *The Golden Age of Capitalism: Reinterpreting the Postwar Experience*, Oxford: Clarendon Press.

Marsden, R. 1999: *The Nature of Capital: Marx after Foucault*, London: Routledge.

Martin, C. J. 1995: Nature or nurture? Sources of firm preference for national health reform. *American Political Science Review*, 43 (4), 898–915.

Martin, R. 1999: *Money and the Space Economy*, Chichester: Wiley.

Martin, R. and Sunley, P. 1997: The post-Keynesian state and the space-economy. In R. Lee and J. Wills (eds), *Geographies of Economies*, London: Arnold, 278–89.

Marx, K. 1967 [1867]: *Capital*, vol. I, London: Lawrence & Wishart.

Marx, K. 1973 [1857]: Introduction to the contribution to the critique of political economy. In idem, *Grundrisse: Foundations of the Critique of Political Economy*, Harmondsworth: Penguin.

Marx, K. 1996 [1867]: *Capital*, vol. I, in *Marx–Engels Collected Works*, vol. 35. London: Lawrence & Wishart.

Maskell, P., Eskelinen, H., Hannibalsson, I., Malmberg, A. and Vatne, E. 1998: *Competitiveness, Localised Learning and Regional Development: Possibilities for Prosperity in Open Economies*, London: Routledge.

Matzner, E. 1994: Instrument-targeting or context-making? A new look at the theory of economic policy. *Journal of Economic Issues*, 28 (2), 461–76.

Mayntz, R. 1993: Modernization and the logic of interorganizational networks. In J. Child, M. Crozier and R. Mayntz (eds), *Societal Change between Market and Organization*, Aldershot: Avebury, 3–18.

Menzies, H. 1998: Challenging capitalism in cyberspace. In R. W. McChesney, E. M. Wood and J. F. Bellamy (eds), *Capitalism and the Information Age*, New York: Monthly Review Press, 87–98.

Messner, D. 1998: *The Network Society*, London: Cass.

Milward, A. S., Brennan, G. and Romero, F. 1993: *The European Rescue of the Nation State*, London: Routledge.

Minzberg, H. 1983: *Structures in Fives: Designing Effective Organization*, Englewood Cliffs, NJ: Prentice-Hall.

Mishra, R. 1985: *The Welfare State in Crisis*, Brighton: Harvester.

Mitchell, T. 1991: The limits of the state: beyond statist approaches and their critics. *American Political Science Review*, 85 (1), 77–96.

Mittelman, J. H. 1996: Rethinking the 'new regionalism' in the context of globalization. *Global Governance*, 2 (2), 189–213.

Morin, E. 1980: *La méthode: la vie de la vie*, vol 2. Paris: Seuil.

Moulaert, F., Swyngedouw, E. A. and Wilson, P. 1988: Spatial responses to Fordist and post-Fordist accumulation and regulation. *Papers of the Regional Science Association*, 64 (1), 11–23.

Müller, C. and Neusüss, W. 1975: The illusion of state socialism and the contradiction between wage labor and capital. *Telos*, 25, 13–90.

Munro, R. 1997: Ideas of difference: stability, social spaces and the labour of division. In K. Hetherington and R. Munro (eds), *Ideas of Difference: Social Spaces and the Labour of Division*, Blackwell: Oxford, 3–26.

Murphy, A. 1993: Emerging regional linkages within the European Community: challenging the dominance of the state. *Tijdschrift voor Economische en Sociale Geografie*, 84 (2), 103–18.

Myles, J. and Pierson, P. 2001: The comparative political economy of pension reform. In P. Pierson (ed.), *The New Politics of the Welfare State*, Oxford: Oxford University Press, 305–34.

Nelson, R. R. and Romer, P. M. 1996: Science, economic growth, and public policy. *Challenge*, March–April, 9–21.

Nitzan, J. 1998: Differential accumulation: toward a new political economy of capital. *Review of International Political Economy*, 5 (2), 169–216.

Nitzan, J. 2001: Regimes of differential accumulation: mergers, stagflation and the logic of globalization. *Review of International Political Economy*, 8 (2), 226–74.

Notermans, T. 2000: *Money, Markets, and the State: Social Democratic Economic Policies since 1918*, Cambridge: Cambridge University Press.

O'Connor, J. 1973: *The Fiscal Crisis of the State*, New York: St Martin's Press.

OECD 1981: *The Crisis of Welfare*, Paris: OECD.

OECD 1985: *Social Expenditure 1960–1990: Problems of Growth and Control*, Paris: OECD.

OECD 1994: *New Orientations for Social Policy*, Paris: OECD.

OECD 1996: *Social Expenditure Statistics of OECD Member Countries*, Paris: OECD.

OECD 1999: *A Caring World: The New Social Policy Agenda*, Paris: OECD.

Offe, C. 1972: *Strukturprobleme des kapitalistischen Staates*, Frankfurt: Suhrkamp.

Offe, C. 1975: The theory of the capitalist state and the problem of policy formation. In L. N. Lindberg, R. Alford, C. Crouch and C. Offe (eds), *Stress and Contradiction in Modern Capitalism*, Lexington: D. C. Heath, 125–44.

Offe, C. 1984: *Contradictions of the Welfare State*, London: Hutchinson.

Offe, C. 1985b: New social movements: challenging the boundaries of institutional politics. *Social Research*, 54 (2), 817–68.

Ohlin, B. 1938: Economic progress in Sweden. *The Annals of the American Academy of Political and Social Science*, 197, 1–6.

Ohmae, K. 1991: The rise of the region state. *Foreign Affairs*, 72, Spring, 78–87.

Ohmae, K. 1995: *The End of the Nation State: the Rise of Regional Economies*. New York: Harper Collins.

Orszag, P. R. and Stiglitz, J. E. 2001: Rethinking pension reform: ten myths about social security systems. In R. Holzman and J. E. Stiglitz (eds), *New Ideas about Old Age Security*, Washington DC: World Bank, 17–56.

Osiander, A. 2001: Sovereignty, international relations, and the Westphalian myth. *International Organization*, 55 (2), 251–87.

Overbeek, H. 1990: *Global Capitalism and National Decline: The Thatcher Decade in Perspective*, London: Hutchinson.

Oxley, H. and Martin, J. 1991: Controlling government spending and deficits: trends in the 1980s and prospects in the 1990s. *OECD Economic Studies*, 17, 145–89.

Painter, J. 1991: Regulation theory and local government. *Local Government Studies*, 17 (6), 23–44.

Palan, R. 1998: The emergence of an offshore economy. *Futures*, 30 (1), 63–73.

Palier, B. and Sykes, R. 2000: Challenges and change: issues and perspectives in the analysis of globalization and the European welfare states. In R. Sykes, B. Palier and P. M. Prior (eds), *Globalization and the European Welfare State: Challenges and Change*, Basingstoke: Palgrave, 1–16.

Pankoke, E. 1970: *Soziale Bewegung – Soziale Frage – Soziale Politik. Grundfragen der deutschen 'Sozialwissenschaft' im 19. Jahrhundert*, Stuttgart: Klett.

Parkinson, M. and Harding, A. 1995: European cities toward 2000: entrepreneurialism, competition and social exclusion. In M. Rhodes (ed.), *The Regions and the New Europe: Patterns in Core and Periphery Development*, Manchester: Manchester University Press, 53–77.

Parsonage, J. 1992: Southeast Asia's 'growth triangle': a subregional response to global transformation. *International Journal of Urban and Regional Research*, 16 (3), 307–17.

Pashukanis, E. B. 1978: *Law and Marxism: A General Theory*, London: Ink Links.

Peck, J. 2001: *Workfare States*. New York: Guilford Press.

Peck, J. and Jones, M. 1995: Training and enterprise councils: Schumpeterian workfare state, or what? *Environment and Planning A* 27: 1361–96.

Peck, J. and Theodore, N. 2000: Work first: workfare and the regulation of contingent labour markets. *Cambridge Journal of Economics*, 24 (1), 119–38.

Peck, J. and Theodore, N. 2001: Exporting workfare/importing welfare-to-work: exploring the politics of Third Way policy transfer. *Political Geography*, 20 (4), 427–60.

Peck, J. and Tickell, A. 2002: Neoliberalizing space. *Antipode*, 34 (2), 380–404.

Perkmann, M. 2000: Euroregions. Strategies of Institution-Building in the New European Polity. Lancaster University, Ph.D. thesis.

Perkmann, M. and Sum, N. L. (eds) 2002: *Globalization, Regionalization, and Cross-Border Regions*, Basingstoke: Palgrave.

Perrin, J.-C. 1988: New technologies, local synergies and regional policies in Europe. In P. Aydelot and D. Keeble (eds), *High Technology Industry and Innovative Environments*, London: Routledge, 139–62.

Petit, P. 1999: Structural forms and growth regimes of the post-Fordist era. *Review of Social Economy*, 57 (2), 220–43.

Petit, P. and Soete, L. 1999: Globalization in search of a future. The contemporary challenge to national policies. *International Social Science Journal*, 160, 165–81.

Pierson, P. 1995: *Dismantling the Welfare State? Reagan, Thatcher and the Politics of Retrenchment*, Cambridge: Cambridge University Press.

Pierson, P. 2001a: Coping with permanent austerity: welfare state restructuring. In P. Pierson (ed.), *The New Politics of the Welfare State*, Oxford: Oxford University Press, 410–56.

Pierson, P. 2001b: Post-industrial pressures on the mature welfare states. In idem (ed.), *The New Politics of the Welfare State*, Oxford: Oxford University Press, 80–104.

Piore, M. J. and Sabel, C. F. 1985: *The Second Industrial Divide*, New York: Basic Books.

Pitruzello, S. 1999: Decommodification and the worlds of welfare capitalism. a cluster analysis. Florence: European Forum (European University Institute), Seminar Paper WS/90.

Piven, F. F. and Cloward, R. 1971: *Regulating the Poor: The Functions of Public Welfare*, New York: Pantheon Books.

Piven, F. F. and Cloward, R. 1993: *Regulating the Poor: The Functions of Public Welfare* (2nd edition), New York: Anchor.

Polanyi, K. 1944: *The Great Transformation: The Political and Economic Origins of our Time*, New York: Rinehart and Company.

Portelli, H. 1973: *Gramsci y el Bloque Histórico*, Mexico: Siglio Ventiuno.

Porter, M. E. 1990: *The Competitive Advantage of Nations*, Basingstoke: Macmillan.

Porter, M. E. 1995: The competitive advantage of the inner city. *Harvard Business Review*, 73, May–June, 55–71.

Porter, M. E., Sachs, J. D., Warner, A. M., Moore, C., Tudor, J. M., Vasquez, D., Schwab, K., Cornelius, P. K., Levinson, M. and Ryder, B. 2000: *The Global Competitiveness Report 2000*, Oxford: Oxford University Press.

Postone, M. 1993: *Time, Labor, and Social Domination: a Reinterpretation of Marx's Critical Theory*, Cambridge: Cambridge University Press.

Poulantzas, N. 1973: *Political Power and Social Classes*, London: New Left Books.

Poulantzas, N. 1974a: *Fascism and Dictatorship: The Third International and the Problem of Fascism*, London: New Left Books.

Poulantzas, N. 1974b: The internationalization of capitalist relations and the nation state. *Economy and Society*, 3 (2), 145–79.

Poulantzas, N. 1975: *Classes in Contemporary Capitalism*, London: New Left Books.

Poulantzas, N. 1978: *State, Power, Socialism*, London: New Left Books.

Power, M. 1997: *The Audit Society: Rituals of Verification*, Oxford: Oxford University Press.

Putnam, R. D. 2000: *Bowling Alone: The Collapse and Revival of American Community*, New York: Simon and Schuster.

Radice, H. 1984: The national economy: a Keynesian myth? *Capital and Class*, 22, 111–40.

Rasch, W. 2000: *Niklas Luhmann's Modernity: The Paradox of Differentiation*, Stanford: Stanford University Press.

Regini, M. 2000: Between deregulation and social pacts: the responses of European economies to globalization. *Politics and Society*, 28 (1), 5–33.

Reuten, G. and Williams, M. 1989: *Value-Form and the State: The Tendencies of Accumulation and the Determination of Economic Policy in a Capitalist Society*, London: Routledge.

Rhodes, 1998: Globalization, labour markets and welfare states: a future of 'competitive corporatism'? In M. Rhodes and Y. Mény (eds), *The Future of European Welfare: A New Social Contract?* Basingstoke: Macmillan, 178–203.

Ringer, F. 1997: *Max Weber's Methodology: The Unification of the Cultural and Social Sciences*, Cambridge, MA: Harvard University Press.

Robins, K. and Gillespie, A. 1992: Communication, organisation and territory. In K. Robins (ed.), *Understanding Information: Business, Technology, and Geography*, London: Belhaven, 148–62.

Robins, K. and Webster, F. 1987: Information as capital: a critique of Daniel Bell. In J. Slack and F. Fejes (eds), *The Ideology of the Information Age*, Norwood, NJ: Ablex Publishing, 95–117.

Robins, K. and Webster, F. 1989: *The Technical Fix: Education, Computers and Industry*, London: Macmillan.

Robinson, P. 1998: Beyond workfare. Active labour-market policies. *Institute of Development Studies Bulletin*, 29 (1), 89–98.

Robinson, P. 2000: Active labour-market policies: a case of evidence-based policy-making? *Oxford Review of Economic Policy*, 16 (1), 13–26.

Rodrik, D. 1997: Has globalization gone too far? *California Management Review*, 39 (3), 29–53.

Rokkan, S. 1999: *State Formation, Nation-Building and Mass Politics in Europe: The Theory of Stein Rokkan*, Oxford: Oxford University Press.

Rose, R. and Davies, P. L. 1994: *Inheritance in Public Policy: Change without Choice in Britain*, New Haven: Yale University Press.

Ruggie, J. G. 1982: International regimes, transactions, and change: embedded liberalism in the postwar economic order. *International Organization*, 36 (2), 379–415.

Ruggie, J. 1993: Territoriality and beyond: problematizing modernity in international relations. *International Organization*, 47 (1), 139–74.

Ruigrok, W. and van Tulder, R. 1995: *The Logic of International Restructuring*, London: Routledge.

Ruigrok, W. and van Tulder, R. 1996: The price of diversity: rival concepts of control as a barrier to an EU industrial strategy. In P. Devine, Y. Katsoulacos and R. Sugden (eds), *Competitiveness, Subsidiarity, and Industrial Policy*, London: Routledge, 79–103.

Rupert, M. 1994: *Producing Hegemony: The Politics of Mass Production and American Global Power*, Cambridge: Cambridge University Press.

Sabel, C. F. 1989: Flexible specialisation and the re-emergence of regional economies. In P. Q. Hirst and J. Zeitlin (eds), *Reversing Industrial Decline?*

Industrial Structure and Policy in Britain and Her Competitors, Leamington Spa: Berg Publishers, 17–70.

Sainsbury, D. 1996: *Gender, Equality and Welfare State*, Cambridge: Cambridge University Press.

Sassen, S. 1994: *Global Cities*, New York: Oxford University Press.

Sassen, S. 1996: The state and the global city: notes towards a conception of place-centered governance. *Competition and Change*, 1 (1), 31–50.

Sayer, A. 2000: *Realism and Social Science*, London: Sage.

Sbragia, A. 2000: The European Union as coxswain: governance by steering. In J. Pierre (ed.), *Debating Governance: Authority, Steering, and Democracy*, Oxford: Oxford University Press, 219–40.

Scharpf, F. W. 1991: *Crisis and Choice in European Social Democracy*, Ithaca: Cornell University Press.

Scharpf, F. W. 1994: Games real actors could play: positive and negative coordination in embedded negotiations. *Journal of Theoretical Politics*, 6 (1), 27–53.

Scharpf, F. W. 1997: Employment and the welfare state: a continental dilemma. Köln: Max Planck Institut für Sozialforschung, MPIfG Working Paper 97/7.

Scharpf, F. W. 2000: Economic changes, vulnerabilities, and institutional capabilities. In idem and V. A. Schmidt (eds), *Welfare and Work in the Open Economy. Vol. I: From Vulnerability to Competitiveness*, Oxford: Oxford University Press, 21–124.

Scharpf, F. W. and Schmidt, V. A. 2000b: Introduction. In idem (eds), *Welfare and Work in the Open Economy. Vol. I: From Vulnerability to Competitiveness*, Oxford: Oxford University Press, 1–19.

Scharpf, F. W. and Schmidt, V. A. (eds) 2000c: *Welfare and Work in the Open Economy. Vol. II: Diverse Responses to Common Challenges*, Oxford: Oxford University Press.

Schiller, D. 1988: How to think about information. In V. Mosco and J. Wasko (eds), *The Political Economy of Information*, Madison: University of Wisconsin Press, 27–44.

Schiller, D. 1999: *Digital Capitalism: Networking the Global Market System*, Cambridge, MA: MIT Press.

Schmid, J. 1996: *Wohlfahrtsstaaten in Vergleich: Soziale Sicherungssysteme in Europa: Organisation, Finanzierung, Leistungen und Probleme*, Opladen: Buske & Ledrich.

Schmidt, V. A. 2000: Values and discourses in the politics of adjustment. In F. W. Scharpf and V. A. Schmidt (eds), *Welfare and Work in the Open Economy. Vol. I: From Vulnerability to Competitiveness*, Oxford: Oxford University Press, 239–309.

Schulz, M., Söderbaum, F. and Öjendal, J. (eds) 2001: *Regionalization in a Globalizing World: A Comparative Perspective on Forms, Actors and Processes*, London: Zed Books.

Schumpeter, J. A. 1934: *Theory of Economic Development: An Inquiry into Profits, Capital, Credit, Interest and the Business Cycle*, Cambridge, MA: Harvard University Press.

Scott, A. J. 1998: *Regions and the World Economy. The Coming Shape of*

Global Production, Competition and Political Order, Oxford: Oxford University Press.

Scott, A. J. (ed.) 2001: *Global City-regions: Trends, Theory, Policy*, Oxford: Oxford University Press.

Shaw, M. 2000: *Theory of the Global State: Globality as an Unfinished Revolution*, Cambridge: Cambridge University Press.

Shy, O. 2001: *Economics of Network Industries*, Cambridge: Cambridge University Press.

Siegel, T. 1988: Introduction (to Fordism and Fascism). *International Journal of Political Economy*, 18 (1), 2–9.

Sigurdson, J. 1990: The Internationalisation of R&D – an interpretation of forces and responses. In J. Sigurdson (ed.), *Measuring the Dynamics of Technological Change*, London: Pinter, 171–95.

Siim, B. 2000: *Gender and citizenship. Politics and agency in France, Britain and Denmark*, Cambridge: Cambridge University Press.

Slaughter, S. and Leslie, G. 1997: *Academic Capitalism*, Baltimore, MD: Johns Hopkins University Press.

Smith, M. P. 2000: *Transnational Urbanism: Locating Globalization*, Oxford: Blackwell.

Smith, N. J. 1988: The region is dead! Long live the region! *Political Geography Quarterly*, 7 (2), 141–52.

Smith, S. 1997: The Indonesia–Malaysia–Singapore growth triangle: a political and economic equation. *Australian Journal of International Affairs*, 51 (3), 369–82.

Smyslov, D. 1992: Economic problems of Eastern Europe within the context of the East–West relationships. *Journal of Regional Policy*, 12 (2), 239–50.

Sohn-Rethel, A. 1978: *Intellectual and Manual Labour: A Critique of Epistemology*, London: Macmillan.

Somers, M. 1994: The narrative constitution of identity: a relational and network approach. *Theory and Society*, 23 (4), 605–49.

Soskice, D. 1999: Divergent production regimes: coordinated and uncoordinated market economies in the 1980s and 1990s. In H. Kitschelt, P. Lange, G. Marks and J. D. Stephens (eds), *Continuity and Change in Contemporary Capitalism*, Cambridge: Cambridge University Press, 101–34.

Soysal, Y. N. 1994: *Limits of Citizenship: Migrants and Postnational Membership in Europe*, Chicago: Chicago University Press.

Sparkes, M. 2002: Not a state, but more than a state of mind: cascading Cascadia and the geoeconomics of cross-border regionalism. In M. Perkmann and N. Sum (eds), *Globalization, Regionalization, and Cross-Border Regions*, Basingstoke: Palgrave, 212–38.

Stahel, A. W. 1999: Time contradictions of capitalism. *Capitalism, Nature, Socialism*, 10 (1), 101–32.

Stella, D. 2000: Globalization, think tanks and policy transfer. In D. Stone (ed.), *Banking on Knowledge: The Genesis of the Global Development Network*, London: Routledge, 203–20.

Storper, M. J. 1997: *Regional Worlds*, New York: Guilford.

Streeck, W. 1992: *Social Institutions and Economic Performance. Studies of Industrial Relations in Advanced Capitalist Economies*, London: Sage.

Streeck, W. 1995: Neo-voluntarism: a new European social policy regime? In S. Leibfried and P. Pierson (eds), *European Social Policy: Between Fragmentation and Integration*, Washington, DC: Brookings Institution, 389–431.

Streeck, W. and Crouch, C. (eds) 1997: *Political Economy of Modern Capitalism*, London: Sage.

Streeck, W. and Schmitter, P. C. 1985: Community, market, state – and associations? The prospective contribution of interest governance to social order. In idem (eds), *Private Interest Government*, London: Sage, 1–29.

Streeck, W. and Schmitter, P. C. 1991: From national corporatism to transnational pluralism: organized interests in the Single European Market. *Politics and Society*, 19 (2), 133–64.

Sum, N. L. 1997: Time–space embeddedness and geo-governance of cross-border regional modes of growth: their nature and dynamics in East Asian cases. In A. Amin and J. Hausner (eds), *Beyond Markets and Hierarchy: Interactive Governance and Social Complexity*, Cheltenham: Edward Elgar, 159–95.

Sum, N. L. 1998: Theorizing export-oriented economic development in East Asian newly industrializing countries: a regulationist perspective. In I. Cook, M. Doel, R. Li and Y. Yang (eds), *Dynamic Asia*, Aldershot: Avebury, 41–77.

Sum, N. L. 1999: Re-articulating spatial scale and temporal horizons of trans-border spaces. In K. Olds, P. Dicken, P. F. Kelly, L. Kong and H. W. C. Yeung (eds), *Globalisation and the Asia Pacific*, London: Routledge, 129–45.

Sum, N. L. 2001: An integral approach to the Asian crisis: the (dis)articulation of the production and financial (dis)order. *Capital and Class*, 74, 139–64.

de Swaan, A. 1988: *In Care of the State: Health Care, Education and Welfare in Europe and the USA in the Modern Era*, Cambridge: Polity.

de Swaan, A. 1992: Perspectives for transnational social policy. *Government and Opposition*, 27 (1), 33–51.

Swank, D. 2001: Political institutions and welfare state restructuring: the impact of institutions on social policy change in developed democracies. In P. Pierson (ed.), *The New Politics of the Welfare State*, Oxford: Oxford University Press, 197–237.

Swank, D. 2002: *Global Capital, Political Institutions, and Policy Change in Developed Welfare States*, Cambridge: Cambridge University Press.

Swedberg, R. 1998: *Max Weber and the Idea of Economic Sociology*, Princeton: Princeton University Press.

Swyngedouw, E. A. 1997: Neither global nor local: 'glocalization' and the politics of scale. In K. R. Cox (ed.), *Spaces of Globalization: Reasserting the Power of the Local*, New York: Guilford, 137–66.

Sykes, R., Palier, B. and Prior, P. M. 2001: *Globalization and European Welfare States: Challenges and Change*, Basingstoke: Palgrave.

Taylor, P. J. 1991: A theory and practice of regions: the case of Europe. *Environment and Planning D: Society and Space*, 9 (2), 184–95.

Taylor, P. J. 1994: The state as container: territoriality in the modern world-system. *Progress in Human Geography*, 18 (2), 151–62.

Taylor-Gooby, P. 1996: Paying for welfare: the view from Europe. *Political Quarterly*, 67 (2), 116–26.

Taylor-Gooby, P. 1997: European welfare futures: the views of key influentials in six European countries on likely developments in social policy. *Social Policy and Administration*, 31 (1), 1–19.

Taylor-Gooby, P. 2001a: The politics of welfare in Europe. In idem (ed.), *Welfare States under Pressure*, London: Sage, 1–28.

Taylor-Gooby, P. (ed.) 2001b: *Welfare States under Pressure*, London: Sage.

Teichler, U. 1999: Higher education and changing job requirements: a comparative view. In M. Henkel and B. Little (eds), *Changing Relationships between Higher Education and the State*, London: Jessica Kingsley, 69–89.

Thant, M., Tang, M. and Kakazu, H. (eds) 1998: *Growth Triangles in Asia: A New Approach to Regional Economic Cooperation*, Oxford: Oxford University Press.

Thelen, K. 2001: Varieties of labor politics in the developed democracies. In P. A. Hall and D. Soskice (eds), *Varieties of Capitalism: the Institutional Foundations of Comparative Advantage*, Oxford: Oxford University Press, 71–103.

Therborn, G. and Roebroek, J. 1986: The irreversible welfare state: its recent maturation, its encounter with the economic crisis, and its future prospects. *International Journal of Health Services*, 16 (3), 319–57.

Théret, B. 1992: *Régimes économiques de l'ordre politique*, Paris: Presses Universitaires Françaises.

Thornhill, C. 2000: *Political Theory in Modern Germany*, Cambridge: Polity.

Tölölyan, K. 1991: The nation-state and its others. *Diaspora*, 1 (1), 1–9.

Tomlinson, J. 1985: *British Macroeconomic Policy since 1940*, London: Croom Helm.

Tömmel, I. 1992: System-Entwicklung und Politikgestaltung in der Europäischen Gemeinschaft am Beispiel der Regionalpolitik. In M. Kreile (ed.), *Die Integration Europas*, Opladen: Westdeutscher Verlag, 185–208.

Tömmel, I. 1994: Interessenartikulation und transnationale Politik-kooperation im Rahmen der EU. In V. Eichener and H. Voelkoz (eds), *Europäische Integration und verbändliche Regulierung*, Marburg: Metropolis.

Tömmel, I. 1998: Transformation of governance: the European Commission's strategy for creating a 'Europe of the Regions'. *Regional and Federal Studies*, 8 (2), 52–80.

Torfing, J. 1999: Workfare with welfare: recent reforms of the Danish welfare state. *Journal of European Social Policy*, 9 (1), 5–28.

UNESCO 1995: *Policy Paper for Change and Development in Higher Education*, Paris: UNESCO.

UNESCO 1996: *Learning: The Treasure Within*. Report to UNESCO of the International Commission on Education for the Twenty-First Century, Paris: UNESCO.

van Apeldoorn, S. 1998: Transnationalization and the restructuring of Europe's socioeconomic order. *International Journal of Political Economy*, 28 (1), 12–53.

van der Pijl, K. 1984: *The Making of an Atlantic Ruling Class*, London: New Left Books.

310 References

Van Hoogstraten, P. 1983: *De Ontwikkeling van het Regionaal Beleid in Nederland 1949–1977*, Nijmegen: Stichting Politiek en Ruimte.

Van Kersbergen, K. 1995: *Social Capitalism. A Study of Christian Democracy and the Welfare State*, London: Routledge.

Veblen, T. 1958 [1904]: *The Theory of Business Enterprise*, New York: Mentor.

Veblen, T. 1967 [1923]: *Absentee Ownership and Business Enterprise in Recent Times. The Case of America*, Boston: Beacon Press.

Vellinga, M. (ed.) 2000: *The Dialectics of Globalization*, Boulder: Westview.

Veltz, P. 1996: *Mondialisation villes et territoires: l'économie archipel*, Paris: Presses Universitaires de France.

Visser, J. 2000: From Keynesianism to the Third Way: labour relations and social policy in postwar Western Europe. *Economic and Industrial Democracy*, 21 (4), 421–56.

Vobruba, G. 1995: Social policy on tomorrow's Euro-corporatist stage. *Journal of European Social Policy*, 5 (4), 303–15.

Wallace, H. 2000: The institutional setting: five variations on a theme. In H. Wallace and W. Wallace (eds), *Policy-making in the European Union*, Oxford: Oxford University Press, 3–37.

Warr, P. G. 1994: Comparative and competitive advantage. *Asia-Pacific Economic Literature*, 8 (2), 1–15.

Weber, M. 1948: Politics as a vocation. In H. Gerth and C. W. Mills (eds), *From Max Weber: Essays in Sociology*, London: Routledge and Kegan Paul, 77–128.

Weber, M. 1978: *Economy and Society: An Outline of Interpretive Sociology*, 3 vols, Berkeley: University of California Press.

Weiss, L. 1998: *The Myth of the Powerless State. Governing the Economy in a Global Era*, Cambridge: Polity.

Wessels, W. 2000: *Die Öffnung des Staates. Modelle und Wirklichkeit grenzüberschreitender Verwaltungspraxis 1960–1995*, Opladen: Buske & Ledrich.

Western, B. 1997: *Between Class and Market. Postwar Unionization in the Capitalist Democracies*, Princeton: Princeton University Press.

Wilding, P. 1997: Globalization, regionalization and social policy. *Social Policy and Administration*, 31 (4), 410–28.

Williams, K., Williams, J. and Thomas, D. 1983: *Why are the British Bad at Manufacturing?* London: Routledge.

Williams, F. 1995: Race/ethnicity, gender, and class in welfare states: a framework for comparative analysis. *Social Politics*, 2 (2), 126–59.

Willke, H. 1992: *Die Ironie des Staates*, Frankfurt: Campus Verlag.

Willke, H. 1997: *Supervision des Staates*, Frankfurt: Campus Verlag.

Wilthagen, T. 1998: Flexicurity: a new paradigm for labour market policy reform? Berlin: Wissenschaftszentrum Berlin, FSI-98-202.

Windolf, P. 1990: Productivity coalitions and the future of unionism: disintegration of generalized political exchange? In B. Marin (ed.), *Governance and Generalized Exchange: Self-Organizing Policy Networks in Action*, Frankfurt: Campus, 249–73.

Wirth, M. 1977: Towards a critique of the theory of state monopoly capitalism. *Economy and Society*, 6 (3), 284–313.

Wolf, C. 1979: A theory of nonmarket failure. *Journal of Law and Economics*, 22 (1), 107–39.

Wood, E. M. 1981: The separation of the economic and the political in capitalism. *New Left Review*, 127, 66–93.

Woodiwiss, A. 1998: *Globalization, Human Rights and Labour Law in Pacific Asia*, Cambridge: Cambridge University Press.

World Bank 1994: *Higher Education: The Lessons of Experience*, Washington, DC: the World Bank.

World Bank 1994: *Averting the Old Age Crisis: Policies to Protect the Old and Promote Growth*, Oxford: Oxford University Press.

Zacher, H. F. 1985: Verrechtlichung im Bereich des Sozialrechts. In F. Kübler (ed.), *Verrechtlichung von Wirtschaft, Arbeit und sozialer Solidarität*, Frankfurt: Suhrkamp, 11–72.

Ziebura, G. 1992: Über den Nationalstaat. *Leviathan*, 4, 1992, 467–89.

Index

Note: The index combines names and subjects. Page numbers printed in bold refer to a major discussion of a given topic. Specific page numbers (e.g. 31–3) indicate that the discussion continues over the relevant pages; non-specific page numbers indicate several separate references on two (31f) or more (31ff) pages. The index is thematic so that entries sometimes refer to a relevant theme rather than an exact use of a given word, concept or phrase. Authors are indexed only when they are directly quoted or discussed at length, not when they are simply cited in support of one or another argument.